Choral Literature for Sundays and Seasons

Bradley Ellingboe, editor

Augsburg Fortress
Minneapolis

Contents

Preface	3
From the publisher	4
Key to Music Publishers	5
Key to Music Abbreviations	6

Music Listings

Advent	8
Christmas	16
Epiphany	23
Lent	42
Holy Week/Three Days	54
Easter	62
Time after Pentecost	80
Lesser Festivals	136

Indexes

Index to the Revised Common Lectionary	142
Index of Composers	161
Index of Titles	223

Choral Literature for Sundays and Seasons
Bradley Ellingboe, editor

Copyright © 2004 Augsburg Fortress. All rights reserved. Unless otherwise noted, no part of this book may be reproduced in any manner without prior written permission from the publisher or from the other copyright holders. Write to: Permissions, Augsburg Fortress, P.O. Box 1209, Minneapolis, MN 55440-1209.

Scripture quotations, unless otherwise noted, are from the New Revised Standard Version (NRSV) Bible, copyright © 1989 Division of Christian Education of the National Council of Churches of Christ in the United States of America. Used by permission.

Editors: Carol Carver, Robert Buckley Farlee, Becky Lowe

Printed in the USA.
ISBN 0-8066-4689-6

Preface

Lists can be both objective and subjective. A list of the ten tallest mountain peaks in the world is an objective, quantifiable list. A list of the ten greatest novels of all time is, of course, subjective. The book that follows falls into the second category.

Having stated this from the outset I nevertheless hope that you will find this resource to be a useful tool. Since it represents subjective opinion, it may be helpful to know both the genesis of the project, as well as the criteria applied when choosing the anthems and solos found herein.

For the past nine years Augsburg Fortress has published *Sundays and Seasons*, an extraordinarily valuable compendium for all of us who work in the church. In an almost Trinitarian bit of serendipity they have by now gone through the three-year lectionary cycle three times. As you may know, *Sundays and Seasons* contains suggested anthems and vocal solos for each possible church day of the liturgical year. These pieces are meant to correspond to, and illuminate, the readings for that day. Many of the finest choral musicians of our time have been contributors to the lists of musical suggestions.

In 2003 the music editors of *Sundays and Seasons* struck upon the idea of editing material from these nine volumes to create one book of "classic" choral literature that corresponds to the three-year lectionary cycle. Knowing it would be a subjective list they sought an outside person to make the final deliberations. In the summer of 2003 they approached me and I accepted.

The staff then did a great deal of preliminary editing to cull the nine years of material into a manageable amount for me to begin my work. After their first winnowing, the list was sent to me with the instruction that each liturgical occasion should offer not less than 10 and not more than 12 anthems or solos.

A structural decision such as this ("not less than 10, not more than 12") has its own implications. For example, it is difficult to limit oneself to only 12 "classic" choral anthems for Christmas Eve. Conversely, there are Sundays during what our Catholic brothers and sisters so aptly call "ordinary time" where even reaching the number 10 was difficult. Despite that, overall it was a good guideline and one I held to as much as possible.

As we neared finalizing the contents of the book we were suddenly fortunate to be able to draw upon the extensive repertoire lists accumulated by the nationally broadcast radio program "Sing for Joy," now produced by WCAL-FM at Saint Olaf College under the general purview of Professor John Ferguson. We happily accepted the chance to incorporate even more suggestions into our work. But by now it is undoubtedly apparent to the reader that we suffered from an embarrassment of riches!

With the wealth of material available, I made the following decisions, in descending order:

1) All suitable music by an acknowledged master (e.g., Bach) was automatically included. The only deviation from this might come when there were multiple titles written by the same composer. In such a case I would sometimes omit some titles so as to not have the entire list for that day dominated by a single name—however great a name that might be.
2) All suitable music by minor masters or pre-Baroque composers (such as Stanford or Byrd) was generally included.
3) Music by the great twentieth-century chorus masters was generally included. For example, the Christiansens, Willcocks, and so on. In this same category I included composers writing some of the best music for the liturgical church in our time. Here you find names like Schalk, Lauridsen, Rutter, Proulx, Jennings, Ferguson, and Manz.
4) Whenever possible I included choral music from folk music traditions.
5) For the sake of balance and interest, I tried to include as many female composers as possible.

There is a great deal of fine music listed here, and much more that had to be omitted. For any sins of omission, I apologize.

Two thoughts occur to me as to how to make even further use of this book. First, let titles inspire you to consider music with the same title by other composers not listed. For example, many fine settings of "Create in me a clean heart, O God" (Psalm 51) exist beyond those found here. Seek the others out, as well. Also, consider referring to similar occasions in the lectionaries of other years. Thus, if you are in the First Sunday of Advent in lectionary A, you might also check for suggestions for this Sunday in cycle C.

In conclusion, I wish to thank my editor at Augsburg Fortress, Carol Carver, as well as her colleague Robert Buckley Farlee for approaching me with this idea. I also wish to thank John Ferguson and the production staff of the "Sing for Joy" radio program. And finally, thanks to all those who contributed to the original editions of *Sundays and Seasons* from which the contents of this book were largely gleaned.

Bradley Ellingboe
Spring 2004

From the publisher

In the listings of choral music, we have made an effort to include mainly music that is in print. But since choral libraries include various editions and can span many years and many directors, we have included listings that may be out of print. Also note that when a piece of music includes separate instrumental parts, we have included only the publisher code for the choral edition. With codes and publishers, we have tried to be as accurate as time and resources would allow, but we cannot guarantee that errors did not creep in. Publishers and retailers will be able to help you order the piece that you want.

The Sundays in the Time after Pentecost are named in three ways. The first ("Sunday N") corresponds to lectionary numbering systems in which Baptism of Our Lord is Sunday 1. The second ("Proper N") corresponds to the system used in *Lutheran Book of Worship*. The third is the most universal: the dates between which that lectionary Sunday may fall, if after Holy Trinity.

Our plan is for this to be an ongoing product that, in time, you will be able to access at the Augsburg Fortress website. If you know of a piece of choral music that you think works well for a certain Sunday or season, please send the title and publisher information to us at musicsub@augsburgfortress.org. The selection may be included in a future edition of this resource.

Key to Music Publishers

ABI	Abingdon	EBOR	Eboracum	PM	Peer Music
AFP	Augsburg Fortress	ECS	E. C. Schirmer	PET	Peters
AG	Agape (Hope)	EV	Elkan-Vogel	PLY	Plymouth
ALF	Alfred	FLA	Flammer (Shawnee)	PRE	Presser
AMC	Arista	GAL	Galaxy	PVN	Pavanne (Intrada)
AMSI	AMSI (Lorenz)	GEN	Gentry	Ricordi	
Assoc	Associated Music Publishers	GIA	GIA Publications	RK	Robert King
AUR	Aureole (MSM)	GSCH	G. Schirmer (Hal Leonard)	RSCM	Royal School of Church Music
BAR	Bärenreiter	GVX	Genevox		
BBL	Broude Brothers	HAL	Hal Leonard	SCH	Schott (European American)
BEC	Beckenhorst	HÄN	Hänssler	SEL	Selah
BEL	Belwin (Warner)	HIN	Hinshaw	SHW	Shawnee
B&H	Boosey & Hawkes	HOP	Hope	SMP	Sacred Music Press (Lorenz)
BOR	Bornemann	HWG	H. W. Gray (Warner)	S&B	Stainer & Bell
BRD	Broadman	ION	Ionian Arts	TetraAB	Tetra A Broude
BRE	Breitkopf & Härtel	KAL	Kalmus	VIV	Vivace
BRN	Bourne	KJO	Kjos	WAL	Walton
BST	Boston	LAW	Lawson-Gould Publishing	WAR	Warner (Plymouth)
CFI	Carl Fischer	LED	Leduc	WLP	World Library
CV	Carus Verlag	LEM	Lemoine	WRD	Word Music
CFP	C. F. Peters	LOR	Lorenz		
CG	Choristers Guild (Lorenz)	MFS	Mark Foster	§ = also in other editions	
CHA	Chantry (Augsburg Fortress)	MC	Mercury		
CHE	Chester	MSM	MorningStar Music		
CLP	Warners: CCP/Belwin	MR	Musica Russica		
CPH	Concordia	NOV	Novello (Shawnee)		
Dover		OCP	Oregon Catholic Press		
DUR	Durand (Presser)	OXF	Oxford University Press		
EarthSongs		PAR	Paraclete		

Key to Music Abbreviations

acc	accompaniment	gtr	guitar	qrt	quartet
bar	baritone	hb	handbells	rec	recorder
bng	bongos	hc	handchimes	sax	saxophone
bsn	bassoon	hp	harp	sop	soprano
br	brass	hpd	harpsichord	str	strings
CT	countertenor	hrn	horn	synth	synthesizer
cant	cantor	inst	instrument	tamb	tambourine
ch	chimes	kybd	keyboard	tba	tuba
ch chr	childrens choir	M	medium	tbn	trombone
cl	clarinet	MH	medium high	ten	tenor
clo	cello	ML	medium low	tpt	trumpet
cong	congregation	mar	marimba	timp	timpani
cont	continuo	mxd	mixed	trbl	treble
cym	cymbal	narr	narrator	tri	triangle
DB	double or string bass	ob	oboe	U	unison
dbl	double	oct	octave	vc	violoncello
desc	descant	opt	optional	vcs	voices
div	divisi	orch	orchestra	voc	vocal
drm	drum	org	organ	vla	viola
eng hrn	English horn	perc	percussion	vln	violin
fc	finger cymbals	picc	piccolo	ww	woodwind
fl	flute	pno	piano	wndchm	windchimes
fr hrn	french horn	pt	part	xyl	xylophone
glock	glockenspiel	qnt	quintet		

Where a piece of music is tied particularly to a certain lectionary reading for the day, that is indicated by a letter in parentheses.

    F   First Reading   S   Second Reading   PrG   Processional Gospel
    P   Psalm   G   Gospel

§ = also in other editions

Music Listings

First Sunday in Advent

Year A

    Isaiah 2:1-5   *Weapons of war transformed into instruments of peace*
    Psalm 122   *I was glad when they said to me, "Let us go to the house of the Lord"*
    Romans 13:11-14   *Salvation is near; time to wake from sleep*
    Matthew 24:36-44   *The sudden coming of the Son of Man*

Bach, Johann Sebastian. "Zion Hears the Watchmen Singing." *Bach for All Seasons*. U, kybd, opt C inst. AFP 080065654X. § (G)
Boyce, William. "I Was Glad." SATB. NOV 29-0454-0. (P)
Distler, Hugo. "A Little Advent Music." SAB, fl, ob, clo, vln. CPH 97-6438.
———. "O Savior, Rend the Heavens Wide." *Chantry Choirbook*. SATB. AFP 0800657772.
Hovhaness, Alan. "Watchman, Tell Us of the Night." SATB, bar, org. CFP 6460. (G)
Howells, Herbert. "O Pray for the Peace of Jerusalem." SATB, org. OXF 42.064. (P)
Manz, Paul. "E'en So, Lord Jesus, Quickly Come." SATB. MSM 50-0001. SSAA. MSM 50-0450. TTBB. MSM50-0900. (G)
Parry, Charles Hubert H. "I Was Glad When They Said unto Me." SSATTB, org. HWG GCMR 2404. (P)
Proulx, Richard. "I Rejoiced When I Heard Them Say." 2 pt mxd, cong, kybd, fl, opt DB. GIA G-3780. (P)
Rameau, Jean Philippe. "Come, Thou Long-Expected Jesus." *To God Will I Sing*. MH, kybd. AFP 0800674332. ML, kybd. AFP 0800674340. (S, G)
Schalk, Carl. *Chorales for Advent*. U or SAB, kybd, adaptable. AFP 6000101112.
Thomas, André. "Keep Your Lamps." SATB, 3 conga drms. HIN HMC577. (G)
Willan, Healey. "Rejoice, O Jerusalem. Behold, Thy King Cometh." SATB, org. CPH 98-1506. (F)

Year B

    Isaiah 64:1-9   *Prayer that God would come with power and compassion*
    Psalm 80:1-7, 17-19   *Show the light of your countenance, and we shall be saved*
    1 Corinthians 1:3-9   *Gifts of grace sustain those who wait for the end*
    Mark 13:24-37   *The sudden coming of the Son of Man*

Bach, Johann Sebastian. "Savior of the Nations, Come." *Bach for All Seasons*. SATB, org. AFP 080065854X. (F)
———. "Wake, Awake, for Night Is Flying." *Bach for All Seasons*. SATB. AFP 080065854X.
Brahms, Johannes. "O Savior Rend the Heavens Wide/O Heiland, reiss die Himmel auf." Op. 74, no. 2. SATB. ECS 382. (F) §
Burleigh, Harry T. "My Lord What a Mornin'." *The Spirituals of Harry T. Burleigh*. L, kybd. WAR EL 03150. H, kybd. WAR EL 03151. (G)
Gieseke, Richard. "Lift Up Your Heads." U or 2 pt, cong. CPH 98-2959.
Helgen, John. "Keep Silence." SATB, pno, ten rec (C inst), opt wndchm. KJO 8891.
How, Martin. "Advent Message." SATB or U, org. *The New Oxford Easy Anthem Book*. OXF 0193533189.
Sirett, Mark G. "Thou Shalt Know Him When He Comes." SSAA. AFP 0800675304. SATB. AFP 0800655206. *The Augsburg Choirbook*. AFP 0800656784.
Thomas, André. "Keep Your Lamps." SATB, 3 conga drms. HIN HMC577.
Weiland, Brent. "Christ Is Coming." SATB, fl, org. AFP 0800654587. (G)

§ = *also in other editions*

Year C

Jeremiah 33:14-16	*A righteous branch springing up from David*
Psalm 25:1-10	*To you, O LORD, I lift up my soul*
1 Thessalonians 3:9-13	*Strengthen hearts of holiness for the coming of the Lord*
Luke 21:25-36	*Be alert for the coming of the Son of Man*

Bach, Johann Sebastian. "Savior of the Nations, Come." *Bach for All Seasons.* SATB, org. AFP 080065854X. (S, G)

———. "Wake, Awake, for Night Is Flying." *Bach for All Seasons*. SATB. AFP 080065854X. (G)

Burleigh, Harry T. "My Lord What a Mornin'." *The Spirituals of Harry T. Burleigh*. L, kybd. WAR EL 03150. H, kybd. WAR EL 03151. (G)

Christiansen, F. Melius. "Wake, Awake." SSAATTBB. AFP 0800645065. (G)

Distler, Hugo. "Lo! How a Rose E'er Blooming." *Chantry Choirbook*. SATB. AFP 0800657772. (F)

Hopson, Hal H. "Advent Prayer." 2 pt mxd, kybd, opt solo. AFP 0800658469.

Howells, Herbert. "A Spotless Rose." SATB, T or B solo. GAL 1.5014. (F)

Manz, Paul. "E'en So, Lord Jesus, Quickly Come." SATB. MSM 50-0001. SSAA. MSM 50-0450. TTBB. MSM50-0900. (G)

Pelz, Walter L. "Show Me Thy Ways." SATB, gtr, ob or fl. AFP 0800645421. (P)

Rossi, Richard Robert. "Conditor alme siderum." SATB, hb. GIA G-4725.

Schalk, Carl. "As the Dark Awaits the Dawn." SATB, org. AFP 0800658450.

Sirett, Mark G. "Thou Shalt Know Him When He Comes." SSAA. AFP 0800675304. SATB. AFP 0800655206. *The Augsburg Choirbook*. AFP 0800656784.

Thiman, Eric H. "Hark! A Thrilling Voice Is Sounding." SATB, org. NOV M.T.993.

Thomas, André. "Keep Your Lamps." SATB, 3 conga drums. HIN HMC577.

Thompson, Randall. "Howl Ye." *Peaceable Kingdom*. SSAATTBB. ECS 1750. (G)

Second Sunday in Advent

Year A

    Isaiah 11:1-10   *From David's line, a ruler bringing justice and peace*
    Psalm 72:1-7, 18-19   *In his time the righteous shall flourish*
    Romans 15:4-13   *Live in harmony, welcoming one another*
    Matthew 3:1-12   *A voice cries: Prepare the way of the Lord*

Bach, Johann Sebastian. "Comfort, Comfort Ye My People." U, SATB, 2 vln, vla, cont. CPH 98-2045. Str, fl, ob. CPH 98-2046. (F, P)
Billings, William. "Rejoice Ye Shining Worlds on High." SATB, kybd. CPH 98-3281.
Bunjes, Paul. "Comfort, Comfort Ye My People." SATB. CPH 98-1388. (F, P)
Busarow, Donald. "On Jordan's Banks the Baptist's Cry." SAB, ob, org, cong. CPH 98-2639. (G)
Cherwien, David. "On Jordan's Banks." SATB, org, opt br, hb, timp, cong, inst pts. AMSI 2020. (G)
Distler, Hugo. "Lo! How a Rose E'er Blooming." SATB. CPH 98-1925. (F)
Ferguson, John. "Comfort, Comfort." SATB, opt picc, 2 cl, tamb or opt kybd. AFP 0800646355. (F, P)
Gallus, Jacobus (Handl). "Enredietur virga." SATB. AMC AE244.
Howells, Herbert. "A Spotless Rose." *100 Carols for Choirs*. SATB, T or B solo. OXF 0-19-353227-1. (F)
Jean, Martin. "Advent Hymn." SATB. AFP 0800656628.
Praetorius, Michael. "Lo, How a Rose E'er Blooming." SATB. GSCH 2484. (F)
Thompson, Randall. "Blessed Be the Lord God." SATB. PRE 392-03021.

Year B

    Isaiah 40:1-11   *Good news of God's coming to a people in exile*
    Psalm 85:1-2, 8-13   *Righteousness and peace shall go before the L*ORD
    2 Peter 3:8-15a   *Waiting for and hastening the day of God*
    Mark 1:1-8   *John appears from the wilderness*

Bach, Johann Sebastian/arr. Hal H. Hopson. "The Lord Will Soon Appear." SATB, kybd. AFP 0800657527. (S)
Britten, Benjamin. "A New Year's Carol." *100 Carols for Choirs*. U, kybd. OXF 0-19-353227-1.
Ellingboe, Bradley. "Soul, Adorn Yourself with Gladness/Vengo a ti, Jesús amado." SATB. AFP 0800658477.
Ferguson, John. "Comfort, Comfort." SATB, opt picc, 2 cl, tamb or opt kybd. AFP 0800646355. (F)
Fleming, Larry L. "His Voice." SATB div. AFP 0800656504.
Handel, George Frideric. "And the Glory of the Lord." *Messiah*. SATB kybd or orch. § (F)
Jennings, Carolyn. "Climb to the Top of the Highest Mountain." SATB, opt ch chr or solo, kybd. CUR C-8118.
Larkin, Michael. "O Child of Promise Come." SATB, kybd. AFP 0800658442.
Rutter, John. "What Sweeter Music." SATB, org. OXF X319.
Walter, Johann. "Rise Up, Rise Up!" *Chantry Choirbook*. SATB. AFP 0800657772.

Year C

Malachi 3:1-4	*My messenger is a refiner and purifier*
or Baruch 5:1-9	*The return of scattered Israel*
Luke 1:68-79	*In the tender compassion of our God, the dawn from on high shall break upon us*
Philippians 1:3-11	*A harvest of righteousness on the day of Jesus Christ*
Luke 3:1-6	*Prepare the way of the Lord*

Dietterich, Philip R. "Carol of the Advent." SATB, org. HOP APM-216.
Ellingboe, Bradley. "Soul, Adorn Yourself with Gladness/Vengo a ti, Jesús amado." SATB. AFP 0800658477.
Ferguson, John. "Advent Processional." SATB. AFP 080065238X.
———. "Comfort, Comfort." SATB, opt picc, 2 cl, tamb or opt kybd. AFP 0800646355.
Goudimel, Claude/ed. Anne Heider. "Comfort, Comfort Ye My People." SATB GIA G-2893.
Handel, George Frideric. "And He Shall Purify." *Messiah*. SATB, kybd or orch. § (F)
———. "And the Glory of the Lord." *Messiah*. SATB, kybd or orch. § (F, G)
———. "But Who May Abide." *Messiah*. B solo, kybd or orch. § (F)
Mathews, Peter. "Blest Be the King." U, pno, opt fl. MSM 50-0400. (P)
Niedmann, Peter. "Lift Up Your Heads, Ye Mighty Gates." SATB, org. AFP 0800656350.
Stanford, Charles Villiers. "Benedictus." Op. 115, No. 2. SATB. S&B. (P)

Third Sunday in Advent

Year A

    Isaiah 35:1-10   *The desert blooms as God's people return from exile*
    Psalm 146:5-10   *The L*ORD *lifts up those who are bowed down*
    or Luke 1:47-55   *My spirit rejoices in God my Savior*
    James 5:7-10   *Patience until the coming of the Lord*
    Matthew 11:2-11   *The forerunner of Christ*

Berthier, Jacques. "Magnificat." *Songs and Prayers from Taizé.* Canon or chorale. GIA G-3719-P. (P)
Distler, Hugo. "Lo! How a Rose E'er Blooming." SATB. CPH 98-1925. §
———. "Maria Walks amid the Thorn." *Chantry Choirbook.* SATB. AFP 0800657772. §
Ferguson, John. "Advent Processional." SATB, adaptable. AFP 080065238X.
———. "He Comes to Us as One Unknown." SATB, org. AFP 0800656008. (G)
Fleming, Larry L. "Go and Tell John." SATB div. AFP 0800651464. (G)
Gibbs, Armstrong C. "Bless the Lord, O My Soul." *The Oxford Easy Anthem Book.* SATB, org. OXF 3533219. (P)
Hassler, Hans Leo. "My Soul Proclaims the Greatness of the Lord." *Chantry Choirbook.* SATB. AFP 080065772. (P)
Jennings, Arthur. "Springs in the Desert." SATB, T solo, org. HWG GCMR580. (F)
Jennings, Carolyn. "A New Magnificat." SATB, org, opt cong, opt soli. AFP 080065255X. (P)
Purcell, Henry. "Thou Knowest, Lord, the Secrets of Our Hearts." SATB. CPH 98-2321.
Schalk, Carl. "A Parish Magnificat." U, org, cong. CPH 98-2887. (P)
———. "As the Dark Awaits the Dawn." SATB, org. AFP 0800658450. (F)
———. "Hail, O Favored One." SATB, opt solo. AFP 080064705X.
Willan, Healey. "Magnificat and Nunc dimittis." SATB, org. CPH 98-144. (P)
Wood, Charles. "O Thou, the Central Orb." OXF 0-19-353109-0.
Zacharia, Cesare de/arr. Larry Long. "Magnificat." SATB. AFP 0800653882. (P)

Year B

    Isaiah 61:1-4, 8-11   *Righteousness and praise flourish like a garden*
    Psalm 126   *The L*ORD *has done great things for us*
    or Luke 1:47-55   *The Lord has lifted up the lowly*
    1 Thessalonians 5:16-24   *Kept in faith until the coming of Christ*
    John 1:6-8, 19-28   *A witness to the light*

Gibbons, Orlando. "This Is the Record of John." SAATB, T solo. OXF TCM 42R 352084-2. (G)
Hopson, Hal H. "O Day of Peace." SAB, kybd, opt 3 oct hb. AFP 0800653750.
How, Martin. "Advent Message." U. OXF W.161.
Jean, Martin. "Advent Hymn." SATB. AFP 0800656628.
Manz, Paul. "E'en So, Lord Jesus, Quickly Come." SATB. MSM 50-0001.
Nystedt, Knut. "I Will Greatly Rejoice." SATB. HMC 226.
Schalk, Carl. "As the Dark Awaits the Dawn." SATB, org. AFP 0800658450.
Susa, Conrad. "El Desembre Congelat/On December's Frozen Ground." *Carols and Lullabies.* SATB, org or hp, gtr, mar. ECS 4839.

Year C

Zephaniah 3:14-20 *Rejoice, the Lord is in your midst*
Isaiah 12:2-6 *In your midst is the Holy One of Israel*
Philippians 4:4-7 *Rejoice, the Lord is near*
Luke 3:7-18 *One more powerful is coming, baptizing with fire*

Anonymous sixteenth century/arr. John Redford. "Rejoice in the Lord Always." OXF 43.243. (S)
Bach, Johann Sebastian. "Zion Hears the Watchmen Singing." *Bach for All Seasons.* U, kybd. AFP 080065654X. (F)
Bach, Johann Sebastian/arr. Michael Burkhardt. "Prepare Thyself, Zion." U, kybd, opt clo/bsn. MSM 50-0415. (F)
Byrd, William. "Laetentur coeli." NOV 16006.
Crotch, William. "Be Peace on Earth." *The Oxford Easy Anthem Book.* SA, org. OXF 3533219.
Erickson, Richard. "Light One Candle to Watch for Messiah." SATB, org. AFP 0800657519.
Jacob, Gordon. "O Lord I Will Praise Thee." *The Oxford Easy Anthem Book.* SATB, org. OXF 3533219.
Jean, Martin. "Advent Hymn." SATB. AFP 0800656628.
Jennings, Carolyn. "Climb to the Top of the Highest Mountain." SATB, opt children, org. KJO C-8118.
Organ, Anne Krentz. "Come My Light." 2 pt, pno. AFP 0800675819.
Purcell, Henry. "Rejoice in the Lord Always." SATB, org, opt str. CPH 97-6344. (S)
Willan, Healey. "Lift Up Your Heads, Ye Mighty Gates." SATB. CPH 98-2003.

Fourth Sunday in Advent

Year A

Isaiah 7:10-16	*The sign of Immanuel*
Psalm 80:1-7, 17-19	*Show the light of your countenance and we shall be saved*
Romans 1:1-7	*Paul's greeting to the church at Rome*
Matthew 1:18-25	*A God near at hand*

Bairstow, Edward C. "Let All Mortal Flesh Keep Silence." SATB. S&B CCL 294.
Dawson, William. "Mary Had a Baby." SATB, S solo. KJO T 142. (G)
Distler, Hugo. "Maria Walks amid the Thorn." SAB. CPH 98-2306. (G)
Ferguson, John. "He Comes to Us as One Unknown." SATB, org. AFP 0800656008. (G)
———. "O Come, O Come, Emmanuel." SSATBB, vla. MSM 50-0015. (G)
Hallock, Peter. "The 'O' Antiphons." SATB, org, hb. ION CH-1030.
Handel, George Frideric. "Behold, a Virgin Shall Conceive." *Messiah*. SATB, A solo, kybd. § (F, G)
———. "O Thou That Tellest." *Messiah*. SATB, A solo, kybd. §
Hillert, Richard. "Come, Thou Long-Expected Jesus." *Church Choir Book II*. SAB. CPH 97-56.
Isaac, Heinrich/arr. Anthony G. Petti. "Ecce virgo concipies." *Christmas and Advent Motets for 4 Voices*, 3rd ed. SATB. CHE CH55110. (F, G)
Kemp, Helen. "A Waiting Carol." U, kybd, fl, drm. CGA-555.
Mathias, William H. "Hear, O Thou Shepherd of Israel." SAATTB, org. OXF A339. (P)
Nester, Leo. "Magnificat." SATB. MSM 80-077.
Schütz, Heinrich. "O Gracious Lord, Our God." SS, org. CPH 98-155.
Scott, K. Lee. "Peace Came to Earth." SATB, org, opt cong, opt hrn. CPH 98-3376. (G)
Thompson, Randall. "My Soul Doth Magnify the Lord." S solo. ECS 124.
Willan, Healey/ed. Carl Schalk. "The Great O Antiphons of Advent." SATB. CPH 97-584.

Year B

2 Samuel 7:1-11, 16	*The Lord's promise to David*
Luke 1:47-55	*The Lord has lifted up the lowly*
or Psalm 89:1-4, 19-26	*Your love, O Lord, forever will I sing*
Romans 16:25-27	*The mystery of God revealed in Jesus Christ*
Luke 1:26-38	*The angel appears to Mary*

Biebl, Franz. "Ave Maria." SATB. HIN 1251. TTBB. HIN 1253.
Brahms, Johannes. "A Dove Flew Down from Heaven." *Chantry Choirbook*. SATB. AFP 0800657772. § (G)
Distler, Hugo. "Lo! How a Rose E'er Blooming." *Chantry Choirbook*. SATB. AFP 0800657772. §
———. "Maria Walks amid the Thorn." *Chantry Choirbook*. SAB. AFP 0800657772. §
Ellingboe, Bradley. "Magnificat." SSAA, S solo, ob, mar. KJO 6274. (P)
Ferguson, John. "Advent Processional." SATB. AFP 080065238X.
Jennings, Carolyn. "A New Magnificat." SATB cong, org. AFP 080065255X. *The Augsburg Choirbook*. AFP 0800656784. (P, G)
Proulx, Richard. "Festival Magnificat." SATB, org, opt cong, br. SEL 410-866. (P)
Schalk, Carl. "My Soul Gives Glory to the Lord." SATB, U, kybd, children, opt fl or hb. MSM 50-1058. (P)
Schroeder, Hermann. "The Angel Gabriel." SATB. CPH 98-2381. (G)
Schütz, Heinrich/arr. Robert Buckley Farlee. "My Soul Exalts Your Name, O Lord." SATB, kybd. AFP 080067524X. (P)

Year C

Micah 5:2-5a — *From Bethlehem comes a ruler*
Luke 1:47-55 — *The Lord has lifted up the lowly*
or Psalm 80:1-7 — *Show the light of your countenance and we shall be saved*
Hebrews 10:5-10 — *I have come to do your will*
Luke 1:39-45 [46-55] — *Blessed are you among women/My soul magnifies the Lord*

Bach, Johann Sebastian. "Magnificat anima mea." *Magnificat in D Major.* SATB, kybd or orch. § (P, G)
Brahms, Johannes. "A Dove Flew Down from Heaven." *Chantry Choirbook.* SATB. AFP 0800657772.
Carter, Andrew. "Mary's Magnificat." SATB, org. OXF X299. (P, G)
Eccard, Johannes. "Over the Hills Maria Went." SSATB. GSCH 8420. (G)
Goetze, Mary. "The Angel Gabriel." U, kybd. B&H OCTB6256.
Hassler, Hans Leo. "Then Mary Said to the Angel." *Chantry Choirbook.* SATB. AFP 0800657772. §
Jennings, Carolyn. "A New Magnificat." SATB cong, org. AFP 080065255X. *The Augsburg Choirbook.* AFP 0800656784. (P, G)
Mathias, William H. "Hear, O Thou Shepherd of Israel." SAATTB, org. OXF A339. (P)
Prower, Anthony. "The Angel Gabriel from Heaven Came." SATB, org. CPH 98-2853.
Rachmaninoff, Sergei. "Magnificat." *All Night Vigil. Songs of the Church.* SATB, div. HWG GCMR GB 640. (P, G)
Schalk, Carl. "Mary Went Up to Hill Country." SATB, org. CPH 98-3172. (G)
———. "My Soul Gives Glory to the Lord." SATB, U, kybd, children, opt fl or hb. MSM 50-1058. (P, G)
Schütz, Heinrich/arr. Robert Buckley Farlee. "My Soul Exalts Your Name, O Lord." SATB, kybd. AFP 080067524X. (P, G)
Willcocks, David. "Gabriel's Message." *Carols for Choirs 2.* OXF 3535653.

Nativity of Our Lord, Christmas Eve (I)

Years A, B, C

Isaiah 9:2-7 — *Light shines: a child is born for us*
Psalm 96 — *Let the heavens rejoice and the earth be glad*
Titus 2:11-14 — *The grace of God has appeared*
Luke 2:1-14 [15-20] — *God with us*

Bach, Johann Sebastian. "From Heaven Above." *Christmas Oratorio, part 2*. SATB, kybd. BÄR BA5014.90 § (G)
———. "From Heaven Above to Earth I Come." *Bach for All Seasons*. SSATB. AFP 080065854X. § (G)
———. "Gloria in excelsis Deo." *Bach for All Seasons*. SATB. AFP 080065854X. (G)
Britten, Benjamin. "A Boy Was Born." SATB. OXF X92.
Burkhardt, Michael. "From Heaven Above to Earth I Come." (S)SATB, solo, 2 trbl inst, opt strgs, kybd, inst. MSM 50-1040. (G)
Christiansen, F. Melius. "Lullaby on Christmas Eve." SATB, S solo. AFP 0800645103.
Ebeling, Johann Georg. "All My Heart This Night Rejoices: Be Glad and Sing." SATB, 2 trbl inst, kybd. CPH 97-537. (G)
Ellingboe, Bradley. "Jesus, Jesus, Rest Your Head." AFP 0800655796. *The Augsburg Choirbook*. AFP 0800656784.
Farlee, Robert Buckley. "This Is the Night." SATB, org. AFP 0800656393.
Gardner, John. "Tomorrow Shall Be My Dancing Day." SATB, kybd. OXF X356.
Handel, George Frideric. "For Unto Us a Child Is Born." *Messiah*. SATB, kybd or orch. § (F)
Hassler, Hans Leo. "O Sing unto the Lord." SATB. ECS 708. (P)
Mathias, William H. "A Babe Is Born." SATB, org (or pno duet). OXF 3430231.
———. "In excelsis gloria." SATB. OXF X364 343168. (G)
Near, Gerald. "O magnum mysterium." U, org. CAL 6003. (G)
Pinkham, Daniel. "Christmas Cantata." SATB, org, 2 tpt, 2 tbn. Robert King 602.
Poulenc, Francis. "O magnum mysterium." SATB. Salabert 12525.
Praetorius, Michael. "Psallite." *Chantry Choirbook*. SATB. AFP 0800657772.
Proulx, Richard. "It Came upon the Midnight Clear." SAB, cong, org, tpt. GIA G-4323. (G)
Purcell, Henry. "O Sing unto the Lord." SATB, soloists, str, org. NOV 29 0146 03. (P)
Rameau, Jean Philippe/ed. Ronald A. Nelson. "Wake, O Shepherds." U, kybd, C inst. AFP 0800675967. (G)
Reger, Max. "The Virgin's Slumber Song." SSA, kybd. GSC HL50482659. (G)
———/ed. K. Lee Scott. "The Virgin's Slumber Song." *Sing a Song of Joy*. MH, kybd. AFP 0800647882. ML, kybd. AFP 0800652827.
Rutter, John. "Christmas Night." SATB. OXF 84.316. (G)
Schalk, Carl. "Before the Marvel of This Night." SATB, org, opt inst pts: fl or ob, hrn, str, hb, hp or gtr, and DB. AFP 0800646037. (G)
Schein, Johann H. "From Heaven Above." SSB, org. GIA G-300. (G)
Schroeder, Hermann. "In Bethlehem a Wonder." SATB, fl, vln or ob. CPH 98-2063.
Scott, K. Lee. "Infant Holy, Infant Lowly." SATB. AFP 0800650271. (G)
Sweelinck, Jan Pieterszoon. "Hodie Christus natus est." SSATB. Columbo FC338.
Victoria, Tomás Luis de. "O magnum mysterium." SATB. GSCH 10193. (G)
Wetzler, Robert. "Still, Still, Still." U, org, opt fl. AFP 0800645219. SATB, org, opt fl. AFP 0800645227
Willcocks, David. "Sussex Carol." SATB, org. OXF X75. (G)

Nativity of Our Lord, Christmas Dawn (II)

Years A, B, C

Isaiah 62:6-12	*God comes to restore the people*
Psalm 97	*Light has sprung up for the righteous*
Titus 3:4-7	*Saved through water and the Spirit*
Luke 2:[1-7] 8-20	*The birth of the Messiah revealed to shepherds*

Bach, Johann Sebastian. "Break Forth, O Beauteous Heavenly Light." *Bach for All Seasons*. SATB, kybd. AFP 080065854X.

———. "From Heaven Above to Earth I Come." *Bach for All Seasons*. SATB. AFP 080065854X. (G)

———. "The Savior of the World Is Born." SATB or 2 pt, org. CPH 97-470. (G)

Barnett, Steve. "Go! Tell It On the Mountain." SATB, opt str and perc. OCT B6396. (G)

Batastini, Robert J. "Gaudete." SATB, hb, fc, drm. GIA G-3056.

Berger, Jean. "Behold, the Lord Hath Proclaimed." SATB. KJO 5398.

Binkerd, Gordon. "Third Mass of Christmas." SATB, org. B&H 5829.

Burt, Alfred. "All on a Christmas Morning." *The Alfred Burt Carols*, Set I. SATB or solo, kybd. SHW A-449. (G)

Chilcott, Bob. "Shepherd's Carol." SATB, div. OXF 343296X.

Ellingboe, Bradley. "Jesus, Jesus, Rest Your Head." SATB. AFP 0800655796. *The Augsburg Choirbook*. AFP 0800656784. (G)

Ferguson, John. "Good Christian Friends, Rejoice." SATB, kybd. CPH 98-3069. (G)

———. "Unto Us Is Born God's Son." SATB, org. AFP 0800652398. (G)

Franck, César/ed. K. Lee Scott. "Nativity Carol." *Rejoice Now, My Spirit*. MH, kybd. AFP 0800651081. ML, kybd. AFP 080065109X.

Hillert, Richard. "On This Day Earth Shall Ring." SATB, kybd. CPH 98-3149.

Holst, Gustav. "In the Bleak Midwinter." SATB. GSCH 50483537. (G)

———/arr. Brad Printz. "In the Bleak Midwinter." 2 pt mxd, pno, perc, hb. HOP 6540408341. (G)

Mathias, William H. "Hodie Christus natus est." SATB. OXF A400.

Morton, Graeme. "In the Splendor of the Dawn." SATB. AFP 0800675312.

———. "Ring Glad Bells." SATB, org or pno. AFP 0800675894.

Nelson, Ronald A. "Choral Fanfare for Christmas." SATB or TTBB, org or br. B&H OCTB5337.

Nestor, Leo. "A Child Is Born." SATB, org. ECS 4389. (G)

Nystedt, Knut. "Your Savior Comes." *Four Liturgical Songs*. SATB, kybd. MSM 80-904. (G)

Pergolesi, Giovanni. "Glory to God in the Highest." SAB, org. LOR 7380. (G)

Praetorius, Michael. "Psallite." *Chantry Choirbook*. SATB. AFP 0800657772.

———. "To Us Is Born Emmanuel/Enatus est Emanuel." *Chantry Choirbook*. SATB. AFP 0800657772. §

Proulx, Richard. "A Child Is Born in Bethlehem." SAB, hb. GIA G-4156. (G)

———. "Once in Royal David's City." SATB, org, fl. AFP 0800645839. (G)

Scott, K Lee. "When Christmas Morn Is Dawning. SATB, org. MSM 50-1010.

Shaw, Martin. "Fanfare for Christmas Day." SATB, org, 2 tpt. GSCH 8745.

Sirett, Mark G. "What Sweeter Music." SATB. AFP 0800659287.

Vivaldi, Antonio/arr. S. Drummond Wolff. "Gloria in excelsis Deo." SATB, org, tpt. AFP 0800654625. (G)

Walter, Johann. "Now Sing We, Now Rejoice." SATB. CPH 98-204.

Werner, Gregor Joseph. "Puer natus in Bethlehem." SATB, vln or fl, cont. CPH 98-2313. (G)

Willan, Healey. "What Is This Lovely Fragrance?" SATB, kybd. OXF 42.171.

Willcocks, David. "Once in Royal David's City." *100 Carols for Choirs*. SATB, desc, org. OXF 0193532271. (G)

Nativity of Our Lord, Christmas Day (III)

Years A, B, C

Isaiah 52:7-10 — *Heralds announce God's salvation*
Psalm 98 — *All the ends of the earth have seen the victory of our God*
Hebrews 1:1-4 [5-12] — *God has spoken by a Son*
John 1:1-14 — *The Word became flesh*

Bach, Johann Sebastian. "Gloria in excelsis Deo." *Bach for All Seasons.* SATB, kybd. AFP 080065854X.
———. "O Little One, Sweet." *100 Carols for Choirs.* OXF 0193532771.
Bell, John L. "Sing a New Song to the Lord/Psalm 98." SATB, cong, org. GIA G-4380. (P)
Bertalot, John. "See Amid the Winter's Snow." SATB, kybd, 2 tpt, opt cong. AFP 0800653238.
Bouman, Paul. "A Babe Is Born." SATB. CPH 98-1058.
Caldwell, Paul/arr. Sean Ivory. "Hope for Resolution." SATB or 2 or 3 pt, fl, pno, sax, perc. EAR.
Carter, Andrew. "Hodie Christus natus est." SATB, org. OXF X382. (G)
Distler, Hugo. "Lo! How a Rose E'er Blooming." *Chantry Choirbook.* SATB. AFP 0800657772. §
Farlee, Robert Buckley. "Christmas Day." *To God Will I Sing.* MH, kybd. AFP 0800674332. ML, kybd. AFP 0800674340.
Ferguson, John. "In the Beginning." SATB, org, opt ob. KJO 8885. (G)
———. "Rejoice, Rejoice, This Happy Morn." SATB, vla. MSM 50-1053.
Gieschen, Thomas. "Of the Father's Love Begotten." SATB, cong, ob, vln, org. CPH 98-2723. (G)
Handel, George Frideric. "Let All the Angels of God Worship Him." *Messiah.* SATB, kybd or orch. §
Hassler, Hans Leo. "God Now Dwells among Us." SAB or TTB, kybd. MF MF129. (G)
Holst, Gustav. "Christmas Day." SATB, orch or kybd. NOV A 6435.
Hovland, Egil. "The Glory of the Father." SATB. WAL W-2973. (G)
Hurd, David. "Cantate Domino/Psalm 98." SATB, opt cong, opt kybd. AFP 0800650468. (P)
Manz, Paul. "Peace Came to Earth." SATB, opt cong. MSM 50-1020.
Morton, Graeme. "Ring Glad Bells." SATB, org or pno. AFP 0800675894.
Praetorius, Michael. "Let All Together Praise Our God." SATB. CPH 98-3136. (G)
———. "To Us Is Born Emmanuel/Enatus est Emanuel." *Chantry Choirbook.* SATB. AFP 0800657772. § (G)
Ryan-Wenger, Michael. "In the Beginning Was the Word." SATB, kybd. AFP 0800649230. (G)
Schalk, Carl. "Let Our Gladness Have No End." SATB, hb. CPH 98-3164.
Scheidt, Samuel. "Sing, Rejoice/Psallite unigenito." SATB, org. CPH 98-2806. (G)
Schulz-Widmar, Russell. "Midnight Clear." SATB, org. AFP 0800651235.
Sedio, Mark. "There Is No Rose of Such Vertu." SATB, org. AFP 0800656458.
Stainer, John. "How Beautiful upon the Mountains." SATB, org. NOV 018330. (F)
Sweelinck, Jan Pieterszoon. "Hodie Christus natus est." SSATB. HWG GCMR 01855.
Thomas, André. "African Noel." SATB div, perc. LAW 52747.
———. "Here's a Pretty Little Baby." SATB, solo, synth, opt DB. EAR S-80.
Victoria, Tomás Luis de. "O magnum mysterium. SATB. GSCH 10193. (G)
Warland, Dale. "Wexford Carol." SATB, fl. AFP 0800647203.
Willan, Healey. "The Word Was Made Flesh." SA, kybd. CPH 97-6160. (G)
Willcocks, David. "Hark! The Herald Angels Sing." *100 Carols for Choirs.* SATB, org. OXF 0193532271.
Zimmermann, Heinz Werner. "And the Word Became Flesh." SATB. CPH 98-2177. (G)

First Sunday after Christmas

Year A

    Isaiah 63:7-9   *Israel saved by God's own presence*
    Psalm 148   *The splendor of the Lord is over earth and heaven*
    Hebrews 2:10-18   *Christ shares flesh and blood to free humankind*
    Matthew 2:13-23   *The slaughter of innocent children*

Bach, Johann Sebastian. "Break Forth, O Beauteous Heavenly Light." *Bach for All Seasons*. SATB, kybd. AFP 080065854X.
Eccard, Johannes. "Raise a Song, Let Praise Abound." *Chantry Choirbook*. SATTB. AFP 0800657772.
Ferguson, John. "Good Christian Friends, Rejoice." SATB, vla. MSM 50-4025.
Howells, Herbert. "Here Is the Little Door." SATB. GAL 1-5227.
Pelz, Walter L. "Coventry Carol." SATB, hp or kybd. AFP 0800646088. (G)
Praetorius, Michael. "To Us Is Born Emmanuel/Enatus est Emmanuel." *Chantry Choirbook*. SATB. AFP 0800657772.
Rorem, Ned. "Psalm 148." *Cycle of Holy Songs for Voice and Piano*. Solo. Peer 01-073794-212. (P)
Shaw, Martin. "Coventry Carol." *100 Carols for Choirs*. SATB. OXF 0193532271. (G)
Stevens, Halsey. "Psalm 148/Praise Ye the Lord." SATB. MSF EH 2. (G)
Vaughan Williams, Ralph. "The Blessed Son of God." *Two Chorals from the Cantata "This Holy Day."* SATB. OXF 43.929. *Carols for Choirs 1*. OXF 0193532220.
Warland, Dale. "Coventry Carol." SATB. CPH 98-1928. (G)

Year B

    Isaiah 61:10—62:3   *Clothed in garments of salvation*
    Psalm 148   *The splendor of the Lord is over earth and heaven*
    Galatians 4:4-7   *Children and heirs of God*
    Luke 2:22-40   *The presentation of the child*

Bass, Claude L. "At Bethlehem." SATB, kybd. AFP 080065742X.
Britten, Benjamin. "This Little Babe." *Ceremony of Carols*. SATB, hp or pno. B&H OCTB1830
Clausen, René. "Nunc dimittis." SATB, org or orch. AFP 0800676432. (G)
Desamours, Emile. "Noel Ayisyen." SATB. MF 582.
Ellingboe, Bradley. "Simeon's Song." SATB, pno. KJO 8988. (G)
Marshall, Jane. "Song of Simeon." SATB, org. ECS 4956. (G)
Scholz, Robert. "Nunc dimittis." SSATB, kybd, opt full orch. AFP 6000001215. (G)
Willcocks, David. "Sussex Carol." SATB, org. OXF X75.

Year C

1 Samuel 2:18-20, 26 — *The boy Samuel grew in favor with the L*ORD *and the people*
Psalm 148 — *The splendor of the L*ORD *is over earth and heaven*
Colossians 3:12-17 — *Clothe yourselves in love; let the peace of Christ rule your hearts*
Luke 2:41-52 — *The boy Jesus increased in wisdom, and in divine and human favor*

Averitt, William. "He Is Born the Divine Christ Child." SATB. CPH 98-2953.
Britten, Benjamin. "A Boy Was Born." SATB. OXF 84.092.
Carnahan, Craig. "The Christ-Child Lay on Mary's Lap." SATB, pno or harp. AFP 0800659260.
Ellingboe, Bradley. "Teach Each Other in Wisdom." SATB, org. KJO 8986. (S, G)
Heim, Bret. "All Glory Be to God Alone." U, kybd. CPH 98-3619.
Joubert, John. "Torches." *Carols for Choirs 1*. SATB, org. OXF 3532220.
Laster, James. "Sing of Mary, Pure and Lowly." SATB, org. AFP 0800674235. (G)
Pinkham, Daniel. "Let the Word of Christ Dwell in You." *Letters from Saint Paul*. ECS 142. (S)
Sutcliffe, James. "What Child Is This?" SATB. KJO 8751.
Vaughan Williams, Ralph. "The Blessed Son of God." *Two Chorals from the Cantata "This Holy Day."* SATB. OXF 43.929. *Carols for Choirs 1*. OXF 0193532220.

Second Sunday after Christmas

Years A, B, C

Jeremiah 31:7-14	*Joy at the gathering of God's scattered flock*
or Sirach 24:1-12	*Wisdom lives among God's people*
Psalm 147:12-20	*Worship the L<small>ORD</small>, O Jerusalem; praise your God, O Zion*
or Wis. of Sol. 10:15-21	*We sing, O Lord, to your holy name; we praise with one accord your defending hand*
Ephesians 1:3-14	*The will of God made known in Christ*
John 1:[1-9] 10-18	*God with us: the incarnation of the Word*

Bach, Johann Sebastian. "O Jesus Christ, My Life, My Light/O Jesu Christ, meins Lebens Licht." *Bach for All Seasons*. SATB, org. AFP 080065854X.

Behnke, John. "Of the Father's Love Begotten." SATB, cong, hb, org. MSM 60-1000. (G)

Bengtson, Bruce. "Behold My Servant." SATB, org, opt cong. AFP 0880659120.

Bisbee, B. Wayne. "O Splendor of God's Glory Bright." 2 pt trbl or mxd, pno. AFP 0800659252. (G)

Bouman, Paul. "God Is Light." SATB, org. AFP 0800653254. (G)

Ferguson, John. "Unto Us Is Born God's Son." SATB, org. AFP 0800652398.

Folkening, John. "Psalm 147." *Six Psalm Settings with Antiphons*. SATB, cong, opt kybd. MSM 80-700. (P)

Gardner, John. "Tomorrow Shall Be My Dancing Day." SATB, kybd, opt perc. OXF 40.107.

Hovland, Egil. "The Glory of the Father." SATB. WAL 2973. (G)

Marshall, Jane. "Sing to God." SATB, org. BEL GCMR03548.

Martinson, Joel. "And the Word Became Flesh." SATB. SEL 410-541. (G)

Mendelssohn, Felix. "There Shall a Star Come Out of Jacob." *Chantry Choirbook*. SATB, org. AFP 0800657772. §

Neswick, Bruce. "The Blessed Son of God." SATB, org. AFP 0800656482.

Powell, Rosephayne. "The Word Was God." SATB div. HAL 08738700. (G)

Proulx, Richard, ed. "Verbum caro factum est." SATB. GIA G-4158. (G)

Roberts, Paul. "The Word Became Flesh." SATB, fl. AFP 0800657659. *The Augsburg Choirbook*. AFP 0800656784. (G)

Ryan-Wenger, Michael. "In the Beginning Was the Word." SATB, kybd. AFP 0800649230. (G)

Saint-Saëns, Camille. "A Christmas Alleluia." SATB. FB 8738842.

Schalk, Carl. "Let Our Gladness Have No End." SATB, hb. CPH 98-3164.

Sedio, Mark. "Wexford Carol." SATB and U, fl or other C inst, org. AFP 080065465X.

Vivaldi, Antonio. "Domine fili unigenite." *Gloria in D*. SATB, org or str, cont. RIC R131415. §

Willan, Healey. "The Word Was Made Flesh." *We Praise Thee II*. SA, org. CPH 97-7610. (G)

Willcocks, David. "Of the Father's Love Begotten." *100 Carols for Choirs*. SATB div, org. OXF 3532271. (G)

Zimmermann, Heinz Werner. "And the Word Became Flesh." SATB. CPH 97-2177. (G)

Epiphany of Our Lord

Years A, B, C

Isaiah 60:1-6 — *Nations come to the light*
Psalm 72:1-7, 10-14 — *All kings shall bow down before him*
Ephesians 3:1-12 — *The gospel's promise extends to all*
Matthew 2:1-12 — *Revelation of Christ to the nations of the earth*

Bach, Johann Sebastian. "O Morning Star, How Fair and Bright." *Bach for All Seasons.* SATB. AFP 080065854X. (F)
———. "The Only Son from Heaven" (alt. text for "Bring Low Our Ancient Adam"). *The Augsburg Choirbook.* SATB, kybd, opt inst. AFP 0800656784. *Bach for All Seasons.* AFP 080065854X. §
Busarow, Donald. "O Morning Star, How Fair and Bright." SAB, org, trbl inst, cong. CPH 98-2819. (F)
Christiansen, F. Melius. "Beautiful Savior." SSAATTBB, A solo. AFP 0800652584. *Augsburg Choirbook.* AFP 0800656784.
Erickson, Richard. "I Want to Walk as a Child of the Light." SATB, org. AFP 0800658396.
Fleming, Larry L. "Lord of the Dance." SATB. AFP 0800655354.
Forsberg, Charles. "Fairest Lord Jesus." SATB, pno. AFP 0800656962.
Hirten, John Karl. "For Glory Dawns upon You." *The Augsburg Choirbook.* 2 pt mxd, kybd. AFP 0800656784. (F)
Hobby, Robert A. "O Morning Star, How Fair and Bright." SAB, cong, 2 trbl inst, org. MSM 60-2000A. (F)
How, Martin. "Arise, Shine, for Your Light Has Come." 2 pt mxd, org, cong. ION CH-1009. (F)
Jennings, Kenneth. "Arise, Shine, for Thy Light Has Come." *The Augsburg Choirbook.* SATB. AFP 0800656784. (F)
Lassus, Rudolph de/arr. Richard Proulx. "Stars in the Sky Proclaim." SAB. AFP 0800672445. (G)
Lauridsen, Morten. "O nata lux." SATB. PM 619081210.
Martinson, Joel. "Arise, Shine!" SATB, org. AFP 0800652401. (F)
Mendelssohn, Felix. "There Shall a Star Come Out of Jacob." *Chantry Choirbook.* SATB, org. AFP 0800657772. §
Neswick, Bruce. "Epiphany Carol." U, kybd. AFP 0800653912. *The Augsburg Choirbook.* AFP 0800656784.
Praetorius, Michael. "O Morning Star, How Fair and Bright!" *Chantry Choirbook.* SSATB. AFP 0800657772.
Schalk, Carl. "How Lovely Shines the Morning Star." 2 pt mxd. CPH 97-7618.
Tallis, Thomas. "O nata lux." SATTB. OXF 43.228.
Thomerson, Kathleen. "I Want to Walk as a Child of the Light." SATB, kybd. GIA G-2786.
Weaver, John. "Epiphany Alleluias." SATB, org. B&H. (G)
White, David Ashley. "Star in the East." SATB, org, opt perc. SEL 405-316. (G)
Willan, Healey. "Arise, Shine, for Thy Light Is Come." SATB, org. CPH 98-1508. (F)
———. "The Three Kings." SSATB. OXF OCS 718.340498-2. (G)
Wood, Dale. "Rise, Shine!" SATB, org. AFP 0800655923. *The Augsburg Choirbook.* AFP 0800656784.
Zgodava, Richard. "Out of the Orient Crystal Skies." SATB, opt perc. AFP 0800652711. (G)

Baptism of Our Lord (Sunday 1 / Epiphany 1)

Year A

    Isaiah 42:1-9   *The servant of the Lord brings justice*
    Psalm 29   *The voice of the Lord is upon the waters*
    Acts 10:34-43   *Jesus' ministry after his baptism*
    Matthew 3:13-17   *Revelation of Christ as God's servant*

Bach, Johann Sebastian. "The Only Son from Heaven" (alt. text for "Bring Low Our Ancient Adam"). *The Augsburg Choirbook*. SATB, kybd, opt inst. AFP 0800656784. *Bach for All Seasons*. AFP 080065854X. §
Biery, James. "The Waters of Life." SATB, org. AFP 0800657683.
Callahan, Charles. "The Baptism of Our Lord." U, opt desc, org. MSM 50-2003. (G)
Cleobury, Stephen. "Joys Seven." SATB, org. OXF 019 353 227 1.
Ellingboe, Bradley. "Spirit of God, Descend upon My Heart." SATB, clar, bells, opt wndchm. KJO 8856.
Hallock, Peter. "The Baptism of Christ." SATB. GIA G-2331. (G)
Mathias, William H. "Arise, Shine, for Your Light Has Come." SATB, org. OXF A327.
Neswick, Bruce. "Jesus Came from Nazareth." 2 pt, solo, org. AFP 0800655192. (G)
Pinkham, Daniel. "For the Gift of Water." SATB, opt org. ECS 5204.
Schütz, Heinrich. "The Voice of the Lord Sounds upon the Waters." SATB, kybd. MC40. (P)
Wyton, Alec. "When Jesus Went to Jordan's Stream." SATB, fl, hb, org. PAR PPM8606. (G)

Year B

    Genesis 1:1-5   *God creates light*
    Psalm 29   *The voice of the Lord is upon the waters*
    Acts 19:1-7   *Baptized in the name of the Lord Jesus*
    Mark 1:4-11   *Revelation of Christ as God's servant*

Bach, Johann Sebastian. "Christ unser Herr zum Jordan kam." *Cantata BWV 7*. SATB, kybd or str, oboe d'amore, cont. HÄN 31 007/03. § (G)
Busarow, Donald. "The Baptism Carol." SATB, kybd. CPH 98-3223. (G)
Callahan, Charles. "The Baptism of Our Lord." U, opt desc, org. MSM 50-2003. (G)
Neswick, Bruce. "Epiphany Carol." U, org. AFP 0800653912. *The Augsburg Choirbook*. AFP 0800656784.
Ore, Charles W. "This Is My Son." SATB, opt cong, tpt, org. CPH 98-3288. (G)
Plag, Johannes/arr. Richard Proulx. "Jesus Went to Jordan's Stream." 2 pt mxd, org. AFP 0800655249. (G)
Uhl, Dan. "This Is My Beloved Son." *The Augsburg Choirbook*. SATB, org. AFP 0800656784. (G)

Year C

Isaiah 43:1-7	*When you pass through the waters, do not fear, for I am with you*
Psalm 29	*The voice of the Lord is upon the waters*
Acts 8:14-17	*Prayer and laying on of hands for the Holy Spirit*
Luke 3:15-17, 21-22	*The baptism of Jesus with the descent of the Holy Spirit*

Bach, Johann Sebastian. "The Only Son from Heaven" (alt. text for "Bring Low Our Ancient Adam"). *The Augsburg Choirbook*. SATB, kybd, opt inst. AFP 0800656784. *Bach for All Seasons*. AFP 080065854X. §

Biery, James. "The Waters of Life." SATB, org. AFP 0800657683. (F)

Busarow, Donald, "The Baptism Carol." SATB, kybd. CPH 98-3223.

Helman, Michael. "Christ, When for Us You Were Baptized." SAB, kybd. AFP 0800674057. (G)

Hogan, Moses. "I'm Gonna Sing 'til the Spirit Moves in My Heart." SATB. HAL 08740284.

Nystedt, Knut. "This Is My Beloved Son." SAB, org. CPH 98-1805

Plag, Johannes/arr. Richard Proulx. "Jesus Went to Jordan's Stream." 2 pt mxd, org. AFP 0800655249. (G)

Schütz, Heinrich. "Psalm 29." SATB. PRE 312-40072. (P)

Uhl, Dan. "This Is My Beloved Son." *The Augsburg Choirbook*. SATB, org. AFP 0800656784. (G)

Vaughan Williams, Ralph. "The Blessed Son of God." *Carols for Choirs 1*. SATB. OXF 3532220.

Wyton, Alec. "When Jesus Went to Jordan's Stream." SATB, fl, hb, org. PAR PPM0806. (G)

Sunday 2 / Second Sunday after Epiphany

Year A

    Isaiah 49:1-7   *The servant brings light to the nations*
    Psalm 40:1-11   *I love to do your will, O my God*
    1 Corinthians 1:1-9   *Paul's greeting to the church at Corinth*
    John 1:29-42   *Revelation of Christ as the Lamb of God*

Bach, Johann Sebastian. "The Only Son from Heaven" (alt. text for "Bring Low Our Ancient Adam"). *The Augsburg Choirbook*. SATB, kybd, opt inst. AFP 0800656784. *Bach for All Seasons*. AFP 080065854X. §
Basler, Paul. "Agnus Dei." SATB, pno, hrn, perc. PLY PJMS-106.
Bender, Mark. "Hail to the Lord's Anointed." SAB, opt desc, cong, org, tpt, opt add br & timp, inst pts. CPH 98-2888. (G)
Bouman, Paul. "Behold the Lamb of God." SA, org. CPH 98-1088. (G)
Christiansen, F. Melius. "Lamb of God." SATB. AFP 0800652592. *The Augsburg Choirbook*. AFP 0800656784.
Christiansen, Olaf C. "Light Everlasting." SATB. KJO 5110.
Diemer, Emma Lou. "Sing, O Heavens." SATB. CFI CM 7923.
Goss, John. "These Are They Which Follow the Lamb." *Anthems for Choirs I*. SATB, org. OXF 353214X.
Handel, George Frideric. "And He Shall Purify." *Messiah*. SATB, org. §
Moore, Undine Smith/arr. Kenneth Jennings. "I Believe This Is Jesus." SATB. AFP 0800645286. *The Augsburg Choirbook*. AFP 0800656784.
Morley, Thomas. "Agnus Dei." SATB. KJO 21.

Year B

    1 Samuel 3:1-10 [11-20]   *The calling of Samuel*
    Psalm 139:1-6, 13-18   *You have searched me out and known me*
    1 Corinthians 6:12-20   *Glorify God in your body*
    John 1:43-51   *The calling of the first disciples*

Archer, Malcolm. "Christ, Whose Glory." *Anthems Old & New*. SATB, org. Kevin Mayhew 0786648767.
Byrd, William/arr. Austin Lovelace. "Lord, Make Me to Know Thy Ways." SATB. CPH 98-2935.
Ferguson, John. "He Comes to Us as One Unknown." SATB, org, opt cong. AFP 0800656008. (F)
Handel, George Frideric. "For Unto Us a Child Is Born." *Messiah*. SATB, kybd or orch. § (G)
Moore, Undine Smith/arr. Kenneth Jennings. "I Believe This Is Jesus." SATB. AFP 0800645286. *The Augsburg Choirbook*. AFP 0800656784. (G)
Schutte, Daniel L./arr. Ovid Young. "Here I Am, Lord." SATB, kybd. AFP 0800656059. (F)
Sedio, Mark. "Take My Life, That I May Be/Toma, oh Dios, mi voluntad." SATB, pno, fl, opt gtr. AFP 0800658299.

Year C

Isaiah 62:1-5 — *As bridegroom and bride rejoice, so shall God rejoice over you*
Psalm 36:5-10 — *We feast on the abundance of your house, O Lord*
1 Corinthians 12:1-11 — *There are a variety of gifts but the same Spirit*
John 2:1-11 — *The wedding at Cana*

Byrd, William. "Surge illuminare." NOV TM 6.
Clausen, René. "Set Me As a Seal." SATB. SHW 8MA2047. *A New Creation*. MF 2047.
Edwards, Paul. "Thy Mercy, O Lord, Reacheth unto the Heavens." SATB, org. GSCH A.404. (P)
Ellingboe, Bradley. "Soul, Adorn Yourself with Gladness/Vengo a ti, Jesús amado." SATB. AFP 0800658477. (F)
Handel, George Frideric. "All My Spirit Longs to Savor." *Chantry Choirbook*. SATB, kybd. AFP 0800657772.
Jennings, Kenneth. "Arise, O Zion." KJO 5135.
Mozart, Wolfgang Amadeus. "Laudate Dominum." SATB, sop, pno. LAW 51165.
Schalk, Carl. "This Touch of Love." SATB, cong, org. MSM 50-8301.
Sedio, Mark. "Take My Life, That I May Be/Toma, oh Dios, mi voluntad." SATB, pno, fl, opt gtr. AFP 0800658299.
Stearns, Peter Pindar. "Your Love, O Lord, Reaches to the Heavens." SATB, org. SEL 410-836. (P)
Zipp, Friedrich. "Soul, Adorn Yourself with Gladness." *Chantry Choirbook*. SATB. AFP 0800657772. (F)

Sunday 3 / Third Sunday after Epiphany

Year A

Isaiah 9:1-4	*Light shines for those in darkness*
Psalm 27:1, 4-9	*The Lord is my light and my salvation*
1 Corinthians 1:10-18	*Appeal for unity in the gospel*
Matthew 4:12-23	*Revelation of Christ as a prophet*

Busarow, Donald. "Thy Strong Word." SAB, cong, 2 tpt, org, inst pts. MSM 60-9000.
Christiansen, Olaf C. "Light Everlasting." SATB. KJO 5110.
Ellingboe, Bradley. "Let Us Talents and Tongues Employ." SATB, kybd, fl, drm. KJO Ed. 8833.
Ferguson, John. "He Comes to Us as One Unknown." SATB, org. AFP 0800656008.
Handel, George Frideric. "His Yoke Is Easy." *Messiah*. SATB, org or orch. §
———. "The People That Walked in Darkness." *Messiah*. B solo, org or orch. § (F)
Kopylow, Alexander/arr. Peter Wilhousky. "Heavenly Light." SATB. CFI CM 497.
Manz, Paul. "I Want to Walk as a Child of the Light." SATB, org, opt cong. MSM 60-9019. (G)
Schalk, Carl. "Thy Strong Word." SATB, tpts, org, inst pts. CPH 97-5167.
Schutte, Daniel L./arr. Ovid Young. "Here I Am, Lord." SATB, kybd. AFP 0800656059.
Wesley, Samuel Sebastian. "Thou Wilt Keep Him in Perfect Peace." *The New Church Anthem Book*. SATTB, org. OXF 0193531097. (P)
Wood, Dale. "Rise, Shine!" SATB, org. AFP 0800655923. *The Augsburg Choirbook*. AFP 0800656784.
Zimmermann, Heinz Werner. "The Lord Is My Light." SATB. CPH 98-2174. (P)

Year B

Jonah 3:1-5, 10	*Repentance at Nineveh*
Psalm 62:5-12	*In God is my safety and my honor*
1 Corinthians 7:29-31	*Living in the end times*
Mark 1:14-20	*The calling of the disciples at the sea*

Bach, Johann Sebastian/ed. Patrick Liebergen. "Dedication Prayer/Bist du bei mir." *Favorite Sacred Classics for Solo Singers*. ML, kybd. ALF 11482. MH, kybd. ALF 11481.
Christiansen, F. Melius. "O Day Full of Grace." SSATTBB. AFP 080064512X.
Ellingboe, Bradley. "There's a Wideness in God's Mercy." SATB, kybd. AFP 0800676548. (F)
Erickson, Richard. "I Want to Walk as a Child of the Light." SATB, org. AFP 0800658396. (G)
Farrant, Richard or John Hilton. "Lord, for Thy Tender Mercy's Sake." SATB. OXF OCCO31. § (F, G)
Hovland, Egil. "The Glory of the Father." SATB. WAL W 2973.
Kopylow, Alexander/arr. Peter Wilhousky. "Heavenly Light." SATB. CFI CM 497.
Telemann, Georg Philipp. "O Praise the Lord, All Ye Nations." SATB, kybd, str. CPH 97-4838.
Thomerson, Kathleen. "I Want to Walk as a Child of the Light." SATB, acc. GIA G-2786. (G)
Wood, Dale. "Rise, Shine!" SATB, org. AFP 0800655923. *The Augsburg Choirbook*. AFP 0800656784.

Year C

Nehemiah 8:1-3, 5-6, 8-10 — *Ezra reads the law of Moses before the people*
Psalm 19 — *The law of the L ORD revives the soul*
1 Corinthians 12:12-31a — *You are the body of Christ*
Luke 4:14-21 — *Jesus reads from the scroll of the prophet Isaiah*

Bach, Johann Sebastian. "All Who Believe and Are Baptized." *Bach for All Seasons*. SATB. AFP 080065854X.
Bender, Jan. "O God, O Lord of Heaven and Earth." SATB, opt cong, org, opt tpt. AFP 0800652509. *The Augsburg Choirbook*. AFP 0800656784. (G)
Bender, Mark. "Hail to the Lord's Anointed." SAB, tpt, kybd, cong. CPH 98-2888. (G)
Elgar, Edward. "The Spirit of the Lord Is upon Me." SATB, org. NOV 29-0216. (G)
Fauré, Gabriel. "Cantique de Jean Racine." *European Sacred Music*. SATB, kybd or hp. OXF 0193436957. § (F, G)
Rotermund, Melvin. "O God of Light." SATB, kybd. CPH 98-3375.

Sunday 4 / Fourth Sunday after Epiphany

Year A

    Micah 6:1-8   *The offering of justice, kindness, humility*
    Psalm 15   *Lord, who may abide upon your holy hill?*
    1 Corinthians 1:18-31   *Christ crucified, the wisdom and power of God*
    Matthew 5:1-12   *The teaching of Christ: Beatitudes*

Ashdown, Franklin D. "Jesus, the Very Thought of Thee." SATB, org, opt C inst. AFP 0800657500.
Davies, H. Walford. "Blessed Are the Pure in Heart." *New Church Anthem Book*. SATB, org. OXF 0193531097. (G)
Ferguson, John. "Be Thou My Vision." SATB, org. AFP 0800657934.
Handel, George Frideric. "Exceeding Glad." *Coronation Anthems*. SATB, org. OXF.
Hillert, Richard. "You Are the Light of the World." 2 pt. MSM 50-2006.
Martinson, Joel. "Psalm 15." 2 pt mxd, cant, org, ob, opt cong. SEL 421-015. (P)
Pelz, Walter L. "Who Shall Abide." SAB, fl, gtr. AFP (P)
Powell, Robert J. "Jesu, the Very Thought of Thee." SATB, org. MSM 50-9070.
Routley, Erik/arr. John Hakes. "What Does the Lord Require?" SATB, org. MF2054. (F)
Wood, Dale. "Rise, Shine!" SATB, org. AFP 0800655923. *The Augsburg Choirbook*. AFP 0800656784.

Year B

    Deuteronomy 18:15-20   *The prophet speaks with God's authority*
    Psalm 111   *The fear of the Lord is the beginning of wisdom*
    1 Corinthians 8:1-13   *Limits to liberty: the case of food offered to idols*
    Mark 1:21-28   *The healing of one with an unclean spirit*

Bach, Johann Sebastian. "Bring Low Our Ancient Adam." *Bach for All Seasons*. SATB, kybd. AFP 080065854X.
Haan, Raymond H. "I Want Jesus to Walk with Me." SATB, pno. MSM 50-9002.
Kallman, Daniel. "Just a Closer Walk." SATB, pno. MSM 50-9064.
Lovelace, Austin. "Hope of the World." SATB or 2 pt mxd, kybd. CPH 98-2434.
Mendelssohn, Felix. "How Lovely Are the Messengers." *St. Paul*. SATB, kybd or orch. $
———. "On God Alone My Hope I Build." *Chantry Choirbook*. SATB. AFP 0800657772.
Poston, Elizabeth. "The Apple Tree." SATB. Ebor141.
Schulz-Widmar, Russell. "God Remembers." SATB, org. AFP 0800657462.
Titcomb, Everett. "O Love, How Deep." SATB, org. HWG 2226.
Wood, Dale. "Rise, Shine!" SATB, org. AFP 0800655923. *The Augsburg Choirbook*. AFP 0800656784.

Year C

Jeremiah 1:4-10 — *I appointed you a prophet to the nations*
Psalm 71:1-6 — *From my mother's womb you have been my strength*
1 Corinthians 13:1-13 — *If I speak without love, I am a noisy gong*
Luke 4:21-30 — *Jesus says a prophet is not accepted in his hometown*

Bach, Johann Sebastian. "O God, You Are My Refuge." 2 pt mxd, kybd. HOP MW1239. (P)
Bairstow, Edward C. "I Sat Down under His Shadow." SATB. OXF 43.002.
Clausen, René. "The Greatest of These Is Love." *A New Creation*. U, kybd. MSF 2047. (S)
Duruflé, Maurice. "Ubi caritas." SATB. DUR. (S)
Ferguson, John. "He Comes to Us as One Unknown." SATB, org, cong, C inst. AFP 0800656008. (G)
Hobby, Robert A. "O God of Light." SATB, org, br, timp, cong. MSM 60-8002A.
Hopp, Roy H. "God of Grace and God of Laughter." SATB, pno. AFP 0800659570.
———. "Not for Tongues of Heaven's Angels." SATB, org, opt cong. SEL 425-812. (S)
McKie, William. "We Wait for Thy Loving Kindness, O God." SATB, solo, org. OXF 42.081.
Mendelssohn, Felix. "See What Love." SATB, kybd. AFP 0800645618. § (S)
Thomas, André. "Go Where I Send Thee." SATB. MF 2044. (F)
Titcomb, Everett. "Jesus, Name of Wondrous Love." SATB, org. WAR 44-669.

Sunday 5 / Fifth Sunday after Epiphany

Year A

    Isaiah 58:1-9a [9b-12]   *The fast God chooses*
    Psalm 112:1-9 [10]   *Light shines in the darkness for the upright*
    1 Corinthians 2:1-12 [13-16]   *God's wisdom revealed through the Spirit*
    Matthew 5:13-20   *The teaching of Christ: salt and light*

Beethoven, Ludwig van/arr. Richard Proulx. "Give Thanks to God." SAB, kybd. AFP 0800655230.
Buxtehude, Dietrich. "God Shall Do My Advising." U, SATB, org. CPH 98-144. (S)
Carter, Andrew. "The Light of the World." SATB, org. OXF E161. (G)
Clausen, René. "My God, How Wonderful Thou Art." SATB, div. AFP 0800676998. (S)
Routley, Erik. "Light and Salt." SATB, org. GIA G-2300. (G)
Rudolph, Glen. "Arise, Shine." SATB, opt org. OXF 3859920.
Wood, Dale. "Rise, Shine!" SATB, org. AFP 0800655923. *The Augsburg Choirbook* AFP 0800656784.

Year B

    Isaiah 40:21-31   *The creator of all cares for the powerless*
    Psalm 147:1-11, 20c   *The Lord heals the brokenhearted*
    1 Corinthians 9:16-23   *A servant for the sake of the gospel*
    Mark 1:29-39   *The healing of Peter's mother-in-law*

Busarow, Donald. "Jesus Has Come and Brings Pleasure." SATB, B solo, hrn, org. CPH 98-3160.
Ellingboe, Bradley. "How Can I Keep from Singing?" SATB, pno, ob. KJO 8884.
Lovelace, Austin. "Hope of the World." SATB or 2 pt mxd, kybd. CPH 98-2434.
Nelson, Eric. "How Can I Keep from Singing?" SATB. AFP 0800675177.
Nystedt, Knut. "Get You Up." SATB div. HIN HMC-439. (G)
Pote, Allen. "A Song of Joy." SATB, pno. HOP AP450.
Powell, Robert J. "The Great Creator of the Worlds." SATB, org. AFP 0800657470.
Thompson, Randall. "Have Ye Not Known/Ye Shall Have a Song." SATB. ECS 1035.
Zimmermann, Heinz Werner. "The Lord Is My Light." SATB. CPH 98-2174.

Year C

Isaiah 6:1-8 [9-13]	*Isaiah says, Here am I; send me*
Psalm 138	*I will bow down toward your holy temple*
1 Corinthians 15:1-11	*I am the least of the apostles*
Luke 5:1-11	*Jesus calls the disciples to fish for people*

Bairstow, Edward C. "Let All Mortal Flesh Keep Silence." SATB. ECS 1.5095. (F)

Duruflé, Maurice. "Sanctus." *Requiem.* SATB, kybd or orch. DUR. (F)

Hammerschmidt, Andreas. "Heilig ist der Herr/Holy Is the Lord." SSATB, 2 tpt or ob, org. CPH 97-6314. (F)

Helgen, John. "Keep Silence." SATB, pno, rec (C inst). KJO 8891. (F)

Holst, Gustav. "Let All Mortal Flesh." SATB, opt orch, org. PRE 392-03013. (F)

Mendelssohn, Felix. "Heilig/Holy." SSAATTBB. HL 12005. §(F)

Nelson, Ronald A. "Whoever Would Be Great among You." SAB, kybd or gtr. AFP 0800645804. *The Augsburg Choirbook.* AFP 0800656784.

Schutte, Daniel L./arr. Ovid Young. "Here I Am, Lord." SATB, kybd. AFP 0800656059. (F)

Williams, David McKinley. "In the Year That King Uzziah Died." SATB, org. HWG. (F)

Sunday 6 / Sixth Sunday after Epiphany

Year A

    Deuteronomy 30:15-20   *Choose life*
    or Sirach 15:15-20   *Choose between life and death*
    Psalm 119:1-8   *Happy are they who walk in the law of the Lord*
    1 Corinthians 3:1-9   *God gives the growth*
    Matthew 5:21-37   *The teaching of Christ: forgiveness*

Buxtehude, Dieterich. "Everything You Do." *Chantry Choirbook*. SATB, org. AFP 0800657772.
Hayes, Mark. "Day by Day." SATB, kybd. AFP 0800658345.
How, Martin. "Day by Day." *The New Oxford Easy Anthem Book*. SATB, org. OXF 0193533189. §
———. "Day by Day." U, 2 or 3 pt, kybd. GIA G4178.
Powell, Robert J. "The Lord Will Guide Our Ways." SATB, kybd. AFP 0800654757.
Proulx, Richard. "Strengthen for Service." *The Augsburg Choirbook*. SATB. AFP 0800656784.
Wilby, Philip. "If Ye Love Me." SSATB, org. ECS 191.

Year B

    2 Kings 5:1-14   *Naaman is healed of leprosy*
    Psalm 30   *My God, I cried out to you, and you restored me to health*
    1 Corinthians 9:24-27   *Run the race for an imperishable prize*
    Mark 1:40-45   *The healing of one with leprosy*

Bach, Johann Sebastian. "Jesu, Joy—My Joy Forever." *Bach for All Seasons*. SATB. AFP 080065854X. §
Burleigh, Harry T. "Balm in Gilead." *The Spirituals of Harry T. Burleigh*. L, kybd. WAR EL 03150. H, kybd. WAR EL 03151. (F, G)
Dawson, William. "There Is a Balm in Gilead." SATB. KJO T105. (F, G)
Gardner, John. "Fight the Good Fight." SATB, pno. OXF 3531402. (S)
Mendelssohn, Felix. "All Ye That Cried Unto the Lord." *Hymn of Praise*. SATB, org. NPM 102. (P)
———/ed. Susan Palo Cherwien. "For the Lord Will Lead." *To God Will I Sing*. MH, kybd. AFP 0800674332. ML, kybd. AFP 0800674340.
Pinkham, Daniel. "Wash Yourself in the Jordan." *Alleluia for the Waters*. SATB, org. ESC 4971. TTBB. ECS 4970. (F, G)
Shepperd, Mark. "Balm in Gilead." SATB, kybd. AFP 0800657918. (F, G)
Wienhorst, Richard. "Lord, Whose Love in Humble Service." SATB, kybd. MSM 50-9059.
Wood, Dale. "Arise, My Soul, Arise!" SATB. SMP S-181.
Zimmermann, Heinz Werner. "Praise the Lord." SATB. CPH 98-2176.

Year C

Jeremiah 17:5-10	*Blessed are those who trust the Lord, they are like trees by water*
Psalm 1	*They are like trees planted by streams of water*
1 Corinthians 15:12-20	*Christ has been raised, the first fruits of those who have died*
Luke 6:17-26	*Jesus speaks blessings on the poor and hungry; woes on the rich and full*

Ashdown, Franklin D. "Jesus, the Very Thought of Thee." SATB, org, opt C inst. AFP 0800657500.
Haas, David. "Blest Are They." U/SAB, cong, 2 C inst, gtr. GIA G-2958. (G)
Handel, George Frideric. "I Know that My Redeemer Liveth." *Messiah*. Solo, kybd or orch. §
Noble, T. Tertius. "The Risen Christ." SATB, org. HWG GCMR 383.
Rachmaninoff, Sergei. "Blessed Is the Man." *All Night Vigil. Songs of the Church*. SATB, div. HWG GCMR GB 640. § (G)
Victoria, Tomás Luis de. "Jesu, the Very Thought of Thee." *The Oxford Easy Anthem Book*. OXF 0193533189.
Vierne, Louis/ed. Charles Callahan. "Let All Mortal Flesh Keep Silence." SAB, org. MSM 50-0209.
White, David Ashley. "This Glimpse of Glory." SATB, org, opt tpt. AFP 0800650891.
Willcock, Christopher. "Give Us a Pure Heart." SATB, org. OCP 4529.

Sunday 7 / Seventh Sunday after Epiphany

Year A

Leviticus 19:1-2, 9-18 — *Holiness revealed in acts of mercy and justice*
Psalm 119:33-40 — *Teach me, O Lord, the way of your statutes*
1 Corinthians 3:10-11, 16-23 — *Allegiance to Christ, not human leaders*
Matthew 5:38-48 — *The teaching of Christ: love*

Attwood, Thomas. "Teach Me, O Lord." *The New Oxford Easy Anthem Book.* SATB, org. OXF 0193533189. (P) §
Bisbee, B. Wayne. "O Splendor of God's Glory Bright." 2 pt trbl or mxd, kybd. AFP 0800659252.
Byrd, William. "Teach Me, O Lord." SAATB or SSATB, ST solos, org. OXF CMS 23. (P)
Farrant, Richard or John Hilton. "Lord, for Thy Tender Mercy's Sake." SATB. OXF OCCO31. § (F, G)
Fleming, Larry L. "Humble Service." SATB. AFP 0800646223.
Vulpius, Melchior. "O Spirit of God, Eternal Source." *Chantry Choirbook.* SATB. AFP 0800657772. (S)
Willcocks, David. "Love Divine, All Loves Excelling." *The New Oxford Easy Anthem Book.* SATB, org. OXF 019533198. (G)

Year B

Isaiah 43:18-25 — *Like rivers in the desert, God makes new*
Psalm 41 — *Heal me, for I have sinned against you*
2 Corinthians 1:18-22 — *Every promise of God is a "Yes"*
Mark 2:1-12 — *The healing of a paralyzed man*

Bertalot, John. "Amazing Grace." SATB, org. AFP 0800649141. *The Augsburg Choirbook.* AFP 0800656784. (G)
Britten, Benjamin. "Jubilate Deo." SATB, org. OXF 3515776.
Burkhardt, Michael. "Go, My Children, with My Blessing." U, 2 or 3 pt, pno. MSM 50-9416.
Dawson, William. "There Is a Balm in Gilead." SATB. KJO T105. (G)
Fleming, Larry L. "Humble Service." SATB. AFP 0800646223.
Hampton, Keith. "He's Got the Whole World." SATB. AFP 0800659600.
Hopp, Roy H. "God of Grace and God of Laughter." SATB, pno or hp, ob or C inst. AFP 0800659570.
Hurford, Peter. "Litany to the Holy Spirit." U, org. OXF E164.
Powell, Robert J. "The Great Creator of the Worlds." SATB, org. AFP 0800657470.
Schalk, Carl. "Who Is the One We Love the Most." SATB, org. CPH 98-3404.
Shepperd, Mark. "Balm in Gilead." SATB, kybd. AFP 0800657918. (G)
White, David Ashley. "There's a Wideness in God's Mercy." SATB, org. SEL 420-243. (G)

Year C

Genesis 45:3-11, 15 — *Joseph forgives his brothers*
Psalm 37:1-11, 39-40 — *The lowly shall possess the land; they will delight in abundance of peace.*
1 Corinthians 15:35-38, 42-50 — *The mystery of the resurrection of the body*
Luke 6:27-38 — *Love your enemies*

Bender, Jan. "O God, O Lord of Heaven and Earth." SATB, org, opt cong, opt 2 tpts. AFP 0800652509. *The Augsburg Choirbook*. AFP 0800656784.
Ellen, Jane. "Love One Another." 2 pt trbl, pno, opt fl. KJO 6271. (F, G)
Farrant, Richard or John Hilton. "Lord, for Thy Tender Mercy's Sake." SATB, opt org. OXF 3418053. § (F, G)
Fleming, Larry L. "Humble Service." SATB. AFP 0800646223. (G)
Hobby, Robert A. "Forgive Our Sins as We Forgive." SAB. CPH 98-2870. (F, G)
Howells, Herbert. "My Eyes for Beauty Pine." *Oxford Easy Anthem Book*. SATB, org. OXF 42.008.
Mendelssohn, Felix. "Grant Peace We Pray/Verleih uns Frieden." SATB, org. *Chantry Choirbook*. AFP 0800657772. §
Proulx, Richard. "Psalm 133." SATB, org. HOP FPC 126.
Schulz-Widmar, Russell. "We Are Not Our Own." SATB, kybd. AFP 0800657810.

Sunday 8 / Eighth Sunday after Epiphany

Year A

    Isaiah 49:8-16a   *God's motherly compassion for the people*
    Psalm 131   *Like a child upon its mother's breast, my soul is quieted within me*
    1 Corinthians 4:1-5   *Servants accountable to God for their stewardship*
    Matthew 6:24-34   *The teaching of Christ: trust in God*

Bach, Johann Sebastian. "Jesus, My Sweet Pleasure/Jesu, meine Freude." *Bach for All Seasons*. SATB. AFP 080065854X. §
Carter, Andrew. "Deep Peace." SATB, kybd, opt cong. OXF 3504790. (G)
Glarum, L. Stanley. "Sing Praises." SATB. BEL 1656.
Handel, George Frideric. "Ev'ry Valley." *Messiah*. T solo, org or orch. §
Scholz, Robert. "Children of the Heavenly Father." SATB. AFP 0800659112. (G)

Year B

    Hosea 2:14-20   *The covenant renewed by God's persistent love*
    Psalm 103:1-13, 22   *The Lord is full of compassion and mercy*
    2 Corinthians 3:1-6   *Equipped as ministers of God's new covenant*
    Mark 2:13-22   *Eating and drinking with tax collectors and prostitutes*

Bach, Johann Sebastian. "Jesus, My Sweet Pleasure/Jesu, meine Freude." *Bach for All Seasons*. SATB. AFP 080065854X. §
———. "Salvation unto Us Has Come." *Bach for All Seasons*. SATB. AFP 080065854X.
Busarow, Donald. "Day by Day." SATB. MSM 50-6004.
Cherubini, Luigi/arr. Austin Lovelace. "Like as a Father." SAB or combined U or 2 pt mxd, kybd. CGA-156.
Distler, Hugo. "Salvation unto Us Has Come." *Chantry Choirbook*. SATB. AFP 0800657772. §
Ellingboe, Bradley. "There's a Wideness in God's Mercy." SATB, pno. AFP 0800676548. §
Hurd, David. "Love Bade Me Welcome." SATB. SEL 418-610. (G)

Year C

Isaiah 55:10-13	*The word goes forth from the mouth of God*
or Sirach 27:4-7	*Wisdom rules both heaven and earth*
Psalm 92:1-4, 12-15	*The righteous shall flourish like a palm tree*
1 Corinthians 15:51-58	*The mystery of the resurrection*
Luke 6:39-49	*Take the speck from your eye; build your house on a firm foundation*

Ellingboe, Bradley. "The Chief Cornerstone." 2 pt mxd, kybd. AFP 0800676394. *Augsburg Easy Choirbook.* AFP 0800676025.

Ferguson, John. "What Then." SATB, org. KJO 8827. (G)

Kallman, Daniel. "In Thee Is Gladness." SATB, org, opt U choir, C inst. MSM 50-9058.

Widor, Charles Marie/ed. David Cherwien. "Tu es Petrus." SATBB, org. MSM 50-6512.

Transfiguration of Our Lord
(Sunday before Lent / Last Sunday after Epiphany)

Year A

    Exodus 24:12-18 — *Moses enters the cloud of God's glory on Mount Sinai*
    Psalm 2 — *You are my son; this day have I begotten you*
    or Psalm 99 — *Proclaim the greatness of the Lord; worship upon God's holy hill*
    2 Peter 1:16-21 — *The apostle's message confirmed on the mount of transfiguration*
    Matthew 17:1-9 — *Revelation of Christ as God's beloved Son*

Bach, Johann Sebastian. "Alleluia." *Bach for All Seasons.* SATB, kybd. AFP 080065854X.
Bairstow, Edward C. "Jesus, the Very Thought of Thee." SATB. OXF 43.003.
Bertalot, John. "Christ upon the Mountain Peak." 2 pt, pno, ob, fl or other C inst. AFP 0800653793. (G)
Bouman, Paul. "Christ upon the Mountain Peak." SATB, org. CPH 98-2856. (G)
Christiansen, F. Melius. "Beautiful Savior." SSAATTBB or SATB, A solo. AFP 0800645138. *The Augsburg Choirbook.* AFP 0800656784.
Farlee, Robert Buckley. "Farewell to Alleluia." U, org, opt cong, opt tpt. AFP 0800649486.
———. "The Lightener of the Stars." *To God Will I Sing.* MH, kybd. AFP 0800674332. ML, kybd. AFP080067434X.
Forsberg, Charles. "Fairest Lord Jesus." SATB, pno. AFP 0800656962.
Gastoldi, Giovanni. "In You Is Gladness." *Let All Together Praise.* SATB, kybd. CPH 97-585S.
Helman, Michael. "Go Up to the Mountain of God." SATB, pno, opt fl. AFP 0800658353. (G)
Hobby, Robert A. "Offertory for the Transfiguration of Our Lord." SATB, hb, org. MSM 80-225.
Martinson, Joel. "Transfiguration." U, org. PAR PPM 09511. (G)
Nystedt, Knut. "This Is My Beloved Son." SAB, org. CPH 98-1805. (S, G)
Pachelbel, Johann. "Der Herr ist König/The Lord God Reigneth (Psalm 99)." SATB dbl choir. CPH 97-7568.
Praetorius, Michael. "O Morning Star, How Fair and Bright!" *Chantry Choirbook.* SSATB. AFP 0800657772.
Proulx, Richard. "Alleluia, Song of Gladness." U, hb, perc. GIA G-3984.
Schalk, Carl. "Jesus, Take Us to the Mountain." SATB, opt cong, org. MSM 50-2601. (G)
Thompson, Randall. "Alleluia." SATB. ECS 1786.
Uhl, Dan. "This Is My Beloved Son." *Augsburg Choirbook.* SATB, org. AFP 0800656784. (S, G)

Year B

    2 Kings 2:1-12 — *Elijah taken up to heaven and succeeded by Elisha*
    Psalm 50:1-6 — *Out of Zion, perfect in beauty, God shines forth in glory*
    2 Corinthians 4:3-6 — *God's light seen clearly in the face of Christ*
    Mark 9:2-9 — *Revelation of Christ as God's beloved Son*

Bairstow, Edward C. "Let All Mortal Flesh Keep Silence." SATB. S&B (ECS) CC 294.
Beethoven, Ludwig van. "Hallelujah." *Christ on the Mount of Olives.* SATB, kybd or orch. § (G)
Bouman, Paul. "Christ upon the Mountain Peak." SATB, org. CPH 98-2856. (G)
Busarow, Donald. "Farewell to Alleluia." SATB, org, opt cong. CPH 98-2995.
Cherwien, David. "Beautiful Savior." SATB, org, cong, opt fl. AFP 0800675088.
Christiansen, F. Melius. "Beautiful Savior." SATB div, A solo. AFP 0800652584. *The Augsburg Choirbook.* AFP 0800656784.
Ferguson, John. "Let All Mortal Flesh." SATB, hb. AFP 0800646681.
Forsberg, Charles. "Fairest Lord Jesus." SATB, pno. AFP 080656952.
Helman, Michael. "Go Up to the Mountain of God." SATB, pno, opt fl. AFP 0800658353. (G)

Lallouette, Jean François/arr. Richard Proulx. "Christ the Glory." 2 pt mxd, org. GIA 2288.
Martinson, Joel. "Transfiguration." U, org. PAR PPM 09511.
Schalk, Carl. "Jesus, Take Us to the Mountain." SATB, opt cong, org. MSM 50-2601. (G)
———. "Oh, Wondrous Type, Oh, Vision Fair." SATB, kybd. CPH 98-1524. (G)
Willan, Healey. "Grant Us Thy Light." SATB. CPH 98-1014.

Year C

Exodus 34:29-35 — *Coming down from Mount Sinai, Moses' face shone*
Psalm 99 — *Proclaim the greatness of the Lord; worship upon God's holy hill*
2 Corinthians 3:12—4:2 — *With unveiled faces we see the Lord's glory as we are transformed*
Luke 9:28-36 [37-43] — *Jesus is transfigured on the mountain*

Bach, Johann Sebastian. "Transcendent, Holy God." *Bach for All Seasons.* SATB, kybd. AFP 080065854X.
Bisbee, B. Wayne. "O Splendor of God's Glory Bright." 2 pt trbl or mxd, pno. AFP 0800659252. (F, G)
Bouman, Paul. "Christ upon the Mountain Peak." SATB, org. CPH 98-2856. (G)
Cherwien, David. "Beautiful Savior." SATB, org, cong, opt fl. AFP 0800675088. (G)
Farlee, Robert Buckley. "Farewell to Alleluia." U, org, opt tpt, cong. AFP 0800649486.
Forsberg, Charles. "Fairest Lord Jesus." SATB, pno. AFP 0800656962. (G)
Helman, Michael. "Go Up to the Mountain of God." SATB, pno, opt fl. AFP 0800658353. (G)
Hobby, Robert A. "Offertory for the Transfiguration of Our Lord." SATB, hb, org. MSM 80-225.
Mendelssohn, Felix. "And Then Shall Your Light Break Forth." *Elijah.* SATB, kybd. § (G)
Schalk, Carl. "Jesus, Take Us to the Mountain." SATB, opt cong, org. MSM 50-2601. (G)
Scholz, Robert. "Oh, Wondrous Type! Oh, Vision Fair." SATB, hb. MSM 50-2600. (G)
Tallis, Thomas. "O nata lux." SATTB. OXF 43.228.
White, David Ashley. "This Glimpse of Glory." SATB, org, opt tpt. AFP 0800650891.
Wolff, S. Drummond. "Oh, Wondrous Type! Oh, Vision Fair." SATB, org, cong, tpts. CPH 98-2690. (G)

Ash Wednesday

Years A, B, C

Joel 2:1-2, 12-17 — *Return to the L<small>ORD</small>, your God*
or Isaiah 58:1-12 — *The fast that God chooses*
Psalm 51:1-17 — *Have mercy on me, O God, according to your lovingkindness*
2 Corinthians 5:20b—6:10 — *Now is the day of salvation*
Matthew 6:1-6, 16-21 — *The practice of faith*

Allegri, Gregorio. "Miserere mei, Deus." SSATB. CHE CH55059. § (P)
Attwood, Thomas. "Turn Thy Face from My Sins." *The New Church Anthem Book*. SATB. OXF 0193531097. (P)
Bach, Johann Sebastian. "Bring Low Our Ancient Adam." *Bach for All Seasons*. SATB, kybd. AFP 080065854X.
———. "Jesus, My Sweet Pleasure/Jesu, meine Freude." *Bach for All Seasons*. SATB, opt kybd. AFP 080065854X. §
Brahms, Johannes. "Create in Me, O God." SATBB. GSCH 50297770. § (P)
———. "O World So Vain." *Chantry Choirbook*. SATB. AFP 0800657772.
Byrd, William. "Miserere mei/Mercy Grant unto Me." SATB. OXF 3520532 or TCM 26. (P)
Christiansen, Paul J. "Create in Me a Clean Heart." SATB. AFP 0800645847. (P)
Farrant, Richard or John Hilton. "Lord, for Thy Tender Mercy's Sake." SATB. GIA G-3049. §
Ferguson, John. "Psalm 130/Out of the Depths." *Psalm Set.* SATB, org. AFP 0800656075.
Gerike, Henry V. "Create in Me." SAB, org. AFP 0800656040. (P)
Haas, David. "Dust and Ashes." 2 pt, kybd, gtr. GIA G-3655.
Hallock, Peter. "Wash Me Through and Through." SATB, opt U, opt hb. ION CH-1014. (P)
Hopson, Hal H. "A Psalm of Confession." SATB, opt solo. AFP 080065952X. (P)
Moore, Bob. "Have Mercy, O Lord: Music for the Imposition of Ashes." SATB, cant, cong, gtr, acc. GIA G-3670.
Nelson Ronald A. "Create in Me a Clean Heart." SATB. KJO 8808. (P)
Oldham, Kevin. "Out of the Depths Have I Cried to Thee." SATB, org, hp. KJO EDJ11.
Rorem, Ned. "Lay Up for Yourselves." *Seven Motets for the Church Year*, No. 3. SATB. B&S OCTB6444 (G)
Schalk, Carl. "Have Mercy on Me, O God." SATB. AFP 0800657845. (P)
———. "Out of the Depths." SAB, org. MSM 50-3410.
Scott, K. Lee. "Out of the Depths I Cry to Thee." 2 pt mxd, kybd. AFP 0800647327.
———. "Out of the Depths I Cry to Thee." *Rejoice Now My Spirit*. MH, kybd. AFP 0800651081. ML, kybd. 080065109X.
Tallis, Thomas. "Purge Me, O Lord." SATB. OXF TCM67. (P)
Telemann, Georg Philipp/ed. Susan Palo Cherwien. "Make Me Pure, O Sacred Spirit." *To God Will I Sing*. MH, kybd. AFP 0800674332. ML, kybd. 0800674340.
Wesley, Samuel Sebastian. "Wash Me Thoroughly." *The New Church Anthem Book*. SATB, cong. OXF 0193531097. (P)

First Sunday in Lent

Year A

Genesis 2:15-17. 3:1-7	*Eating of the tree of the knowledge of good and evil*
Psalm 32	*Mercy embraces those who trust in the Lord*
Romans 5:12-19	*Death came through one; life comes through one*
Matthew 4:1-11	*The temptation of Jesus in the wilderness for forty days*

Bach, Johann Sebastian. "Lord, Keep Us Steadfast." *Bach for All Seasons*. SATB. AFP 080065854X.
Below, Robert. "The Glory of These Forty Days." SATB, org. AFP 600010152X.
Bender, Jan. "Begone, Satan." SA or TB, org. CPH 98-1848. (G)
Busarow, Donald. "A Mighty Fortress." SAB, cong, tpt, org. MSM 60-8000.
Ferguson, John. "A Mighty Fortress." SATB, org, tpt. AFP 0800676424.
Haan, Raymond H. "I Want Jesus to Walk with Me." SATB, pno. MSM 50-9002.
Handel, George Frideric. "Since by Man Came Death." *Messiah*. SATB, kybd or orch. § (S)
Hassler, Hans Leo. "A Mighty Fortress Is Our God/Ein feste Burg ist unser Gott." *Chantry Choirbook*. SATB. AFP 0800657772. §
Hilton, John/ed. K. Lee Scott. "Wilt Thou Forgive?/A Hymne to God the Father." *Sing Forth God's Praise*. MH, kybd. AFP 0800675266. ML, kybd. AFP 080067538X.
Hopson, Hal H. "A Mighty Fortress Is Our God." SATB, cong, org, opt 2 tpt, 2 tbn, timp. AFP 0800646150.
Trinkley, Bruce. "I Want Jesus to Walk with Me." *Augsburg Choirbook for Men*. TB, kybd. AFP 0800676831.

Year B

Genesis 9:8-17	*The rainbow, sign of God's covenant*
Psalm 25:1-10	*Your paths are love and faithfulness to those who keep your covenant*
1 Peter 3:18-22	*Saved through water*
Mark 1:9-15	*The temptation of Jesus in the wilderness for forty days*

Bach, Johann Sebastian. "Lord Jesus Christ, God's Only Son." *Bach for All Seasons*. SATB, kybd. AFP 080065854X. (G)
Busarow, Donald. "Lord Keep Us Steadfast in Your Word." 2 pt mxd, inst. CPH 98-2602.
Erickson, Karle. "Thy Holy Wings." SATB, 2 fl. AFP 0800645359.
Farrant, Richard. "Call to Remembrance." SATB. ECS 1639. § (P)
Ferguson, John. "A Mighty Fortress." SATB, org, tpt. AFP 0800676424. (G)
Hampton, Keith. "Give Me Jesus." SATB, div. AFP 0800659554.
Hopson, Hal H. "A Lenten Walk." 2 pt mxd, opt timp, hb. AFP 080065448X. *The Augsburg Choirbook*. AFP 0800656784.
Parker, Alice. "Take Me to the Water." SAATB. GIA G-4238.
———. "We Will March thro' the Valley." SSATB, solo. GIA G-4242.
Pelz, Walter L. "Show Me Thy Ways." SATB, gtr, ob or fl. AFP 0800645421. *The Augsburg Choirbook*. AFP 0800656784. (P)
Schalk, Carl. "Show Me Your Ways, O Lord." SATB. CPH 98-3207. (P)
Scott, K. Lee. "Redeeming Grace." *Sing a Song of Joy*. MH, kybd. AFP 0800647882. ML, kybd. AFP 0800652827.
Wesley, Samuel Sebastian. "O Lord My God." *The New Church Anthem Book*. SATB, org. OXF 0193531097.

Year C

Deuteronomy 26:1-11 — *The Lord brought us out of Egypt with a mighty hand*
Psalm 91:1-2, 9-16 — *God shall charge the angels to keep you in all your ways*
Romans 10:8b-13 — *If you confess that Jesus is Lord, you will be saved*
Luke 4:1-13 — *The temptation of Jesus in the wilderness for forty days*

Gibbons, Orlando. "Almighty and Everlasting God." OXF TCM 36.
Haan, Raymond H. "I Want Jesus to Walk with Me." SATB, pno. MSM 50-9002. (G)
Hassler, Hans Leo. "A Mighty Fortress Is Our God/Ein feste Burg ist unser Gott." *Chantry Choirbook*. SATB. AFP 0800657772. (G)
Hillert, Richard. "He Shall Give His Angels Charge." U, org, ob, opt str. GIA G-3983. (P)
Hopson, Hal H. "A Lenten Walk." 2 pt mxd, opt timp, hb. AFP 080065448X. *The Augsburg Choirbook*. AFP 0800656784.
Kitson, C. H. "Jesu, Grant Me This, I Pray." SATB, org. OXF 42-041.
Mendelssohn, Felix. "For He Shall Give His Angels Charge Over Thee." *Elijah*. SATB, kybd or orch. § (P)
Near, Gerald. "A Lenten Prayer." 2 pt, org. MSM AUR AE91.
Rowan, William P. "With the Lord, There Is Mercy." SATB, kybd. AFP 0800675584.
Sitton, Michael. "Tantum ergo." U, org. PAR PPM 09111.
Walter, Johann. "I Build on God's Strong Word." *Chantry Choirbook*. SATB. AFP 0800657772.

Second Sunday in Lent

Year A

    Genesis 12:1-4a   *The blessing of God upon Abram*
    Psalm 121   *It is the L*ORD *who watches over you*
    Romans 4:1-5, 13-17   *The promise to those who share Abraham's faith*
    John 3:1-17   *The mission of Christ: to save the world*

Adler, Samuel. "God's Promise." SSA, kybd. OXF 94-404.
Berger, Jean. "I to the Hills Lift Up Mine Eyes." SATB. AFP 0800645448. *The Augsburg Choirbook.* AFP 0800656784. (P)
Bouman, Paul. "I Lift Up My Eyes to the Hills." 2 pt, org. B&H OCTB6550. (P)
Bruckner, Anton/ed. Maynard Klein. "God So Loved the World." SATB, org ad lib. GIA G-1438. (G)
Distler, Hugo. "For God So Loved the World/Also hat Gott die Welt geliebet." *Chantry Choirbook.* SAB. AFP 0800657772. (G) §
Ellingboe, Bradley. "There's a Wideness in God's Mercy." SATB, kybd. AFP 0800676548.
Goss, John. "God So Loved the World." *The New Church Anthem Book.* SATB. OXF 0193531097. (G)
Martinson, Joel. "God So Loved the World." SA, org. CPH 98-3098. (G)
Mendelssohn, Felix. "Lift Thine Eyes." *Elijah.* SSA. § (P)
Rutter, John. "I Will Lift Up Mine Eyes." SATB, org. OXF A313. (P)
Schütz, Heinrich. "God So Loved the World/Also hat Gott die Welt geliebet." *Chantry Choirbook.* SATTB. AFP 0800657772. § (G)
Scott, K. Lee. "Jesus, Thou Joy of Loving Hearts." SATB, org. CPH 98-3009.
Stainer, John. "God So Loved the World." *The Crucifixion.* SATB. GSCH 3798. (G)
Tye, Christopher. "To Our Redeemer's Glorious Name." *Parish Choir Book.* SATB. CPH 97-7574.

Year B

    Genesis 17:1-7, 15-16   *God blesses Abraham and Sarah*
    Psalm 22:23-31   *All the ends of the earth shall remember and turn to the L*ORD
    Romans 4:13-25   *The promise to those who share Abraham's* faith
    Mark 8:31-38   *The passion prediction*

Bach, Johann Sebastian. "Lord, Thee I Love with All My Heart." *Bach for All Seasons.* SATB. AFP 080065854X.
Distler, Hugo. "A Lamb Goes Uncomplaining Forth." *Chantry Choirbook.* SATB. AFP 0800657772.
Farrant, Richard or John Hilton. "Lord, for Thy Tender Mercy's Sake." *The New Church Anthem Book.* SATB. OXF 0193531097. §
Ferguson, John. "Lord, in All Love." SATB, org, opt cong. AFP 0800656490.
———. "When I Survey the Wondrous Cross." *St. John Passion.* SATB, org. AFP 0800658582. (G)
Martinson, Joel. "God So Loved the World." SA, org. CPH 98-3098.
Neswick, Bruce. "Hearken to My Voice, O Lord, When I Call." *The Augsburg Choirbook.* 2 pt, kybd. AFP 0800656784.
Reger, Max. "Meinen Jesum lass ich nicht/I Stand Fast with Jesus Christ." S solo, SATB, vln, vla, org. CV 50.406/05.
Schalk, Carl. "All the Ends of the Earth." SATB, org. CPH 98-3546. (P)

Year C

Genesis 15:1-12, 17-18 — *The covenant with Abram and his descendants*
Psalm 27 — *In the day of trouble, the* LORD *shall keep me safe*
Philippians 3:17—4:1 — *Our citizenship is in heaven from where we expect a Savior*
Luke 13:31-35 — *I have desired to gather Jerusalem as a hen gathers her brood*

Bach, Johann Sebastian. "Lord, Thee I Love with All My Heart." *Bach for All Seasons*. SATB. AFP 080065854X.
Distler, Hugo. "For God So Loved the World/Also hat Gott die Welt geliebet." *Chantry Choirbook*. SAB. AFP 0800642772. §
Ellingboe, Bradley. "Thy Holy Wings." SATB. KJO C9001. (G)
Farlee, Robert Buckley. "When Twilight Comes." 2 pt mixed, pno. AFP 0800675576. (G)
Helgen, John. "That Priceless Grace." SATB, pno. AFP 0800658590. 2 pt mxd, pno. *Augsburg Easy Choirbook*. AFP 0800676025.
Hopp, Roy H. "May I Love You, Lord." SATB, kybd. AFP 080067541X.
Marcello, Benedetto. "Give Ear unto Me." SS, pno. HWG GCMR01522.
Mendelssohn, Felix. "Jerusalem, Jerusalem." *St. Paul*. S solo, kybd. § (G)
Schütz, Heinrich. "God So Loved the World/Also hat Gott die Welt geliebet." *Chantry Choirbook*. SATTB. AFP 0800642772. §
Stainer, John. "God So Loved the World." SATB, kybd. NOV 29.0234.06. §
Vierne, Louis. "Benedictus." *Solemn Mass*. SATB, org. MF 190.
Zimmermann, Heinz Werner. "The Lord Is My Light." SATB, org. CPH 98-2174. (P)

Third Sunday in Lent

Year A

    Exodus 17:1-7   *Water from the rock in the wilderness*
    Psalm 95   *Let us shout for joy to the rock of our salvation*
    Romans 5:1-11   *Reconciled to God by Christ's death*
    John 4:5-42   *Baptismal image: the woman at the well*

Bertalot, John. "Amazing Grace." SATB, org. AFP 0800649141. *The Augsburg Choirbook.* AFP 0800656784.
Busarow, Donald. "I Heard the Voice of Jesus Say." SATB, fl, org, opt cong. CPH 98-2619.
Christiansen, Paul J. "Wondrous Love." SATB. AFP 0800652665. *The Augsburg Choirbook.* AFP 0800656784.
Farlee, Robert Buckley. "O Blessed Spring." SATB, ob (vln or cl), org, opt cong. AFP 0800654242. *The Augsburg Choirbook.* 0800656784.
Farrant, Richard or John Hilton. "Lord for Thy Tender Mercy's Sake." SATB. GIA G-3049. §
Handel, George Frideric. "Surely He Hath Borne Our Griefs." *Messiah.* SATB, kybd or orch. §
How, Martin. "O Come, Let Us Sing Unto the Lord." 2 pt, org. MSM 50-73012. (P)
Mendelssohn, Felix. "O Come, Every One that Thirsteth." *Elijah.* SATB, org. §
Rachmaninoff, Sergei. "O Come Let Us Worship." *All Night Vigil. Songs of the Church.* SSAATTBB. Musica Russica § (P)
Rorem, Ned. "Sing, My Soul, His Wondrous Love." SATB. PET 6386.

Year B

    Exodus 20:1-17   *The commandments are given at Sinai*
    Psalm 19   *The commandment of the L*ORD *gives light to the eyes*
    1 Corinthians 1:18-25   *Christ crucified, the wisdom of God*
    John 2:13-22   *The cleansing of the temple*

Bertalot, John. "Amazing Grace." SATB, org. AFP 0800649141. *The Augsburg Choirbook.* AFP 0800656784.
Bruckner, Anton. "Christus factus est." SATB. AMC AE 157. §
Elgar, Edward. "Ave verum corpus." *The New Church Anthem Book.* SATB, org. OXF 019353170. § (G)
Fleming, Larry L. "Give Me Jesus." SATB div. AFP 0800645278. *The Augsburg Choirbook.* AFP 0800656784.
Kodály, Zoltán. "Jesus and the Traders." SATB. Universal Editions 10739. § (G)
Mozart, Wolfgang Amadeus. "De profundis clamavi/From the Depths I Have Called unto Thee." *A First Motet Book.* SATB, org. CPH 97-5230.
Schalk, Carl. "Lord, It Belongs Not to My Care." SATB. AFP 0800645901.
Schütz, Heinrich. "Praise to You, Lord Jesus." *Chantry Choirbook.* SATB. AFP 0806642772. §
Willcocks, Jonathan. "O Holy Jesus." SATB, org. SMP 10/1937S.
Yarrington, John. "O Savior of the World." SATB, org. AFP 0800673158. OP

Year C

Isaiah 55:1-9	*Everyone who thirsts, come to the water; seek the Lord*
Psalm 63:1-8	*O God, eagerly I seek you; my soul thirsts for you*
1 Corinthians 10:1-13	*Israel, baptized in cloud and seas, ate the same spiritual food as Christians*
Luke 13:1-9	*Unless you repent, you will perish: parable of the fig tree*

Bach, Johann Sebastian. "O Bread of Life from Heaven." *Bach for All Seasons*. SATB. AFP 080065854X. (F)

Christiansen, Paul J. "Wondrous Love." SATB. AFP 0800652665. *The Augsburg Choirbook*. AFP 0800656784.

Dowland, John. "He That Is Down Need Fear No Fall." *Oxford Easy Anthem Book*. SATB. OXF 3533219.

Goudimel, Claude. "As the Deer, for Water Yearning." *Chantry Choirbook*. SATB. AFP 0800642772.

Halloran, Jack. "Witness." SSAATTBB. HAL JG2010.

Howells, Herbert. "Like As the Hart." SATB, org. OXF 3501635.

Mendelssohn, Felix. "O Come, Every One that Thirsteth." *Elijah*. SATB, kybd or orch. § (F)

Moore, Philip. "He That Is Down Need Fear No Fall." SATB, org. Randall M. Egan.

Paulus, Stephen. "Built on a Rock." SATB. WAR 1408152

Purcell, Henry. "O God, Thou Art My God." SATB, org. NOV 1064.

White, David Ashley. "Come, Ye Sinners." 2 pt, kybd, ob or other C inst. AFP 0800653246.

Fourth Sunday in Lent

Year A

1 Samuel 16:1-13	*David is chosen and anointed*
Psalm 23	*You have anointed my head with oil*
Ephesians 5:8-14	*Awake from sleep, live as children of light*
John 9:1-41	*Baptismal image: the man born blind*

Ellingboe, Bradley. "Jesus, Good Shepherd." SATB, pno or harp. AFP 0800658272. (P)
Haydn, Franz Joseph. "Lo, My Shepherd's Hand Divine." SATB, org. ECS 1019. (P)
How, Martin. "Psalm 23." U or B solo, kybd, opt desc. B&H W.180. (P)
Lowenberg, Kenneth. "Blessed Are the Pure in Spirit." U or 2 pt, kybd. SEL 410-557.
Manz, Paul. "On My Heart Imprint Thine Image." SATB. MSM 50-3037.
Rutter, John. "Open Thou Mine Eyes." SATB. HMC-467. (G)
———. "The Lord Is My Shepherd." SATB, org. OXF 94.216. (P)
Schütz, Heinrich. "O Lord, I Trust Your Shepherd Care." *Chantry Choirbook*. SATB. AFP 0800657772. (P)
Smith, Gregg. "The Lord Is My Shepherd." 2 pt, kybd. GSCH 12325. (P)
Vulpius, Melchior. "Jesus Said to the Blind Man." SATB. CPH 98-1027. (G)
Zimmermann, Heinz Werner. "Psalm 23." SATB, org, DB. AFP 0800645383. *The Augsburg Choirbook*. AFP 0800656784. (P)

Year B

Numbers 21:4-9	*The lifting up of the serpent*
Psalm 107:1-3, 17-22	*The L ORD delivered them from their distress*
Ephesians 2:1-10	*Saved by grace through faith for good works*
John 3:14-21	*The lifting up of the Son of Man*

Beethoven, Ludwig van/arr. Richard Proulx. "Give Thanks to God." SAB, kybd. AFP 0800655230. (P)
Bertalot, John. "Amazing Grace." SATB, org. AFP 0800649141. *The Augsburg Choirbook*. AFP 0800656784. (S, G)
Cherwien, David. "My Song Is Love Unknown." SAB, org, fl, opt cong. AFP 0800655486. (G)
Christiansen, Paul J. "Wondrous Love." SATB. AFP 0800652665. *The Augsburg Choirbook*. AFP 0800656784. (S, G)
Distler, Hugo. "For God So Loved the World/Also hat Gott die Welt geliebet." *Chantry Choirbook*. SAB. AFP 0806642772. § (G)
Ellingboe, Bradley. "There Is a Green Hill Far Away." 2 pt mxd, pno. KJO 5765.
Scholz, Robert. "What Wondrous Love." SATB, div. MSM 50-9017. (S, G)
Schütz, Heinrich. "For God So Loved the World/Also hat Gott die Welt geliebet." *Chantry Choirbook*. SATTB. AFP 0800657772. § (G)
Stainer, John. "God So Loved the World." *The Crucifixion*. SATB. GSCH 50294340. § (G)

Year C

Joshua 5:9-12 — *Israel eats bread and grain, the produce of the land*
Psalm 32 — *Be glad, you righteous, and rejoice in the Lord*
2 Corinthians 5:16-21 — *The mystery and ministry of reconciliation*
Luke 15:1-3, 11b-32 — *The parable of the prodigal father and the repentant son*

Bertalot, John. "Amazing Grace." SATB, org. AFP 0800649141. *The Augsburg Choirbook.* AFP 0800656784. (G)
Clausen, René. "A New Creation." *A New Creation.* SATB div, kybd. MF 2047. (S)
Nelson, Ronald A. "Create in Me a Clean Heart." SATB. KJO 8808.
Parker, Alice/Robert Shaw. "Amazing Grace." SATB. WAR WBLG00918. (G)
Purcell, Henry. "Thou Knowest, Lord, the Secrets of Our Hearts." SATB. CPH 98-2321.
Thompson, J. Michael. "Taste and See the Lord Is Good." SATB, org, ob. AFP 0800657039.
Viadana, Lodovico. "Shout for Joy, Ye Righteous/Exsultate justi." SATB. OXF 0-19-343695-7. (P)

Fifth Sunday in Lent

Year A

Ezekiel 37:1-14	*The dry bones of Israel brought to life*
Psalm 130	*With the* Lord *there is mercy and plenteous redemption*
Romans 8:6-11	*Life in the Spirit*
John 11:1-45	*Baptismal image: the raising of Lazarus*

Bach, Johann Sebastian. "Ye Are Not of the Flesh." *Jesu, Meine Freude*. SSATB GSCH 14354. § (S)
Dressler, Gallus. "I Am the Resurrection." *Chantry Choirbook*. SATB. AFP 0800657772. (G) §
Ferguson, John. "Psalm 130/Out of the Depths." SATB, org. AFP 0800656075. (P)
Hassler, Hans Leo. "Lord, Let at Last Thine Angels Come." SSAATTBB. CPH 98-1026.
Pinkham, Daniel. "De profundis." SATB, vla, opt org. ECS 4156. (P)
Rowan, William P. "With the Lord, There Is Mercy." SATB, kybd. AFP 0800675584. (P)
Rutter, John. "Agnus Dei." *Requiem*. SATB, org, opt orch. HIN MH-164.
Schalk, Carl. "Lord, It Belongs Not to My Care." SATB, org. AFP 0800645901.
———. "Out of the Depths." SAB, org. MSM 50-3410. (P)
Schütz, Heinrich. "I Am the Resurrection." SATB dbl choir. CFP 6591. (G)
Scott, K. Lee. "Out of the Depths I Cry to Thee." 2 pt mxd, kybd. AFP 0800647327. (P)
Thompson, J. Michael. "Taste and See the Lord Is Good." SATB, org, ob. AFP 0800657039.
Vaughan Williams, Ralph. "O Taste and See." SATB, S solo, org, OXF 3535114.
Willaert, Adrian. "The Raising of Lazarus." SATB. RIC 1873. (G)

Year B

Jeremiah 31:31-34	*A new covenant written on the heart*
Psalm 51:1-12	*Create in me a clean heart, O God*
or Psalm 119:9-16	*I treasure your promise in my heart*
Hebrews 5:5-10	*Through suffering Christ becomes the source of salvation*
John 12:20-33	*The grain of wheat dying in the earth*

Allegri, Gregorio. "Miserere mei, Deus." *European Sacred Music*. SSAATTBB. OXF 0193436957. (P)
Bach, Johann Sebastian. "Jesus, My Sweet Pleasure/Jesu, meine Freude." *Bach for All Seasons*. SATB. AFP 080065854X. §
Beethoven, Ludwig van/ed. K. Lee Scott. "A Contrite Heart." *Sing a Song of Joy*. MH, kybd. AFP 0800647882. ML, kybd. AFP 0800652827. (P)
Brahms, Johannes. "Create in Me, O God." SATBB. GSCH 50297770. § (P)
Christiansen, F. Melius. "Lamb of God." SATB. AFP 0800652592. *The Augsburg Choirbook*. AFP 0800656784.
Hogan, Moses. "Lord, I Want to Be a Christian." SATB. HAL 08703140.
How, Martin. "Lenten Litany." U, opt solos, kybd. B&H 6080.
Monteverdi, Claudio. "Christe, adoramus te." SATB, cont. NOV 19653.
Schalk, Carl. "Have Mercy on Me, O God." SATB. AFP 0800657845. (P)
Tchesnokov, Pavel. "Salvation Is Created." SATB. GSCH 50308470. §
Vantine, Bruce. "Now the Green Blade Rises." SATB, opt kybd. MSM 50-4010. (G)
Wesley, Samuel Sebastian. "Wash Me Thoroughly." *The New Church Anthem Book*. SATB, org. OXF 0193531097. (P)

Year C

Isaiah 43:16-21	*The Lord gives water in the wilderness to the chosen people*
Psalm 126	*Those who sowed with tears will reap with songs of joy*
Philippians 3:4b-14	*To know Christ and his resurrection, to share in his sufferings*
John 12:1-8	*Mary anoints Jesus for his burial*

Ashdown, Franklin D. "Jesus, the Very Thought of Thee." SATB, org, opt C inst. AFP 0800657500.

Ferguson, John. "Lord, in All Love." SATB, org, opt cong. AFP 0800656490.

Fleming, Larry L. "Humble Service." SATB. AFP 0800646223. (G)

Gibbs, Armstrong C. "Bless the Lord, O My Soul." *Oxford Easy Anthem Book*. SATB in 2 pts, org. OXF 3533219.

Martin, Gilbert. "When I Survey the Wondrous Cross." SATB, org. PRE 312-40785.

Mozart, Wolfgang Amadeus. "Adoramus te." SATB, opt kybd. AMC 112.

Proulx, Richard. "Weary of All Trumpeting." SAB, org, opt cong and br qnt. AFP 0800657632. *The Augsburg Choirbook*. AFP 0800656784.

Saylor, Bruce. "When I Survey the Wondrous Cross." SATB. CPH 98-2776.

Schütz, Heinrich. "Praise to You, Lord Jesus." *Chantry Choirbook*. SATB. AFP 08006427772. §

Scott, K. Lee. "Jesu, Our Hope, Our Heart's Desire." SATB, org. CPH 98-2951.

Walton, William. "A Litany/Drop, Drop Slow Tears." *Anthems for Choirs IV*. SATB. OXF 353018X.

Sunday of the Passion / Palm Sunday

Year A

Isaiah 50:4-9a	*The servant of the Lord submits to suffering*
Psalm 31:9-16	*Into your hands, O Lord, I commend my spirit*
Philippians 2:5-11	*Humbled to the point of death on a cross*
Matthew 26:14—27:66	*The passion of the Lord*
or Matthew 27:11-54	*The passion of the Lord*

Bach, Johann Sebastian. "Crucifixus." *Mass in B Minor. Bach for All Seasons.* SATB, org. AFP 0800656784. § (G)
Benson, Robert A. "Ride On! Ride On in Majesty!" SATB, org, opt cong. AFP 0800674634. (PrG)
Bertalot, John. "Passion of Our Lord According to St. Matthew." SATB, 6 solo vcs, cong, org. AFP 0800651391. (G)
Bruckner, Anton. "Christus factus est." SATB. AMC AE-157. (G) §
Ferguson, John. "Ah, Holy Jesus." SATB (div), vla. MSM 50-3012.
———. "Ah, Holy Jesus." SATB, org, opt cong. AFP 0800654528. *The Augsburg Choirbook.* 0800656784. (F, G)
Ferko, Frank. "Motet for Passion Sunday." SATB. ECS 4916.
Fleming, Larry L. "Ride On, King Jesus." *Three About Jesus.* SATB, S solo. AFP 0800652622. (PrG)
Gounod, Charles. "Blessed Is He Who Cometh." SATB, solo, org. GSCH 3423. (PrG)
Handel, George Frideric. "He Was Despised." *Messiah.* A solo, org or orch. §
Jennings, Carolyn. "My Song Is Love Unknown." U. CG 559.
Kern, Jan. "Chants of the Passion." 3 solo vcs. GSCH G-1795.
Mathias, William H. "Lift Up Your Heads, O Ye Gates." SATB, org. OXF 3503441. *Anthems for Choirs 1.* OXF 353214X.
Morgan, David C. "A Palm Sunday Antiphon/Hosanna to the Son of David." *The New Church Anthem Book.* SATB, org. OXF 0193531097. (PrG)
Near, Gerald. "Christ for Us Became Obedient unto Death." 2 pt mxd, org. MSM AE112.
Proulx, Richard. "Entrance into Jerusalem and Hymn." SATB, cong, org, timp, opt tpt. OXF 94.248. (PrG)
———. "Were You There." SATB, sop solo, opt cong. AFP 080065451X. *The Augsburg Choirbook.* AFP 0800656784.
Schütz, Heinrich. "St. Matthew Passion." SATB, solos, org. CPH 97-751. (G)
Tchaikovsky, Pyotr Il'yich. "The Crown of Roses." *100 Carols for Choirs.* SATB. OXF 1193532271.
Victoria, Tomás Luis de. "Hosanna to the Son of David." SATB. CPH 98-1993. (PrG)
Willan, Healey. "Hosanna to the Son of David." SATB. CPH 98-101. (PrG)

Year B

Isaiah 50:4-9a	*The servant of the Lord submits to suffering*
Psalm 31:9-16	*Into your hands, O Lord, I commend my spirit*
Philippians 2:5-11	*Humbled to the point of death on a cross*
Mark 14:1—15:47	*The passion of the Lord*
or Mark 15:1-39 [40-47]	*The passion of the Lord*

Adams, Stephen. "The Holy City." *Sing Solo Sacred.* ML, kybd. OXF 0193457857. MH, kybd. OXF 0193457849.
Bell, John L. "O the Lamb." SATB, pno. GIA G-4533.
Bruckner, Anton. "Christus factus est." SATB. AMC AE-157. (G) §
Distler, Hugo. "A Lamb Goes Uncomplaining Forth." SATB. CPH 67-5892. (F, G)
Farlee, Robert Buckley. "Solemn Reproaches of the Cross." SATB, solo, pno. AFP 0800674723.
Ferguson, John. "Ah, Holy Jesus." SATB div, vla. MSM 50-3012. (F, G)
———. "Ah, Holy Jesus." SATB, org, opt cong. AFP 0800654528. *The Augsburg Choirbook.* 0800656784. (F, G)
Fleming, Larry L. "Ride On, King Jesus." *Three About Jesus.* SATB, S solo. AFP 0800652622. (PrG)

Gesius, Bartholomäus. "Sing Hosanna to the Son of David." SATB. PRE 312-41450. (PrG)
Gibbons, Orlando. "Hosanna to the Son of David." SSAATTB. OXF 43.079. (PrG)
Jennings, Carolyn. "Ah, Holy Jesus." SA, clo. AFP 0800645154. (F, G)
Johnson, David N. "O Dearest Lord, Thy Sacred Head." SATB, org, opt S or T solo, opt fl. AFP 0800645790.
Leaf, Robert. "O Sacred Head, Now Wounded." SATB, org, cl. AFP 0800652738. (F, G)
Vaughan Williams, Ralph. "At the Name of Jesus." SATB, org or br qnt. OXF A158. (S)

Year C

Isaiah 50:4-9a — *The servant of the Lord submits to suffering*
Psalm 31:9-16 — *Into your hands, O Lord, I commend my spirit*
Philippians 2:5-11 — *Humbled to the point of death on a cross*
Luke 22:14—23:56 — *The passion of the Lord*
or Luke 23:1-49 — *The passion of the Lord*

Benson, Robert A. "Ride On! Ride On in Majesty!" SATB, org, opt cong. AFP 0800674634. (PrG)
Bertalot, John. "Passion of Our Lord According to St. Luke." SATB, cong, org. AFP 0800654455. (G)
Casals, Pablo. "O vos omnes." SSAATTBB. TetraAB 128.
Dering, Richard. "O vos omnes." SSATTB, org. OXF 3953668.
Gesius, Bartholomäus. "Hosanna to the Son of David." *Chantry Choirbook*. SATB. AFP 0800642772. (PrG)
Gibbons, Orlando. "Hosanna to the Son of David." SSAATTBB. OXF 3520788. (PrG)
Mathias, William H. "Lift Up Your Heads, O Ye Gates." SATB, org. OXF 3503441. *Anthems for Choirs 1*. OXF 353214X.
Niedmann, Peter. "Lift Up Your Heads, Ye Mighty Gates." *The Augsburg Choirbook*. SATB, org. AFP 0800656784.
Petrich, Roger. "Ah, Holy Jesus." *Anthems for Choirs IV*. SSATB. OXF 353018X. (G)
Pinkham, Daniel. "Hosanna to the Son of David." SAB, org. ECS 4040. (PrG)
Proulx, Richard. "Entrance into Jersualem and Hymn." SATB, cong, org, timp, opt tpt. OXF 94-248. (PrG)
———. "We Adore You O Christ." SATB. PAR PPM09836.
Taranto, Steven. "Into Jerusalem." U, kybd, Orff inst. CG CGA735. (PrG)
Vaughan Williams, Ralph. "At the Name of Jesus." SATB, org, br, cong. OXF 350197X. (S)

Monday in Holy Week

Years A, B, C

Isaiah 42:1-9	The servant brings forth justice
Psalm 36:5-11	Your people take refuge under the shadow of your wings
Hebrews 9:11-15	The redeeming blood of Christ
John 12:1-11	Mary anoints the feet of Jesus

Ellingboe, Bradley. "Thy Holy Wings." SATB. KJO C9001.
Erickson, Karle. "Thy Holy Wings." SATB, 2 fl. AFP 0800645359.

Tuesday in Holy Week

Years A, B, C

Isaiah 49:1-7	The servant brings salvation to earth's ends
Psalm 71:1-14	From my mother's womb you have been my strength
1 Corinthians 1:18-31	Christ crucified, the wisdom of God
John 12:20-36	The hour has come

Ellingboe, Bradley. "The Chief Cornerstone." 2 pt mxd, org, tpt. AFP 0800676394. *Augsburg Easy Choirbook.* AFP 0800676025.
Martin, Gilbert. "When I Survey the Wondrous Cross." SATB, kybd. PRE 312407850.

Wednesday in Holy Week

Years A, B, C

Isaiah 50:4-9a	The servant is vindicated by God
Psalm 70	Be pleased, O God, to deliver me
Hebrews 12:1-3	Look to Jesus, who endured the cross
John 13:21-32	The departure of Jesus' betrayer

Copland, Aaron. "Help Us, O Lord." SATB. B&H 6018.
Ferguson, John. "Ah, Holy Jesus." SATB, org, opt cong. AFP 0800654528. *The Augsburg Choirbook.* AFP 0800656784. (F)
Handel, George Frideric. "He Was Despised." *Messiah.* CT or A solo, kybd or orch. §

Maundy Thursday

Years A, B, C

Exodus 12:1-4 [5-10] 11-14   *The passover of the Lord*
Psalm 116:1-2, 12-19   *I will take the cup of salvation and call on the name of the Lord.*
1 Corinthians 11:23-26   *Proclaim the Lord's death until he comes*
John 13:1-17, 31b-35   *The service of Christ: footwashing and meal*

Aston, Peter. "I Give You a New Commandment." 2 pt, org. GIA G-4331. (G)
Basler, Paul. "Ubi caritas." SATB, pno, hrn. PLY PJMS-121. (G)
Benson, Robert A. "Wondrous Love." SATB, org. AFP 0800658604.
Bouman, Paul. "Lord of Lords, Adored by Angels." SATB, org. MSM 50-9025.
Cherwien, David. "Psalm 22." *To God Will I Sing*. ML, kybd. AFP 0800674340. MH, kybd. AFP 0800674332.
Christiansen, F. Melius. "Lamb of God." SATB. AFP 0800652592. *The Augsburg Choirbook*. AFP 0800656784.
Duruflé, Maurice. "Ubi caritas." SATTBB. DUR 312-41253. (G)
Elgar, Edward. "Ave verum corpus." *The New Church Anthem Book*. SATB, org. OXF 0193531097.
Farlee, Robert Buckley. "Mandatum." SATB. AFP 0800654153. (G)
———. "When Twilight Comes." 2 pt mxd, pno. AFP 0800675576. (G)
Fleming, Larry L. "Sing and Ponder." SATB, hb. AFP 0800653491.
Haugen, Marty. "Triduum Hymn: Wondrous Love." SATB, cong, gtr, kybd, bass inst. GIA G-3544.
Heim, Bret. "Lord of Lords Adored by Angels." SATB, org. CPH 98-3309.
Kemp, Helen. "A Lenten Love Song." U, kybd. CGA 486.
Leighton, Kenneth. "Solus ad victimam/Alone to Sacrifice." SATB, org. OXF 42.384.
Lienas, Juan de/ed. Bradley Ellingboe. "Coenantibus autem illis." SATB. KJO 8820.
Mendelssohn, Felix. "See What Love." SATB, kybd. AFP 0800645618. §
Messiaen, Olivier. "O sacrum convivium." SATB. DUR 12.742.
Moore, Philip. "O sacrum convivium." SATB, A solo. Kevin Mayhew 5101193M.
Mozart, Wolfgang Amadeus. "Ave verum corpus." *Chantry Choirbook*. SATB. AFP 0800657772. § (S, G)
Near, Gerald. "Christ for Us Became Obedient unto Death." 2 pt mxd, org. MSM AE112.
Nelson, Ronald A. "If You Love One Another." U or 2 pt, kybd. SEL 422-841. (G)
Organ, Anne Krentz. "Love One Another." SATB. AFP 0800659643. (G)
Peloquin, Alexander. "Psalm for Holy Week." SATB, cant, cong, acc. GIA G-1658.
Praetorius, Michael. "O Lord, We Praise Thee." SATB, solos, inst or org. CPH 97-509.
Proulx, Richard. "God Is Love." SATB, cant, cong, org, ob. GIA G-4853.
———. "Ubi caritas et amor." SATB, hb. GIA G-1983.
Raminsh, Imant. "Ubi caritas." SATB. Jaymar 02.285. (G)
Saint-Saëns, Camille. "Ave verum corpus." SATB, opt kybd. MSM 50-3005.
Schalk, Carl. "Where Charity and Love Prevail." 2 pt, org. CPH 98-2701.
Schütz, Heinrich. "My God, My God." *Ten Psalms from the Becker Psalter*. SATB. CPH 97-6303.
Tallis, Thomas. "O sacrum convivium." SAATB. OXF TCM74.
Walton, William. "A Litany/Drop, Drop Slow Tears." SATB. OXF 3594366.
Zipp, Friedrich. "Soul, Adorn Yourself with Gladness." *Chantry Choirbook*. SATB, kybd or inst. AFP 0800657772.

Good Friday

Years A, B, C

Isaiah 52:13—53:12	*The suffering servant*
Psalm 22	*My God, my God, why have you forsaken me?*
Hebrews 10:16-25	*The way to God is opened by Jesus' death*
or Hebrews 4:14-16; 5:7-9	*Jesus, the merciful high priest*
John 18:1—19:42	*The passion and death of Christ*

Bach, Johann Sebastian. "Crucifixus." *Mass in B Minor. Bach for All Seasons*. SATB, org. AFP 080065854X. § (G)
Bouman, Paul. "Behold the Lamb of God." SA, org. CPH 98-1088.
Burleigh, Harry T. "Were You There." *The Spirituals of Harry T. Burleigh*. L, kybd. WAR EL 03150. H, kybd. WAR EL 03151.(G)
Burleigh, Harry T. "Were You There?" SSATTBB. RIC NY 423. (G)
Byrd, William. "The Passion According to St. John." SAB, 3 solo vcs. CPH 97-4868. (G)
Casals, Pablo. "O vos omnes." SATB. TetraAB 128.
Chilcott, Bob. "Were You There." SATB, div. OXF 3432900. (G)
Christiansen, F. Melius. "Lamb of God." SATB. AFP 0800652592. *The Augsburg Choirbook*. AFP 0800656784. (F)
Copley, R. Evan. "Surely He Has Borne Our Griefs." SATB, kybd. AFP 0800646185. (F)
Distler, Hugo. "A Lamb Goes Uncomplaining Forth." *Chantry Choirbook*. SATB. AFP 0800657772.
Ellingboe, Bradley. "There Is a Green Hill Far Away." 2 pt mxd, pno. KJO 5765. (G)
Farlee, Robert Buckley. "Solemn Reproaches of the Cross." SATB, solo, pno. AFP 0800674723.
Ferguson, John. "Ah, Holy Jesus." SATB, org, opt cong. AFP 0800654528. (G)
———. *St. John Passion*. SATB, org, opt cong. AFP 0800658582. (G)
Fleming, Larry L. "Sing and Ponder." SATB, hb. AFP 0800653491.
Handel, George Frideric. "Surely He Hath Borne Our Griefs." *Messiah*. SATB. §
Hillert, Richard. "Surely He Hath Borne Our Griefs." SATB. CPH 98-159. (F)
Isaac, Heinrich. "Upon the Cross Extended." SATB, opt kybd. GIA G-293. (G)
Jennings, Carolyn. "Ah, Holy Jesus." SA, cl. AFP 0800645154. (F, G)
Johnson, David N. "O Dearest Lord, Thy Sacred Head." SATB, opt fl, org. AFP 0800645790.
Kern, Jan. "Chants of the Passion." 3 solo vcs. GIA G-1795.
Leaf, Robert. "O Sacred Head, Now Wounded." SATB, org, cl. AFP 0800652738.
Leighton, Kenneth. "Solus ad victimam/Alone to Sacrifice." SATB, org. OXF 42.384.
Manz, Paul. "I Caused Thy Grief." SATB, org. MSM 50-3036.
Mathias, William H. "Ah, Holy Jesus." SATB. OXF 3-7800.
Moore, Undine Smith. "Oh, That Bleeding Lamb." SATB. AFP 0800656032.
Mozart, Wolfgang Amadeus. "Agnus Dei." U, kybd. KJO 8736.
Palestrina, Giovanni Pierluigi da. "Adoramus te Christe." SATB. CFI CM6578.
Paulus, Stephen. "Carol of the Hill." SATB, kybd. AMSI 312. (G)
Pinkham, Daniel. "Near the Cross of Jesus/Stabat mater." SATB, pno. ECS 4588.
Proulx, Richard. "Were You There." SATB, S solo, opt cong. AFP 080065451X. (G)
Rickard, Jeffrey H. "Let Thy Blood in Mercy Poured." SAATB. CFI C.M.447.
Schütz, Heinrich. "Praise to You, Lord Jesus." *Chantry Choirbook*. SATB. AFP 08066427772.
Scott, K. Lee. "Blessed Lamb, on Calvary's Mountain." *Sing Forth God's Praise*. MH, kybd. AFP 0800675266. ML, kybd. AFP 080067538X.
Shaw, Robert/Alice Parker. " 'Tis Finished." SA(T)B. LAW 9944.
Victoria, Tomás Luis de. "The Passion According to St. John." SATB, solos. CPH 97-5430. (G)
Willan, Healey. "Behold the Lamb of God." SATB, org. CPH 98-1509.

Resurrection of Our Lord: Vigil of Easter

Years A, B, C

Psalm 114	*Tremble, O earth, at the presence of the Lord*
Romans 6:3-11	*Dying and rising with Christ*
(A) Matthew 28:1-10	*Proclaim the resurrection*
(B) Mark 16:1-8	*The resurrection of Jesus is announced*
(C) Luke 24:1-12	*The women proclaim the resurrection*

Around the Light of Christ

Batastini, Robert J. "Exsultet/Easter Proclamation." U chant. GIA G-2351.

Repulski, John. "Exsultet." SATB, hb. OCP 11059GC.

Weaver, John. "The Easter Proclamation/The Exsultet." *Psalter—Psalms & Canticles for Singing*. Solo, org. Westminster/John Knox.

Around the Readings

Creation
Hopson, Hal H. "O Praise the Lord Who Made All Beauty." U, kybd. CG CGA 143.

Flood
Cherwien, David. "God Is Our Refuge and Strength." U, org. MSM 80-800.

Testing of Abraham
Britten, Benjamin. "Canticle II: Abraham and Isaac." A and T solo, pno. B&H 1408.

Deliverance at the Red Sea
Barker, Michael. "Miriam's Song." U, kybd, opt tamb. CG 740.

Cherwien, David. "Go Down, Moses." U, kybd. AMSI.

Salvation Freely Offered to All
DeLong, Richard P. "Seek Ye the Lord." *Five Sacred Songs*. Solo, kybd. ECS 4759.

Hopson, Hal H. "For as the Rain and Snow Come Down." SATB. AFP 080065868X.

New Heart, New Spirit
Goudimel, Claude. "As the Deer, for Water Yearning." *Chantry Choirbook*. SATB. AFP 0800642772.

Howells, Herbert. "Like As the Hart." SATB, org. OXF 42.066.

Gathering of God's People
Marshall, Jane. "Psalm 98." U, kybd. CGA-427.

Fiery Furnace
Jennings, Kenneth. "All You Works of the Lord, Bless the Lord." *The Augsburg Choirbook*. SATB, org. AFP 0800656784.

Proulx, Richard. "Song of the Three Children." U, opt 2 pt, cant, cong, perc, org. GIA G-1863.

Around the Font

Cherwien, David/Susan Palo Cherwien. "Life Tree." SAB, org, opt fl. CPH 98-3190.

Farlee, Robert Buckley. "O Blessed Spring." SATB, ob, vln or cl, org, opt cong. AFP 0800654242. *The Augsburg Choirbook*. AFP 0800656784.

Trapp, Lynn. "Music for the Rite of Sprinkling." SATB, org. MSM 80-901.

Other music

Anerio, Felice. "Angelus autem Domini." SATB. ECS 2975.
Bach, Johann Sebastian. "Lord Jesus Christ, God's Only Son." *Bach for All Seasons*. SATB. AFP 080065854X.
Bairstow, Edward C. "Sing Ye to the Lord." SATB, org. NOV.
Berthier, Jacques. "Surrexit Christus." *Music from Taizé*, vol 2. Choir, cant, gtr. GIA G-2778.
Biery, James. "Easter Sequence." U, br qrt or org. MSM 80-404.
———. "O sacrum convivium." SATB. MSM 50-8311.
Cherwien, David. "At the Lamb's High Feast We Sing." SATB, opt tpt, org, cong. CPH. 98-2864.
Erickson, Richard. "Come Away to the Skies." SATB, fl, fc. AFP 0800656776.
———. "When Long Before Time." SATB, org, fl. AFP 0800656768.
Gerike, Henry V. "The Strife Is O'er, the Battle Done." SATB, kybd, tpt, cong. CPH 98-2446.
Handel, George Frideric. "Since by Man Came Death." *Messiah*. SATB, org. §
Hobby, Robert A. "Now All the Vault of Heaven Resounds/Ye Watchers and Ye Holy Ones." SAB, org, 2 tr, opt 2 oct hb, cong. AFP 0800658655.
Leavitt, John. "At the Lamb's High Feast." SATB, cong, br qrt, timp, org. GIA G-2980.
Ley, Henry G. "The Strife Is O'er." SATB, org. OXF 3532522. §
Neswick, Bruce. "O Taste and See." SATB, S solo, kybd. AFP 0800654714.
Proulx, Richard. "Our Paschal Lamb, That Sets Us Free." SATB, org. AFP 0800656113.
Rachmaninoff, Sergei. "Today Hath Salvation Come." *All Night Vigil. Songs of the Church*. SSAATTB. §
Schein, Johann H. "Christ Lay in Death's Dark Tomb." SAB, cont. BBL.
Smith, Byron J. "Worthy to Be Praised." SATB, pno. LAW 52654.
Stanford, Charles Villiers. "We Know That Christ Is Raised." SATB, org, opt cong. AFP 6000106432.
Willan, Healey. "Christ Our Passover." *First Motet Book*. SATB. CPH 97-484.
Wolff, S. Drummond. "At the Lamb's High Feast." SATB, tpts, cong, kybd. CPH 98-2300.
———. "We Know That Christ Is Raised." SATB, tpts. CPH 98-2609.

Resurrection of Our Lord: Easter Day

Year A

    Acts 10:34-43   *God raised Jesus on the third day*
    or Jeremiah 31:1-6   *Joy at the restoration of God's people.*
    Psalm 118:1-2, 14-24   *On this day the L*ORD *has acted; we will rejoice and be glad in it*
    Colossians 3:1-4   *Raised with Christ to seek the higher things*
    or Acts 10:34-43   *God raised Jesus on the third day.*
    John 20:1-18   *Seeing the risen Christ*
    or Matthew 28:1-10   *Proclaim the resurrection*

Anerio, Felice. "Angelus autem Domini." SATB. ECS 2975.
Bach, Johann Sebastian/arr. Michael Burkhardt. "Christ Jesus Lay in Death's Strong Bands." SATB and U, org, vln, opt clo. MSM 50-4021.
Bairstow, Edward C. "The Day Draws on the Golden Light." SATB, org. OXF 0193531097.
Benson, Robert A. "On Earth Has Dawned This Day of Days." SATB, organ, opt br qrt. AFP 0800676289.
Billings, William. "Easter Anthem." SATB. GSCH 9949.
Brahms, Johannes. "Magdalena." SATB. GSCH 9953.
Burkhardt, Michael. "Christ the Lord Is Risen Again." SATB, opt br qrt, org. MSM 50-4024.
Busarow, Donald. "At the Lamb's High Feast We Sing." SAB, org, cong. AFP 6000105096.
Cherwien, David. "At the Lamb's High Feast We Sing." SATB, opt tpt and timp, org, cong. CPH 98-2864.
Christiansen, Paul J. "Easter Morning." SATB. AFP 080064557X. *The Augsburg Choirbook*. AFP 0800656784.
Crüger, Johann. "Awake, My Heart, with Gladness." *Chantry Choirbook*. SATB, 2 C insts. AFP 0800657772.
Ellingboe, Bradley. "Mary at the Tomb." SATB, pno. AFP 0800656946. (G)
———. "The Chief Cornerstone." 2 pt mixed, kybd, opt tpt. AFP 0800676394. (P)
Erickson, Richard. "Come Away to the Skies." SATB, fl, fc. AFP 0800656776.
Ferguson, John. "Christ the Lord Is Risen Today!" SATB, opt kybd, snare drm, picc. AFP 0800646363.
Gallus, Jacobus (Handl). "This Is the Day." SATB, dbl choir or choir and brass qrt. CPH 98-1702. (P)
Goemanne, Noël. "Fanfare for Festivals (choral pts)." SATB, org, 3 tpts, timp. AG 7137.
Handel, George Frideric. "Alleluia." *Coronation Anthems*. SAATB, org. OXF.
Martinson, Joel. "Three Days Had Passed." SATB, br qnt, timp, org. PAR PPM00212. (G)
Mendelssohn, Felix. "Jesus Christ, My Sure Defense—Alleluia." *Chantry Choirbook*. SATB. AFP 0800657772.
Parker, Alice/Robert Shaw. "On Easter Morn." SATB. GSCH 995.
Pote, Allen. "On the Third Day." SATB, br, hb. HOP F-1000.
Praetorius, Michael. "The Strife Is O'er, the Battle Done." SAB. GIA G-279.
Rutter, John. "Christ the Lord Is Risen Again." SATB, org. OXF 42.362.
Stanford, Charles Villiers. "Ye Choirs of New Jerusalem." *Anthems for Choirs I*. SATB, org. OXF 353214.
Vaughan Williams, Ralph. "Christ Our Passover." SATB or U, br, org. PAR PPM 08702.
Vulpius, Melchior. "Arisen Is Our Blessed Lord." *Chantry Choirbook*. SATB, dbl chorus or inst. AFP 0800657772.

Year B

Acts 10:34-43	*God raised Jesus on the third day*
or Isaiah 25:6-9	*The feast of victory*
Psalm 118:1-2, 14-24	*On this day the Lord has acted; we will rejoice and be glad in it*
1 Corinthians 15:1-11	*Witnesses to the risen Christ*
or Acts 10:34-43	*God raised Jesus on the third day*
John 20:1-18	*Seeing the risen Christ*
or Mark 16:1-8	*The resurrection of Jesus is announced*

Bach, Johann Sebastian. "Awake, Thou Wintry Earth." *The New Church Anthem Book*. SATB, org, kybd. OXF 0193531097. §

Benson, Robert A. "Good Christians All, Rejoice and Sing." SATB, org, br qrt. AFP 0800659597.

Billings, William. "Easter Anthem." SATB. GSCH 9949.

Byrd, William. "Sing Praise to God This Holy Day." SSATB. CPH 98-2091.

Cherwien, David. "At the Lamb's High Feast We Sing." SATB, opt tpt and timp, org, cong. CPH 98-2864.

Clausen, René. "At the Name of Jesus." SATB, org, br qrt. MF 2052.

Fedak, Alfred V. "Begin the Song of Glory Now." SATB, org, opt br. MSM 50-4014.

Hancock, Gerre. "Christ Our Passover/Pascha nostrum." SATB, org, cong. OXF 3861747.

Harris, William H. "This Joyful Eastertide." SATB, org. NOV 29-0151.

Hovhannes, Alan. "Jesus Christ Is Risen Today." SATB, org. Assoc. 196/59.

Leavitt, John. "Easter." SATB, pno, opt 2 tpt, hrn, 2 tbn, timp, xyl, glock, sus cym, tri. AFP 0800647238.

Mathias, William H. "Alleluia! Christ Is Risen." SATB, br, perc, org. OXF 42.479.

Nelson, Ronald A. "He Rose." U, kybd. SEL 422-401.

Telemann, Georg Philipp/ed. Susan Palo Cherwien. "Halleluja." *To God Will I Sing*. MH, kybd. AFP 0800674332. ML, kybd. AFP 080067434X.

Wolff, S. Drummond. "At the Lamb's High Feast." SATB, tpts, cong. CPH 98-2300.

Year C

Acts 10:34-43	*God raised Jesus on the third day*
or Isaiah 65:17-25	*God promises a new heaven and a new earth*
Psalm 118:1-2, 14-24	*On this day the Lord has acted; we will rejoice and be glad in it*
1 Corinthians 15:19-26	*Christ raised from the dead, the first fruits*
or Acts 10:34-43	*God raised Jesus on the third day*
John 20:1-18	*Seeing the risen Christ*
or Luke 24:1-12	*The women proclaim the resurrection*

Byrd, William. "Haec dies." SSATTB, opt org. OXF 3521008. (P)

Farlee, Robert Buckley. "Christ Is Living!/Cristo vive." SATB, org, gtr, perc, opt cong. AFP 0800658833.

Gallus, Jacobus (Handl). "This Is the Day." SATB, dbl choir or choir and brass qrt. CPH 98-1702. (P)

Gesius, Bartholomäus. "Today in Triumph Christ Arose." *Chantry Choirbook*. SATB. AFP 0800642772.

Handel, George Frideric. "I Know that My Redeemer Liveth." *Messiah*. Solo, kybd or orch. §

———. "Since by Man Came Death." *Messiah*. SATB, kybd or orch. §

Hayes, Mark. "Alleluia, Christ Is Risen." SATB, kybd. AFP 0800659538.

Near, Gerald. "Arise, My Love, My Fair One." *The Augsburg Choirbook*. SATB. AFP 0800656784.

Nystedt, Knut. "Now Is Christ Risen." SATB, org, tpt, fl, hb. AFP 6000103239.

Peeters, Flor. "Entrata Festiva." U, org, opt br. PET 6159.

Proulx, Richard. "Our Paschal Lamb, That Sets Us Free." SATB, org. AFP 0800656113.

Rachmaninoff, Sergei. "Today Hath Salvation Come." *All Night Vigil. Songs of the Church*. SATB. HWG GCMR GB640.

Vulpius, Melchior. "Arisen Is Our Blessed Lord." *Chantry Choirbook*. SATB, dbl chorus or inst. AFP 0800657772.

Resurrection of Our Lord: Easter Evening

Years A, B, C

>   Isaiah 25:6-9 *The feast of victory*
>   Psalm 114 *Hallelujah*
>   1 Corinthians 5:6b-8 *Celebrating with sincerity and truth*
>   Luke 24:13-49 *At evening, the risen Christ is revealed*

Bertalot, John. "Abide with Me." SATB, org. AFP 0800647106.
Dirksen, Richard. "Christ, Our Passover." SATB, br qrt, org, timp. HWG CMR 2874.
Farlee, Robert Buckley/ed. Susan Palo Cherwien. "We Are a Garden Walled Around." *To God Will I Sing*. MH, kybd. AFP 0800674332. ML, kybd. 080067434X.
Hovland, Egil. "Stay with Us." SATB, org. AFP 0800658825. (G)
Jordan, Alice. "See the Land, Her Easter Keeping." SATB, org. Randall M. Egan EC92-107.
Owens, Sam Batt. "O Paschal Lamp of Radiant Light." *The Augsburg Choirbook*. SATB, org. AFP 08000656784.
Pelz, Walter L. "Stay with Us." SATB, fl, org. CPH 98-2920. (G)
Philips, Craig. "On This Bright Easter Morn." SATB, org. OCP 10258.
Praetorius, Michael. "Stay with Us, Lord/Bleib bei uns, Herr." *Chantry Choirbook*. SATB. AFP 0800657772. (G)
Sirett, Mark G. "Thou Shalt Know Him When He Comes." SSAA. AFP 0800675304. SATB. AFP 0800655206. *The Augsburg Choirbook*. AFP 0800656784.
Thompson, Randall. "Alleluia." SATB. ECS 1786.
Vulpius, Melchior. "Arisen Is Our Blessed Lord." *Chantry Choirbook*. SATB. AFP 0800657772.

Second Sunday of Easter

Year A

>   Acts 2:14a, 22-32 *Christ's resurrection: the fulfillment of God's promise to David*
>   Psalm 16 *In your presence there is fullness of joy*
>   1 Peter 1:3-9 *New birth to a living hope through the resurrection*
>   John 20:19-31 *Beholding the wounds of the risen Christ*

Christiansen, Paul J. "Easter Morning." SATB. AFP 080064557X. *The Augsburg Choirbook*. AFP 0800656784.
Conlon, Joan. "Come, Enjoy God's Festive Springtime." U, kybd, opt C inst. AFP 0800646487.
Davies, H. Walford. "O Sons and Daughters." SATB. RSCM AO19.1 (G)
Ellingboe, Bradley. "Mary at the Tomb." SATB, pno. AFP 0800656946.
Hassler, Hans Leo. "Because You Have Seen Me, Thomas." *Ten Renaissance Motets*. SATB. WLP ESA-1635-8. (G)
Hillert, Richard. "Image of the Unseen God." SATB, kybd. AFP 0800659627.
Marenzio, Luca. "Quia vidisti me, Thomas/Because You Have Seen Me, Thomas." SATB. CPH 98-2617. (G)
Nystedt, Knut. "Peace I Leave with You." SSATB. AFP 0800652673.
Pelz, Walter L. "Peace I Leave with You." SATB. AFP 0800645650. *The Augsburg Choirbook*. AFP 0800656784.
Schalk, Carl. "I Have Set the Lord Always Before Me." SATB, opt kybd. MSM 50-9019.
Wetzler, Robert. "Peace Be with You." SATB, org. AMSI 178. (G)

Year B

Acts 4:32-35 — *The believers' common life*
Psalm 133 — *How good and pleasant it is to live together in unity*
1 John 1:1—2:2 — *Walking in the light*
John 20:19-31 — *Beholding the wounds of the risen Christ*

Billings, William. "The Lord Is Risen Indeed." SATB. CPH 98-3273.
Bouman, Paul. "God Is Light." SATB, org. AFP 0800653254. (S)
Christiansen, Paul J. "Easter Morning." SATB. AFP 080064557X. *The Augsburg Choirbook.* AFP 0800656784.
Crüger, Johann. "Awake, My Heart, with Gladness." *Chantry Choirbook.* SATB. AFP 0800657772.
Ellingboe, Bradley. "Mary at the Tomb." SATB, pno. AFP 0800656946.
Gallus, Jacobus (Handl). "Stetit Iesus/There Came Jesus." SATB. GIA G-2460. (G)
Helman, Michael. "We Walk by Faith." SATB, pno, opt fl, hb. AFP 0800659759. (G)
Hillert, Richard. "O Sons and Daughters of the King." SAB, cong, opt trp, org. CPH 98-3117. (G)
Leavitt, John. "An Easter Gloria!" SATB, kybd, perc. AFP 0800654161.
Marenzio, Luca. "Quia vidisti me, Thomas/Because You Have Seen Me, Thomas." SATB. CPH 98-2617. (G)
Pelz, Walter L. "Peace I Leave with You." SATB. AFP 0800645650. *The Augsburg Choirbook.* AFP 0800656784. (G)
Proulx, Richard. "Easter Carol." 2 pt, fl, kybd. GIA G-4465.
Roberts, William Bradley. "In All These You Welcomed Me." U, org, opt ob or inst. AFP 6000001207.
Wolff, S. Drummond. "Come, You Faithful, Raise the Strain." SATB, kybd, tpt. CPH 98-2522.

Year C

Acts 5:27-32 — *The God of our ancestors raised up Jesus*
Psalm 118:14-29 — *This is the Lord's doing and it is marvelous in our eyes*
or Psalm 150 — *Let everything that has breath praise the Lord*
Revelation 1:4-8 — *Jesus Christ, the firstborn of the dead, is coming*
John 20:19-31 — *Beholding the wounds of the risen Christ*

Aguiar, Ernani. "Psalm 150/Salmo 150." SATB. EAR. (P)
Christiansen, Paul J. "Easter Morning." SATB. AFP 080064557X. *The Augsburg Choirbook.* AFP 0800656784.
Clausen, René. "All That Hath Life and Breath, Praise Ye the Lord." SATB div, S solo. SHW 8MF0223. (P)
Ellingboe, Bradley. "Mary at the Tomb." SATB, pno. AFP 0800656946.
Handel, George Frideric. "Thine Is the Glory." SATB, 2 tpt, kybd. CPH 98-2831.
Hobby, Robert A. "Psalm 150." SATB, cong, opt br, org. MSM 50-7014. (P)
Manz, Paul. "E'en So, Lord Jesus, Quickly Come." SATB. MSM 50-0001. TTBB. MSM 50-0900.
Marenzio, Luca. "Quia vidisti me, Thomas/Because You Have Seen Me, Thomas." SATB. CPH 98-2617. (G)
Noble, T. Tertius. "Grieve Not the Holy Spirit." SATB, solo, org. HWG GCMR 00409.
Pelz, Walter L. "Peace I Leave with You." SATB. AFP 0800645650. *The Augsburg Choirbook.* AFP 0800656784. (G)
Proulx, Richard. "Easter Carol." 2 pt, fl, org. GIA G-4465.
Young, Gordon. "My Master from a Garden Rose." SATB. SHW A-6087.

Third Sunday of Easter

Year A

    Acts 2:14a, 36-41   *Receiving God's promise through baptism*
    Psalm 116:1-4, 12-19   *I will call upon the name of the Lord*
    1 Peter 1:17-23   *Born anew through the living word of God*
    Luke 24:13-35   *Eating with the risen Christ*

Bach, Johann Sebastian. "Christ Is Arisen." *Bach for All Seasons*. SATB, kybd. AFP 080065854X.
———. "Sing Praise to Christ." SATB, org. CPH 98-1377. *With High Delight*. CPH 97-5047.
Bertalot, John. "Come, Risen Lord." SATB, org. AFP 0800657667. *The Augsburg Choirbook*. AFP 0800656784.
Byrd, William. "Cognoverunt discipuli/The Disciples with Wondering Eyes." SATB. NOV TM18.
Carter, Andrew. "Love One Another." SATB, org. OXF A422.
Crüger, Johann. "Awake, My Heart, with Gladness." *Chantry Choirbook*. SATB, C inst, org. AFP 0800657772.
Hovland, Egil. "Stay with Us." SATB, org or pno. AFP 0800658825. (G)
Pelz, Walter L. "Stay with Us." SATB, fl, org. CPH 98-2920. (G)
———. "With High Delight Let Us Unite." Concertato w opt SATB. CPH 97-5853.
Petrich, Robert. "Alleluia! Risen Indeed." 2 pt mxd, kybd. MSM 80-401.
Popora, Niccolo/arr. E. Hyde. "Credidi." SSA, str. NOV 19923.
Praetorius, Michael. "Stay with Us, Lord/Bleib bei uns, Herr." *Chantry Choirbook*. SATB. AFP 0800657772. (G)
Schalk, Carl. "Day of Arising." SATB, org. AFP 0800658671. (G)
Telemann, Georg Philipp. "Halleluja." *To God Will I Sing*. MH, kybd. AFP 0800674332. ML, kybd. AFP 0800674340.
Tiefenbach, Peter. "What Shall I Render to the Lord?" *The Augsburg Choirbook*. SATB. AFP 0800656784.
Tye, Christopher/arr. Carl Schalk. "The Man We Crucified." *Easter Motets*, Series A. SATB. AFP 0800647645.
Vaughan Williams, Ralph. "O Taste and See." *First Motet Book*. SATB, org. CPH 97-484. §
Wesley, Samuel Sebastian. "Blessed Be the God and Father." *The New Church Anthem Book*. SATB, org. OXF 0193531097.

Year B

    Acts 3:12-19   *Health and forgiveness through the risen Jesus*
    Psalm 4   *The Lord does wonders for the faithful*
    1 John 3:1-7   *The revealing of the children of God*
    Luke 24:36b-48   *Eating with the risen Christ*

Bertalot, John. "Come, Risen Lord." SATB, org. AFP 0800657667. *The Augsburg Choirbook*. AFP 0800656784.
Crüger, Johann. "Awake, My Heart, with Gladness." *Chantry Choirbook*. SATB, 2 C inst. AFP 08000657772.
Farlee, Robert Buckley. "Christ Is Living!/Cristo vive." SATB, org, gtr, perc. AFP 0800652479. (G)
Gerike, Henry V. "The Strife Is O'er, the Battle Done." SATB, kybd, tpt, cong. CPH 98-2446.
Lassus, Orlande de. "Christ Has Arisen/Christ ist erstanden." SATB. SCH AP 520.
Lau, Robert. "Christ Is Risen! Alleluia!" 2 pt, kybd, opt hb. CGA 674.
Martinson, Joel. "Awake, Arise!" SATB. OXF 94.349.
Mendelssohn, Felix. "See What Love." SATB, kybd. AFP 0800645618. §(S)
Pelz, Walter L. "Stay with Us." SAB, org. CPH 98-3073.
Philips, Peter. "Surgens Jesus/He Is Risen." *The New Church Anthem Book*. SATB. OXF 0193531097.

Year C

Acts 9:1-6 [7-20] *Paul's conversion, baptism, and preaching*
Psalm 30 *You have turned my wailing into dancing*
Revelation 5:11-14 *The song of the living creatures to the Lamb*
John 21:1-19 *Jesus appears to the disciples at the Sea of Tiberias*

Bertalot, John. "Come, Risen Lord." SATB, org. AFP 0800657667. *The Augsburg Choirbook.* AFP 0800656784.
Ellingboe, Bradley. "The Chief Cornerstone." *Augsburg Easy Choirbook.* 2 pt mxd, kybd. AFP 0800676025.
Handel, George Frideric. "Worthy Is the Lamb." *Messiah.* SATB, kybd. § (S)
Hovland, Egil. "Saul." SATB, org, narr. WAL WM-126. (F)
Johnson, Carolyn. "Now the Green Blade Rises." SATB, kybd, tpt. AFP 0800675428. (G)
Josquin Desprez. "O Mighty Word from God Come Down." *Chantry Choirbook.* SATB. AFP 0800642772.
Parker, Alice/Robert Shaw. "John Saw Duh Numbuh." SATB. LG 51109. (S)
Proulx, Richard. "Our Paschal Lamb, That Sets Us Free." SATB, org. AFP 0800656113.
Sweelinck, Jan Pieterszoon. "Sing to the Lord, New Songs Be Raising." *Chantry Choirbook.* SATB. AFP 0806642772.
Willan, Healey. "O Sacred Feast." SATB. HWG CGMR 715.

Fourth Sunday of Easter

Year A

Acts 2:42-47 — *The believers' common life*
Psalm 23 — *The Lord is my shepherd; I shall not be in want*
1 Peter 2:19-25 — *Follow the shepherd, even in suffering*
John 10:1-10 — *Christ the shepherd*

Archer, Malcolm. "The Lord's My Shepherd." 2 pt. RSCM AO274. (P)
Bach, Johann Sebastian. "Sheep May Safely Graze." SATB, kybd. GAL 127.
Bairstow, Edward C. "The King of Love My Shepherd Is." SATB, org. OXF A4. (P)
Bender, Jan. "I Am the Good Shepherd." 2 pt, kybd. CPH 98-1992.
DeLong, Richard P. "Loving Shepherd of Thy Sheep." U, kybd. ECS 4795.
Ellingboe, Bradley. "Jesus, Good Shepherd." SATB, pno or hp. AFP 0800658272.
———. "The Lord's My Shepherd." SATB, opt pno. KJO 8956. (P)
Handel, George Frideric. "All We Like Sheep Have Gone Astray." *Messiah*. SATB, org §
———. "And with His Stripes We Are Healed." *Messiah*. SATB, org §
———. "He Shall Feed His Flock." *Messiah*. S or A solo §
How, Martin. "Psalm 23." U or bar solo, kybd, opt desc. B&H W.180. (P)
Ireland, John. "Greater Love Hath No Man." SATB, B solo, org. GAL 1.5030.1.
Krapf, Gerhard. "The King of Love My Shepherd Is." SATB, org. CPH 98-267. (P)
McFerrin, Bobby. "The 23rd Psalm." SATB, orch. HAL 0859551. (P)
Pelz, Walter L. "The King of Love My Shepherd Is." SATB, kybd, fl, opt cong. AFP 0800646010. (P)
Pote, Allen. "The Lord Is My Shepherd." SATB, pno. CGA-551. (P)
Proulx, Richard. "Though We Are Many, in Christ We Are One." SATB. MSM 80-834.
Ray, Robert. "He Never Failed Me Yet." SATB, br, perc. JEN 447080167.
Roberts, William Bradley. "Savior, Like a Shepherd Lead Us." U, kybd, opt fl, vln or other C inst. AFP 0800646983. *The Augsburg Easy Choirbook*. AFP 0800676025. (P, G)
Tavener, John. "The Lamb." SATB. CHE 55570.
Thompson, Randall. "The Lord Is My Shepherd." SATB, pno, org or hp. ECS 2688. (P)
Thomson, Virgil. "My Shepherd Will Supply My Need." SATB. HWG GCMR 2046. (P)
Tomkins, Thomas. "My Shepherd Is the Living Lord." SATB, org. CPH 98-141A. (P)
Tye, Christopher/arr. Carl Schalk. "The Man We Crucified." *Easter Motets*, Series A. SATB. AFP 0800647645.
Zimmermann, Heinz Werner. "Psalm 23." SATB, org, DB. AFP 0800645383. *The Augsburg Choirbook*. AFP 0800656784. (P)

Year B

Acts 4:5-12	*Salvation in the name of Jesus*
Psalm 23	*The LORD is my shepherd; I shall not be in want*
1 John 3:16-24	*Love in truth and action*
John 10:11-18	*Christ the shepherd*

Cherwien, David. "Psalm 23/The Lord Is My Shepherd." U, cong, org. MSM 80-840. (P)
Ellingboe, Bradley. "Jesus, Good Shepherd." SATB, pno or hp. AFP 0800658272. (P)
Haugen, Marty. "Shepherd Me, O God." SATB, cong, kybd, C inst, opt glock and str. GIA G-2950. (P)
Pote, Allen. "The Lord Is My Shepherd." SATB, pno. CGA 551. (P)
Roberts, William Bradley. "Savior, Like a Shepherd Lead Us." U, kybd, opt fl, vln or other C inst. AFP 0800646983.
   The Augsburg Easy Choirbook. AFP 0800676025. (P, G)
Schalk, Carl. "The God of Love My Shepherd Is." SATB, 2 vln, org. MSM 50-8812. (P, G)
Schubert, Franz. "The Lord Is My Shepherd." SATB. GSCH 50304810. SSAA. GSCH 5302. (P)
Schütz, Heinrich. "O Lord, I Trust Your Shepherd Care." *Chantry Choirbook*. SATB, org. AFP 0806642772. (P, G)
Thompson, Randall. "The Lord Is My Shepherd." SATB, org, pno or hp. ECS 2688. (P)

Year C

Acts 9:36-43	*Peter raises Tabitha/Dorcas from the dead*
Psalm 23	*The LORD is my shepherd; I shall not be in want*
Revelation 7:9-17	*A white-robed multitude sings before the Lamb*
John 10:22-30	*Jesus promises eternal life to his sheep*

Bach, Johann Sebastian. "Flocks in Pastures Green Abiding." *Oxford Easy Anthem Book*. SATB, org. OXF. § (F, G)
Bouman, Paul. "The Lord Is My Shepherd." U, kybd. CPH 98-2911. (P, G)
Cherwien, David. "Psalm 23/The Lord Is My Shepherd." U, org. MSM 80-840. (P)
Goodall, Howard. "The Lord Is My Shepherd." SATB, org. NOV 29 0680. (P, G)
Krapf, Gerhard. "The King of Love My Shepherd Is." SATB, org. CPH 98-2671. (P, G)
Pelz, Walter L. "The King of Love My Shepherd Is." SATB, kybd, fl, opt cong. AFP 0800646010. (P, G)
Roberts, William Bradley. "Savior, Like a Shepherd Lead Us." U, kybd, opt fl, vln or other C inst. AFP 0800646983.
   The Augsburg Easy Choirbook. AFP 0800676025. (P, G)
Rutter, John. "The Lord Is My Shepherd." SATB, org, opt ob. OXF 94-216. (P, G)
Schalk, Carl. "Thine the Amen, Thine the Praise." SATB, opt cong, org. AFP 0800646126. (S)
Schumann, Georg/ed. Paul Christiansen. "Yea Though I Wander." SATB. AFP 0800655664, OP (P)
Schütz, Heinrich. "O Lord, I Trust Your Shepherd Care." *Chantry Choirbook*. SATB, org. AFP 0806642772. (P, G)
Thomson, Virgil. "My Shepherd Will Supply My Need." SATB. HWG GCMR 2046. (P, G)
Vaughan Williams, Ralph. "The Twenty-third Psalm." SATB, solo, kybd. OXF 43-913. (P)

Fifth Sunday of Easter

Year A

Acts 7:55-60 — *The martyrdom of Stephen*
Psalm 31:1-5, 15-16 — *Into your hands, O Lord, I commend my spirit*
1 Peter 2:2-10 — *God's people chosen to proclaim God's mighty acts*
John 14:1-14 — *Christ the way, truth, and life*

Buszin, Walter. "Jesus Is Our Joy, Our Treasure." SATB. CPH 98-107.
Carter, Andrew. "The Light of the World." SATB, org. OXF E161.
Ellingboe, Bradley. "The Chief Cornerstone." 2 pt mixed, kybd, opt tpt. AFP 0800676394. (S)
Ferguson, John. "Jesus, My Lord and God." U, kybd. AFP 0800646193.
Haydn, Franz Joseph. "In Thee, O Lord." SATB, pno or org. Sam Fox PS 103.
How, Martin. "An Easter Greeting." U or 2 pt mxd. Robertson 312-41257.
Hurd, David. "Alleluia for a Festival." SATB, br or org. GIA G-2618.
Jennings, Kenneth. "With a Voice of Singing." *The Augsburg Choirbook*. SATB. AFP 0800656784.
Mendelssohn, Felix. "Jesus Christ, My Sure Defense—Alleluia." *Chantry Choirbook*. SATB. AFP 0800657772.
Parker, Alice. "The Wells of Salvation." SATB, org, hb. OXF 02.245.
Paynter, John. "The Call." 2 pt, org. OXF 351125-8. (G)
Pelz, Walter L. "Peace I Leave with You." SATB. AFP 0800645650.
Schalk, Carl. "Christ Goes Before." SATB, br, org. MSM 50-9049 (G)
Schütz, Heinrich. "In Thee, O Lord, Do I Put My Trust." SATB. PLY SC-117.
Scott, K. Lee. "The Call." *Sing a Song of Joy: Vocal Solos for Worship*. MH, kybd. AFP 0800647882. ML, kybd. AFP 0800652827. (G)
Shaw, Martin. "With a Voice of Singing." SATB, org. Gsch 810.
Vaughan Williams, Ralph. "The Call." *Five Mystical Songs*. B solo, org, pno, or orch. GAL. § (G)
———. "This Is the Truth." 2 pt, kybd. OXF 44.087.
White, David Ashley. "The Call." SATB, org. SEL 418-606. (G)
Wood, Dale. "Jubilate Deo/Psalm 100." *Augsburg Easy Choirbook*, vol. 1. 2 pt mxd, org. AFP 0800676025.
Young, Gordon. "Let Not Your Heart Be Troubled." SATB, kybd. PRE 312-41024. (G)

Year B

    Acts 8:26-40   *Philip teaches and baptizes an Ethiopian*
    Psalm 22:25-31   *All the ends of the earth shall remember and turn to the Lord*
    1 John 4:7-21   *God's love perfected in love for one another*
    John 15:1-8   *Christ the vine*

Basler, Paul. "Alleluia." SATB, hrn, perc. PLY PJMS-116.
Buxtehude, Dietrich. "Everything You Do." *Chantry Choirbook*. SATB, org. AFP 0806642772.
Carter, Andrew. "Thou Art the Vine." SATB or U, kybd, opt cong, hb. MSM 50-8504.
Distler, Hugo. "Dear Christians, One and All Rejoice." SATB. CPH 98-1901.
Farlee, Robert Buckley. "O Blessed Spring." SATB, ob, vln or cl, org, opt cong. AFP 0800654242. *The Augsburg Choirbook*. AFP 0800656784. (G)
Poston, Elizabeth. "Jesus Christ the Apple Tree." SATB. PVN. (G)
Rutter, John. "Christ the Lord Is Risen Again." SATB. OXF 42.362.
Scott, K. Lee. "God Shall the Broken Heart Repair." SATB, kybd. AFP 0800654102.
Vaughan Williams, Ralph. "Come Down, Love Divine." SATB, org. HWG CGMR 0356

Year C

    Acts 11:1-18   *Peter's vision: God gives the Gentiles repentance that leads to life*
    Psalm 148   *The splendor of the Lord is over earth and heaven*
    Revelation 21:1-6   *New heaven, new earth: springs of living water in the new Jerusalem*
    John 13:31-35   *Jesus gives a new commandment: Love one another as I have loved you*

Aston, Peter. "I Give You a New Commandment." 2 pt, org. GIA G-4331. (P)
Bainton, Edgar L. "And I Saw a New Heaven." SATB, org. NOV 29 0342 03. (S)
Burkhardt, Michael. "Praise the Lord! O Heavens Adore Him." U, trbl inst, kybd. MSM 50-9305. (P)
Duruflé, Maurice. "Ubi caritas." SATTBB. DUR 312-41253. (G)
Farlee, Robert Buckley. "Mandatum." SATB. AFP 0800654153. (G)
Holst, Gustav. "Psalm 148." SATB div, org, opt str. GAL 15353. (P)
Schalk, Carl. "I Saw a New Heaven and a New Earth." SATB. AFP 0800656644. (S)
Tallis, Thomas. "If Ye Love Me." SATB. OXF 42.60. (G)
Vaughan Williams, Ralph. "O How Amiable." SATB, org. OXF 42.056.
———. "O Taste and See." SATB, S solo. OXF 44.415.
———. "The Call." *Five Mystical Songs*. U, kybd. MSM 1.5038. §

Sixth Sunday of Easter

Year A

    Acts 17:22-31   *Paul's message to the Athenians*
    Psalm 66:8-20   *Be joyful in God, all you lands*
    1 Peter 3:13-22   *The days of Noah, a sign of baptism*
    John 14:15-21   *Christ our advocate*

Byrd, William. "I Will Not Leave You Comfortless." SSATB. NOV 29-0123. (G)
Hassler, Hans Leo/Hugo Distler. "Dear Christians, One and All, Rejoice." SATB. CPH 98-190.
Near, Gerald. "Awake, O Sleeper, Rise from Death." SATB, org, opt br. MSM 50-4033.
Pelz, Walter L. "Peace I Leave with You." SATB. AFP 0800645650.
Scholz, Robert. "Children of the Heavenly Father." SATB. AFP 0800659112.
Scott, K. Lee. "So Art Thou to Me." SATB, kybd. AFP 0800674308.
Sjolund, Paul. "Children of the Heavenly Father." *The Augsburg Choirbook*. SATB, org, opt trbl choir. AFP 0800656784.
Tallis, Thomas. "If Ye Love Me." SAB. GIA G-2290. OXF 42.60. (G)
Wilby, Philip. "If Ye Love Me." SSATB, org. ECS 191. (G)

Year B

    Acts 10:44-48   *The Spirit poured out on the Gentiles*
    Psalm 98   *Shout with joy to the L*ORD*, all you lands*
    1 John 5:1-6   *The victory of faith*
    John 15:9-17   *Christ the friend and lover*

Bach, Johann Sebastian. "Alleluia." *Bach for All Seasons*. SATB, kybd. AFP 080065854X.
Bengtson, Bruce. "O Sing to the Lord a New Song." SATB, org. AFP 08000676270. (P)
Busarow, Donald. "All Creatures of Our God and King." SATB, 2 tpts, org. MSM 60-9011. (P)
Duruflé, Maurice. "Ubi caritas." SATB. DUR 50561415. (G)
Hobby, Robert A. "Now All the Vault of Heaven Resounds/Ye Watchers and Ye Holy Ones." SAB, org, 2 tpt, opt 2 oct hb, cong. AFP 0800658655.
Ireland, John. "Greater Love Hath No Man." SATB, org. ECS 1.5030. (G)
Jennings, Kenneth. "With a Voice of Singing." SATB. AFP 0800645669. *The Augsburg Choirbook*. AFP 0800656784.
Pachelbel, Johann/ed. Donald Rotermund. "Sing to the Lord a New Song." SATB dbl choir. CPH 98-3329. (P)
Rorem, Ned. "Sing, My Soul, His Wondrous Love." SATB. PET 6386.
Rutter, John. "All Things Bright and Beautiful." 2 pt, kybd. HIN HMC-663. (P)
Tallis, Thomas. "If Ye Love Me." SATB. OXF TCM69. (G)
Wolff, S. Drummond. "Now All the Vault of Heaven Resounds." SATB, br. CPH 98-2785.

Year C

Acts 16:9-15 — *Lydia and her household are baptized by Paul*
Psalm 67 — *Let the nations be glad and sing for joy*
Revelation 21:10, 22—22:5 — *The Lamb is the light of the city of God*
John 14:23-29 — *The Father will send the Holy Spirit*
or John 5:1-9 — *Jesus heals on the Sabbath*

Åhlén, Waldemar. "The Earth Adorned/Sommersalm." SATB. WAL 8500102. (S)
Boyle, Malcolm. "Thou O God Art Praised in Zion." SATB, org. PAR PPM 08618.
Clausen, René. "Peace I Leave with You." SATB div. MF 2079. (G)
Erickson, Richard. "Come Away to the Skies." SATB, fl, fc. AFP 0800656776. (S)
Harris, William H. "Come Down, O Love Divine." SATB, org. NOV 29 0470 05.
———. "Faire Is the Heaven." SATB dbl choir. OXF 353018X.
Manz, Paul. "E'en So, Lord Jesus, Quickly Come." SATB. MSM 50-0001. TTBB. MSM 50-0900.
Mathias, William H. "Let the People Praise Thee, O God." SATB, org. OXF 3503727. (P)
Nelson, Ronald A. "If You Love One Another." 2 pt, kybd. SEL 422-841.
Nystedt, Knut. "Peace I Leave with You." SSATB. AFP 0800652673. (G)
Proulx, Richard. "Our Paschal Lamb, That Sets Us Free." SATB, org. AFP 0800656113.
Schalk, Carl. "Thine the Amen, Thine the Praise." SATB, opt cong, org. AFP 0800646126. (S)
Wilby, Philip. "If Ye Love Me." SSATB, org. PVN 8300561. (G)

Ascension of Our Lord

Years A, B, C

Acts 1:1-11 — *Jesus sends the apostles*
Psalm 47 — *God has gone up with a shout*
or Psalm 93 — *Ever since the world began, your throne has been established*
Ephesians 1:15-23 — *Eyes to see the risen and ascended Christ*
Luke 24:44-53 — *Christ present in all times and places*

Benson, Robert A. "O Lord Most High, Eternal King." SATB, org. AFP 0800674200. (P, S)
Billings, William. "Rejoice Ye Shining Worlds on High." SATB. CPH 98-3281.
Busarow, Donald. "All Creatures of Our God and King" (choir score). SATB, 2 tpts, org. MSM 60-9011.
———. "Love Divine, All Loves Excelling." SATB. MSM 50-9046.
———. "O Lord, You Are My God and King." SATB, org, tpt, 4 oct hb, opt cong. AFP 080065756X.
Cherwien, David. "Up Through Endless Ranks of Angels." SAB, org, opt tr and cong. AFP 0800658817. (F, G)
Croft, William. "God Is Gone Up with a Merry Noise." SSAATB, org. NOV 88 0034 00. (P1)
Dengler, Lee. "O Clap Your Hands." *Songs of David*. M, kybd. AFP 0800654846. (P)
Erickson, Richard. "Come Away to the Skies." SATB, fl, fc. AFP 0800656776.
Farlee, Robert Buckley. "The Lightener of the Stars." *To God Will I Sing*. ML, kybd. AFP 080067434X. MH, kybd. AFP 0800674332.
Fleming, Larry L. "Lord of the Dance." SATB. AFP 0800655354.
Gallus, Jacobus (Handl). "Ascendit Deus." SATBB. Associated Music Publishers A-83. (F, P, G)
Gerike, Henry V. "Up through Endless Ranks of Angels." SAB, cong, tpt, org. CPH 98-270. (F, G)
Gibbons, Orlando. "O Clap Your Hands." SSAATTBB, opt org. OXF TCM40. (P)
Haydn, Franz Joseph. "Achieved Is the Glorious Work." *Creation*. SATB, org. WAL W6001. § (F)
Hopson, Hal H. "God Has Gone Up with a Shout." SATB, org, opt tpt, hb. HWG GCMR 03586. (P)
Hurd, David. "The Lord Shall Reign." 2 vcs, cong, acc. GIA G-2717.
Hutchings, Arthur. "God Is Gone Up with a Merry Noise." *Shorter Anthems*. SATB. NOV 296. (P1)
Josquin Desprez/ed. Leonard Van Camp. "God, the Lord, Now Reigneth." SATB. CPH 98-3213. (P, S)
Mathias, William H. "Lift Up Your Heads, O Ye Gates." SATB, org. OXF 3503441. *Anthems for Choirs 1*. OXF 353214X
———. "O Clap Your Hands." SATB, org. OXF 3503883. (P)
Mendelssohn, Felix. "Above All Praise and All Majesty." SATB, org. *Oxford Book of Easy Anthems* OXF 3533219. *The New Church Anthem Book* OXF 3531097.
Moore, Philip. "The Ascension/Lift Up Your Heads." SATB, org. PVN 1006. (G)
Pelz, Walter L. "Up through Endless Ranks of Angels." SATB, 2 tpts, opt timp, org. CPH 98-2324. (F, G)
Powell, Robert J. "Ye Watchers and Ye Holy Ones." SATB, br, org, timp. GIA G-2427.
Riegal, Friedrich Samuel. "See God to Heaven Ascending." *Chantry Choirbook*. SATB. AFP 0800657772. (G)
Roberts, William Bradley. "In All These You Welcomed Me." U, org, opt ob or other C or B-flat inst. AFP 6000001207.
Rose, Michael. "Ye Choirs of New Jerusalem." SATB, org. OXF A412.
Rutter, John. "O Clap Your Hands." SATB, org. OXF A307. (P1)
Scott, K. Lee. "Jesus, My All, to Heaven Is Gone." *Rejoice Now My Spirit*. MH, kybd. AFP 0800651081. ML, kybd. AFP 080065109X. (F, G)
Titcomb, Everett. "God Is Gone Up." SATB. HWG GCMR 2192. (P1)
———"I Will Not Leave You Comfortless." SATB, org. CFI CM 441.
Vaughan Williams, Ralph. "At the Name of Jesus." SATB, org. OXF 40.100.
——— "O Clap Your Hands." SATB, br, org, perc. ECS 1-5000. (P1)

Seventh Sunday of Easter

Year A

  Acts 1:6-14 — *Jesus' companions at prayer after his departure*
  Psalm 68:1-10, 32-35 — *Sing to God, who rides upon the heavens*
  1 Peter 4:12-14; 5:6-11 — *God will sustain and restore those who suffer*
  John 17:1-11 — *Christ's prayer for his disciples*

Berger, Jean. "A Rose Touched by the Sun's Warm Rays." *Devotional Songs No. 3*. SATB. AFP 0800645553.
Biery, James. "The Waters of Life." *The Augsburg Choirbook*. SATB, org. AFP 0800656784. Octavo AFP 0800657683.
Ferguson, John. "The Head That Once Was Crowned with Thorns." SATB, org, br qrt. GIA G-3750.
Fetler, Paul. "Sing unto God." SATB, opt kybd. AFP 0800645588.
Handel, George Frideric. "Glory and Worship." *Coronation Anthems*. SSATTBB, org. OXF.
Hillert, Richard. "Alleluia! Voices Raise!" SATB, opt cong, org, inst. OXF 94.231.
Jennings, Kenneth. "With a Voice of Singing." SATB. AFP 0800645669.
Johnson, David N. "The Lone, Wild Bird." *The Augsburg Choirbook*. SATB. AFP 0800656784.
Peloquin, Alexander. "A Great Harvest." SATB, org. GIA G-2875.
Pinkham, Daniel. "Thou Art Ascended Up on High." *Easter Cantata*. SATB, pno or br. CFP 6393. (F)
Purcell, Henry. "O God the King of Glory." *Anthems for Choirs I*. SATB, org. OXF 019535214X.
Rorem, Ned. "God Is Gone Up." SATB. B&H 11-MO51464463. (F)
Schalk, Carl. "O Love, How Deep, How Broad, How High." SATB. CPH 98-1524.
———. "Thine the Amen, Thine the Praise." SATB, opt cong. org. AFP 0800646126.
Willan, Healey. "I Will Not Leave You Comfortless." *We Praise Thee II*. SA, org. CPH 97-76.
Wolff, S. Drummond. "Look, Oh, Look, the Sight Is Glorious." SATB. CPH 98-2611.

Year B

  Acts 1:15-17, 21-26 — *Matthias added to the apostles*
  Psalm 1 — *The Lord knows the way of the righteous*
  1 John 5:9-13 — *Life in the Son of God*
  John 17:6-19 — *Christ's prayer for his disciples*

Davies, H. Walford. "God Be in My Head." *The New Church Anthem Book*. SATB. OXF 0193531097.
Ferguson, John. "Come, Labor On." SATB, org. MSM 50-6502.
———. "Jesus, My Lord and God." U, org. AFP 0800646193.
Handel, George Frideric. "All My Spirit Longs to Savor." *Chantry Choirbook*. SATB, kybd. AFP 0800657772.
Harrison, Benjamin. "Alleluia! Sing to Jesus." SATB, org. MSM 50-9004.
Jennings, Kenneth. "Thee Will I Love." SATB. KJO 8724.
Nelson, Ronald A. "I Will Not Leave You Comfortless." *Four Anthems for Young Choirs*. U, org. B&H 5576.
Pelz, Walter L. "Alleluia! Sing to Jesus." SATB, br, timp, opt 3 oct hb. CPH 98-3185.
———. "Peace I Leave with You." SATB. AFP 0800645650. *The Augsburg Choirbook*. AFP 0800656784.
Schalk, Carl. "Christ Is Made the Sure Foundation." SATB, org, br, qrt, cong. MSM 60-9003.

Year C

Acts 16:16-34	*While in prison, Paul speaks to the jailer, who is then baptized*
Psalm 97	*Rejoice in the LORD, you righteous*
Rev. 22:12-14, 16-17, 20-21	*Blessed are those who wash their robes*
John 17:20-26	*Jesus prays that the disciples will be one and abide in his love*

Busarow, Donald. "O Morning Star, How Fair and Bright." SAB, kybd, cong. CPH 98-2819.
Farlee, Robert Buckley. "O Blessed Spring." SATB, ob, opt cong. AFP 0800654242.
Manz, Paul. "E'en So, Lord Jesus, Quickly Come." SATB. MSM 50-0001. (S)
Pelz, Walter L. "O Morning Star, How Fair and Bright." SATB, cong, org. MSM 60-2001.
Schalk, Carl. "Thine the Amen, Thine the Praise." SATB, opt cong, org. AFP 0800646126.
Schütz, Heinrich. "Psalm 97." SATB. EAR. (P)
Scott, K. Lee. "Thy Perfect Love." *Sing Forth God's Praise*. ML, kybd. AFP 080067538X. MH, kybd. AFP 0800675266.
Wilby, Philip. "If Ye Love Me." SSATB, org. ECS 191.

Vigil of Pentecost

Years A, B, C

Exodus 19:1-9	*The covenant at Sinai*
or Acts 2:1-11	*Filled with the Spirit to tell God's deeds*
Psalm 33:12-22	*The LORD is our help and our shield*
or Psalm 130	*There is forgiveness with you*
Romans 8:14-17, 22-27	*Praying with the Spirit*
John 7:37-39	*Jesus is the true living water*

Attwood, Thomas. "Come, Holy Ghost." *New Church Anthem Book*. SATB, org. OXF 0193533189.
Bach, Johann Sebastian. "Come, Holy Ghost, God and Lord." *Bach for All Seasons*. SATB. AFP 080065854X.
Baldwin, Anthony. "Holy Spirit, Ever Dwelling." SATB, org. OXF 3864053.
Biery, James. "The Waters of Life." SATB, org. *The Augsburg Choirbook*. AFP 0800656784. (G)
Burkhardt, Michael. "Filled with the Spirit." 3 pt, opt hb or kybd. MSM 50-7402.
Christiansen, F. Melius. "O Day Full of Grace." SSAATTBB. AFP 080064512X.
Helgen, John. "Breath of God." SATB, pno. KJO 8977.
———. "Spirit of God, Descend." SATB, pno. AFP 0800676378.
Mathias, William H./arr. Donald D. Livingston. "Come Down, O Love Divine." SSATB, org. AFP 0800675355. (F, G)
Proulx, Richard. "Christ Sends the Spirit." SAB, opt cong, org, fl. AFP 0800652703.
Rorem, Ned. "Breathe on Me, Breath of God." SATB. B&H OCTB6543.
Schalk, Carl. "Creator Spirit, Heavenly Dove." SATB, kybd, br, cong. CPH 98-2582.
———. "O Day Full of Grace." SATB, org, 2 tpt, 2 tbn, opt cong. AFP 0800645928. (F)
Scott, K. Lee. "Gracious Spirit, Dwell with Me." 2 pt mxd, org. AFP 0800646134. *The Augsburg Choirbook*. AFP 0800656784.
Tallis, Thomas. "If Ye Love Me." HWG GCMR 1629. §
———. "O Lord, Give Thy Holy Spirit." SATB. CPH 98-2249.

Day of Pentecost

Year A

Acts 2:1-21	*Filled with the Spirit to tell God's deeds*
or Numbers 11:24-30	*The Spirit comes upon the elders of Israel*
Psalm 104:24-34, 35b	*Alleluia.* or *Send forth your Spirit and renew the face of the earth*
1 Corinthians 12:3b-13	*Varieties of gifts from the same Spirit*
or Acts 2:1-21	*Filled with the Spirit to tell God's deeds*
John 20:19-23	*The Spirit poured out*
or John 7:37-39	*Jesus is the true living water*

Attwood, Thomas/ed. K. Lee Scott. "Come, Holy Ghost." *Sing Forth God's Praise.* MH, kybd. AFP 0800675266. ML, kybd. AFP 080067538X.

Bach, Johann Sebastian. "Come, Holy, Quickening Spirit." *Cantata 22.* SAB, kybd. CPH 98-283.

———. "Dona nobis pacem." *Bach for All Seasons.* SATB, kybd. AFP 080065854X.

Berger, Jean. "The Eyes of All Wait upon Thee." SATB. AFP 0800645596. *The Augsburg Choirbook.* AFP 0800656784. (P)

Christiansen, F. Melius. "O Day Full of Grace." SSAATTBB, S solo. AFP 080064512X. (F)

Dawson, William. "Ev'ry Time I Feel the Spirit." SATB. KJO T117.

Distler, Hugo. "Come, Holy Ghost, God and Lord." *Chantry Choirbook.* SATB. AFP 0800657772.

———. "Creator Spirit, Heavenly Dove." *Chantry Choirbook.* SAB. AFP 0800657772.

Farlee, Robert Buckley. "O Blessed Spring." SATB, ob, opt cong. AFP 0800654242.

Gibbons, Orlando. "Come, Holy Spirit." SATB, org. GIA G-1540.

Hogan, Moses. "I'm Gonna Sing 'til the Spirit Moves in My Heart." SATB. HAL 08740284.

How, Martin. "O Holy Spirit, Lord of Grace." SATB, org. GIA G-4314.

Hurford, Peter. "Litany to the Holy Spirit." SATB, org or pno. OXF E164.

Jennings, Carolyn. "Creator Spirit, by Whose Aid." SATB, 3 tpts, timp. AFP 0800646371.

Josquin Desprez. "Come, O Creator Spirit, Come." SATB. CPH 98-1944.

Nystedt, Knut. "Peace I Leave with You." *Three Motets.* SATB. AFP 0800652673.

Palestrina, Giovanni Pierluigi da. "When Fully Came the Day of Pentecost." SSATBB. CPH 98-3339. (F)

Proulx, Richard. "Christ Sends the Spirit." SAB, opt cong, org, fl. AFP 0800652703. *The Augsburg Choirbook.* AFP 0800656784.

Schalk, Carl. "Lord God, the Holy Ghost." SATB, org. AFP 0800646215.

———. "O Day Full of Grace." SATB, br, org, cong. AFP 080064591X.

Schein, Johann H. "Come, Holy Ghost, God and Lord." *Third Morning Star Choir Book.* SSB, cont. CPH 97-497.

Scott, K. Lee. "Gracious Spirit, Dwell with Me." 2 pt mxd, org. AFP 0800646134.

Willan, Healey. "The Spirit of the Lord." *Second Motet Book.* SATB. CPH 97-5205.

Year B

Acts 2:1-21	*Filled with the Spirit to tell God's deeds*
or Ezekiel 37:1-14	*Life to dry bones*
Psalm 104:24-34, 35b	*Alleluia.* or *Send forth your Spirit and renew the face of the earth*
Romans 8:22-27	*Praying with the Spirit*
or Acts 2:1-21	*Filled with the Spirit to tell God's deeds*
John 15:26-27; 16:4b-15	*Christ sends the Spirit of truth*

Bach, Johann Sebastian/ed. K. Lee Scott. "Come, Holy, Quickening Spirit." SAB, kybd. CPH 98-2838.
Burkhardt, Michael. "Come, Holy Ghost, Our Souls Inspire." 2 pt, hb. MSM 50-5551.
Carter, Andrew. "Come, Holy Ghost, Creator Blest." SATB, org. OXF A427.
Christiansen, F. Melius. "O Day Full of Grace." SSAATTBB, S solo. AFP 080064512X. (F)
Distler, Hugo. "Creator Spirit, Heavenly Dove." *Chantry Choirbook*. SATB. AFP 0800657772.
Gallus, Jacobus (Handl). "Repleti sunt omnes/And They All Were Filled." SATB dbl choir or SATB and br. CPH 98-2394. (F)
Grieg, Edvard. "Pentecost Hymn." *Peer Gynt*. SATB. KJO 8825. §
Helgen, John. "Praise the Living God Who Sings." SATB, org. AFP 0800674618.
Maddux, David. "O Sifuni Mungu." SATB, kybd, perc. HL 403263306.
Proulx, Richard. "Christ Sends the Spirit." SAB, opt cong, org, fl. AFP 0800652703. *The Augsburg Choirbook*. AFP 0800656784. (G)
Schalk, Carl. "O Day Full of Grace." SATB, org, 2 tpt, 2 tbn, opt cong. AFP 080064591X. (F)
Vulpius, Melchior. "O Spirit of God, Eternal Source." *Chantry Choirbook*. SATB. AFP 0806642772.

Year C

Acts 2:1-21	*Filled with the Spirit to tell God's deeds*
or Genesis 11:1-9	*God destroys the tower of Babel*
Psalm 104:24-34, 35b	*Alleluia.* or *Send forth your Spirit and renew the face of the earth*
Romans 8:14-17	*The Spirit makes us children of God*
or Acts 2:1-21	*Filled with the Spirit to tell God's deeds*
John 14:8-17 [25-27]	*The Father will give you another Advocate, the Spirit of truth*

Berger, Jean. "The Eyes of All Wait upon Thee." SATB. AFP 0800645596. *The Augsburg Choirbook*. AFP 0800656784. (P)
Burleigh, Harry T. "Every Time I Feel the Spirit." L, kybd. WAR EL 03150. H, kybd. WAR EL 03151.
Dawson, William. "Ev'ry Time I Feel the Spirit." SATB. KJO T117.
Distler, Hugo. "Come, Holy Ghost, God and Lord." *Chantry Choirbook*. SATB. AFP 0806642772. (F, G)
Gallus, Jacobus (Handl). "Repleti sunt omnes/And They All Were Filled." SATB, opt 2 tpt, 2 tbn. CPH 98-2394. (F)
Jennings, Carolyn. "Creator Spirit, by Whose Aid." SATB, 3 tpts, timp. AFP 0800646371.
Mathias, William H./arr. Donald D. Livingston. "Come Down, O Love Divine." SSATB, org. AFP 0800675355. (F, G)
Schalk, Carl. "Creator Spirit, Heavenly Dove." SATB, br qrt, cong, kybd. CPH 98-2582.
Tallis, Thomas. "If Ye Love Me." SATB. OXF 3521385. §
Telemann, Georg Philipp. "Make Me Pure, O Sacred Spirit." *To God Will I Sing*. MH, kybd. AFP 0800674332. ML, kybd. AFP 0800674340.
Vulpius, Melchior. "O Spirit of God, Eternal Source." *Chantry Choirbook*. SATB. AFP 0806642772.
Wilby, Philip. "If Ye Love Me." SSATB, org. ECS 191.

The Holy Trinity (First Sunday after Pentecost)

Year A

> Genesis 1:1—2:4a *The creation of the heavens and the earth*
> Psalm 8 *How exalted is your name in all the world!*
> 2 Corinthians 13:11-13 *Paul's farewell to the church at Corinth*
> Matthew 28:16-20 *Living in the community of the Trinity*

Arnatt, Ronald. "Holy God, We Praise Thy Name." SATB, cong, org, opt br, timp, orch bells. MSM 60-9016.
———. "When the Morning Stars Together." SATB, org, opt cong. ECS 4870.
Burkhardt, Michael. "Hymn to the Trinity." SATB, opt cong, org. MSM 50-7004.
Busarow, Donald. "Holy God, We Praise Your Name." SATB, br qrt, timp, org, inst parts. CPH 98-2530.
Copland, Aaron. "In the Beginning." SATB, A solo. B&H. (F)
Ellingboe, Bradley. "The Holy Trinity." 2 pt mxd, pno. KJO 6298.
Ferguson, John. "Holy God, We Praise Thy Name." SATB, org, opt br, cong. GIA G-3167.
Friedell, Harold. "Draw Us in the Spirit's Tether." SATB, org. HWG GCMR 2472.
Glinka, Mikhail. "Cherubic Hymn." SATTBB. PAR PPM 09501.
Goemanne, Noël. "Holy God, We Praise Thy Name." SA(T)B, cong, acc, opt 1 or 2 tpts. GIA G-1903.
Hanson, Howard. "O Lord Our Lord, How Excellent Thy Name." *Four Psalms.* B solo, pno or org, opt str orch. CFI 4608. (P)
Hurd, David. "Creating God." SATB, org. GIA G-2891.
Leavitt, John. "Festival Sanctus." SATB, pno. BEL CPP SV8821.
Neswick, Bruce. "Magna et mirabilia." S(S)ATB, org. PAR PPM 09504.
Pinkham, Daniel. "In the Beginning of Creation." SATB, audio acc. ECS 2902. (F)
Praetorius, Michael. "Praise the Lord." SATB. GSCH 9817.
Reger, Max. "We Bless the Father and the Son and the Holy Ghost." SATB, org. CPH 97-5205.
Schalk, Carl. "Go Therefore and Make Disciples of All Nations." 2 pt mxd, kybd. MSM 50-6200. (G)
Schütz, Heinrich. "A Song of Praise to the Holy Trinity." SATB. CPH BA 24.
Scott, K. Lee. "Trinitarian Blessings." SATB, kybd, opt solo. AFP 0800654269. *Sing Forth God's Praise.* MH, kybd. AFP 0800675266. ML, kybd. AFP 080067538X.
Sowerby, Leo. "All Hail, Adored Trinity." SATB, org. OXF A165.
Turner, Kenneth C. "O Trinity, Most Blessed Light." *Anthems for Choirs 1.* SATB div, org. OXF 353214X.
Wyton, Alec. "Go Ye Therefore." SATB, org. HWG 2755. (G)

Year B

> Isaiah 6:1-8 *Isaiah's vision and call*
> Psalm 29 *Worship the Lord in the beauty of holiness*
> Romans 8:12-17 *Living by the Spirit*
> John 3:1-17 *Entering the reign of God through water and the Spirit*

Bernstein, Leonard. "Sanctus." *Mass.* SA, SATB, pno. GSCH 11973. (F)
Distler, Hugo. "For God So Loved the World/Also hat Gott die Welt geliebet." *Chantry Choirbook.* SAB. AFP 0800657772. § (G)
Johnson, Hall. "Ev'ry Time I Feel de Spirit." M solo, pno. GSCH 1939. (S)
Palestrina, Giovanni Pierluigi da. "O Holy and Glorious Trinity." SSATB. OXF 3952920.
Scott, K. Lee. "Holy, Holy, Holy." SATB, org, opt cong, 2 tpt, 2 tbn, timp. SEL 425-612 (F)
———. "Trinitarian Blessings." SATB, kybd, opt solo. AFP 0800654269. *Sing Forth God's Praise.* MH, kybd. AFP 0800675266. ML, kybd. AFP 080067538X.

Smith, Carl. "Trinity Sunday." *Four George Herbert Songs*. MH, kybd. MSM 40-905.
Stainer, John. "God So Loved the World." SATB. GSCH 50294340. § (G)
Tallis, Thomas. "O Lord, Give Thy Holy Spirit." SATB. AMC 524.
Tchaikovsky, Pyotr Il'yich. "Holy, Holy, Holy." *The New Church Anthem Book*. SATB. OXF 0193531097. (F)
Vaughan Williams, Ralph. "The Old Hundredth Psalm Tune." SATB, org or orch. OXF 3535084.
Willan, Healey. "Te Deum laudamus/We Praise Thee, O God." SATB, org. CPH 98-1126.
Wolff, S. Drummond. "Holy, Holy, Holy." SATB, org, tpt. CPH 98-2129. (F)

Year C

Proverbs 8:1-4, 22-31	*Wisdom rejoices in the creation*
Psalm 8	*Your majesty is praised above the heavens*
Romans 5:1-5	*God's love poured into our hearts through the Holy Spirit*
John 16:12-15	*The Spirit will guide you into the truth*

Britten, Benjamin. "Te Deum in C." SATB, org, S solo. OXF 42.141.
Ellingboe, Bradley. "The Holy Trinity." 2 pt mxd, pno. KJO 6298.
Erickson, Richard. "When Long Before Time." SATB, org, fl. AFP 0800656768. (F)
Handel, George Frideric. "How Excellent Thy Name." SATB, org. MC 286. (P)
Hanson, Howard. "O Lord Our Lord, How Excellent Thy Name." *Four Psalms*. B solo, pno or org, opt str orch. CFI 4608. (P)
Haydn, Franz Joseph. "Achieved Is the Glorious Work." *Creation*. SATB, org. GSCH S-003-02358-00. (F)
Marcello, Benedetto. "O Lord, Our Governor." U, kybd. CPH 98-1045.
Mozart, Wolfgang Amadeus. "Mighty Are Your Works, O God." 2 pt mxd, kybd. SEL 410-808.
Proulx, Richard. "You Are God: We Praise You." U, cong, hb. GIA G-4577.
Purcell, Henry. "We Sing to Him." *Harmonia Sacra*. voice, pno. § (P)
Scott, K. Lee. "Trinitarian Blessings." SATB, kybd, opt solo. AFP 0800654269. *Sing Forth God's Praise*. MH, kybd. AFP 0800675266. ML, kybd. AFP 080067538X.
Sowerby, Leo. "All Hail, Adored Trinity." SATB, org. OXF A165.
Willan, Healey. "Holy, Holy, Holy Is the Lord." SATB, org. CPH 98-1553.

Sunday 8 / Proper 3 / May 24–28

Year A

    Isaiah 49:8-16a   *God's motherly compassion for the people*
    Psalm 131   *Like a child upon its mother's breast, my soul is quieted within me*
    1 Corinthians 4:1-5   *Servants accountable to God for their stewardship*
    Matthew 6:24-34   *The teaching of Christ: trust in God*

Ferguson, John. "Thy Holy Wings." *Three Swedish Folk Hymns.* M, pno or org. AFP 0800647955. (P)
Glarum, L. Stanley. "Seek Ye First the Kingdom of God." SAB. H. T. Fitzsimmons 2210. (G)
Helgen, John. "Praise the Living God Who Sings." SATB, org. AFP 0800674618.
Kallman, Daniel. "In Thee Is Gladness." SATB, kybd. MSM 50-9058.
Mozart, Wolfgang Amadeus. "Quaerite primum regnum Dei/Seek Ye First." *Mozart Anthem Book.* SATB. CPH 97-5230. § (G)
Scholz, Robert. "Children of the Heavenly Father." SATB. AFP 0800659112. (G)

Year B

    Hosea 2:14-20   *The covenant renewed by God's persistent love*
    Psalm 103:1-13, 22   *The Lord is full of compassion and mercy*
    2 Corinthians 3:1-6   *Equipped as ministers of God's new covenant*
    Mark 2:13-22   *Eating and drinking with tax collectors and prostitutes*

Bach, Johann Sebastian/ed. Fritz Oberdoerffer. "Bridegroom of My Soul." *Sacred Songs.* H solo, pno or org. CPH 97-9334. (F)
Chilcott, Bob. "Just As I Am." SATB, org. OXF 3511495.
Ellingboe, Bradley. "There's a Wideness in God's Mercy." SATB, kybd. AFP 0800676548. (G)
Ferguson, John. "Children of the Heavenly Father." *Three Swedish Folk Hymns.* M solo, pno or org. AFP Children of the Heavenly Father. (P)
Helgen, John. "That Priceless Grace." SATB, pno. AFP 0800658590. 2 pt mxd, pno. *Augsburg Easy Choirbook.* AFP 0800676025.
Hilton, John/ed. K. Lee Scott. "Wilt Thou Forgive?/A Hymne to God the Father." *Sing Forth God's Praise.* ML, kybd. AFP 080067538X. MH, kybd. AFP 0800675266

Year C

Isaiah 55:10-13 — *The word goes forth from the mouth of God*
or Sirach 27:4-7 — *Wisdom rules both heaven and earth*
Psalm 92:1-4, 12-15 — *The righteous shall flourish like a palm tree*
1 Corinthians 15:51-58 — *The mystery of the resurrection*
Luke 6:39-49 — *Take the speck from your eye; build your house on a firm foundation*

Adler, Samuel. "Mizmor shir l'yom ha-Shabat." *Three Psalms.* M solo, pno or org. Southern Music Company. (P)
Ellingboe, Bradley. "The Chief Cornerstone." 2 pt mxd, pno, opt tpt. AFP 0800676394. *Augsburg Easy Choirbook.* AFP 0800676025.
Ferguson, John. "What Then." SATB org. KJO 8827.
Lekberg, Sven. "For as the Rain Cometh Down." SATB. GSCH 11509. (F)
Wood, Dale. "Built on a Rock." SATB, org. LOR 3201191. (G)

Sunday 9 / Proper 4 / May 29–June 4

Year A

Deuteronomy 11:18-21, 26-28 — *Keeping the words of God at the center of life*
Psalm 31:1-5, 19-24 — *Be my strong rock, a castle to keep me safe*
Rom. 1:16-17; 3:22b-28 [29-31] — *Justified by God's grace as a gift*
Matthew 7:21-29 — *The teaching of Christ: doing the works of God*

Semicontinuous first reading/psalm

Genesis 6:9-22; 7:24; 8:14-19 — *The great flood*
Psalm 46 — *The LORD of hosts is with us; the God of Jacob is our stronghold.*

Bach, Johann Sebastian. "All Who Believe and Are Baptized." *Bach for All Seasons.* SATB, kybd. AFP 080065854X.
———. "Salvation unto Us Has Come." *Bach for All Seasons.* SATB. AFP 080065854X.
Bertalot, John. "Thy Word Is a Lantern." SATB, org, opt br and perc. AFP 0800674251.
Chemin-Petit, Hans. "Salvation unto Us Has Come." *The SAB Chorale Book.* SAB. CPH 97-7575.
Ferguson, John. "Word of God Come Down on Earth." SATB, org. GIA G-3764.
Hanson, Howard. "God Is Our Refuge and Strength." *Four Psalms.* B solo, pno or org, opt str orch. CFI 4608. (P)
Haydn, Franz Joseph. "In Thee, O Lord." SATB, pno or org. Sam Fox PS 103. (P)
Mendelssohn, Felix. "On God Alone My Hope I Build." *Chantry Choirbook.* SATB. AFP 0800657772. (G)
Sowerby, Leo. "Thou Art My Strength." *Songs of Faith and Penitence,* S solo, org. HWG. (P)
Stevens, Halsey. "In Thee, O Lord, Have I Put My Trust." SATB, org. CFP 6520. (P)
Walter, Johann. "I Build on God's Strong Word." *Chantry Choirbook.* SATB. AFP 0800657772. (G)

Year B

Deuteronomy 5:12-15 — *The commandment regarding the sabbath*
Psalm 81:1-10 — *Raise a loud shout to the God of Jacob*
2 Corinthians 4:5-12 — *Treasure in clay jars*
Mark 2:23—3:6 — *Doing the work of God on the sabbath*

Semicontinuous first reading/psalm

1 Samuel 3:1-10 [11-20] — *The calling of Samuel*
Psalm 139:1-6, 13-18 — *You have searched me out and known me*

Bach, Johann Sebastian/ed. Fritz Oberdoerffer. "'Tis Well with Me, for by Thy Might." *Sacred Songs.* H solo, pno or org. CPH 97-9334. (S)
Bairstow, Edward C. "Let All Mortal Flesh Keep Silence." SATB. S&B CCL 294. (S)
Ferguson, John. "He Comes to Us as One Unknown." SATB, org. AFP 0800656008.
Petker, Allan. "Grace Above All." SATB, kybd. PVN 8301589. (P)
Piccolo, Anthony. "O Come, Let Us Sing unto the Lord." SATB, org. OXF 3505700. *The New Church Anthem Book.* OXF 0193531097.
Proulx, Richard. "Sing We Merrily." SATB, 2 tpt, 2 tbn, kybd. GIA G-2403.
Scott, K. Lee. "Thy Perfect Love." *Sing Forth God's Praise.* ML, kybd. 080067538X. MH, kybd. 0800675266.
Wolff, S. Drummond. "O Day of Rest and Gladness." SATB, kybd, tr. CPH 98-2907. (F, G)

Year C

1 Kings 8:22-23, 41-43	*God's everlasting covenant is for all people*
Psalm 96:1-9	*Declare the glory of the Lord among the nations*
Galatians 1:1-12	*Beware of contrary gospels*
Luke 7:1-10	*Jesus heals the centurion's slave*

Semicontinuous first reading/psalm

1 Kings 18:20-21 [22-29] 30-39	*Elijah and the prophets of Baal*
Psalm 96	*Ascribe to the Lord honor and power*

Carter, Andrew. "For the Beauty of the Earth." U, fl, pno. PXF 3420724.
Distler, Hugo. "Salvation unto Us Has Come." *Chantry Choirbook*. SATB. AFP 0800657772. (S)
Fleming, Larry L. "Humble Service." SATB. AFP 0800646223.
Mendelssohn, Felix. "Lord, God of Abraham." *Elijah*. B solo, kybd. § (F)
Sweelinck, Jan Pieterszoon. "Sing to the Lord, New Songs Be Raising." SATB. *Chantry Choirbook*. AFP 0800657772.
White, David Ashley. "In Christ There Is No East or West." SATB, kybd. AFP 0800654749.

Sunday 10 / Proper 5 / June 5–11

Year A

Hosea 5:15—6:6	*God desires steadfast love*
Psalm 50:7-15	*To those who keep in my way will I show the salvation of God.*
Romans 4:13-25	*The promise to those who share Abraham's faith*
Matthew 9:9-13, 18-26	*Christ heals a woman and raises a synagogue leader's daughter*

Semicontinuous first reading/psalm

Genesis 12:1-9	*Abram's journey in the promise*
Psalm 33:1-12	*Happy is the nation whose God is the LORD!*

Bach, Johann Sebastian. "Jesus Is My Joy, My All." SATB. ECS 2214.

Beethoven, Ludwig van/ed. K. Lee Scott. "The Heavens Sing Praises." *Sing Forth God's Praise*. MH, kybd. AFP 0800675266. ML, kybd. AFP 080067538X.

Bisbee, B. Wayne. "Teach Me Your Way, O Lord." 2 pt mxd, kybd. AFP 080065479X.

Dvořák, Antonín. "Songs of Gladness I Will Sing Thee." *Biblical Songs*. § (P)

Ellingboe, Bradley. "There's a Wideness in God's Mercy." SATB, kybd. AFP 0800676548.

Handel, George Frideric. "Keep Me Faithfully in Thy Paths." 2 pt mxd, org. GIA G-2355.

Harris, David S. "Come, and Let Us Return unto the Lord." SAB, org. HWG CMR3346.

Johnson, J. Rosamond. "Little David Play On Your Harp." M solo, pno. Edward B. Marks. (P)

Marcello, Benedetto. "Oh, Hold Thou Me Up." SS, org. CPH 98-1046.

Mendelssohn, Felix. "I Will Sing of Thy Great Mercies." *Sing a Song of Joy*. MH, kybd. AFP 0800647882. ML, kybd. AFP 0800652827.

Parker, Alice. "I Know the Lord." SATB, S solo. GIA G-4229.

Pelz, Walter L. "Have No Fear, Little Flock." Org, cong. CPH 97-5692.

Scott, K. Lee. "God Shall the Broken Heart Repair." SATB, kybd. AFP 0800654102.

———. "Gracious Spirit, Dwell with Me." 2 pt mxd, org. AFP 0800646134.

Telemann, Georg Philipp/arr. Joan Conlon. "Come, Enjoy God's Festive Springtime." U, cont, vln or C inst. AFP 0800646487.

Zimmermann, Heinz Werner. "Have No Fear, Little Flock." *Five Hymns*. U or SATB, kybd. CPH 97-5131.

Year B

Genesis 3:8-15	*God confronts Adam and Eve in the garden*
Psalm 130	*With the Lord there is mercy and plenteous redemption*
2 Corinthians 4:13—5:1	*Renewed in the inner nature*
Mark 3:20-35	*Doing the work of God as brothers and sisters of Christ*

Semicontinuous first reading/psalm

1 Samuel 8:4-11 [12-15] 16-20 [11:14-15]	*Israel determined to have a king*
Psalm 138	*Your love endures forever; do not abandon the work of your hands.*

Busarow, Donald. "A Mighty Fortress." SAB, cong, tpt, org. MSM 60-8000.
Ferguson, John. "O God, Our Help in Ages Past." SATB, cong, br, org. GIA G-3892 (P)
Handel, George Frideric. "I Know that My Redeemer Liveth." *Messiah.* S solo, kybd. §
Mendelssohn, Felix. "Be Thou Faithful to the Truth." *St. Paul.* T solo, kybd. (S) §
Proulx, Richard. "Strengthen for Service." *The Augsburg Choirbook.* SATB. AFP 0800656784.
Schalk, Carl. "A Mighty Fortress." SATB, kybd. CPH 98-1842.
Scott, K. Lee. "Out of the Depths I Cry to Thee." 2 pt, kybd. AFP 0800647327. In *Rejoice Now, My Spirit.* ML, kybd. AFP 080065109X. MH, kybd. AFP 0800651081. (P)

Year C

1 Kings 17:17-24	*Elijah revives a widow's son*
Psalm 30	*My God, I cried out to you, and you restored me to health*
Galatians 1:11-24	*The gospel is received through a revelation of Jesus Christ*
Luke 7:11-17	*Jesus revives a widow's son*

Semicontinuous first reading/psalm

1 Kings 17:8-16 [17-24]	*A widow offers hospitality to Elijah*
Psalm 146	*The Lord lifts up those who are bowed down*

Bach, Johann Sebastian. "Salvation unto Us Has Come." SATB. *Bach for All Seasons.* AFP 080065854X.
———. "Take Heart, Contented Be, and Restful." *To God Will I Sing.* ML, kybd. AFP 0800674340. MH, kybd. AFP 0800674332.
Burleigh, Harry T. "I Know De Lord's Laid His Hands On Me." *The Spirituals of Harry T. Burleigh.* L, kybd. WAR EL 03150. H, kybd. WAR EL 03151. (F, G)
Ives, Charles. "Hymn." *114 Songs.* Solo, kybd. Merion Music. (P)
Mendelssohn, Felix. "I Will Sing of Thy Great Mercies." *Sing a Song of Joy.* ML, kybd. AFP 0800652827. MH, kybd. AFP 0800647882.

Sunday 11 / Proper 6 / June 12–18

Year A

    Exodus 19:2-8a   *The covenant with Israel at Sinai*
    Psalm 100   *We are God's people and the sheep of God's pasture*
    Romans 5:1-8   *While we were sinners, Christ died for us*
    Matthew 9:35—10:8 [9-23]   *The sending of the Twelve*

Semicontinuous first reading/psalm

    Genesis 18:1-15 [21:1-7]   *The LORD appears to Abraham and Sarah*
    Psalm 116:1-2, 12-19   *I will call upon the name of the LORD. (Ps. 116:11)*

Bender, Jan. "O God, O Lord of Heaven and Earth." *The Augsburg Choirbook*. SATB, cong, tpt. AFP 0800656784.
Britten, Benjamin. "Jubilate Deo." SATB, org. OXF 3515776. (P)
Dvořák, Antonín. "I Will Sing New Songs of Gladness." *Third Morning Star Choir Book*. U, kybd. CPH 97-4972.
Head, Michael. "Make a Joyful Noise unto the Lord." H voice, pno, org. PRE 1014. L voice PRE 1015. (P)
Laster, James. "Forgive Our Sins as We Forgive." SATB, org. AFP 0800646894.
Mendelssohn, Felix. "Jerusalem, Thou That Killest the Prophets." *St. Paul*. S solo, kybd. GSCH 321.
———. "They That Shall Endure to the End." *Chantry Choirbook*. SATB. AFP 0800657772.
Mezzogorri, Giovanni Nicolò. "Jubilate Deo." *Sing to God*. SA or TB, kybd. CPH 98-2470. (P)
Scott, K. Lee. "Come, O Thou Traveler Unknown." *Rejoice Now My Spirit*. MH, kybd. AFP 0800651081. ML, kybd. AFP 080065109X.
Sowerby, Leo. "O Be Joyful in the Lord." *Three Psalms*. Contralto or B solo, org. HWG. (P)
Sweelinck, Jan Pieterszoon. "Psalm 100." SATB, org. ECS 2791. (P)
Tallis, Thomas. "All People That on Earth Do Dwell." *Anthems for Choirs 1*. SATB, org. OXF. (P)
Vaughan Williams, Ralph. "The Old Hundredth Psalm Tune." SATB, cong, org, opt br or orch. OXF 42-953. (P)

Year B

    Ezekiel 17:22-24   *The sign of the cedar, planted on the mountain of Israel*
    Psalm 92:1-4, 12-15   *The righteous shall spread abroad like cedar of Lebanon*
    2 Cor. 5:6-10 [11-13] 14-17   *In Christ, a new creation*
    Mark 4:26-34   *The parable of the mustard seed*

Semicontinuous first reading/psalm

    1 Samuel 15:34—16:13   *David anointed by Samuel*
    Psalm 20   *The LORD gives victory to the anointed one*

Adler, Samuel. "Mizmor shir l'yom ha-Shabat." *Three Psalms*. M solo, pno or org. Southern Music Company. (P)
Bach, Johann Sebastian. "All Who Believe and Are Baptized." SATB. *Bach for All Seasons*. AFP 080065854X.
Bonnemère, Edward V. "I'm Going on a Journey." U, opt 2 pt, pno or kybd, opt fl. AFP 0800675525. 2 pt mxd, pno, opt fl. *Augsburg Easy Choirbook*. AFP 0800676025.
Ferguson, John. "The Head That Once Was Crowned with Thorns." SATB, org, br. GIA G-3750
Hopson, Hal H. "We Know That Christ Is Raised." SATB, kybd. HWG GCMR 03566
Scott, K. Lee. "So Art Thou to Me." *Rejoice Now, My Spirit*. MH, kybd. AFP 0800651081. ML, kybd. AFP 080065109X.
Wolff, S. Drummond. "We Know That Christ Is Raised." SATB, tpt, kybd, cong. CPH 98-2609

Year C

2 Samuel 11:26—12:10, 13-15	*Nathan tells the story of the lamb to David*
Psalm 32	*Then you forgave me the guilt of my sin*
Galatians 2:15-21	*Crucified with Christ; justification through grace*
Luke 7:36—8:3	*The woman anointing the feet of Jesus is forgiven*

Semicontinuous first reading/psalm

1 Kings 21:1-10 [11-14] 15-21a	*Ahab kills the owner of a vineyard*
Psalm 5:1-8	*Lead me, O Lord, in your righteousness; make your way straight before me*

Bach, Johann Sebastian/ed. Fritz Oberdoerffer. "The Wise Confine Their Choice in Friends." *Sacred Songs.* H solo, pno or org. CPH 97-9334. (S)

Dengler, Lee. "Sing unto the Lord." *Songs of David.* M, kybd. AFP 0800654846.

Handel, George Frideric. "O Zion, Herald of Good News." SATB. CGA-323.

Jennings, Kenneth. "Thee Will I Love." SATB. KJO 8724.

Rutter, John. "Thy Perfect Love." SATB, org. OXF 42-392.

Scott, K. Lee. "Gracious Spirit, Dwell with Me." 2 pt mxd, org. AFP 0800646134. *The Augsburg Choirbook.* AFP 0800656784.

Sunday 12 / Proper 7 / June 19–25

Year A

Jeremiah 20:7-13	*The prophet must speak despite opposition*
Psalm 69:7-10 [11-15] 16-18	*Answer me, O Lord, for your love is kind*
Romans 6:1b-11	*Buried and raised with Christ by baptism*
Matthew 10:24-39	*The cost of discipleship*

Semicontinuous first reading/psalm

Genesis 21:8-21	*The rescue of Hagar and Ishmael*
Psalm 86:1-10, 16-17	*Have mercy upon me. give strength to your servant*

Åhlén, Waldemar. "The Earth Adorned/Sommersalm." SATB, kybd. WAL WH126.
Bisbee, B. Wayne. "Teach Me Your Way, O Lord." 2 pt mxd, kybd. AFP 080065479X.
Ferguson, John. "The Church's One Foundation." SATB, org, br qrt, opt cong. AFP 0800658310.
Handel, George Frideric. "Since by Man Came Death." *Messiah*. SATB, kybd. §
Johnson, Hall. "This Is de Healin' Water." M solo, pno. GSCH 1939. (S)
Mendelssohn, Felix. "Cast Thy Burden upon the Lord." *Church Choir Book*. SATB. CPH 97-6320.
———/ed. Susan Palo Cherwien. "For the Lord Will Lead." *To God Will I Sing*. ML, kybd. AFP 0800674340. MH, kybd. AFP 0800674332.
Proulx, Richard. "Strengthen for Service." SATB. AFP 0800672453.
———. "Weary of All Trumpeting." SAB, org, opt cong, opt br qnt. AFP 0800657632.
Schalk, Carl. "Lord of Feasting and of Hunger." SATB, org. CPH CPH 98-2863.
Scheidt, Samuel. "My Inmost Heart Now Raises." 2 pt mxd, kybd. CPH 98-3564.
Sedio, Mark. "Once He Came in Blessing." 2 pt mxd, org, fl. AFP 080065241X.
Willan, Healey. "Christ Being Raised from the Dead." *We Praise Thee I*. SSA. CPH CC 1032. (S)

Year B

Job 38:1-11	*The creator of earth and sea*
Psalm 107:1-3, 23-32	*God stilled the storm and quieted the waves of the sea*
2 Corinthians 6:1-13	*Paul's defense of his ministry*
Mark 4:35-41	*Christ calming the sea*

Semicontinuous first reading/psalm

1 Sam. 17:[1a, 4-11, 19-23] 32-49	*The Lord's victory over Goliath*
or 1 Samuel 17:57—18:5, 10-16	*David and Jonathan; Saul fears David's success*
Psalm 9:9-20	*The Lord will be a refuge in time of trouble*
or Psalm 133	*How good and pleasant it is to live together in unity*

Archer, Malcolm. "Author of Life Divine." *Five Anthems for Mixed Voices and Organ*. SATB. MAY 1450033. (F)
Beethoven, Ludwig van/arr. Richard Proulx. "Give Thanks to God." SAB, kybd. AFP 0800655230. (P)
Bisbee, B. Wayne. "Teach Me Your Way, O Lord." 2 pt mxd, kybd. AFP 080065479X.
Busarow, Donald. "How Firm a Foundation." *A Sacred Harp Quartet*. SATB div. MSM 50-9840.
Christiansen, F. Melius. "Praise to the Lord." SSAATTBB, kybd ad lib. AFP 0800645049.
Dengler, Lee. "Sing unto the Lord." *Songs of David*. Med vocal solo, kybd. AFP 0800654846.
Ellingboe, Bradley. "How Can I Keep from Singing?" SATB, pno, ob. KJO 8884. (G)
Gibbons, Orlando. "Almighty and Everlasting God." SATB. OXF TCM36.
Haydn, Franz Joseph. "Rolling In Foaming Billows." *The Creation*. B solo, kybd. § (F, P, S)

How, Martin. "Day by Day." U, 2 or 3 pt, kybd. GIA G-4178.
Johnson, Hall. "Witness." SATB. GEN JG2010. (G)
Mendelssohn, Felix/ed. Susan Palo Cherwien. "For the Lord Will Lead." *To God Will I Sing*. ML, kybd. AFP 0800674340. MH, kybd. AFP 0800674332.
Nelson, Eric. "How Can I Keep from Singing?" SATB. AFP 0800675177. (G)
Schalk, Carl. "Evening and Morning." SATB, org, br, opt cong. CPH 98-3314.
Viadana, Ludovico. "Sing, Ye Righteous." SATB. CPH 98-1527.
Walker, Gwyneth. "Sounding Joy." SATB. ECS 4318.

Year C

Isaiah 65:1-9	*The prophet sent to a rebellious people*
Psalm 22:19-28	*In the midst of the congregation I will praise you*
Galatians 3:23-29	*In baptism, clothed with Christ; no longer Jew or Greek*
Luke 8:26-39	*Jesus casts out demons possessing a man of the Gerasenes*

Semicontinuous first reading/psalm

1 Kings 19:1-4 [5-7] 8-15a	*Elijah hears the word of the Lord in the midst of silence*
Psalm 42 and 43	*Send out your light and truth that they may lead me*

Bach, Johann Sebastian. "All Who Believe and Are Baptized." *Bach for All Seasons*. SATB. AFP 080065854X.
———. "Salvation unto Us Has Come." *Bach for All Seasons*. SATB. AFP 080065854X.
Berger, Jean. "The Eyes of All Wait upon Thee." SATB. AFP 0800645596. *The Augsburg Choirbook*. AFP 0800656784.
Copland, Aaron. "Help Us, O Lord." SATB. B&H 6018.
Ferguson, John. "By Gracious Powers." SATB, fl, org, cong. AFP 0800675495.
Friedell, Harold. "Draw Us in the Spirit's Tether." SATB, org. HWG GCMR 2472.
Grieg, Edvard. "God's Son Has Made Me Free." SATB. AFP 0800645561. *The Augsburg Choirbook*. AFP 0800656784.
Scott, K. Lee. "Redeeming Grace." *Sing a Song of Joy*. ML, kybd. AFP 0800652827. MH, kybd. AFP 0800647882.
Sowerby, Leo. "O God of Light." *Songs of Faith and Penitence*. S solo, org. HWG. (P)
Weelkes, Thomas. "Early Will I Seek Thee." SATB. BRD 931.
Wood, Dale. "Rise, Shine!" SATB, org. AFP 0800655923. *The Augsburg Choirbook*. 0800656784.
Zingarelli, Niccolò Antonio. "Go Not Far from Me, O God." SATB. GSCH 4889. (P)

Sunday 13 / Proper 8 / June 26–July 2

Year A

Jeremiah 28:5-9	*The test of a true prophet*
Psalm 89:1-4, 15-18	*Your love, O Lord, forever will I sing*
Romans 6:12-23	*No longer under law but under grace*
Matthew 10:40-42	*Welcome Christ in those he sends*

Semicontinuous first reading/psalm

Genesis 22:1-14	*The testing of Abraham*
Psalm 13	*I put my trust in your mercy, O Lord*

Beethoven, Ludwig van/ed. K. Lee Scott. "Prayer." *Rejoice Now My Spirit.* MH, kybd. AFP 0800651081. ML, kybd. AFP 080065109X.

Farrant, Richard. "Hide Not Thou Thy Face." SATB, org. OXF.

Grieg, Edward/arr. Oscar Overby. "God's Son Has Made Me Free." SATB. AFP 0800645561.

Hallock, Peter. "Your Love, O Lord, For Ever I Will Sing." SATB, acc. GIA G-2078. (P)

Handel, George Frideric. "But Thanks Be to God." *Messiah.* SATB, kybd. §

———. "O Death, Where Is Thy Sting?" *Messiah.* AT duet, kybd. §

Lamberton, Dodd. "I Want to Walk as a Child of the Light." SATB, org. MSM 50-8813.

Lynn, George. "I Want Jesus to Walk with Me." SATB, S solo. PRE 312-40113.

Manz, Paul. "Let Us Ever Walk with Jesus." U, org. MSM 50-9405.

Sampson, Godfrey. "My Song Shall Be Alway of the Lovingkindness." U, SATB, org. NOV 29 0244 03. (P)

Schickele, Peter. "Amazing Grace." SATB. PRE 362-03402.

Scott, K. Lee. "Gracious Spirit, Dwell with Me." 2 pt mxd, org. AFP 0800646134.

———. "I Will Sing of Thy Great Mercies." *Sing a Song of Joy.* MH, kybd. AFP 0800647882. ML, kybd. AFP 0800652827. (P)

———. "Thy Perfect Love." *Sing Forth God's Praise.* MH, kybd. AFP 0800675266. ML, kybd. AFP 080067538X.

Year B

Lamentations 3:22-33	*Great is the Lord's faithfulness*
or Wis. of Sol. 1:13-15; 2:23-24	*God created humankind for immortality*
Psalm 30	*I will exalt you, O Lord, because you have lifted me up*
2 Corinthians 8:7-15	*Excel in generosity, following the Lord Jesus*
Mark 5:21-43	*Christ healing a woman and Jairus' daughter*

Semicontinuous first reading/psalm

2 Samuel 1:1, 17-27	*Lamentation over Saul and Jonathan*
Psalm 130	*Out of the depths have I called to you, O Lord*

Beethoven, Ludwig van/ed. K. Lee Scott. "Prayer." *Rejoice Now My Spirit.* MH, kybd. AFP 0800651081. ML, kybd. AFP 080065109X.

Cherwien, David. "Healing River." SATB, pno. AFP 0800675886.

Corfe, Joseph. "I Will Magnify Thee, O Lord." 2 equal voices, kybd. NOV 29.019708.

Hellerman, Fred and Fran Minkoff/arr. David Cherwien. "O Healing River." *To God Will I Sing.* MH, kybd. AFP 0800674332. ML, kybd. AFP 080067434X.

Hobby, Robert A. "I Lift My Soul." U, fl, pno. MSM 50-9453.

Kallman, Daniel. "Amazing Grace." SATB, pno. MSM 50-9073.

Manz, Paul. "Let Us Ever Walk with Jesus." U, org. MSM 50-9405.
Palestrina, Giovanni Pierluigi da. "Jesu! Rex admirabilis/Jesus, Thou Wondrous King." *Eleven Motets for Treble Voices*. SSA. GIA G-2143.
Roberts, William Bradley. "In All These You Welcomed Me." U, org, opt ob or other C or B-flat inst. AFP 6000001207.
Scholz, Robert. "Children of the Heavenly Father." SATB. AFP 0800659112. (F)
Schütz, Heinrich. "Herr, ich hoffe darauf/Lord, My Hope Is in Thee." 2 pt, cont. CV 20.312.
———. "Lift Up Your Voice." *Chantry Choirbook*. SATB. AFP 0800657772.
Weber, Paul D. "I Will Sing the Story of Your Love." SATB or U, org, opt cong. AFP 0800657004.

Year C

1 Kings 19:15-16, 19-21 — *Elijah says to Elisha, Follow me and do not continue plowing*
Psalm 16 — *I have set the Lord always before me*
Galatians 5:1, 13-25 — *Love is the whole law, gift of the Spirit*
Luke 9:51-62 — *Jesus says, Follow me and do not look back*

Semicontinuous first reading/psalm

2 Kings 2:1-2, 6-14 — *Elijah ascends into heaven in a whirlwind*
Psalm 77:1-2, 11-20 — *By your strength you have redeemed your people*

Callahan, Charles. "In Your Mercy, Lord, You Called Me." U, kybd. CPH 98-2861.
Duruflé, Maurice. "Ubi caritas." SATTBB. DUR 312-41253.
Fleming, Larry L. "Give Me Jesus." SATB. AFP 0880645278. *The Augsburg Choirbook*. SATB. AFP 0800656784. (G)
Friedell, Harold. "Draw Us in the Spirit's Tether." SATB, org. HWG GCMR 2472.
———. "The Way to Jerusalem." SATB, solo, org. HWG CMR 2328. (G)
Handel, George Frideric. "Jesus, Sun of Life, My Splendor." SATB, org. CPH 98-1445.
Hobby, Robert A. "Beloved, God's Chosen." *To God Will I Sing*. MH, kybd. AFP 0800674332. ML, kybd. AFP 080067434X.
Rutter, John. "Open Thou Mine Eyes." SATB. HIN HMC 467.
Wood, Charles. "Jesus Had a Garden." *Carols for Choirs 1*. SATB. OXF 353220.

Sunday 14 / Proper 9 / July 3–9

Year A

    Zechariah 9:9-12　　　　　　　*The king will come in humility and peace*
    Psalm 145:8-14　　　　　　　　*The Lord is gracious and full of compassion*
    Romans 7:15-25a　　　　　　　*The struggle within the self*
    Matthew 11:16-19, 25-30　　　　*The yoke of discipleship*

Semicontinuous first reading/psalm

    Genesis 24:34-38, 42-49, 58-67　　*The marriage of Isaac and Rebekah*
    Psalm 45:11-18　　　　　　　　*God has anointed you with the oil of gladness*

Cherubini, Luigi. "Come Unto Me, All Ye Heavy Laden." SAB, kybd. HTF F6019. (G)
Handel, George Frideric. "Come unto Him." *Messiah*. S solo. § (G)
———. "His Yoke Is Easy." *Messiah*. SATB, kybd. § (G)
———. "Rejoice Greatly, O Daughter of Zion." *Messiah*. S solo. § (F)
Howells, Herbert. "O, Pray for the Peace of Jerusalem." SATB, org. OXF 42.064.
Kallman, Daniel. "Lord of All Hopefulness." SAB, fl, org. CPH 98-2680.
Leaf, Robert. "Come with Rejoicing." U, kybd. AFP 0800645758.
Schalk, Carl. "Gather Your Children, Dear Savior, in Peace." SATB, org. MSM 50-8500.
Schütz, Heinrich. "To Thee We Turn Our Eyes." SATB, opt kybd. CPH 98-1885.
Scott, K. Lee. "A Song of Trust." *Sing a Song of Joy*. MH, kybd. AFP 0800647882. ML, kybd. AFP 0800652827.
Willan, Healey. "Come unto Me, All Ye That Labor." U, kybd. CPH 98-2359. (G)

Year B

    Ezekiel 2:1-5　　　　　　　　*The call of Ezekiel*
    Psalm 123　　　　　　　　　　*Our eyes look to you, O God, until you show us your mercy*
    2 Corinthians 12:2-10　　　　　*God's power made perfect in weakness*
    Mark 6:1-13　　　　　　　　　*Sending of the Twelve to preach and heal*

Semicontinuous first reading/psalm

    2 Samuel 5:1-5, 9-10　　　　　*The reign of David*
    Psalm 48　　　　　　　　　　*God shall be our guide forevermore*

Bach, Johann Sebastian. "Nations, Listen to God's Calling." *Bach Arias for the Church Year*. U or 2 pt, kybd. CPH 97-6055.
Bell, John L. "Will You Come and Follow Me." SATB, solo, opt kybd, cong. GIA G-4384.
Bender, Jan. "O God, O Lord of Heaven and Earth." SATB, org, opt tpt, cong. AFP 0800652509.
Bisbee, B. Wayne. "Teach Me Your Way, O Lord." 2 pt mxd, kybd. AFP 080065479X.
Bouman, Paul. "I Lift Up My Eyes to the Hills." 2 pt, org. B&H OCTB6550. (P)
Friedell, Harold. "Draw Us in the Spirit's Tether." SATB, org. HWG GCMR 2472.
Hobby, Robert A. "O Christ, Our Light, O Radiance True/Jesus, Thy Church with Longing Eyes." 2 pt, ob, kybd. CPH 98-2891.
Hobby, Robert A./ed. Susan Palo Cherwien. "Beloved, God's Chosen." *To God Will I Sing*. MH, kybd. AFP 0800674332. ML, kybd. 080067434X.
Marcello, Benedetto. "Oh, Hold Thou Me Up." *The Morning Star Choir Book*. SA, org. CPH 97-6287.
Powell, Robert J. "The Wisdom, Riches, and Knowledge of God." *Surely the Lord Is In This Place*. Med. vocal solo, kybd. AFP 0800654838.

Schütz, Heinrich. "Praise God in Heaven." 2 pt, kybd. CPH 98-3587.
Sedio, Mark. "Teach Me Your Way, O Lord." U or 2 pt, kybd. AMSI 711.

Year C

Isaiah 66:10-14	*Jerusalem, a nursing mother giving life to her children*
Psalm 66:1-9	*God holds our souls in life*
Galatians 6:[1-6] 7-16	*Do what is right now and reap at the harvest time*
Luke 10:1-11, 16-20	*Jesus sends out seventy disciples into the harvest*

Semicontinuous first reading/psalm
2 Kings 5:1-14	*Elisha heals a warrior with leprosy*
Psalm 30	*My God, I cried out to you, and you restored me to health*

Copland, Aaron. "Sing Ye Praises to Our King." SATB. B&H OCTB6021.
———. "Zion's Walls." SATB, kybd. B&H MO5146-700.
Dawson, William. "There Is a Balm in Gilead." SATB. KJO T105. (F)
Hancock, Gerre/arr. Paul Bouman. "O God of Mercy." *To God Will I Sing*. MH, kybd. AFP 0800674332. ML, kybd. AFP 0800674340.
Handel, George Frideric. "Rejoice Greatly, O Daughter of Zion." *Messiah*. S solo, kybd. § (F)
Jennings, Kenneth. "With a Voice of Singing." SATB. AFP 0800645669. *The Augsburg Choirbook*. AFP 0800656784.
Mendelssohn, Felix. "For the Lord Will Lead." *To God Will I Sing*. MH, kybd. AFP 0800674332. ML, kybd. AFP 0800674340.
Rutter, John. "Praise Ye the Lord." SATB, org. OXF E120.
Schütz, Heinrich. "Praise God, Ye Lands." *Ten Psalms (Becker Psalter)*. SATB. CPH 97-6303. (P)
Scott, K. Lee. "God Shall the Broken Heart Repair." SATB, kybd. AFP 0800654102.

Sunday 15 / Proper 10 / July 10–16

Year A

Isaiah 55:10-13	*The growth of the word to accomplish God's purpose*
Psalm 65:[1-8] 9-13	*Your paths overflow with plenty*
Romans 8:1-11	*Living according to the Spirit*
Matthew 13:1-9, 18-23	*The parable of the sower and the seed*

Semicontinuous first reading/psalm

Genesis 25:19-34	*Esau sells his birthright to Jacob*
Psalm 119:105-112	*Your word is a lantern to my feet and a light upon my path.*

Bach, Johann Sebastian. "For There Is Now No Condemnation." *Jesu, meine Freude.* SATB. § (S)
———. "Ye Are Not of the Flesh." *Jesu, Meine Freude.* SATB. § (S)
Bertalot, John. "Thy Word Is a Lantern." SATB, org, opt br and perc. AFP 0800674251.
Clausen, René. "Seek the Lord." SATB, kybd. MFS MF 2009.
DeLong, Richard P. "Almighty God, Your Word Is Cast." SATB. AFP 0800650921.
Farlee, Robert Buckley. "O My People, Turn to Me." *Three Biblical Songs.* U, kybd. AFP 0800654803.
Ferguson, John. "Word of God Come Down on Earth." SATB, org. GIA G-3764.
Greene, Maurice/ed. K. Lee Scott. "You Visit the Earth." *Sing Forth God's Praise.* MH, kybd. AFP 0800675266. ML, kybd. AFP 080067538X. (P)
Haugen, Marty. "Come to the Feast." SATB, gtr, kybd, trbl inst, opt br and hb. GIA G-3543.
Hopson, Hal H. "For as the Rain and Snow Come Down." SATB. AFP 080065868X. (F)
Lekberg, Sven. "For as the Rain Cometh Down." SATB. GSCH 11509. (F)
Mendelssohn, Felix. "I Will Sing of Thy Great Mercies." *Sing a Song of Joy.* MH, kybd. AFP 0800647882. ML, kybd. AFP 0800652827.
Rutter, John. "For the Beauty of the Earth." SATB, kybd (2 pt also available). HIN HMC 550.
Sedio, Mark. "The Thirsty Fields Drink In the Rain." SATB, org. AFP 0800657063. OP
Willan, Healey. "The Seed Is the Word of God." *We Praise Thee II.* U, org. CPH 97-7610. (G)
Willcocks, David. "Thou, O God, Art Praised in Zion." SATB, org. OUP A360. (P)
Williamson, Malcolm. "Thou Art Praised in Zion." U, cong, org. B&H 5954. (P)

Year B

Amos 7:7-15	*The sign of the plumb line: God's judgment on Israel*
Psalm 85:8-13	*I will listen to what the L*ORD *God is saying*
Ephesians 1:3-14	*Chosen in Christ to live to the praise of God's glory*
Mark 6:14-29	*The death of John the Baptist*

Semicontinuous first reading/psalm

2 Samuel 6:1-5, 12b-19	*David and the house of Israel dance before the Lord*
Psalm 24	*Lift up your heads, O gates, and the King of glory shall come in*

Bouman, Paul. "Blest Are They." SAB. SEL 410-113.
Buxtehude, Dietrich. "My Jesus Is My Lasting Joy." U, org. HWG CGMR 02727.
Ellingboe, Bradley. "The Prayer of St. Francis." SAB, pno. KJO 5767.
Ferguson, John. "Jesus, My Lord and God." U, kybd. AFP 0800646193.
Hampton, Calvin. "Fairest Lord Jesus." U, org. GIA G-2766.
Handel, George Frideric. "All My Spirit Longs to Savor." *Chantry Choirbook.* SATB, kybd. AFP 0800657772.

Mathews, Peter. "The Prayer of St. Francis." Vocal solo, kybd. MSM 40-902.
Schalk, Carl. "Christ Be Our Seed." SATB, ob. CPH. 98-3602.
Sedio, Mark. "The Thirsty Fields Drink In the Rain." SATB, org. AFP 0800657063. OP

Year C

Deuteronomy 30:9-14 — *The Lord will take delight in your fruitfulness*
Psalm 25:1-10 — *Show me your ways, O Lord, and teach me your paths*
Colossians 1:1-14 — *The gospel is growing, bearing fruit in the whole world*
Luke 10:25-37 — *The parable of the merciful Samaritan*

Semicontinuous first reading/psalm

Amos 7:7-17 — *A plumb line will judge the people*
Psalm 82 — *Arise, O God, and rule the earth*

Attwood, Thomas. "Teach Me, O Lord." SATB, org. GIA G-3045.(P)
Bouman, Paul. "O God of Mercy." *To God Will I Sing*. MH, kybd. AFP 0800674332. ML, kybd. AFP 0800674340.
Farrant, Richard. "Call to Remembrance." SATB. ECS 1639. § (P)
Haydn, Franz Joseph. "Show Me Your Ways, O Lord." *Four Psalms for SAB Choir*. SAB. CPH 98-3019. (P)
Helgen, John. "Spirit of God, Descend." SATB, kybd. AFP 0800676378.
How, Martin. "Day by Day." U or 2-3 pt, org. G-4178.
Jennings, Kenneth. "Thee Will I Love." SATB. KJO 8724.
Pelz, Walter L. "Show Me Thy Ways." SATB, gtr, ob or fl. AFP 0800645421. *The Augsburg Choirbook*. AFP 0800656784. (P)
Purcell, Henry. "Thou Knowest, Lord, the Secrets of Our Hearts." SATB, org. ECS 170.
Rorem, Ned. "Love Divine, All Loves Excelling." SATB. B&H MO51454505.
———. "Sing, My Soul, His Wondrous Love." SATB. PET 6386.
Schalk, Carl. "Show Me Your Ways, O Lord." SATB. CPH 98-3207. (P)
Wilby, Philip. "If Ye Love Me." SSATB, org. PVN 8300561.

Sunday 16 / Proper 11 / July 17–23

Year A

Isaiah 44:6-8 — *There is no other God than the Lord*
or Wisdom of Sol. 12:13, 16-19 — *God's sovereignty: both righteous and forbearing*
Psalm 86:11-17 — *Teach me your way, O Lord, and I will walk in your truth*
Romans 8:12-25 — *The revealing of the children of God*
Matthew 13:24-30, 36-43 — *The parable of the weeds*

Semicontinuous first reading/psalm

Genesis 28:10-19a — *Jacob's dream of the ladder to heaven*
Psalm 139: 1-12, 23-24 — *You have searched me out and known me*

Bach, Johann Christoph Friedrich. "In the Resurrection Glorious." *Chantry Choirbook*. SATB, org. AFP 0800642772.
Bach, Johann Sebastian. "O Mortal World." *Lift Up Your Voice*. M voice solo, kybd. PRE.
Bairstow, Edward C. "I Will Wash My Hands in Innocency." SATB. OXF MA 6.
Bisbee, B. Wayne. "Teach Me Your Way, O Lord." 2 pt mxd, kybd. AFP 080065479X. (P)
Dvořák, Antonín. "Search Me, O God." *Lift Up Your Voice*. M voice solo, kybd. PRE.
Hillert, Richard. "Image of the Unseen God." SATB, org. AFP 0800659627.
Marcello, Benedetto/arr. Dale Grotenhuis. "Teach Me Now, O Lord." 2 pt, kybd. MSM 50-9418. (P)
Mendelssohn, Felix/arr. Wilbur Held. "Then Shall the Righteous Shine Forth." *Elijah. Vocal Solos for Funerals and Memorial Services*. M, kybd. AFP 6000001169.
Nystedt, Knut. "Teach Me, O Lord." U or 2 pt, pno, perc, ad lib. MSM 50-9400. (P)
Purcell, Henry. "Thou Knowest, Lord, the Secrets of Our Hearts." SATB, org. ECS 170.
Scott, K. Lee. "The Call." *Sing a Song of Joy*. MH, kybd. AFP 0800647882. ML, kybd. AFP 0800652827.
Wesley, Samuel Sebastian. "Lead Me, Lord." *The New Church Anthem Book*. SATB, org. OXF 0193531097.

Year B

Jeremiah 23:1-6 — *From David's line, a righteous shepherd for Israel*
Psalm 23 — *The Lord is my shepherd; I shall not be in want*
Ephesians 2:11-22 — *Reconciled to God through Christ, our peace*
Mark 6:30-34, 53-56 — *Christ healing the multitudes*

Semicontinuous first reading/psalm

2 Samuel 7:1-14a — *The promise of the Lord to David*
Psalm 89:20-37 — *Your love, O Lord, forever will I sing*

Bach, Johann Sebastian. "What God Ordains Is Good Indeed." *Bach for All Seasons*. SATB, kybd. AFP 080065854X.
Bisbee, B. Wayne. "Teach Me Your Way, O Lord." 2 pt mxd, kybd. AFP 080065479X.
Busarow, Donald. "The Days of Summer." M solo, kybd. CPH 97-5644.
Dvořák, Antonín. "God Is My Shepherd." *Five Biblical Songs*. Vocal solo, kybd. § (P)
Ellingboe, Bradley. "Jesus, Good Shepherd." SATB, pno. AFP 0800658272. (P)
Haydn, Franz Joseph. "Lo, My Shepherd's Hand Divine." SATB, org. ECS 1019. (P)
Kitson, C. H. "Jesu, Grant Me This, I Pray." SATB, org. OXF 42.041.
Liddle, Samuel. "The Lord Is My Shepherd." *Sing Solo Sacred*. OXF 0193457857. (P)
Marcello, Benedetto/arr. Dale Grotenhuis. "Teach Me Now, O Lord." 2 pt, kybd. MSM 50-9418.
Pelz, Walter L. "The King of Love My Shepherd Is." SATB, kybd, fl, opt cong. AFP 0800646010. (P)

Pote, Allen. "The Lord Is My Shepherd." SATB, pno. CGA 551. (P)
Thomson, Virgil. "My Shepherd Will Supply My Need." SAB, org (also available in SA, SSA, SSAA, SATB, TTBB). HWG 2571 (P)
Zimmermann, Heinz Werner. "Psalm 23." SATB, org, opt DB. AFP 0800645383. *The Augsburg Choirbook.* AFP 0800656784. (P)

Year C

Genesis 18:1-10a	*The hospitality of Abraham and Sarah to three visitors of the LORD*
Psalm 15	*Who may abide upon your holy hill? Whoever leads a blameless life and does what is right*
Colossians 1:15-28	*Hymn to Christ, the firstborn of all creation*
Luke 10:38-42	*Jesus says: Martha, your sister Mary has chosen the better part*

Semicontinuous first reading/psalm

Amos 8:1-12	*A famine of hearing the words of the LORD*
Psalm 52	*I am like a green olive tree in the house of God*

Bach, Johann Sebastian. "Lord, Thee I Love with All My Heart." *Bach for All Seasons.* SATB. AFP 080065854X. (G)
Dawson, William. "There Is a Balm in Gilead." SATB, S solo. KJO T105.
Dvořák, Antonín. "Search Me, O God." *Lift Up Your Voice.* M, kybd. PRE.
Farrar, Sue. "As Long as I Have Breath." SATB, kybd. BEC BP1298.
Ferguson, John. "Lord, in All Love." SATB, org, opt cong. AFP 0800656490.
Hayes, Mark. "Day by Day." SATB, pno. AFP 0800658345. (G)
Hobby, Robert A. "Immortal, Invisible, God Only Wise." U, org. MSM 50-9306.
Lassus, Orlande de. "Adoramus te." SATB. PRE MC76.
Scott, K. Lee. "Redeeming Grace." *Sing a Song of Joy.* MH, kybd. AFP 0800647882. ML, kybd. AFP 0800652827.
Vaughan Williams, Ralph. "The Call." U, kybd. MSM 50-9912.

Sunday 17 / Proper 12 / July 24–30

Year A

1 Kings 3:5-12	*Solomon's prayer for wisdom*
Psalm 119:129-136	*When your word goes forth, it gives light and understanding.*
Romans 8:26-39	*Nothing can separate us from God's love*
Matthew 13:31-33, 44-52	*Parables of the reign of heaven*

Semicontinuous first reading/psalm

Genesis 29:15-28	*Leah and Rachel become Jacob's wives*
Psalm 105:1-11, 45b	*Make known the deeds of the* LORD *among the peoples. Hallelujah!*

Bach, Johann Sebastian. "Jesus, My Sweet Pleasure/Jesu, meine Freude." *Bach for All Seasons*. SATB. AFP 080065854X.
Handel, George Frideric. "If God Is for Us, Who Is against Us." *Messiah*. S solo, kybd. § (S)
Hayes, Mark. "Let the Word Go Forth." SATB, org. AFP 0800674189. (P)
Pinkham, Daniel. "Who Shall Separate Us from the Love of Christ." *Letters from St. Paul*. Solo, kybd. ECS 142. (S)
Schütz, Heinrich. "Sing to the Lord." *Chantry Choirbook*. SATB. AFP 0800657772.
———/ed. Larry Fleming. "Who Shall Separate Us." SATB, cont. AFP 0800656954. OP (S)
Scott, K. Lee. "Open My Eyes." SATB, org. CPH 98-2904.
———. "Redeeming Grace." *Sing a Song of Joy: Vocal Solos for Worship*. MH, kybd. AFP 0800647882. ML, kybd. AFP 0800652827.
———. "So Art Thou to Me." *Rejoice Now, My Spirit*. MH, kybd. AFP 0800651081. ML, kybd. AFP 080065109X.
———. "Teach Me, My God and King." SATB, org. AFP 0800659732.

Year B

2 Kings 4:42-44	*Elisha feeding a hundred people*
Psalm 145:10-18	*You open wide your hand and satisfy the needs of every living creature.*
Ephesians 3:14-21	*Prayer for wisdom, strength, and Christ's indwelling*
John 6:1-21	*Christ feeding the five thousand*

Semicontinuous first reading/psalm

2 Samuel 11:1-15	*Bathsheba and Uriah wronged by David*
Psalm 14	*God is in the company of the righteous*

Bach, Johann Sebastian. "Jesus, My Sweet Pleasure/Jesu, meine Freude." *Bach for All Seasons*. SATB. AFP 080065854X.
Beck, Theodore. "Jesus, Priceless Treasure." SATB, cong, 3 tpts, org. MSM 60-9006A.
Beethoven, Ludwig van/ed. K. Lee Scott. "Prayer." *Rejoice Now, My Spirit*. MH, kybd. AFP 0800651081. ML, kybd. AFP 080065109X.
Berger, Jean. "The Eyes of All Wait upon Thee." SATB. AFP 0800645596. *The Augsburg Choirbook*. AFP 0800656784. (P)
Franck, César/ed. Susan Palo Cherwien. "O Bread of Heaven." *To God Will I Sing*. MH, kybd. AFP 0800674332. ML, kybd. AFP 0800674340. (G)
Haugen, Marty. "Bread to Share." SATB, cant, cong, gtr. GIA G-4279. (F, G)
Praetorius, Michael. "Jubilate Deo." Canon in 2, 3, or 4 pt. B&S OCTB6350.
Proulx, Richard. "The Eyes of All." U, org. AFP 0800656466. (P)
Thomas, Paul. "Jesus, Priceless Treasure." *The SAB Chorale Book*. SAB. CPH 97-7575.

Thompson, J. Michael. "Taste and See the Lord Is Good." SATB, org, ob. AFP 0800657039.
Wold, Wayne L. "As This Broken Bread." *Augsburg Easy Choirbook*. 2 pt mxd, pno. AFP 0800676025.

Year C

Genesis 18:20-32	*Abraham bargains with God for the righteous of Sodom and Gomorrah*
Psalm 138	*Your love endures forever; do not abandon the works of your hands*
Colossians 2:6-15 [16-19]	*Buried with Christ in baptism, raised with him through faith*
Luke 11:1-13	*Jesus teaches the disciples to pray*

Semicontinuous first reading/psalm
Hosea 1:2-10	*Hosea's marriage: a message to Israel*
Psalm 85	*Righteousness and peace shall go before the* LORD

Duruflé, Maurice. "Notre Pére." SATB. DUR 362-03307. (G)
Ellingboe, Bradley. "The Lord's Prayer." SATB, pno. KJO 8952. (G)
Franck, Melchior. "Our Father, Thou in Heaven Above." GSCH 11174. (G)
Organ, Anne Krentz. "Come and Find the Quiet Center." SAB, kybd, opt fl. AFP 0800675096.
Peeters, Flor. "The Lord's Prayer." SATB, kybd. PET 6200. (G)
Proulx, Richard. "The Eyes of All." U, org. AFP 0800656466.
Schubert, Franz. "Lord, to Whom Our Prayers Ascend." *Rejoice Now My Spirit*. MH, kybd. AFP 0800651081. ML, kybd. AFP 080065109X.
Schütz, Heinrich. "Our Father." *Chantry Choirbook*. SATB. AFP 0806642772. (G)

Sunday 18 / Proper 13 / July 31–August 6

Year A

Isaiah 55:1-5	*Eat and drink that which truly satisfies*
Psalm 145:8-9, 14-21	*You open wide your hand and satisfy the needs of every living creature*
Romans 9:1-5	*The glory of God's people Israel*
Matthew 14:13-21	*Christ feeding five thousand*

Semicontinuous first reading/psalm

Genesis 32:22-31	*Jacob receives a blessing from God*
Psalm 17:1-7, 15	*I shall see your face; when I awake, I shall be satisfied*

Berger, Jean. "The Eyes of All Wait upon Thee." SATB. AFP 0800645596. (P)
Berthier, Jacques. "Eat This Bread." SATB, cant, kybd. GIA G-2840. (G)
Franck, César/ed. Susan Palo Cherwien. "O Bread of Life/Panis angelicus." *To God Will I Sing*. MH, kybd. AFP 0800674332. ML, kybd. AFP 0800674340. (G)
Handel, George Frideric. "Deck Thyself, My Soul, with Gladness." SATB, kybd. PRE 392-41707.
Larkin, Michael. "The Eyes of All." SATB. MSM 50-9110. (P)
Marcello, Benedetto. "Give Ear unto Me." *Second Morning Star Choir Book*. SS, org. CPH 97-4702.
Mendelssohn, Felix. "O Come, Every One that Thirsteth." *Elijah*. SATB, org. GSCH 43. (F)
Mozart, Wolfgang Amadeus. "Ave verum corpus." SATB. §
Proulx, Richard. "The Eyes of All." U, org. CHA 12-109. (P)
Wienhorst, Richard. "Lord, Whose Love in Humble Service." SATB, kybd. MSM 50-9059.

Year B

Exodus 16:2-4, 9-15	*The L*ORD *gives manna in the wilderness*
Psalm 78:23-29	*The L*ORD *rained down manna upon them to eat*
Ephesians 4:1-16	*Maintain the unity of the faith*
John 6:24-35	*Christ the bread of life*

Semicontinuous first reading/psalm

2 Samuel 11:26—12:13a	*David rebuked by the prophet Nathan*
Psalm 51:1-12	*Have mercy on me, O God, according to your lovingkindness*

Bach, Johann Sebastian. "O Bread of Life from Heaven." *Bach for All Seasons*. SATB. AFP 080065854X. (G)
Byrd, William. "Ego sum panis vivus." SATB. CHE 8747 (G)
Farlee, Robert Buckley/ed. Susan Palo Cherwien. "We Are a Garden Walled Around." *To God Will I Sing*. MH, kybd. AFP 0800674332. ML, kybd. AFP 080067434X.
Farrell, Bernadette. "Bread of Life." Cant, SATB, kybd, gtr, fl, cl. OCP 7152CC. (G)
Fay, Peter. "O Sacred and Blessed Feast/O sacrum convivium." *The Augsburg Choirbook*. SATB. AFP 0800656784.
Handel, George Frideric/ed. K. Lee Scott "Jesu, Thou Art Watching Ever." *Sing a Song of Joy*. ML, kybd. AFP 0800652827. MH, kybd. AFP 0800647882.
Helgen, John. "In God's Presence." SATB, pno. KJO 8941.
Hobby, Robert A. "Glorious Things of You Are Spoken." SATB, cong, br, org. MSM 60-7007A. (F)
Isaac, Heinrich. "O Bread of Life from Heaven/O esca viatorum." SATB. *Chantry Choirbook*. AFP 0800657772. (F, G)
Toolan, Suzanne. "I Am the Bread of Life." Vocal solo, kybd, opt gtr. GIA G-2054. (G)

Year C

Ecclesiastes 1:2, 12-14; 2:18-23 — *Search out wisdom, for all is vanity*
Psalm 49:1-12 — *We can never ransom ourselves or deliver to God the price of our life*
Colossians 3:1-11 — *Clothed in Christ, your life is hidden with him in God*
Luke 12:13-21 — *Jesus says: Be on guard against greed; be rich toward God, your treasure*

Semicontinuous first reading/psalm

Hosea 11:1-11 — *Like a mother, God will love Israel forever*
Psalm 107:1-9, 43 — *Give thanks to the LORD, all those whom the LORD has redeemed.*

Bach, Johann Sebastian. "Jesus, My Sweet Pleasure/Jesu meine Freude." *Bach for All Seasons*. SATB. AFP 080065854X. § (G)
———. "O Mortal World." *Lift Up Your Voice*. M, kybd. PRE.
Brahms, Johannes. "Ah Thou Poor World." *Anthems for Choirs 1*. SATB. OXF 353214X.
Ellingboe, Bradley. "The Food of Life." SATB, pno. KJO 8966.
Erickson, Richard. "Come Away to the Skies." SATB, fl, fc. AFP 0800656776.
Ferguson, John. "Be Thou My Vision." SATB, org. AFP 0800657934. (G)
Jennings, Kenneth. "If Ye Be Risen Again with Christ." SATB. CPH 98-1798.
Parker, Alice. "Be Thou My Vision." HIN HMC-135. (G)
Rutter, John. "God Be in My Head." SATB. OXF 94.326.
Scott, K. Lee. "Sing a Song of Joy." *Sing a Song of Joy*. ML, kybd. AFP 0800652827. MH, kybd. AFP 0800647882.
Young, Carlton R. "Bread of the World, in Mercy Broken." 2 pt mxd, kybd. AFP 0800675592.

Sunday 19 / Proper 14 / August 7–August 13

Year A

1 Kings 19:9-18	*The Lord speaks to Elijah on Mount Horeb*
Psalm 85:8-13	*I will listen to what the Lord God is saying*
Romans 10:5-15	*Hearing and confessing the word of faith*
Matthew 14:22-33	*Jesus walking on the sea*

Semicontinuous first reading/psalm

Genesis 37:1-4, 12-28	*Joseph sold by his brothers*
Psalm 105:1-6, 16-22, 45b	*Make known the deeds of the Lord among the peoples. Hallelujah!*

Biery, James. "The Waters of Life." *The Augsburg Choirbook*. SATB, org. AFP 0800656784.
Boatner, Edward. "Wade in the Water." *The Story of the Spirituals*. Med range solo, kybd or gtr. MCF. (G)
Cain, Noble. "In the Night, Christ Came Walking." SATB. GSCH 7967. (G)
Davis, Katherine. "Who Was the Man." U. CGA110.
Handel, George Frideric. "How Beautiful Are the Feet." *Messiah*. S solo, kybd or orch. § (S)
Hurd, David. "Show Us Your Kindness." SATB, kybd, gtr. OCP OCP9874CC. (P)
Manz, Paul. "Let Us Ever Walk with Jesus." U, org. MSM 50-9405. (G)
Mendelssohn, Felix/ed. K. Lee Scott. "The Lord Is Ever Watchful." *Sing Forth God's Praise*. MH, kybd. AFP 0800675266. ML, kybd. AFP 080067538X.
Pote, Allen. "The Last Supper." SATB, opt gtr, bass. CGA-532.
Ray, Robert. "He Never Failed Me Yet." SATB, kybd, soloist. HAL 4478014
Stanford, Charles Villiers. "If Thou Shalt Confess with Thy Mouth." *Wonder, Love and Praise*, vol. 1. SATB. NOV 03013808. (S)
Statham, Heathcoat. "Drop Down, Ye Heavens." *The Oxford Easy Anthem Book*. 2 pt, org. OXF 0193533189.

Year B

1 Kings 19:4-8	*Elijah receives bread for his journey*
Psalm 34:1-8	*Taste and see that the Lord is good*
Ephesians 4:25—5:2	*Put away evil, live in love*
John 6:35, 41-51	*Christ the bread of life*

Semicontinuous first reading/psalm

2 Samuel 18:5-9, 15, 31-33	*David laments his son Absalom's death*
Psalm 130	*Out of the depths have I cried to you, O Lord*

Ellingboe, Bradley. "Soul Adorn Yourself with Gladness/Vengo a ti, Jesús amado." SATB. AFP 0800658477.
Haas, David. "I Am the Living Bread." 2 pt, org, gtr, fl. OCP 8730CC. (G)
Isaac, Heinrich. "O Bread of Life from Heaven/O esca viatorum." *Chantry Choirbook*. SATB. AFP 0800657772. (G)
McCabe, Michael. "I Am the Living Bread." SATB. Randall M. Egan 338. (G)
Moore, James. "Taste and See." Cong, cant, acc, gtr. GIA G-2784. (P)
Neswick, Bruce. "O Taste and See." SATB, S solo. AFP 0800654714. (P)
Pinkham, Daniel. "This Is the Bread." 2 pt, org. ECS 4447. (G)
Scott, K. Lee. "So Art Thou to Me." SATB, kybd. AFP 0800674308.
———. "So Art Thou to Me." *Rejoice Now, My Spirit*. MH, kybd. AFP 0800651081. ML, kybd. 080065109X.
Telemann, Georg Philipp/ed. Susan Palo Cherwien. "I Want to Praise the Lord All of My Life." 2 or 3 pt, kybd, opt solo inst. CPH 98-3350. (P)

Vaughan Williams, Ralph. "O Taste and See." SATB. OXF A349. (P)

White, David Ashley. "O Bread of Life from Heaven." 2 pt mxd, org. AFP 0800650913. *The Augsburg Choirbook.* AFP 0800656784. (G)

Year C

    Genesis 15:1-6   *God's promise of a child for Abram and Sarai*
    Psalm 33:12-22   *Let your lovingkindness be upon us, as we have put our trust in you.*
    Hebrews 11:1-3, 8-16   *A model for us: Abraham's faith in a new home given by God*
    Luke 12:32-40   *God will give you the treasure of the kingdom; sell all that you have*

Semicontinuous first reading/psalm

    Isaiah 1:1, 10-20   *Learn to do good, seek justice, and rescue the oppressed*
    Psalm 50:1-8, 22-23   *To those who keep in my way will I show the salvation of God.*

Bach, Johann Sebastian. "Jesus, My Sweet Pleasure/Jesu, meine Freude." *Bach for All Seasons.* SATB, opt kybd. AFP 080065854X. § (G)

———. "Zion Hears the Watchmen Singing." *Bach for All Seasons.* SATB, opt kybd. AFP 080065854X.

Brahms, Johannes. "Ah Thou Poor World." *Anthems for Choirs 1.* SATB. OXF 353214X.

Mendelssohn, Felix. "O Rest in the Lord." *Elijah.* Solo, kybd. §

Mozart, Wolfgang Amadeus. "God Is Our Refuge." BRD 129.

Powell, Rosephanye. "I Wanna Be Ready." SATB. GEN 8738698. (G)

Schalk, Carl. "Our Soul Waits for the Lord." SATB. CPH 98-3252.

Scott, K. Lee. "Keep Your Lamps Trimmed and Burning." *Sing Forth God's Praise.* MH, kybd. AFP 0800675266. ML, kybd. AFP 080067538X. (G)

Viadana, Lodovico. "Exsultate justi in Domino." SATB, org. WAL W2153.

Walter, Johann. "Rise Up, Rise Up!" *Chantry Choirbook.* SATB. AFP 0800657772.

Zimmermann, Heinz Werner. "Have No Fear, Little Flock." *Five Hymns.* U or SATB, kybd. CPH CPH 97-5131. (G)

Sunday 20 / Proper 15 / August 14–August 20

Year A

    Isaiah 56:1, 6-8   *A house of prayer for all peoples*
    Psalm 67   *Let all the peoples praise you, O God*
    Romans 11:1-2a, 29-32   *God's mercy to all, Jew and Gentile*
    Matthew 15:[10-20] 21-28   *The healing of the Canaanite woman's daughter*

Semicontinuous first reading/psalm

    Genesis 45:1-15   *Joseph reconciles with his brothers*
    Psalm 133   *How good and pleasant it is to live together in unity*

Aston, Peter. "God Be Merciful unto Us." SATB, org. NOV 013930. (P)
Bouman, Paul. "God Be Merciful." 2 pt, kybd. CPH 50-7039. (P, G)
———. "God Be Merciful unto Us." SS or SA, org. CPH 98-2471. (P)
Bruckner, Anton. "Locus iste." SATB. PET 6314.
Hammerschmidt, Andreas. "Let the People Praise Thee, O God." U, 2 vln, cont. CPH 98-1826. (P)
Hellerman, Fred and Fran Minkoff/arr. David Cherwien. "O Healing River." *To God Will I Sing*. MH, kybd. AFP 0800674332. ML, kybd. AFP 080067434X.
Howells, Herbert. "Coventry Antiphon." SATB, org. NOV 063230.
Josquin Desprez. "O Jesu, fili David." SA(T)B. TetraAB AB169. (G)
Mathias, William H. "Let the People Praise Thee, O God." SATB org. OXF A 331. (P)
Mendelssohn, Felix. "I Will Sing of Thy Great Mercies." *Sing a Song of Joy*. MH, kybd. AFP 0800647882. ML, kybd. AFP 0800652827.
Neswick, Bruce. "Let the Peoples Praise You, O God." SATB. VIV. (P)
Rowan, William P. "Woman in the Night." SATB, org, opt cong. SEL 425-815. (G)
Rutter, John. "For the Beauty of the Earth." SA, pno. HIN HMC-469.
Schütz, Heinrich. "Lift Up Your Voice." *Chantry Choirbook*. SATB, kybd. AFP 0800657772.
Willan, Healey. "Let the People Praise Thee, O God." *We Praise Thee*. SA, org. CPH 97-7564. (P)

Year B

    Proverbs 9:1-6   *Invited to dine at wisdom's feast*
    Psalm 34:9-14   *Those who seek the L*ord *lack nothing that is good*
    Ephesians 5:15-20   *Filled with the Spirit, sing thanks to God*
    John 6:51-58   *Christ the true food and drink*

Semicontinuous first reading/psalm

    1 Kings 2:10-12; 3:3-14   *Solomon's prayer for wisdom*
    Psalm 111   *The fear of the L*ord *is the beginning of wisdom*

Bairstow, Edward C. "I Sat Down under His Shadow." SATB. OXF 350104X
Burkhardt, Michael. "Filled with the Spirit." 3 pt canon, opt hb or kybd. MSM 50-7402. (S)
Busarow, Donald. "Proclaim with Me." SATB, cong, opt tpt. CPH 98-3127.
DeLong, Richard P. "This Is the Hour of Banquet and of Song." *Hymns of Joy*. SATB, org. HWG GCMR03643.
Fauré, Gabriel. "Benedictus." *Messe Basse*. SA, org. PRE 312-40598.
Haas, David. "I Am the Living Bread." 2 pt, org, gtr, fl. OCP 8730CC. (G)
Haugen, Marty. "Taste and See." SATB, cong, gtr, kybd. OCP G 3555. (P)
Holst, Gustav. "Let All Mortal Flesh." SATB. ECS 1.5019.

Schalk, Carl. "Be Known to Us, Lord Jesus." SATB, cong, U. CPH 98-3202.
Scott, K. Lee. "The Call." *Sing a Song of Joy*. MH, kybd. AFP 0800647882. ML, kybd. AFP 0800652827.
Tallis, Thomas. "Verily, Verily I Say unto You." SATB. OXF A-247.

Year C

Jeremiah 23:23-29	*God's word is like fire, like a hammer that breaks rocks*
Psalm 82	*Arise, O God, and rule the earth*
Hebrews 11:29—12:2	*The faith of the Hebrew people, a great cloud of witnesses*
Luke 12:49-56	*Jesus brings fire on earth and has a baptism with which to be baptized*

Semicontinuous first reading/psalm

Isaiah 5:1-7	*The vineyard of the LORD is destroyed*
Psalm 80:1-2, 8-19	*Look down from heaven, O God; behold and tend this vine*

Åhlén, Waldemar. "The Earth Adorned/Sommersalm." SATB. WAL 8500102. (S)
Attwood, Thomas/ed. K. Lee Scott. "Come, Holy Ghost." *Sing Forth God's Praise*. MH, kybd, kybd. AFP 0800675266. ML, kybd. AFP 080067538X.
Gardner, John. "Fight the Good Fight." SATB, kybd. OXF 42.874. (S)
Handel, George Frideric. "Why Do the Nations So Furiously Rage?" *Messiah*. B solo, kybd or orch. § (G)
Scott, K. Lee. "Redeeming Grace." *Sing a Song of Joy*. MH, kybd. AFP 0800647882. ML, kybd. AFP 0800652827.
Wolff, S. Drummond. "Come Down, O Love Divine." SAB, tpt, kybd. MSM 50-5500.

Sunday 21 / Proper 16 / August 21–August 27

Year A

Isaiah 51:1-6	*The enduring foundation of God's salvation*
Psalm 138	*O Lord, your love endures forever*
Romans 12:1-8	*One body in Christ, with gifts that differ*
Matthew 16:13-20	*The profession of Peter's faith*

Semicontinuous first reading/psalm

Exodus 1:8—2:10	*Pharaoh's daughter takes Moses as her son*
Psalm 124	*We have escaped like a bird from the snare of the fowler*

Bortniansky, Dmitri/ed. Peter Tkach. "We Thank Thee, Lord." SATB. KJO 6513.
Burkhardt, Michael. "Built on the Rock." SATB, cong, hb, tpt, org. MSM 60-9014 (full score). (G)
Christiansen, F. Melius. "Built on the Rock." SSAATTBB. AFP 0800645081. (G)
Duruflé, Maurice. "Tu es Petrus." SATB. DUR. (G)
Ellingboe, Bradley. "You Are Peter!" SATB. MSF MF-2109. (G)
Hewitt-Jones, Tony. "Thou Art Peter." *Anthems from Addington*, vol. 10. SATB, org. RSCM. (G)
Hillert, Richard. "The Lord Is My Light and My Salvation." U, B-flat or C inst. GIA G-4951.
Mendelssohn, Felix. "On God Alone My Hope I Build." *Chantry Choirbook*. SATB. AFP 0800657772. (G)
Morales, Cristóbal de. "Tu es Petrus." SAB. AMC AE168. (G)
Palestrina, Giovanni Pierluigi da. "Tu es Petrus." SSAATB. GSCH 5603. (G)
Pote, Allen. "Many Gifts, One Spirit." SATB (SSA, SAB also available). Coronet 392-41388. (S)
Schalk, Carl. "Christ Is Made the Sure Foundation." SATB, concertato. MSM 60-9003. (G)
Scott, K. Lee. "King of Glory, King of Peace." *Rejoice Now My Spirit*. MH, kybd. AFP 0800651081. ML, kybd. AFP 080065109X.
Wolff, S. Drummond. "Built on the Rock." SATB, br qrt. CPH 97-5446. (G)

Year B

Joshua 24:1-2a, 14-18	*Joshua calls all Israel to serve the Lord*
Psalm 34:15-22	*The eyes of the Lord are upon the righteous*
Ephesians 6:10-20	*Put on the armor of God*
John 6:56-69	*The bread of eternal life*

Semicontinuous first reading/psalm

1 Kings 8:[1, 6, 10-11] 22-30, 41-43	*Solomon's prayer at the temple dedication*
Psalm 84	*How dear to me is your dwelling, O Lord*

Bach, Johann Sebastian. "Jesu, Joy—My Joy Forever." *Bach for All Seasons*. SATB, kybd. AFP 080065854X. §.
Britten, Benjamin. "Jubilate Deo." SATB, org. OXF 3515776. (F)
Busarow, Donald. "Eternal Ruler of the Ceaseless Round." SATB, opt br, opt cong. CPH 98-3078. (S)
Ellingboe, Bradley. "For the Beauty of the Earth." SATB, pno. KJO 9010.
Fleming, Larry L. "Give Me Jesus." SATB. AFP 0800645278. (G)
Haydn, Franz Joseph/arr. Robert Scholz. *God of Life*. SATB, kybd, opt full orch. AFP 0800655990.
How, Martin. "Day by Day." U or 2-3 pt, org. GIA G-4178.
Howells, Herbert. "My Eyes for Beauty Pine." U, opt SATB, org. OXF A14.
Peter, Johann F. "Adorn Yourself, My Soul." SATB, org. HIN HMC-1123.

Proulx, Richard. "Strengthen for Service." *The Augsburg Choirbook*. SATB. AFP 0800656784. (S)
Rutter, John. "For the Beauty of the Earth." 2 pt, pno. HIN HMC-469.
White, David Ashley. "Christians, We Have Met to Worship." SATB, kybd. SEL 410-621.

Year C

Isaiah 58:9b-14	*Do not trample the sabbath, but feed the hungry*
Psalm 103:1-8	*The Lord crowns you with mercy and lovingkindness*
Hebrews 12:18-29	*You have come to the city of the living God and to Jesus*
Luke 13:10-17	*Jesus heals a crippled woman on the sabbath and is condemned*

Semicontinuous first reading/psalm

Jeremiah 1:4-10	*Jeremiah is called to be a prophet*
Psalm 71:1-6	*From my mother's womb you have been my strength*

Bach, Johann Sebastian. "Nun lob, mein Seel." *Gottlob! nun geht das Jahr zu Ende*. Cantata 28. SATB, kybd or orch. BRE 4528.
Beethoven, Ludwig van/ed. K. Lee Scott. "The Heavens Sing Praises." *Sing Forth God's Praise*. MH, kybd. AFP 0800675266. ML, kybd. AFP 080067538X.
Burleigh, Harry T. "Nobody Knows the Trouble I've Seen." *The Spirituals of Harry T. Burleigh*. L, kybd. WAR EL 03150. H, kybd. WAR EL 03150. (G)
Christiansen, F. Melius. "Psalm 50/Offer unto God." SATB. AFP 0800657578. *The Augsburg Choirbook*. AFP 0800656784.
Dowland, John. "He That Is Down Need Fear No Fall." *Oxford Easy Anthem Book*. SATB. OXF 3533219.
Gabrieli, Giovanni. "O Bless the Lord." SATB dbl choir. GIA G-3657. (P)
Handel, George Frideric. "But Who May Abide." *Messiah*. A solo, kybd. §
Ippolitof-Ivanov, Mikhail. "Bless the Lord, O My Soul." GSCH 1100. (P)
Mendelssohn, Felix. "For the Lord Will Lead." *To God Will I Sing*. MH, kybd. AFP 0800674332. ML, kybd. AFP 0800674340.
Moore, Philip. "He That Is Down Need Fear No Fall." SATB, org. Randall M. Egan.
Pachelbel, Johann. "Canon of Praise." 3 pt, kybd. HOP MW1226.
Thompson, Randall. "Alleluia." SATB. ECS 1786.

Sunday 22 / Proper 17 / August 28–September 3

Year A

Jeremiah 15:15-21	*God fortifies the prophet against opposition*
Psalm 26:1-8	*Your love is before my eyes; I have walked faithfully with you*
Romans 12:9-21	*Live in harmony*
Matthew 16:21-28	*The passion prediction and rebuke to Peter*

Semicontinuous first reading/psalm

Exodus 3:1-15	*From the blazing bush God calls Moses*
Psalm 105:1-6, 23-26, 45c	*Make known the deeds of the* LORD *among the peoples. Hallelujah!*

Ashdown, Franklin D. "Jesus, the Very Thought of Thee." SATB, org, opt C inst. AFP 0800657500.
Bender, Mark. "O Lord, I Love the Habitation of Your House." 2 pt. CPH 98-2859. (P)
Bouman, Paul. "Take Up Your Cross, the Savior Said." SATB. SEL 420-617. (G)
Buxtehude, Dietrich. "In God, My Faithful God." *Second Morning Star Choir Book*. U, org. CPH 97-4702.
Handel, George Frideric. "Lord, I Trust Thee." *The New Church Anthem Book*. SATB, org. OXF 0-19-353109-7.
Leavitt, John. "Come, Follow Me." SAB, ob, kybd. GIA G-3028. (G)
Lindley, Simon. "O God, My Heart Is Ready." SS or SA, org. ECS 162.
Parry, Charles Hubert H. "Dear Lord and Father." SATB, org. NOV 29 0247.
Pearce, Thomas. "Son of God, Eternal Savior." SAB, tpt, kybd. CPH 98-2818.
Scott, K. Lee. "So Art Thou to Me." SATB, kybd. AFP 0800674308.

Year B

Deuteronomy 4:1-2, 6-9	*God's law: a sign of a great nation*
Psalm 15	LORD, *who may dwell in your tabernacle?*
James 1:17-27	*Be doers of the word, not hearers only*
Mark 7:1-8, 14-15, 21-23	*Authentic religion*

Semicontinuous first reading/psalm

Song of Solomon 2:8-13	*Song of two lovers*
Psalm 45:1-2, 6-9	*God has anointed you with the oil of gladness*

Bisbee, B. Wayne. "Teach Me Your Way, O Lord." 2 pt mxd, kybd. AFP 080065479X. (F, P)
Carter, Andrew. "God Be in My Head." SATB, org. OXF E159.
Fleming, Larry L. "His Voice." SATB div. AFP 0800656504.
Halloran, Jack. "Witness." SSAATTBB. GEN JG2010.
Harwood, Basil. "I Am the Living Bread." SATB, org. OXF A75.
Moore, Don Andrew. "O Holy Spirit." *The New Anthem Book*, vol. 1. U, kybd. Kevin Mayhew 086209488.
Rachmaninoff, Sergei. "To Thee We Sing." *The Liturgy of St. John Chrysostom*. SATB, S solo. GAL 1.3170.
Scott, K. Lee. "So Art Thou to Me." *Rejoice Now My Spirit*. ML, kybd. AFP 080065109X. MH, kybd. AFP 0800651081.
Telemann, Georg Philipp/ed. Susan Palo Cherwien. "Make Me Pure, O Sacred Spirit." *To God Will I Sing*. MH, kybd. AFP 0800674332. ML, kybd. AFP 0800674340. (G)

Year C

Proverbs 25:6-7	*Do not put yourself forward*
or Sirach 10:12-18	*Judgment upon the proud*
Psalm 112	*The righteous are merciful and full of compassion*
Hebrews 13:1-8, 15-16	*God is with us: let acts of mutual love continue*
Luke 14:1, 7-14	*An image of God's reign: invite the poor, crippled to your banquet*

Semicontinuous first reading/psalm

Jeremiah 2:4-13	*The people of Israel forsake the LORD*
Psalm 81:1, 10-16	*I feed you with the finest wheat and satisfy you with honey from the rock*

Bach, Johann Sebastian. "He Who Would Be Called." *Wer sich selbst erhört.* Cantata 47. S, org, clo. § (G)

———. "Who Himself Exalteth." *Wer sich selbst erhört.* Cantata 47. SATB, kybd or orch. § (G)

Busarow, Donald. "Come Down, O Love Divine." SAB, org. CPH 98-2335.

Fedak, Alfred V. "This Touch of Love." Solo. MSM 40-830.

Hancock, Gerre/arr. Paul Bouman. "O God of Mercy." *To God Will I Sing.* MH, kybd, ob or C inst. AFP 0800674332. ML, kybd, ob or C inst. AFP 0800674340.

Roberts, William Bradley. "In All These You Welcomed Me." U, org, opt ob. AFP 6000001207.

Schalk, Carl. "Here, O My Lord, I See Thee." SATB, inst, kybd. CPH 98-2493.

Vaughan Williams, Ralph. "He That Is Down Need Fear No Fall." SATB, fl or ob. OXF 42.492.

White, David Ashley. "O Bread of Life from Heaven." 2 pt mxd, org. AFP 0800650913. *The Augsburg Choirbook.* AFP 0800656784.

Sunday 23 / Proper 18 / September 4–September 10

Year A

Ezekiel 33:7-11	*The prophet's responsibility to warn the people*
Psalm 119:33-40	*I desire the path of your commandments*
Romans 13:8-14	*Live honorably as in the day*
Matthew 18:15-20	*Reconciliation in the community of faith*

Semicontinuous first reading/psalm

Exodus 12:1-14	*The passover of the Lord*
Psalm 149	*Sing the praise of the Lord in the congregation of the faithful.*

Attwood, Thomas. "Teach Me, O Lord." SATB, kybd. GIA G-3045. (P)
Bach, Johann Sebastian. "Sing Praise to Christ." SATB, org. CPH 98-1377. *With High Delight.* CPH 97-5047.
Bisbee, B. Wayne. "Teach Me Your Way, O Lord." 2 pt mxd, kybd. AFP 080065479X. (P)
Friedell, Harold. "Draw Us in the Spirit's Tether." SATB. CLP CGMR02472. (G)
Handel, George Frideric. "Keep Me Faithfully in Thy Paths." 2 pt mxd, org. GIA G-2355. (P)
Holst, Gustav. "Turn Back O Man." SATB, kybd. GAL S&B 2152. (F, S)
Hurd, David. "Teach Me, O Lord." SATB, org, cong. GIA G-2715. (P)
Marcello, Benedetto/arr. Dale Grotenhuis. "Teach Me Now, O Lord." 2 pt, kybd. MSM 50-9418. (P)
Nystedt, Knut. "Teach Me, O Lord." U or 2 pt, pno, perc, ad lib. MSM 50-9400. (P)
Roff, Joseph. "Put Ye on the Lord Jesus." SATB, opt kybd. Columbo 2356. (S)
Scott, K. Lee. "Teach Me, My God and King." SATB, org. AFP 0800659732. (P)

Year B

Isaiah 35:4-7a	*Like streams in the desert, God comes with healing*
Psalm 146	*I will praise the Lord as long as I live*
James 2:1-10 [11-13] 14-17	*Faith without works is dead*
Mark 7:24-37	*Christ healing a little girl and a deaf man*

Semicontinuous first reading/psalm

Proverbs 22:1-2, 8-9, 22-23	*Sayings concerning a good name and generosity*
Psalm 125	*Those who trust in the Lord stand fast forever*

Brahms, Johannes. "Let Grief Not Overwhelm You." *Chantry Choirbook.* SATB. AFP 0800657772. § (F, G)
Diemer, Emma Lou. "Praise Ye the Lord." SATB, 2 pnos. FLA 5021. (P)
Ferguson, John. "God Is Here." SATB, org, br. HOP DFW 214.
Fleming, Larry L. "Humble Service." SATB. AFP 0800646223. (S, G)
Haugen, Marty. "Healer of Our Every Ill." 2 pt, C inst, pno. GIA G3478. (G)
Purcell, Henry. "Rejoice in the Lord Always." *A Purcell Anthology.* SATB, str, cont. OXF 0193533510.
Rorem, Ned. "Praise the Lord, O My Soul/Psalm 146." SATB div, org. B&H OCTB6105. (P)
Scott, K. Lee. "Giver of Every Perfect Gift." SATB, opt cong, opt C inst, org. CPH 98-3466.
———. "Gracious Spirit, Dwell with Me." 2 pt mxd, org. AFP 0800646134. *The Augsburg Choirbook.* AFP 0800656784.
Thompson, Randall. "Alleluia." SATB. ECS 1786.
Zimmermann, Heinz Werner. "Those Who Trust in the Lord." SATB. CPH 98-2178. (P)

Year C

Deuteronomy 30:15-20	*Walk in the way of life and hold fast to God*
Psalm 1	*Their delight is in the law of the Lord*
Philemon 1-21	*Paul says: Receive Onesimus as a coworker*
Luke 14:25-33	*Jesus says: Disciples, give up your possessions and carry the cross*

Semicontinuous first reading/psalm

Jeremiah 18:1-11	*Like a potter, the Lord will reshape Israel*
Psalm 139:1-6, 13-18	*You have searched me out and known me*

Bouman, Paul. "Take Up Your Cross, the Savior Said." SATB. SEL 420-617. (G)
Hayes, Mark. "Day by Day." SATB, pno. AFP 0800658345.
Helgen, John. "Spirit of God, Descend." SATB, pno. AFP 0800676378. (F)
Loosemore, Henry. "O Lord, Increase Our Faith." *New Church Anthem Book*. SATB. OXF 0193531097.
Pelz, Walter L. "Show Me Thy Ways." SATB, gtr, ob or fl. AFP 0800645421. *The Augsburg Choirbook*. AFP 0800656784.
Schütz, Heinrich/arr. George Lynn. "Psalm 1." SATB, org. MC 352-00143. (P)
Stanford, Charles Villiers. "O for a Closer Walk with God." *Anthems for Choirs 1*. SATB, org. OXF 353214X.
Thompson, Randall. "The Best of Rooms." SATB. ECS 2672.
Wesley, Samuel Sebastian. "Lead Me, Lord." SATB, org, S solo. HWG GCMR 3183. §

Sunday 24 / Proper 19 / September 11–September 17

Year A

Genesis 50:15-21	Joseph reconciles with his brothers
Psalm 103:[1-7] 8-13	The Lord is full of compassion and mercy
Romans 14:1-12	Accepting diversity in the community of faith
Matthew 18:21-35	A parable of forgiveness in the community of faith

Semicontinuous first reading/psalm

Exodus 14:19-31	Israel's deliverance at the Red Sea
Psalm 114	Tremble, O earth, at the presence of the Lord
or Exodus 15:16-11, 20-21	I will sing to the Lord who has triumphed gloriously

Duruflé, Maurice. "Ubi caritas." SATB. PRE 312-41253. (G)
Ehret, Walter. "O My Soul, Bless God the Father." SATB, pno or org. FLA A-680. (P)
Henderson, Ruth Watson. "Bless the Lord, O My Soul." U, kybd. HIN HMC-1171. (P)
Marshall, Jane. "Bless the Lord, My Soul." SATB, org. AFP 0800647343. (P)
Mendelssohn, Felix. "Not unto Him." *St. Paul*. SATB, kybd. GSCH 321
Oldroyd, George. "Prayer to Jesus." SATB. OXF 43 P 037.
Organ, Anne Krentz. "Love One Another." SATB. AFP 0800659643. (G)
Parker, Alice. "Pues si vivimos/While We Are Living." SATB, pno. HAL 08596533. (S)
Peter, Johann F. "Praise the Lord, O My Soul." SATB, kybd. B&H 5891. (P)
Schalk, Carl. "Where Charity and Love Prevail." 2 pt trbl, ob, org. CPH 98-2701. (G)
Schütz, Heinrich. "No Man Liveth to Himself." SSATB. Summy 4696. (S)

Year B

Isaiah 50:4-9a	The servant is vindicated by God
Psalm 116:1-9	I will walk in the presence of the Lord
James 3:1-12	Dangers of the unbridled tongue
Mark 8:27-38	Peter's confession of faith

Semicontinuous first reading/psalm

Proverbs 1:20-33	Wisdom's rebuke to the foolish
Psalm 19	The statutes of the Lord are just and rejoice the heart
or Wis. of Solomon 7:26—8:1	God loves nothing so much as the person who lives with wisdom.

Bouman, Paul. "O God of Mercy." *To God Will I Sing*. MH, kybd. AFP 0800674332. ML, kybd. AFP 0800674340. (P)
Burkhardt, Michael. "Lift High the Cross." SATB, cong, br, timp, opt hb, org. MSM 60-6001. (G)
Busarow, Donald. "Lift High the Cross." 2 pt mxd or SATB, org, opt cong, opt tpt. AFP 0800645898. (G)
Hassler, Hans Leo. "Agnus Dei." SATB. SHW A1482.
Hobby, Robert A. "Take My Life, That I May Be." SATB, fl, org. MSM 50-8820.
Jennings, Carolyn. "The Kingdom of God." SATB, org. AMSI 439.
Mendelssohn, Felix. "On God Alone My Hope I Build." *Chantry Choirbook*. SATB, kybd. AFP 0800657772.
Schalk, Carl. "Lift High the Cross." SATB. CPH 98-2468. Opt br score. CPH 97-5548. (G)

Schubert, Franz. "O Jesus, Crucified for Man/Begrabt dem Leib in seinen Gruft." SATB, org. National Music Publishers CH-10. (G)

Sedio, Mark. "Once He Came in Blessing." 2 pt mxd, org, fl. AFP. 080065241X. (G)

Thompson, R. Paul. "Come, Follow Me." SATB, cong, kybd, opt fl. HIN HMC-1391. (G)

Year C

Exodus 32:7-14	*Moses begs the Lord to turn from anger against the Hebrews*
Psalm 51:1-10	*Have mercy on me, O God, according to your lovingkindness*
1 Timothy 1:12-17	*Christ Jesus came for sinners*
Luke 15:1-10	*Looking for the lost sheep, silver coin: Jesus eating with sinners*

Semicontinuous first reading/psalm

Jeremiah 4:11-12, 22-28	*Judgment is spoken against Jerusalem*
Psalm 14	*The Lord looks down from heaven upon us all*

Bertalot, John. "Amazing Grace." SATB, org. AFP 0800649141. *The Augsburg Choirbook.* AFP 0800656784. (G)

Bouman, Paul. "Create in Me a Clean Heart, O God." SA, org. CPH 98-114. (P)

Brahms, Johannes. "Create in Me, O God." SATBB. GSCH 50297770. § (P)

Christiansen, Paul J. "Create in Me a Clean Heart." SATB. AFP 0800645847. (P)

Decastre, Richard. "Richard de Castre's Prayer to Jesus." SATB, org. GSCH 50300580.

Farlee, Robert Buckley. "Holy God." SATB, org, opt cong. AFP 0800675207.

Kallman, Daniel. "Amazing Grace." SATB, opt solo, pno. MSM 50-9073. (G)

Kosche, Kenneth T. "Come, Thou Fount of Every Blessing." SATB. MSM 50-9830. (G)

Wold, Wayne L. "Rejoice! I Found the Lost." U or 2 pt, kybd. AFP 0800653548. (G)

Sunday 25 / Proper 20 / September 18–September 24

Year A

Jonah 3:10—4:11	*God's concern for the city of Nineveh*
Psalm 145:1-8	*The Lord is slow to anger and of great kindness*
Philippians 1:21-30	*Standing firm in the gospel*
Matthew 20:1-16	*The parable of the vineyard workers*

Semicontinuous first reading/psalm

Exodus 16:2-15	*Manna and quails feed the Israelites in the wilderness*
Psalm 105:1-6, 37-45	*Make known the deeds of the Lord among the peoples. Hallelujah!*

Bach, Johann Sebastian. "Bist du bei mir." *Sing Solo Sacred.* Low vocal solo. OXF 0193457857. High vocal solo. OXF 0193457849.
———. "Salvation unto Us Has Come." *Bach for All Seasons.* SATB. AFP 080065854X.
Carter, Andrew. "Thou Art the Vine." SATB, kybd. MSM 50-8504.
Croft, William. "O Give Thanks unto the Lord." SAB, org. CPH 98-1788.
Diemer, Emma Lou. "I Will Extol You." SATB, org. AFP 0800649222. (P)
Distler, Hugo. "Salvation unto Us Has Come." *Chantry Choirbook.* SATB. AFP0800657772.
Ellingboe, Bradley. "There's a Wideness in God's Mercy." SATB, kybd. AFP 0800676548. (F)
Hallock, Peter. "I Will Exalt You." SATB. GIA G-2186. (P)
Morales, Cristóbal de. "Simile est regnum." *Third Chester Book of Motets.* SATB. CHE JWX CH55104.
Nelson, Ronald A. "Whoever Would Be Great among You." SAB, kybd or gtr. AFP 0800645804. *Augsburg Choirbook.* AFP 0800656784. (G)
Pachelbel, Johann. "On God and Not on Human Trust." SATB. CPH 98-1006.
Sateren, Leland. "O Lord, Thou Art My God and King." SATB, org. AFP 6000108966.
Smith, Byron J. "Worthy to Be Praised." SATB, pno. LAW 52654. (P)
Wienhorst, Richard. "Let Your Manner of Life." SATB. SEL 98-2451. (S)

Year B

Jeremiah 11:18-20	*The prophet led like a lamb to slaughter*
or Wis. of Sol. 1:16—2:1, 12-22	*The righteous shall live*
Psalm 54	*God is my helper; it is the Lord who sustains my life*
James 3:13—4:3, 7-8a	*The wisdom from above*
Mark 9:30-37	*Prediction of the passion*

Semicontinuous first reading/psalm

Proverbs 31:10-31	*Poem celebrating the capable wife*
Psalm 1	*Their delight is in the law of the Lord*

Byrd, William/arr. Austin Lovelace. "Lord, Make Me to Know Thy Ways." SATB. CPH 98-2935.
Ferguson, John. "Be Thou My Vision." SATB, org. AFP 0800657934. (S)
Fleming, Larry L. "Humble Service." SATB. AFP 0800646223. (G)
Franck, Melchior/ed. Carl Schalk. "Come, O Blessed of My Father." SATB. CPH 98-3220.
Nelson, Ronald A. "Whoever Would Be Great among You." SAB, kybd or gtr. AFP 0800645804. *Augsburg Choirbook.* AFP 0800656784. (G)
Roberts, William Bradley. "In All These You Welcomed Me." U, org, opt ob or other C or Bb inst. AFP 6000001207. (G)
Rutter, John. "Open Thou Mine Eyes." SATB. HIN HMC-497.

Scholz, Robert. "Children of the Heavenly Father." U, kybd. AFP 0800647620. (G)
Sjolund, Paul. "Children of the Heavenly Father." *The Augsburg Choirbook*. SATB, kybd. AFP 0800656784. (G)
Tavener, John. "The Lamb." SATB. CHE 55570. (F, G)
Telemann, Georg Philipp. "Make Me Pure, O Sacred Spirit." *To God Will I Sing*. MH, kybd. AFP 0800674332. ML, kybd. AFP 0800674340.
Wienhorst, Richard. "Lord, Whose Love in Humble Service." SATB, kybd. MSM 50-9059. (G)

Year C

Amos 8:4-7	*Warnings to those who trample on the needy and poor*
Psalm 113	*The Lord lifts up the poor from the ashes*
1 Timothy 2:1-7	*One God, one mediator—Christ Jesus—who gave himself for all people*
Luke 16:1-13	*A shrewd manager: faithful in little, faithful in much; serving God/wealth*

Semicontinuous first reading/psalm

Jeremiah 8:18—9:1	*The Lord laments over Judah*
Psalm 79:1-9	*Deliver us and forgive us our sins, for your name's sake*

Bach, Johann Sebastian. "Jesus, My Sweet Pleasure/Jesu, meine Freude." *Bach for All Seasons*. SATB, opt kybd. AFP 080065854X. § (G)
Dawson, William. "Ain'a That Good News." SATB. KJO T103A.
Ferguson, John. "Be Thou My Vision." SATB, org. AFP 0800657934.
Handel, George Frideric. "Laudate pueri Dominum." SSATB, S solo, org, str, 2 ob. NOV 07-0467.
Mozart, Wolfgang Amadeus. "Laudate pueri." SATB, kybd. AMC AE 455.
Rutter, John. "Thy Perfect Love." SATB, org. OXF 42.392.
Scott, K. Lee. "Gracious Spirit, Dwell with Me." 2 pt mxd, org. AFP. 0800646134. *The Augsburg Choirbook*. AFP 0800656784.
Willcock, Christopher. "Give Us a Pure Heart." SATB, org. OCP 4529.
Zimmermann, Heinz Werner. "Praise the Lord." *Five Hymns*. SATB, org. CPH 97-5131.

Sunday 26 / Proper 21 / September 25–October 1

Year A

Ezekiel 18:1-4, 25-32	*The fairness of God's way*
Psalm 25:1-9	*Remember, O Lord, your compassion and love*
Philippians 2:1-13	*Christ humbled to the point of death on a cross*
Matthew 21:23-32	*A parable of doing God's will*

Semicontinuous first reading/psalm

Exodus 17:1-7	*Water from the rock in the wilderness*
Psalm 78:1-4, 12-16	*We will recount to generations to come the power of the Lord*

Anerio, Felice/ed. Walter Ehret. "Christ Became Obedient for Us unto Death." SATB. GIA G-1967. (S)
Bach, Johann Sebastian. "O Thou Sweetest Source of Gladness." SATB, cont. CPH 98-2327.
Bairstow, Edward C. "Jesus, the Very Thought of Thee." SATB. OXF 43.003.
Bruckner, Anton. "Christus factus est." SATB. CFP 6316.
Busarow, Donald. "Lord Keep Us Steadfast in Your Word." 2 pt trbl, fl, org. CPH 98-2602.
Farlee, Robert Buckley. "O Blessed Spring." SATB, ob, opt cong. AFP 0800654242.
Farrant, Richard. "Call to Remembrance." SATB. ECS 1639. § (P)
Ferguson, John. "Jesus Loves Me." SATB, pno. AFP 0800676483.
Gardner, John. "Fight the Good Fight." SATB, pno, opt orch. OXF 42.874.
Handel, George Frideric. "Let Thy Hand Be Strengthened." *Coronation Anthems.* SAATB, kybd. OXF.
Marshall, Jane. "Create in Me, O God." U, kybd. CGA 750.
Pelz, Walter L. "Show Me Thy Ways." SATB, gtr, ob or fl. AFP 0800645421. (P)
Praetorius, Michael/ed. Francis J. Guentner. "Christ Jesus Lord, Thy Name Adored." *Three German Motets.* SATB. AFP 0800649656. (S)
Rachmaninoff, Sergei. "To Thee O Lord." *Anthems for Choirs 1.* SATB. OXF. (P)
Tye, Christopher. "Lord, for Thy Tender Mercy's Sake." *The New Church Anthem Book.* SATB. OXF 0193531097. (P)
Vaughan Williams, Ralph. "At the Name of Jesus." SATB. OXF 40-100. (S)
Willan, Healey. "Christ Hath Humbled Himself." *We Praise Thee.* SA, org. CPH 97-7564. (S)

Year B

Numbers 11:4-6, 10-16, 24-29	*The Lord's spirit comes upon seventy elders*
Psalm 19:7-14	*The commandment of the Lord gives light to the eyes*
James 5:13-20	*Prayer and anointing in the community*
Mark 9:38-50	*Warnings to those who obstruct faith*

Semicontinuous first reading/psalm

Esther 7:1-6, 9-10; 9:20-22	*Esther's intercession spares the lives of her people*
Psalm 124	*We have escaped like a bird from the snare of the fowler*

Ashdown, Franklin D. "Jesus, the Very Thought of Thee." SATB, org, opt C inst. AFP 0800657500. (P)
Hassler, Hans Leo. "Cantate Domino." *Chantry Choirbook.* SATB. AFP 0800657772.
Haydn, Franz Joseph. "The Heavens Are Telling." *Creation.* SATB, kybd. §.
Kallman, Daniel. "Lord, Whose Love in Humble Service." SATB, pno. KJO J17. (S)
Kosche, Kenneth T. "If You Will Trust the Lord to Guide You." SAB, fl, kybd. MSM 50-9108.
Mathias, William H. "Rejoice in the Lord." SATB, org. OXF A359.
Parry, Charles Hubert H. "Dear Lord and Father." SATB, org. NOV 29 0247.

Proulx, Richard. "Strengthen for Service." SATB. *The Augsburg Choirbook*. AFP 0800656784.
Rutter, John. "Open Thou Mine Eyes." SATB. HIN HMC-497. (P)
Schütz, Heinrich. "We Offer Our Thanks and Praise." *Chantry Choirbook*. SATB. AFP 0806642772.
Viner, Alan. "In Heavenly Love Abiding." *The New Anthem Book,* vol. 1. U, kybd. Kevin Mayhew 0-86209-488.

Year C

Amos 6:1a, 4-7	*Warnings to those who are comfortable or wealthy*
Psalm 146	*The Lord gives justice to those who are oppressed*
1 Timothy 6:6-19	*Eager to be rich or eager to pursue richness of God's justice?*
Luke 16:19-31	*Story of poor Lazarus and the wealthy man*

Semicontinuous first reading/psalm

Jeremiah 32:1-3a, 6-15	*Jeremiah buys a field*
Psalm 91:1-6, 14-16	*You are my refuge and my stronghold, my God in whom I put my trust*

Bach, Johann Sebastian. "Lord, Thee I Love with All My Heart." *Bach for All Seasons*. SATB. AFP 080065854X. (S)
Fauré, Gabriel. "In paradisum." *Requiem*. SATB, org. HIN HMB 147A.
Ferguson, John. "Lord, in All Love." SATB, org. AFP 0800656490.
Gardner, John. "Fight the Good Fight." SATB, pno, opt orch. OXF 42.874.
Gibbons, Orlando. "Almighty and Everlasting God." OXF TCM 36.
Hairston, Jester. "Poor Man Laz'rus." SATB. BRN 187567. (G)
Helgen, John. "That Priceless Grace." SATB, pno. AFP 0800658590. 2 pt mxd, pno. *Augsburg Easy Choirbook*. AFP 0800676025.
Marshall, Jane. "A Joyful Psalm." SATB, org. GIA G-3082.
Rorem, Ned. "Praise the Lord, O My Soul/Psalm 146." SATB div, org. B&H OCTB6105. (P)
Rutter, John. "Praise the Lord, O My Soul." SSATB, org, opt 2 tpt, 2 tbn, timp. OXF A330. (P)
Schalk, Carl. "All Things Are Yours, My God." SATB, opt cong, org. MSM 50-9032.
———. "Lord of Feasting and of Hunger." SATB, org. CPH 98-3863.
Schütz, Heinrich/ed. Richard T. Gore. "Father Abraham, Have Mercy on Me." SSAT, T or B solo, 2 vln, cont. CPH 97-9348. (G)

Sunday 27 / Proper 22 / October 2–October 8

Year A

Isaiah 5:1-7	*The song of the vineyard*
Psalm 80:7-15	*Look down from heaven, O God; behold and tend this vine*
Philippians 3:4b-14	*Nothing surpasses the value of knowing Christ*
Matthew 21:33-46	*The parable of the vineyard owner's son*

Semicontinuous first reading/psalm

Exodus 20:1-4, 7-9, 12-20	*The commandments given at Sinai*
Psalm 19	*The statutes of the LORD are just and rejoice the heart*

Ashdown, Franklin D. "Jesus, the Very Thought of Thee." SATB, org, opt C inst. AFP 0800657500.
Handel, George Frideric. "Glory and Worship." *Coronation Anthems*. SAATBB, org. OXF.
———. "Since by Man Came Death." *Messiah*. SATB, kybd. §
Hillert, Richard. "Amid the World's Bleak Wilderness." SATB, org. AFP 0800645995.
Isaac, Heinrich. "O Bread of Life From Heaven/O esca viatorum." *Chantry Choirbook*. SATB. AFP 0800657772.
Lenel, Ludwig. "When I Survey the Wondrous Cross." U, kybd. Randall M. Egan.
Mathias, William H. "Hear, O Thou Shepherd of Israel." SATB, org. OXF A339.
Mendelssohn, Felix. "On God Alone My Hope I Build." *Chantry Choirbook*. SATB. AFP 0800657772. (S)
Moore, Undine Smith. "I Will Trust in the Lord." SATB div. AFP 0800646614.
Neswick, Bruce. "O Taste and See." SATB, kybd. AFP 0800654714.
Scott, K. Lee. "A Vineyard Grows." SATB, opt inst, org. MSM 50-9010. (F, P, G)
Vaughan Williams, Ralph. "The Song of the Tree of Life." *Anthems for Choirs*, vol. 2. U or 2 pt. OXF 0193532409.

Year B

Genesis 2:18-24	*Created for relationship*
Psalm 8	*You adorn us with glory and honor*
Hebrews 1:1-4; 2:5-12	*God has spoken by a Son*
Mark 10:2-16	*Teaching on marriage*

Semicontinuous first reading/psalm

Job 1:1; 2:1-10	*Job's integrity in the face of suffering*
Psalm 26	*Your love is before my eyes; I have walked faithfully with you*

Busarow, Donald. "Our Father, by Whose Name." SAB, fl. CPH 98-2484. (F, G)
Cherwien, David. "Our Father, by Whose Name." SATB, fl. CPH 98-2980. (F, G)
Friedell, Harold. "Draw Us in the Spirit's Tether." SATB. HWG CGMR02472.
Gehring, Philip. "Taste and See." SATB. CPH 98-3585.
Handel, George Frideric/arr. Stephen Andrews. "I Will Praise Forever." U or 2 pt, kybd, fl. LOR 10/1443K.
Hayes, Mark. "Day by Day." SATB, pno. AFP 0800658345.
Hillert, Richard. "How Great Is Your Name." SATB or U, br qrt, timp. GIA G-3187. (P)
Hopson, Hal H. "The Gift of Love." U, opt desc, kybd. HOP CF148.
Rutter, John. "For the Beauty of the Earth." SATB, kybd. HIN HMC550.
Scott, K. Lee. "Open My Eyes." SATB, kybd. CPH 98-2904.

Year C

Habakkuk 1:1-4; 2:1-4	*Wicked surround the righteous; wait for the Lord*
Psalm 37:1-9	*Commit your way to the Lord; put your trust in the Lord*
2 Timothy 1:1-14	*Guard the treasure entrusted to you: faith and love in Christ*
Luke 17:5-10	*Faith the size of a mustard seed*

Semicontinuous first reading/psalm

Lamentations 1:1-6	*Jerusalem is empty and destroyed*
Lamentations 3:19-26	*Great is your faithfulness, O Lord*
or Psalm 137	*Remember the day of Jerusalem, O Lord*

Berger, Jean. "The Eyes of All Wait upon Thee." SATB. AFP 0800645596. *The Augsburg Choirbook*. AFP 0800656784.
Busarow, Donald. "A Nobler Life." SATB or SAB. MSM 50-303.1.
Dengler, Lee. "Look at the Birds of the Air." SATB, kybd, opt fl. CPH 98-3125.
Gibbons, Orlando. "O Lord, Increase My Faith." *A First Motet Book*. CPH 97-4845. (G)
Jennings, Carolyn. "Climb to the Top of the Highest Mountain." SATB or trbl choir, kybd. KJO C8118. (F)
Mueller, Carl F. "An Anthem of Faith." SATB, kybd. HL 12029.
Near, Gerald. "They That Wait upon the Lord." SATB, org. AUR AE17.
Neswick, Bruce. "O Taste and See." SATB, kybd. AFP 0800654714.
Schalk, Carl. "Our Soul Waits for the Lord." SATB. CPH 98-3252.
Vaughan Williams, Ralph. "O Taste and See." SATB, S solo. OXF 43-909.

Sunday 28 / Proper 23 / October 9–October 15

Year A

Isaiah 25:1-9	*The feast of victory*
Psalm 23	*You spread a table before me, and my cup is running over*
Philippians 4:1-9	*Rejoice in the Lord always*
Matthew 22:1-14	*The parable of the unwelcome guest at the wedding feast*

Semicontinuous first reading/psalm

| Exodus 32:1-14 | *The Israelites forge a golden calf* |
| Psalm 106:1-6, 19-23 | *Remember, O Lord, the favor you have for your people* |

Anonymous, sixteenth century/arr. John Redford. "Rejoice in the Lord Always." SATB. OXF 43.243. (S)
Bouman, Paul. "The Lord Is My Shepherd." U, kybd. CPH 98-2911. (P)
Ellingboe, Bradley. "Jesus, Good Shepherd." SATB, pno or hrp. AFP 0800658272. (P)
———. "The Lord's My Shepherd." SATB, opt pno. KJO 8956. (P)
How, Martin. "Psalm 23." U or bar solo, kybd, opt desc. B&H W.180. (P)
Jacob, Gordon. "Brother James's Air." SATB. OXF 94P316.
Mendelssohn, Felix. "I Praise Thee." *St. Paul*. SATB, B solo, kybd. GSCH 321.
Pelz, Walter L. "Psalm 23." SATB, fl, org. CPH 98-2676. (P)
Pote, Allen. "The Lord Is My Shepherd." SATB. CGA-551. (P)
Purcell, Henry. "Rejoice in the Lord Always." SATB, solo ATB, org. CPH 97-6344. Str, cont. CPH 97-4472. (S)
Rachmaninoff, Sergei. "Today Hath Salvation Come." *All Night Vigil. Songs of the Church*. SSAATTB. HWG GB 640. (F)
Rutter, John. "The Lord Is My Shepherd." *Requiem*. SATB, ob, org, opt orch. HIN MH-164. (P)
———. "The Peace of God." SATB, org. OXF E157. (S)
Schalk, Carl. "The God of Love My Shepherd Is." SATB, 2 vln, org. MSM 50-8812. (P)
Schütz, Heinrich. "O Lord, I Trust Your Shepherd Care." *Chantry Choirbook*. SATB, org. AFP 0806642772. (P)
———/arr. Nancy Grundahl. "Rejoice in God." SATB, kybd, fl, perc. AFP 0800676513. (S)
Thomson, Virgil. "My Shepherd Will Supply My Need." SATB. WB 2046. (P)
Willan, Healey. "Rejoice in the Lord Always." *We Praise Thee II*. SA, org. CPH 97-7610. (S)
Zimmermann, Heinz Werner. "Psalm 23." SATB, org, str bass. AFP 0800645383. *The Augsburg Choirbook*. AFP 0800656784. (P)

Year B

Amos 5:6-7, 10-15	*Turn from injustice to the poor, that you may live*
Psalm 90:12-17	*So teach us to number our days that we may apply our hearts to wisdom*
Hebrews 4:12-16	*Approach the throne of grace with boldness*
Mark 10:17-31	*Teaching on wealth and reward*

Semicontinuous first reading/psalm

| Job 23:1-9, 16-17 | *The Almighty hidden from Job's searching* |
| Psalm 22:1-15 | *My God, my God, why have you forsaken me?* |

Bouman, Paul. "Son of God, Eternal Savior." SATB, org, cong, tpt. CPH 98-2818. (G)
Buxtehude, Dietrich. "Everything You Do." *Chantry Choirbook*. SATB, org. AFP 0806642772.
Ferguson, John. "A Song of Thanksgiving/Psalm 90." SATB, org. AFP 0800653858. *The Augsburg Choirbook*. AFP 0800656784.

———. "Be Thou My Vision." SATB, org. AFP 0800657934. (G)
Hobby, Robert A. "Take My Life, That I May Be." SATB, fl, org. MSM 50-8820. (G)
Powell, Robert J. "The Lord Will Guide Our Ways." SATB, kybd. AFP 0800654757.
Proulx, Richard. "Weary of All Trumpeting." SAB, org, opt cong, opt br qnt. AFP 0800657632.
Purcell, Henry. "Thy Word Is a Lantern." *A Purcell Anthology*. SATB, org. OXF 0193533510.
Rutter, John. "All Things Bright and Beautiful." 2 pt, kybd. HIN HMC-663.
Schalk, Carl. "Christ Goes Before." SATB, org, opt cong, br, timp. MSM 50-9049.
Scott, K. Lee. "Nobody Knows the Trouble I See." SATB. OXF 0193864584. (S)
Sedio, Mark. "Take My Life, That I May Be/Toma, oh Dios, mi voluntad." SATB, pno, fl, opt gtr. AFP 0800658299. (G)
Traditional/arr. Robert Shaw, Alice Parker. "My God Is a Rock." SATB. LAW 51107.
Vaughan Williams, Ralph. "He That Is Down Need Fear No Fall." S or B solo, SATB, fl or ob. OXF E138.
———. "Lord, Thou Hast Been Our Refuge." SATB div, org. EV C80592.

Year C

2 Kings 5:1-3, 7-15c   *Naaman washes in the Jordan and is cleansed*
Psalm 111   *I will give thanks to the Lord with my whole heart*
2 Timothy 2:8-15   *If we die with Christ, we will live with Christ*
Luke 17:11-19   *One leper made clean by Jesus gives thanks to God*

Semicontinuous first reading/psalm

Jeremiah 29:1, 4-7   *Israel builds houses and plants gardens in Babylon*
Psalm 66:1-12   *God holds our souls in life*

Bach, Johann Sebastian. "Now Thank We All Our God." *Bach for All Seasons*. SATB, kybd, opt inst. AFP 080065854X. §
Buxtehude, Dietrich. "Everything You Do." *Chantry Choirbook*. SATB, org. AFP 0806642772. §
Distler, Hugo. "Praise to the Lord." *Chantry Choirbook*. SATB. AFP 0806642772. §
Farlee, Robert Buckley. "O Blessed Spring." SATB, ob, opt cong. AFP 0800654242. *The Augsburg Choirbook*. AFP 0800656784.
Ferguson, John. "A Song of Thanksgiving/Psalm 90." SATB, org. AFP 0800653858. *The Augsburg Choirbook*. AFP 0800656784.
Handel, George Frideric. "Since by Man Came Death." *Messiah*. SATB, kybd. §
Helgen, John. "Praise the Living God Who Sings." SATB, org. AFP 0800674618.
Hopson, Hal H. "Sing Praise to the Lord." SATB, org, opt cong, children's choir. AFP 0800676009.
Jennings, Carolyn. "Praise, My Soul, the God of Heaven." SATB, org, opt cong. AFP 0800656725.
Mendelssohn, Felix. "Above All Praise and All Majesty." SATB, org. *Oxford Book of Easy Anthems* OXF 3533219. *The New Church Anthem Book* OXF 3531097.
Scarlatti, Alessandro. "Exsultate Deo." SATB, kybd. PRE MC71.

Sunday 29 / Proper 24 / October 16–October 22

Year A

Isaiah 45:1-7	*An earthly ruler as the instrument of God's will*
Psalm 96:1-9 [10-13]	*Ascribe to the Lord honor and power*
1 Thessalonians 1:1-10	*Thanksgiving for the church at Thessalonica*
Matthew 22:15-22	*A teaching on giving to the emperor and to God*

Semicontinuous first reading/psalm

Exodus 33:12-23	*The glory of God revealed to Moses*
Psalm 99	*Proclaim the greatness of the Lord our God*

Bender, Jan. "O God, O Lord of Heaven and Earth." *The Augsburg Choirbook*. SATB, org, opt 2 tpt, cong. AFP 0800656784.
Busarow, Donald. "Eternal Ruler of the Ceaseless Round." SATB, opt cong, opt br, org. CPH 98-3078.
Clausen, René. "All That Hath Life and Breath, Praise Ye the Lord." SATB. MF 223. (P)
Hassler, Hans Leo/ed. Norman Greyson. "Cantate Domino." SATB. BRN ES18. (P)
Hillert, Richard. "God Whose Giving Knows No Ending." SATB, cong, ob, opt str, org. AG HSA 105. (G)
Hurd, David. "Psalm 96: Sing to the Lord a New Song." 2 pt, kybd, opt cong. AFP 0800649818. (P).
Jennings, Carolyn. "God's Word Is Our Great Heritage." SATB, br or kybd. AFP 0800646495.
Neswick, Bruce. "O Taste and See." SATB, S solo. AFP 0800654714.
Purcell, Henry. "O Sing unto the Lord." SATB, soloists, opt str, org. NOV 29 0146 03. (P)
Schalk, Carl. "Evening and Morning." SATB, org, br, opt cong. CPH 98-3314.
Schein, Johann H. "Sing to the Lord." SAB, org. Randall M.Egan. (P)
Scott, K. Lee. "Sing Aloud to God Our Strength." SATB, org or br qrt. AFP 0800659716. (P)
Sweelinck, Jan Pieterszoon. "Sing to the Lord, New Songs Be Raising." *Chantry Choirbook*. SATB. AFP 0806642772. (P)
Tye, Christopher. "Give Alms of Thy Goods." *Anthems for Choirs 1*. SATB. OXF. (G)

Year B

Isaiah 53:4-12	*The suffering servant*
Psalm 91:9-16	*You have made the Lord your refuge, and the Most High your habitation*
Hebrews 5:1-10	*Through suffering Christ becomes the source of salvation*
Mark 10:35-45	*Warnings to ambitious disciples*

Semicontinuous first reading/psalm

Job 38:1-7 [34-41]	*Challenge to Job from God, the creator*
Psalm 104:1-9, 24, 35c	*O Lord, how manifold are your works! In wisdom you have made them all*

Bach, Johann Sebastian. "Domine Deus." *Mass in G Major*. SA, org, opt vlns. B&HOCTB6552.
Busarow, Donald. "The Church of Christ in Every Age." SATB, opt cong, opt 2 tpt, 2 tbn. AFP 080065210X.
Elgar, Edward. "Ave verum corpus." *The New Church Anthem Book*. SATB, org. OXF 531079.
Fleming, Larry L. "Humble Service." SATB. AFP 0800646223. (G)
Gehring, Philip. "The Cup of Blessing." SATB. CPH 98-3585.
Handel, George Frideric. "Surely He Hath Borne Our Griefs." SATB. *Messiah*. § (F)
Mendelssohn, Felix. "For God Commanded Angels to Watch Over You." *Elijah*. SATB, kybd or orch. § (P)

Nelson, Ronald A. "Whoever Would Be Great among You." SAB, kybd or gtr. AFP 0800645804. *The Augsburg Choirbook*. AFP 0800656784. (G)

Nystedt, Knut. "Teach Me, O Lord." U or 2 pt, pno, perc, ad lib. MSM 50-9400.

Proulx, Richard. "Weary of All Trumpeting." SAB, org, opt cong and br qnt. AFP 0800657632. *The Augsburg Choirbook*. AFP 0800656784.

Victoria, Tomás Luis de. "Vere langoures nostros." SATB. AMC AE 359.

Year C

Genesis 32:22-31	*Jacob's struggle with the angel: I'll not let go until you bless me*
Psalm 121	*My help comes from the Lord, the maker of heaven and earth.*
2 Timothy 3:14—4:5	*In the presence of Christ the judge, proclaim the message*
Luke 18:1-8	*The widow begs for justice; God grants justice to those who cry to him*

Semicontinuous first reading/psalm

Jeremiah 31:27-34	*The Lord promises a new covenant*
Psalm 119:97-104	*Your words are sweeter than honey to my mouth*

Attwood, Thomas. "Teach Me, O Lord." SATB, org. ECS 169.

Berger, Jean. "I to the Hills Lift Up Mine Eyes." SATB. AFP 0800645448. *The Augsburg Choirbook*. AFP 0800656784. (P)

Ferguson, John. "By Gracious Powers." SATB, fl, org cong. AFP 0800675495.

Handel, George Frideric. "Let Justice and Judgment." *Four Coronation Anthems*. SAATB, kybd. OXF 3352591.

Mendelssohn, Felix. "He, Watching Over Israel." *Elijah*. SATB, kybd or orch. ECS 779. § (P)

———. "Lift Thine Eyes." *Elijah*. SSA, kybd or orch. § (P)

Mueller, Carl F. "The New Covenant." SATB, kybd. CFI 6645.

Scott, K. Lee. "Come, O Thou Traveler Unknown." *Rejoice Now My Spirit*. MH, kybd. AFP 0800651081. ML, kybd. AFP 080065109X.

Sunday 30 / Proper 25 / October 23–October 29

Year A

Leviticus 19:1-2, 15-18 — *Holiness revealed in acts of justice*
Psalm 1 — *Their delight is in the law of the Lord*
1 Thessalonians 2:1-8 — *The apostle's tender care for the Thessalonians*
Matthew 22:34-46 — *Two great commandments: love for God and neighbor*

Semicontinuous first reading/psalm

Deuteronomy 34:1-12 — *The death of Moses*
Psalm 90:1-6, 13-17 — *Show your servants your works, and your splendor to their children*

Bach, Johann Sebastian. "Lord, Thee I Love with All My Heart." *Bach for All Seasons*. SATB. AFP 080065854X. (F, G)
Christiansen, F. Melius. "My God, How Wonderful Thou Art." SATB. AFP 6000106106.
Goudimel, Claude. "Psalm 1." SATB. PRE 312-41098. (P)
Hillert, Richard. "Happy Are Those Who Delight." U, org, fl, opt str. GIA G-4259. (P)
Hogan, David. "O Jesus, King Most Wonderful." SA or TB, org. ECS 4886.
Proulx, Richard. "How Blest Are They." U, org, fl. AFP 080064543X. (P)
Schulz-Widmar, Russell. "God Remembers." SATB, kybd. AFP 0800657462.
Stanford, Charles Villiers. "O for a Closer Walk with God." *Anthems for Choirs 1*. SATB, org. OXF 353214X.
Vaughan Williams, Ralph. "The Call." U, kybd. MSM 50-9912.

Year B

Jeremiah 31:7-9 — *The Lord gathers the remnant of Israel*
Psalm 126 — *Those who sowed with tears will reap with songs of joy*
Hebrews 7:23-28 — *Christ the merciful high priest*
Mark 10:46-52 — *Christ healing the blind man Bartimaeus*

Semicontinuous first reading/psalm

Job 42:1-6, 10-17 — *Job's restoration*
Psalm 34:1-8 [19-22] — *Taste and see that the Lord is good*

Bach, Johann Sebastian. "God, the Lord Is Sun and Shield/Gott, der Herr, ist Sonn' und Schild." SATB. §.
Bertalot, John. "Amazing Grace." SATB, org. AFP 0800649141. *The Augsburg Choirbook*. AFP 0800656784. (G)
Campbell, Sidney. "Sing We Merrily Unto God Our Strength." SATB, org. NOV 29 0253.
Copland, Aaron. "Help Us, O Lord." SATB. B&H OCTB6018.
Haugen, Marty. "Healer of Our Every Ill." 2 pt, C inst, pno. GIA G3478. (G)
Hopson, Hal H. "Sing Aloud to God." SATB, org, opt tpt, 4 oct hb. AFP 0800674642.
Proulx, Richard. "Weary of All Trumpeting." SAB, org, opt cong and br qnt. AFP 0800657632. *The Augsburg Choirbook*. AFP 0800656784.
Reger, Max. "Our Lady's Vision." SATB. PET 6601.
Schalk, Carl. "I Saw a New Heaven and a New Earth." SATB. AFP 0800656644. *The Augsburg Choirbook*. AFP 0800656784.

Year C

Jeremiah 14:7-10, 19-22	*Jerusalem will be defeated*
or Sirach 35:12-17	*God is impartial in justice and hears the powerless*
Psalm 84:1-7	*Happy are the people whose strength is in you*
2 Timothy 4:6-8, 16-18	*The good fight of faith*
Luke 18:9-14	*A Pharisee and tax collector pray together*

Semicontinuous first reading/psalm

Joel 2:23-32	*The LORD promises to restore Israel*
Psalm 65	*Your paths overflow with plenty*

Brahms, Johannes. "How Lovely Is Thy Dwellingplace." *Chantry Choirbook*. SATB. AFP 0800657772. § (P)
Dowland, John. "He That Is Down Need Fear No Fall." *Oxford Easy Anthem Book*. SATB. OXF 3533219.
Fauré, Gabriel/ed. Hal H. Hopson. "Psalm 84/Cantique de Jean Racine." SATB, kybd. CFI CM 8042. § (P)
Gardner, John. "Fight the Good Fight." SATB, kybd. OXF 42.874. (S)
Handel, George Frideric. "Ev'ry Valley." *Messiah*. T solo, kybd. §
Marshall, Jane. "How Lovely Is Your Dwelling Place." SATB, org. AFP 0800657489. (P)
Moore, Philip. "He That Is Down Need Fear No Fall." SATB, org. Randall M. Egan.
Schütz, Heinrich. "The Pharisee and the Publican." SATB, org, T and B solos. GSCH 7473. (G)
White, David Ashley. "Come, Ye Sinners." 2 pt, kybd, ob or other C inst. AFP 0800653246.

Sunday 31 / Proper 26 / October 30–November 5

Year A

    Micah 3:5-12 — *Judgment upon corrupt rulers*
    Psalm 43 — *Send out your light and truth that they may lead me*
    1 Thessalonians 2:9-13 — *The apostle's teaching accepted as God's word*
    Matthew 23:1-12 — *All who humble themselves will be exalted*

Semicontinuous first reading/psalm

    Joshua 3:7-17 — *Israel crosses the Jordan into the land of promise*
    Psalm 107:1-7, 33-37 — *Give thanks to the Lord, all those whom the Lord has redeemed*

Bach, Johann Sebastian. "Bring Low Our Ancient Adam." *Bach for All Seasons.* SATB. AFP 080065854X.
———. "Lord Jesus Christ, Thou Prince of Peace." SATB, S solo, vln, cont. CPH 98-1955.
Fleming, Larry L. "Humble Service." SATB. AFP 0800646223. (G)
Handel, George Frideric. "Ev'ry Valley." *Messiah.* T solo, kybd. §
Harris, William H. "Come Down, O Love Divine." *The New Church Anthem Book.* OXF 0-19-353109-7.
Nelson, Ronald A. "Whoever Would Be Great among You." SAB, kybd or gtr. AFP 0800645804. *Augsburg Choirbook.* AFP 0800656784. (G)
Schütz, Heinrich/arr. Robert Buckley Farlee. "My Soul Exalts Your Name, O Lord." SATB, kybd. AFP 080067524X.
Wienhorst, Richard. "Lord, Whose Love in Humble Service." SATB, kybd. MSM 50-9059. (G)
Willan, Healey. "Oh, Send Out Thy Light." *Psalms for the People of God.* Cant, choir, cong, kybd. SMP 45/4037S. (P)

Year B

    Deuteronomy 6:1-9 — *The blessing of keeping the words of God*
    Psalm 119:1-8 — *Happy are they who seek the Lord with all their hearts*
    Hebrews 9:11-14 — *Redeemed through the blood of Christ*
    Mark 12:28-34 — *Two great commandments: loving God and neighbor*

Semicontinuous first reading/psalm

    Ruth 1:1-18 — *Ruth's dedication to her mother-in-law*
    Psalm 146 — *The Lord lifts up those who are bowed down*

Bach, Johann Sebastian. "Lord, Thee I Love with All My Heart." *Bach for All Seasons.* SATB. 080065854X.
Bisbee, B. Wayne. "Teach Me Your Way, O Lord." 2 pt mxd, kybd. AFP 080065479X.
Busarow, Donald. "Lord, Thee I Love with All My Heart." SATB or 2 pt mxd, opt cong, ob or tpt (cl), org. CPH 98-3429. (F, G)
Marcello, Benedetto/arr. Dale Grotenhuis. "Teach Me Now, O Lord." 2 pt, kybd. MSM 50-9418.
Scott, K. Lee. "The Call." *Sing a Song of Joy.* MH, kybd. AFP 0800647882. ML, kybd. AFP 0800652827.
Stanford, Charles Villiers. "Beati quorum via." SSATBB. B&H OCTB 5318.
White, David Ashley. "O Bread of Life from Heaven." 2 pt mxd, org. AFP 0800650913. *The Augsburg Choirbook.* AFP 0800656784.
Willan, Healey. "Behold the Tabernacle of God." SATB. CFI. CM 427.

Year C

Isaiah 1:10-18	*Learn to do good, seek justice, and rescue the oppressed*
Psalm 32:1-7	*All the faithful will make their prayers to you in time of trouble*
2 Thessalonians 1:1-4, 11-12	*Faith and love amid persecution and adversity*
Luke 19:1-10	*Zacchaeus climbs into a tree to see Jesus*

Semicontinuous first reading/psalm

Habakkuk 1:1-4; 2:1-4	*The righteous live by their faith*
Psalm 119:137-144	*Grant me understanding, that I may live*

Clausen, René. "Thank the Lord." SATB. SHW 1207596.
Distler, Hugo. "Salvation unto Us Has Come." *Chantry Choirbook*. SATB. AFP 0806642772.
Grundahl, Nancy. "The Best of Rooms." SATB, org. KJO 8899.
Near, Gerald. "The Best of Rooms." SATB. AUR AE7.
Nelson, Eric. "How Can I Keep from Singing?" SATB. AFP 0800675177.
Ratcliff, Cary. "Come to the Waters." SATB, kybd. KAL K-03.
Satie, Erik/Luigi Zaninelli. "Give Thanks to the Lord." SATB, pno or hp. WAL 3403.
Thompson, Randall. "The Best of Rooms." SATB. ECS 2672.
Vaughan Williams, Ralph. "A Choral Flourish." SATB, kybd. OXF 43-934.

Sunday 32 / Proper 27 / November 6–November 12

Year A

 Amos 5:18-24 *Let justice roll down like waters*
 or Wisdom of Solomon 6:12-16 *Wisdom makes herself known*
 Psalm 70 *You are my helper and my deliverer; O Lord, do not tarry*
 or Wisdom of Solomon 6:17-20 *The beginning of wisdom is the most sincere desire for instruction*
 1 Thessalonians 4:13-18 *The promise of the resurrection*
 Matthew 25:1-13 *The story of the wise and foolish bridesmaids*

Semicontinuous first reading/psalm

 Joshua 24:1-3a, 14-25 *Joshua calls Israel to serve the Lord*
 Psalm 78:1-7 *We will recount to generations to come the power of the Lord. (Ps. 78:4)*

Bach, Johann Sebastian. "Wake, Awake, for Night Is Flying." *Bach for All Seasons*. SATB. AFP 080065854X. (G)
Bender, Jan. "Lord, Lord, Open to Us." U, org. CPH 98-1833. (G)
Bouman, Paul. "Rejoice, Rejoice Believers." SATB, org. MSM 50-0004.
Christiansen, F. Melius. "Wake, Awake." SSAATTBB. AFP 0800645065. (G)
Darst, W. Glen. "Walk Humbly with Thy God." SATB, kybd. CFI CM 7422.
Ellingboe, Bradley. "Soul, adorn yourself with Gladness/Vengo a ti, Jesús amado." SATB. AFP 0800658477.
Handel, George Frideric. "Deck Thyself, My Soul, with Gladness." SATB, kybd. PRE 392-41707.
Hovhaness, Alan. "Make Haste." SATB. CFP 6288.
Johnson, Ralph M. "Be Thou a Smooth Way." SATB, pno. AFP 0800659325.
Martini, Giovanni Battista/ed. John Castellini. "Lord, My God, Assist Me Now." SATB, solos, str. CPH 97-6304. (P)
Mendelssohn, Felix. "Sleeper Wake." *Anthems for Choir 1*. SATB, org. OXF. (G)
Parry, Charles Hubert H. "O Day of Peace." SATB, org, opt br, timp. GIA G-2689.
Proulx, Richard. "Immortal, Invisible." SATB, org, tpt, opt cong. SEL 425-842.
Purcell, Henry. "Thou Knowest, Lord, the Secrets of Our Hearts." SATB, org. ECS 170. SA, kybd. OXF 44.236.
Schalk, Carl. "Thine the Amen, Thine the Praise." SATB. AFP 0800646126.
Tallis, Thomas/ed. R.R. Terry. "Audivi, media nocte." SSTB. OXF TCM2. (G)
Taverner, John/ed. Anthony G. Petti. "Audivi." SATB. CHE CH55103. (G)
Thomas, André. "Keep Your Lamps." SATB, conga drm. HIN HMC577. (G)
———. "When the Trumpet Sounds." SATB, pno, DB. MSF-261. (S)
White, Nicholas. "Steal Away." *The Augsburg Choirbook*. SATB. AFP 0800656784. (S)

Year B

 1 Kings 17:8-16 *God feeds Elijah and the widow at Zarephath*
 Psalm 146 *The Lord lifts up those who are bowed down*
 Hebrews 9:24-28 *The once for all sacrifice of Christ*
 Mark 12:38-44 *A widow's generosity reveals the hypocrisy of the scribes*

Semicontinuous first reading/psalm

 Ruth 3:1-5; 4:13-17 *Ruth wins the favor of Boaz*
 Psalm 127 *Children are a heritage from the Lord*

Ashdown, Franklin D. "Jesus, the Very Thought of Thee." SATB, org, opt C inst. AFP 0800657500.
Beethoven, Ludwig van/arr. Richard Proulx. "Give Thanks to God." SAB, kybd. AFP 0800655230. (G)

Christiansen, F. Melius. "Psalm 50/Offer unto God." SATB, div. AFP 08006 57578. *The Augsburg Choirbook*. AFP 0800656784.

Fauré, Gabriel. "Agnus Dei." *Requiem*. SATB, kybd or orch. § (S)

Fleming, Larry L. "Lord of the Dance." SATB. AFP 0800655354.

Hayes, Mark. "Day by Day." SATB, pno. AFP 0800658345. (F)

Rutter, John. "O Be Joyful in the Lord." SATB, org. OXF A346.

Schalk, Carl. "Lord, It Belongs Not to My Care." SATB, org. AFP 0800645901.

Sedio, Mark. "Take My Life, That I May Be/Toma, oh Dios, mi voluntad." SATB, pno, fl, opt gtr. AFP. 0800658299. (G)

Svedlund, Karl-Erik/ed. Bruce Bengtson. "There'll Be Something In Heaven." SATB. AFP 0800657616.

Victoria, Tomás Luis de. "Jesu, dulcis memoria/Jesus, the Very Thought Is Sweet." SATB. BRN ES48.

White, Nicholas. "Take My Life and Let It Be Consecrated." SATB, kybd, ob. HIN HMC 1336. (G)

Year C

Job 19:23-27a	*I know that my Redeemer lives and I shall see God*
Psalm 17:1-9	*Keep me as the apple of your eye; hide me under the shadow of your wings*
2 Thessalonians 2:1-5, 13-17	*The coming of the Lord Jesus*
Luke 20:27-38	*Jesus speaks of the resurrection; the God of the living*

Semicontinuous first reading/psalm

Haggai 1:15b—2:9	*The L*ORD *promises to restore Judah to prosperity*
Psalm 145:1-5, 17-21	*Great is the L*ORD *and greatly to be praised*
or Psalm 98	*In righteousness shall the L*ORD *judge the world*

Bach, Johann Christoph Friedrich. "In the Resurrection Glorious." *Chantry Choirbook*. SATB, org. AFP 0806642772.

Beck, Theodore. "I Know That My Reedemer Lives." SATB or SAB, 3 tpt, org, cong. MSM 60-4000. (F)

Behnke, John. "I Know That My Redeemer Lives." SAB, cong, opt inst. CPH 98-3197. (F)

Bunjes, Paul. "I Know That My Redeemer Lives." SATB, tpt, cong, org. CPH 98-2933. (F)

Dressler, Gallus. "I Am the Resurrection." *Chantry Choirbook* SATB. AFP 0806642772.

Gerike, Henry V. "Sing with All the Saints in Glory." SATB, org, hrn, opt cong. AFP 0800675835.

Handel, George Frideric. "I Know that My Redeemer Liveth." *Messiah*. S solo, kybd or orch. § (F)

———. "Since by Man Came Death." *Messiah*. SATB, kybd. §

Hopp, Roy H. "From the Apple in the Garden." SATB, org. AFP 0800674138.

Morley, Thomas. "Lamb of God." SATB. KJO 8948.

Schulz-Widmar, Russell. "Jerusalem, Jerusalem." 2 pt mxd, kybd. AFP 0800655214.

Schütz, Heinrich. "We Offer Our Thanks and Praise." *Chantry Choirbook*. SATB. AFP 0806642772.

Svedlund, Karl-Erik/ed. Bruce Bengtson. "There'll Be Something In Heaven." SATB. AFP 0800657616.

Tyler, Edward. "St. Teresa's Bookmark." SSATBB. AFP 0800658329.

Sunday 33 / Proper 28 / November 13–November 19

Year A

Zephaniah 1:7, 12-18	*The day of the* LORD
Psalm 90:1-8 [9-11] 12	*So teach us to number our days that we may apply our hearts to wisdom*
1 Thessalonians 5:1-11	*Be alert for the day of the Lord*
Matthew 25:14-30	*The story of the slaves entrusted with talents*

Semicontinuous first reading/psalm

Judges 4:1-7	*The judgeship of Deborah*
Psalm 123	*Our eyes look to you, O God, until you show us your mercy*

Attwood, Thomas. "Turn Thee Again, O Lord." *The Church Anthem Book*. SATB. OXF 0-19-353109-7.
Bairstow, Edward C. "Lord, Thou Hast Been Our Refuge." SATB div, org. NOV 14430. (P)
Ferguson, John. "A Song of Thanksgiving/Psalm 90." SATB, org. AFP 0800653858.
———. "O God, Our Help in Ages Past." SATB, cong, br, org. GIA G-3892.
Hillert, Richard. "Festival Canticle." U. CPH 98-2305.
Isaac, Heinrich. "O World, I Must Be Parting." SATB. GSCH 8425.
Manz, Paul. "E'en So, Lord Jesus, Quickly Come." SATB. MSM 50-0001. SSAA. MSM 50-0450. TTBB. MSM 50-0900.
Schalk, Carl. "O Lord, Thou Hast Been Our Dwelling Place." SATB. AFP 0800650441. (P)
Sedio, Mark. "Once He Came in Blessing." 2 pt mxd, org, fl. AFP 080065241X.
Stout, Alan. "The Great Day of the Lord." SATB, org. CFP 6883. (F)
Vaughan Williams, Ralph. "Lord, Thou Hast Been Our Refuge." SATB, div, org or orch. GSCH 9720. (P)
Walter, Johann. "Rise Up, Rise Up!" *Chantry Choirbook*. SATB. AFP 0800657772.

Year B

Daniel 12:1-3	*The deliverance of God's people at the end*
Psalm 16	*My heart is glad and my spirit rejoices; my body shall rest in hope*
Hebrews 10:11-14 [15-18] 19-25	*The way to God opened through Christ's death*
Mark 13:1-8	*The end and the coming of the Son*

Semicontinuous first reading/psalm

1 Samuel 1:4-20	*Hannah's prayers for a child answered*
1 Samuel 2:1-10	*My heart exults in the* LORD; *my strength is exalted in my God*

Bach, Johann Sebastian. "O Jesus Christ, My Life, My Light/O Jesu Christ, meins Lebens Licht." *Bach for All Seasons*. SATB. AFP 080065854X.
Crouch, Andraé/Jack Schrader. "Soon and Very Soon." SATB, pno. HOP CG952.
Duruflé, Maurice. "Tantum ergo." *Quatre Motets sur des thèmes Gregoriens, Op. 10*. SATB. DUR.
Fleming, Larry L. "Blessed Are They." SATB div, cong, opt inst or hb. MSM 50-8106.
Haan, Raymond H. "They Shall Shine as the Stars." SATB, org, opt hb. AFP 0800674014. (F)
Hurd, David. "Love Bade Me Welcome." SATB. SEL 418-610.
Mendelssohn, Felix. "He That Shall Endure." *Elijah*. SATB, kybd. GSCH 10713.
Schütz, Heinrich. "I Go My Way to Jesus Christ/So fahr ich hin zu Jesu Christ." SATB, cont. CV 20.379.
Sirett, Mark G. "Thou Shalt Know Him When He Comes." SSAA. AFP 0800675304. SATB. AFP 0800655206. *The Augsburg Choirbook*. AFP 0800656784.

Tyler, Edward. "St. Teresa's Bookmark." SSATBB. AFP 0800658329.
Willan, Healey. "Lo, in the Appointed Time." SATB. OXF 94.310.

Year C

Malachi 4:1-2a	*A day of blistering heat for the arrogant; a day of healing sun for the righteous*
Psalm 98	*In righteousness shall the Lord judge the world*
2 Thessalonians 3:6-13	*Do not be idle, but do what is right for the sake of Christ*
Luke 21:5-19	*Jesus speaks of wars, endurance, betrayal, and suffering for his sake*

Semicontinuous first reading/psalm

Isaiah 65:17-25	*God promises a new heaven and a new earth*
Isaiah 12	*In your midst is the Holy One of Israel*

Bach, Johann Sebastian. "Lord, Thee I Love with All My Heart." *Bach for All Seasons*. SATB. AFP 080065854X.
Bengtson, Bruce. "O Sing to the Lord a New Song." SATB, org. AFP 0800676270. (P)
Dupré, Marcel. "O salutaris." SATB, org. LED AL 15973.
Ellingboe, Bradley. "Soul, Adorn Yourself with Gladness/Vengo a ti, Jesús amado." SATB. AFP 0800658477.
Ferguson, John. "New Songs of Celebration Render." SATB, drm, S rec. HOP DFW215.
Handel, George Frideric. "Why Do the Nations So Furiously Rage?" *Messiah*. B solo, kybd or orch. § (G)
Manz, Paul. "E'en So, Lord Jesus, Quickly Come." SATB. MSM 50-0001. SSAA. MSM 50-0450. TTBB. MSM 50-0900.
Martinson, Joel. "Psalm 98." SATB, cong, tr, org. CPH 98-3225. (P)
Nicholson, Sydney. "O salutaris hostia." *Two Anthems of Communion*. SATB, S or A solo, org. RSCM 255.
Schütz, Heinrich. "Sing to the Lord." *Chantry Choirbook*. SATB. AFP 0806642772. (P)
Tye, Christopher. "Sing to the Lord." SATB, org. CFI CM8216. (P)
White, David Ashley. "When Peace, Like a River." SATB, kybd. AFP 0800654552.

Christ the King / Sunday 34 / Proper 29

Year A

> Ezekiel 34:11-16, 20-24 — *God will shepherd Israel*
> Psalm 95:1-7a — *We are the people of God's pasture and the sheep of God's hand*
> Ephesians 1:15-23 — *The reign of Christ*
> Matthew 25:31-46 — *The coming of the Son of Man; the separation of sheep and goats*

Semicontinuous first reading/psalm

> Ezekiel 34:11-16, 20-24 — *God will shepherd Israel*
> Psalm 100 — *We are God's people and the sheep of God's pasture*

Behnke, John. "The Head That Once Was Crowned." SATB, 2 oct, org, br. CPH 97-6120.
Busarow, Donald. "O Lord, You Are My God and King." SATB, org, tpt, 4 oct hb, opt cong. AFP 080065756X.
Copland, Aaron. "Sing Ye Praises to Our King." SATB. B&H 6021.
Ferguson, John. "The Head That Once Was Crowned with Thorns." SATB, org, br qrt. GIA G-3750.
Handel, George Frideric. "Glory and Worship." *Coronation Anthems.* SSATTBB, org. OXF. (S)
———. "He Shall Feed His Flock." *Messiah.* S solo, kybd. §
———. "My Heart Is Inditing." *Coronation Anthems.* SAATB, kybd. OXF. (P)
———. "The King Shall Rejoice." *Coronation Anthems.* SAATBB, opt soli, kybd, opt orch. DOV 40627. (S)
Josquin Desprez/ed. Leonard Van Camp. "God, the Lord, Now Reigneth." SATB. CPH 98-3213.
Mathias, William H. "Let All the World in Every Corner Sing." SATB, org. OXF A352.
Mendelssohn, Felix/arr. Olaf C. Christiansen. "The Lord Is a Mighty God." SATB, pno or org. KJO 9. (P)
Pelz, Walter L. "Crown Him with Many Crowns." SATB, cong, org, 3 tpt. AFP 080064803X.
Piccolo, Anthony. "O Come, Let Us Sing unto the Lord." SATB, org. OXF A329. (P)
Rachmaninoff, Sergei. "O Come Let Us Worship." *All Night Vigil. Songs of the Church.* SSAATBB. HWG GB 640.
Schalk, Carl. "Lo! He Comes with Clouds Descending." *Second Crown Choir Book.* 2 pt mxd, trbl inst, kybd. CPH 97-4882.
Thomas, André. "The Kingdom." SATB. HIN.
Tye, Christopher. "Give Almes of Thy Goods." *Anthems for Choirs 1.* SATB. OXF.
———. "O Jesus, King Most Wonderful." SATB. GIA A-3113.
Weber, Paul D. "I Will Sing the Story of Your Love." SATB or U, org, opt cong. AFP 0800657004.
Wolff, S. Drummond "Let All the World in Every Corner Sing." SATB, tpt. CPH 98-3011.

Year B

> Daniel 7:9-10, 13-14 — *The one coming with the clouds rules over all*
> Psalm 93 — *Ever since the world began, your throne has been established*
> Revelation 1:4b-8 — *Glory to the one who made us a kingdom*
> John 18:33-37 — *The kingdom of Christ*

Semicontinuous first reading/psalm

> 2 Samuel 23:1-7 — *The just ruler is like the light of morning*
> Psalm 132:1-12 [13-18] — *Let your faithful people sing with joy*

Boulanger, Lili. "Psalm XXIV/Psaume XXIV." SATB, T solo, org, pn or orch. DUR 10.481.
Busarow, Donald. "O Lord, You Are My God and King." SATB, org, tpt, 4 oct hb, opt cong. AFP 080065756X. (F, P, S, G)
Clausen, René. "At the Name of Jesus." SATB, org, br qrt. MF-2052.

Isom, Paul. "King of All Ages, Throned on High." *The New Oxford Easy Anthem Book*. SATB, org. OXF 0193533189. (F, P)
Manz, Paul. "E'en So, Lord Jesus, Quickly Come." SATB. MSM 50-0001. TTBB. MSM 50-0900.
Marshall, Jane. "How Lovely Is Your Dwelling Place." SATB, org. AFP 0800657489.
Rameau, Jean Philippe. "Come, Thou Long-Expected Jesus." *To God Will I Sing*. MH, kybd. AFP 0800674332. ML, kybd. AFP 0800674340.
Rameau, Jean Philippe/ed. Susan Palo Cherwien. "Come, Thou Long-Expected Jesus." *To God Will I Sing*. ML, kybd. AFP 0800674340. MH, kybd. AFP 0800674332.
Rorem, Ned. "Sing, My Soul, His Wondrous Love." SATB. PET 6386.
Sirett, Mark G. "Thou Shalt Know Him When He Comes." SSAA. AFP 0800675304. SATB. AFP 0800655206. *The Augsburg Choirbook*. AFP 0800656784.
Vaughan Williams, Ralph. "Antiphon." *Five Mystical Songs*. SATB, org or orch. ECS 1.5028.
———. "At the Name of Jesus." SATB, kybd. OXF 40.100.
Wolff, S. Drummond. "Christ Is the King." SATB, 2 tpts, org. CPH 98-3216. (G)
Wood, Dale. "Jubilate Deo/Psalm 100." SATB, org, 3 tpt, 2 hrn, perc. AFP 0800645774. *The Augsburg Choirbook*. AFP 0800656784.

Year C

Jeremiah 23:1-6	*Coming of the shepherd and righteous Branch who will execute justice*
Psalm 46	*I will be exalted among the nations*
Colossians 1:11-20	*Hymn to Christ, firstborn of all creation; peace through his blood*
Luke 23:33-43	*Jesus is crucified between two thieves: you will be with me in Paradise*

Semicontinuous first reading/psalm

Jeremiah 23:1-6	*Coming of the shepherd and righteous Branch who will execute justice*
Luke 1:68-79	*God has raised up for us a mighty savior*

Bainton, Edgar L. "And I Saw a New Heaven." SATB, org. NOV 29 0342 03.
Britten, Benjamin. "Festival Te Deum." SATB, org, S solo. B&H 15656.
Cherwien, David. "Beautiful Savior." SATB, org, cong, opt fl. AFP 0800675088.
Dawson, William. "Ain'a That Good News." SATB. KJO T103A.
Fauré, Gabriel. "In paradisum." *Requiem*. SATB, org. HIN HMB 147A. § (G)
Fedak, Alfred V. "Christus Paradox." SATB, org. GIA G 5463.
Ferguson, John. "Psalm 46/The Lord of Hosts." *Psalm Set*. SATB, org. AFP 0800656067. (P)
Finzi, Gerald. "Lo, the Full Final Sacrifice." SSAATTBB, org, STB solos. B&H 3036.
Handel, George Frideric. "The King Shall Rejoice." *Coronation Anthems*. SAATBB, opt soli, kybd, opt orch. DOV 40627. §
Schalk, Carl. "Thine the Amen, Thine the Praise." SATB, opt cong, org. AFP 0800646126. *The Augsburg Choirbook*. AFP 0800656784.
Stanford, Charles Villiers. "Glorious and Powerful God." *New Church Anthem Book*. SATB. OXF 0193531097.
Sweelinck, Jan Pieterszoon. "Sing to the Lord, New Songs Be Raising." *Chantry Choirbook*. SATB. AFP 0806642772.
Vaughan Williams, Ralph. "At the Name of Jesus." SATB, org. OXF 40.100.

The Name of Jesus, January 1

Years A, B, C

    Numbers 6:22-27   *The Aaronic blessing*
    Psalm 8   *How exalted is your name in all the world*
    Galatians 4:4-7   *We are no longer slaves, but children*
    or Philippians 2:5-11   *God takes on human form*
    Luke 2:15-21   *The child is circumcised and named Jesus*

Ashdown, Franklin D. "Jesus, the Very Thought of Thee." SATB, org, opt C inst. AFP 0800657500. (G)
Bach, Johann Sebastian. "From Heaven Above to Earth I Come." *Bach for All Seasons*. SATB, kybd. AFP 080065854X.
Frahm, Frederick. "How Sweet the Name of Jesus Sounds." SAB, kybd. AFP 0800676203.
Kallman, Daniel. "In Thee Is Gladness." SATB, org, opt U, c inst. MSM 50-9058.
Willcocks, David. "Once in Royal David's City." *100 Carols for Choirs*. SATB, org. OXF 0193532271. (S)

The Presentation of Our Lord, February 2

Years A, B, C

    Malachi 3:1-4   *My messenger is a refiner and a purifier*
    Psalm 84   *How dear to me is your dwelling, O Lord*
    or Psalm 24:7-10   *Lift up your heads, O gates and the King of glory shall come in*
    Hebrews 2:14-19   *Jesus shares human flesh and sufferings*
    Luke 2:22-40   *The child is brought to the temple*

Brahms, Johannes. "How Lovely Is Thy Dwellingplace." *Requiem. Chantry Choirbook*. SATB, org or orch. AFP 0800657772. § (P)
Clausen, René. "Nunc dimittis." SATB, org, pno or orch. AFP 0800676432. (G)
Ellingboe, Bradley. "Simeon's Song." SATB, pno. KJO 8988. (G)
Erickson, Richard. "I Want to Walk as a Child of the Light." SATB, org. AFP 0800658396.
Laster, James. "Sing of Mary, Pure and Lowly." SATB, org. AFP 0800674235.
Marshall, Jane. "How Lovely Is Your Dwelling Place." SATB, org. AFP 0800657489. (P)
Rutter, John. "For the Beauty of the Earth." SATB, pno. HIN HMC 550.
Sutcliffe, James. "What Child Is This?" SATB. KJO 8751.

Reformation Day, October 31

Years A, B, C

Jeremiah 31:31-34 — *I will write my law in their hearts, says the Lord*
Psalm 46 — *The Lord of hosts is with us; the God of Jacob is our stronghold*
Romans 3:19-28 — *Justified by God's grace as a gift*
John 8:31-36 — *Jesus says, Continue in my word and you will know the truth*

Bach, Johann Sebastian. "Ein feste Burg/A Mighty Fortress." *Bach for All Seasons.* SATB. AFP 080065854X.
———. "Salvation unto Us Has Come." *Bach for All Seasons.* SATB. AFP 080065854X. (S)
Bertalot, John. "Thy Word Is a Lantern." SATB, org, opt br qnt, perc. AFP 0800674251
Distler, Hugo. "Salvation unto Us Has Come." *Chantry Choirbook.* SATB. AFP 0800657772. § (S)
Ferguson, John. "A Mighty Fortress." SATB, org, tpt. AFP 0800676424. (P)
———. "The Church's One Foundation." SATB, org, br qrt, opt cong. AFP 0800658310.
Grieg, Edvard/arr. Oscar Overby. "God's Son Has Made Me Free." SATB. AFP 0800645561. *The Augsburg Choirbook.* AFP 0800656784. (G)
Hassler, Hans Leo. "A Mighty Fortress Is Our God/Ein feste Burg ist unser Gott." *Chantry Choirbook.* SATB. AFP 0800657772. (P)
Pote, Allen. "God Is Our Refuge." SATB, pno, 2 tpt. HOP A 583. (P)
Powell, Robert J. "The Church's One Foundation." SATB, cong. GIA G-2238.
Schalk, Carl. "The Church's One Foundation." SATB, 2 tr, org, opt cong. CPH 98-2344.
Scott, K. Lee. "Sing Aloud to God Our Strength." SATB, org or br qrt. AFP 0800659716.
Walter, Johann. "I Build on God's Strong Word." *Chantry Choirbook.* SATB. AFP 0800657772.
Weaver, John. "Psalm 46." SATB. MSM 50-8600.
Weber, Paul D. "I Will Sing the Story of Your Love." SATB or U, hop cong, kybd. AFP 0800657004.

All Saints Day, November 1

Year A

Revelation 7:9-17	*The multitudes of heaven worship the Lamb*
Psalm 34:1-10, 22	*Fear the Lord, you saints of the Lord*
1 John 3:1-3	*We are God's children*
Matthew 5:1-12	*Blessed are the poor in spirit*

Bach, Johann Christoph Friedrich. "In the Resurrection Glorious." *Chantry Choirbook*. SATB, org. AFP 0806642772
Ferguson, John. "Holy God, We Praise Your Name." SATB, cong, org, opt br. GIA G-3167.
Harris, William H. "Faire Is the Heaven." *Anthems for Choirs 4*. SATB dbl chorus. OXF 353018X.
Hobby, Robert A. "I Will Bless the Lord." U, cong, org. MSM 80-707. (P)
Johnson, David N. "Souls of the Righteous." *To God Will I Sing*. MH, kybd. AFP 0800674332. ML, kybd. AFP 0800674340.
Kreutz, Robert. "Jesu dulcis/The Taste of Goodness." SATB, cong. GIA G-2304. (P)
Mueller, Jonathan R. "For All the Saints." SATB, org, br qnt, timp, cong. MSM 60-8100.
Neswick, Bruce. "O Taste and See." SATB, kybd. AFP 0800654714. (P)
Rachmaninoff, Sergei. "Blessed Is the Man." *All Night Vigil. Songs of the Church*. SATB, div. HWG GCMR GB 640.
Schalk, Carl. "Blessed Are the Dead Who Die in the Lord." SATB. CPH 98-3214.
Schultz, Donna Gartman. "Shall We Gather at the River." SATB, pno. AFP 0800659376. (F)
Svedlund, Karl-Erik/arr. Bruce Bengtson. "There'll Be Something In Heaven." SATB. AFP 0800657616.
Vaughan Williams, Ralph. "O Taste and See." SATB, sop solo. OXF 43-909. (P)

Year B

Isaiah 25:6-9	*The banquet of the Lord*
or Wisdom of Solomon 3:1-9	*The righteous are with God*
Psalm 24	*They shall receive a blessing from the God of their salvation*
Revelation 21:1-6a	*A new heaven and a new earth*
John 11:32-44	*The raising of Lazarus*

Bainton, Edgar L. "And I Saw a New Heaven." SATB, org. NOV 29 0342. (S)
Parker, Alice/Robert Shaw. "Hark! I Hear the Harps Eternal." SATB. LAW 51331.
Pavlechko, Thomas. "The Souls of the Righteous." SATB, org. AFP 0800676610.
Schalk, Carl. "Blessed Are the Dead Who Die in the Lord." SATB. CPH 98-3214.
Schulz-Widmar, Russell. "Jerusalem, Jerusalem." 2 pt mxd, kybd. AFP 0800655214.
Vaughan Williams, Ralph. "The Souls of the Righteous." SATB or STB. OXF 353516-5.

Year C

Daniel 7:1-3, 15-18 — *The holy ones of the Most High shall receive the kingdom*
Psalm 149 — *Sing the praise of the Lord in the congregation of the faithful*
Ephesians 1:11-23 — *God raised Christ from the dead and made him head over all the church*
Luke 6:20-31 — *Jesus speaks blessings and woes*

Bach, Johann Christoph Friedrich. "In the Resurrection Glorious." *Chantry Choirbook*. SATB, org. AFP 0806642772.
Billings, William. "Universal Praise." SATB, kybd. CPH 98-3321.
Diemer, Emma Lou. "Blessed Are You." SATB, kybd. CFI CM8855. (G)
Fleming, Larry L. "Blessed Are They." SATB div, cong, org, opt hb. MSM 50-8106. (G)
Haas, David. "Blest Are They." SAB or U, cong, 2 C inst, kybd, gtr. GIA G-2958. (G)
Harris, William H. "Faire Is the Heaven." *Anthems for Choirs 4*. SATB dbl chorus. OXF 353018X.
Hobby, Robert A. "Offertory for All Saints Day." 2 pt, org. MSM 80-811.
Marchant, Stanley. "The Souls of the Righteous." *Oxford Easy Anthem Book*. SATB. OXF 3533219.
Nelson, Ronald A. "The Vision of John." SATB, org, hp or pno. KJO 8866.
Pavlechko, Thomas. "The Souls of the Righteous." SATB, org. AFP 0800676610.
Pinkham, Daniel. "Let All His Saints Rejoice." *Wellesley Hills Psalm Book*. U, org. ECS 4035.
Rachmaninoff, Sergei. "Blessed Is the Man." *All Night Vigil. Songs of the Church*. SATB, div. HWG GCMR. GB 640.
Schulz-Widmar, Russell. "Give Rest, O Christ." SATB. GIA G-3819.
Willan, Healey. "Te Deum laudamus/We Praise Thee, O God." SATB, org. CPH 98-1126.

Day of Thanksgiving

Year A

    Deuteronomy 8:7-18   *God will lead you into a land of flowing streams*
    Psalm 65   *You crown the year with your goodness, and your paths overflow with plenty*
    2 Corinthians 9:6-15   *God provides every blessing in abundance*
    Luke 17:11-19   *The healed leper returns to give thanks to Jesus*

Bach, Johann Sebastian. "Now Thank We All Our God." *Bach for All Seasons*. SATB, kybd. AFP 080065854X.
Biery, James. "Now Join We to Praise the Creator." SATB, org, opt inst, cong. AFP 0800675878.
Blake, Leonard. "Sing to the Lord of Harvest." SATB, org. RSCM 215.
Britten, Benjamin. "Jubilate Deo." SATB, org. OXF 3515776.
Goemanne, Noël. "Hymns of Thanks." SATB, org, opt tpts. GIA G-1543.
Greene, Maurice/ed. K. Lee Scott. "You Visit the Earth." *Sing Forth God's Praise*. MH, kybd. AFP 0800675266. ML, kybd. AFP 080067538X.
Head, Michael. "Make a Joyful Noise unto the Lord." High voice, pno, org. PRE 1014. Low voice, pno, org. PRE 1015.
Jennings, Carolyn. "We Praise You, O God." SATB, org, opt tpt. AFP 0800658485.
Kremser, Eduard. "Prayer of Thanksgiving." SATB, pno, org. GSCH 4345.
Pachelbel, Johann. "Now Thank We All Our God." SATB, cont. CPH 98-1944.
Prower, Anthony. "For the Fruits of All Creation." SATB, org, opt cong. AFP 0800649524.
Sweelinck, Jan Pieterszoon. "Sing to the Lord, New Songs Be Raising." *Chantry Choirbook*. SATB. AFP 0800657772.
Vaughan Williams, Ralph. "The Old Hundredth Psalm Tune." SATB, cong, org, opt br or orch. OXF 42-953
Willan, Healey. "Sing to the Lord of Harvest." SATB, org. CPH 98-2013.

Year B

    Joel 2:21-27   *The LORD promises to restore Jerusalem*
    Psalm 126   *The LORD has done great things for us, and we are glad indeed*
    1 Timothy 2:1-7   *Make supplications, prayers, intercessions, and thanksgivings*
    Matthew 6:25-33   *God will care for all our needs*

Aguiar, Ernani. "Psalm 150/Salmo 150." SATB or SSA. EAR.
Bach, Johann Sebastian. "Alles was Odem hat." *Singet dem Herrn*. SATB. MFS 259.
———. "Now Thank We All Our God." *Bach for All Seasons*. SATB, kybd. AFP 080065854X.
Ferguson, John. "A Song of Thanksgiving/Psalm 90." SATB, org. AFP 0800653858. *The Augsburg Choirbook*. AFP 0800656784.
How, Martin. "Praise, O Praise." *The New Church Anthem Book*. 2 pt, org. OXF 0193531097.
Jennings, Carolyn. "We Praise You, O God." SATB, org, opt tpt. AFP 0800658485.
Mozart, Wolfgang Amadeus. "Laudate Dominum." *Sing Solo Sacred*. SATB. OXF 0193457857.
Pachelbel, Johann. "Now Thank We All Our God/Nun danket alle Gott." SATB dbl choir or SATB and br. BAR 2873.
Palestrina, Giovanni Pierluigi da. "Exultate jubilate." SAATB. CHE 8794.
Rutter, John. "All Things Bright and Beautiful." 2 pt, kybd. HIN HMC-663.

Year C

Deuteronomy 26:1-11 — *The offering of the first fruits*
Psalm 100 — *Enter the gates of the Lord with thanksgiving*
Philippians 4:4-9 — *Do not worry about anything*
John 6:25-35 — *Jesus is the bread of life*

Bach, Johann Sebastian. "Now Thank We All Our God." *Bach for All Seasons*. SATB, kybd. AFP 080065854X.
Berger, Jean. "The Eyes of All Wait upon Thee." SATB. AFP 0800645596. *The Augsburg Choirbook*. AFP 0800656784.
Biery, James. "Now Join We to Praise the Creator." SATB, org, opt inst, cong. AFP 0800675878.
Ferguson, John. "A Song of Thanksgiving/Psalm 90." SATB, org. AFP 0800653858. *The Augsburg Choirbook*. AFP 0800656784.
Jennings, Carolyn. "We Praise You, O God." SATB, org, opt tpt. AFP 0800658485.
Pachelbel, Johann. "Now Thank We All Our God." SATB, cont. CPH 98-1944.
Proulx, Richard. "O God Beyond All Praising." SATB, kybd, opt br qnt, cong. GIA G-3190.
———. "The Eyes of All." U, org. AFP 0800656466.
———. "What Shall We Offer." 2 pt mxd, org. KJO 6294.
Schütz, Heinrich. "We Offer Our Thanks and Praise." *Chantry Choirbook*. SATB. AFP 0806642772.
Sweelinck, Jan Pieterszoon. "Sing to the Lord, New Songs Be Raising." *Chantry Choirbook*. SATB. AFP 0806642772.
Wolff, S. Drummond. "Praise and Thanksgiving." SATB. CPH 98-2514.
Wood, Dale. "Jubilate Deo/Psalm 100." SATB, org, perc, opt 3 tpt, 3 tbn. AFP 0800645774. U or SA, org, opt perc. AFP 0800645812. (P)

Index to the Revised Common Lectionary

During the season after Pentecost, Old Testament selections without an asterisk are thematically related to the gospel; the alternate selections, marked with an an asterisk (*), form a semi-continuous pattern of readings. Either series is designed to be read in its entirety.

GENESIS

1:1—2:4a	Holy Trinity		A
1:1—2:4a	Vigil of Easter		A, B, C
1:1-5	Baptism of the Lord		B
2:15-17; 3:1-7	1 Lent		A
2:18-24	S. btwn. Oct. 2 and 8	Pr. 22	B
3:8-15	S. btwn. June 5 and 11	Pr. 5	B
6:9-22; 7:24; 8:14-19	S. btwn. May 29 and June 4*	Pr. 4	A
7:1-5, 11-18; 8:6-18; 9:8-13	Vigil of Easter		A, B, C
9:8-17	1 Lent		B
11:1-9	Day of Pentecost		C
12:1-4a	2 Lent		A
12:1-9	S. btwn. June 5 and 11*	Pr. 5	A
15:1-6	S. btwn. Aug. 7 and 13	Pr. 14	C
15:1-12, 17-18	2 Lent		C
17:1-7, 15-16	2 Lent		B
18:1-10a	S. btwn. July 17 and 23	Pr. 11	C
18:1-15 [21:1-7]	S. btwn. June 12 and 18*	Pr. 6	A
18:20-32	S. btwn. July 24 and 30	Pr. 12	C
21:8-21	S. btwn. June 19 and 25*	Pr. 7	A
22:1-14	S. btwn. June 26 and July 2*	Pr. 8	A
22:1-18	Vigil of Easter		A, B, C
24:34-38, 42-49, 58-67	S. btwn. July 3 and 9*	Pr. 9	A
25:19-34	S. btwn. July 10 and 16*	Pr. 10	A
28:10-19a	S. btwn. July 17 and 23*	Pr. 11	A
29:15-28	S. btwn. July 24 and 30*	Pr. 12	A
32:22-31	S. btwn. July 31 and Aug. 6*	Pr. 13	A
32:22-31	S. btwn. Oct. 16 and 22	Pr. 24	C
37:1-4, 12-28	S. btwn. Aug. 7 and 13*	Pr. 14	A
45:1-15	S. btwn. Aug. 14 and 20*	Pr. 15	A
45:3-11, 15	7 Epiphany		C
50:15-21	S. btwn. Sept. 11 and 17	Pr. 19	A

EXODUS

1:8—2:10	S. btwn. Aug. 21 and 27*	Pr. 16	A
3:1-15	S. btwn. Aug. 28 and Sept. 3*	Pr. 17	A
12:1-14	S. btwn. Sept. 4 and 10*	Pr. 18	A
12:1-4 [5-10] 11-14	Maundy Thursday		A, B, C
14:10-31; 15:20-21	Vigil of Easter		A, B, C
14:19-31	S. btwn. Sept. 11 and 17*	Pr. 19	A
15:1b-11, 20-21	S. btwn. Sept. 11 and 17*	Pr. 19	A
15:1b-13, 17-18	Vigil of Easter		A, B, C
16:2-4, 9-15	S. btwn. July 31 and Aug. 6	Pr. 13	B
16:2-15	S. btwn. Sept. 18 and 24*	Pr. 20	A
17:1-7	3 Lent		A
17:1-7	S. btwn. Sept. 25 and Oct. 1*	Pr. 21	A
19:1-9	Vigil of Pentecost		A, B, C
19:2-8a	S. btwn. June 12 and 18	Pr. 6	A
20:1-4, 7-9, 12-20	S. btwn. Oct. 2 and 8*	Pr. 22	A
20:1-17	3 Lent		B
24:12-18	Transfiguration of the Lord		A
32:1-14	S. btwn. Oct. 9 and 15*	Pr. 23	A
32:7-14	S. btwn. Sept. 11 and 17	Pr. 19	C
33:12-23	S. btwn. Oct. 16 and 22*	Pr. 24	A
34:29-35	Transfiguration of the Lord		C

LEVITICUS
19:1-2, 9-18	7 Epiphany		A
19:1-2, 15-18	S. btwn. Oct. 23 and 29	Pr. 25	A

NUMBERS
11:4-6, 10-16, 24-29	S. btwn. Sept. 25 and Oct. 1	Pr. 21	B
11:24-30	Day of Pentecost		A
21:4-9	4 Lent		B
21:4b-9	Holy Cross		A, B, C

DEUTERONOMY
4:1-2, 6-9	S. btwn. Aug. 28 and Sept. 3	Pr. 17	B
5:12-15	S. btwn. May 29 and June 4	Pr. 4	B
6:1-9	S. btwn. Oct. 30 and Nov. 5	Pr. 26	B
8:7-18	Thanksgiving		A
11:18-21, 26-28	S. btwn. May 29 and June 4	Pr. 4	A
18:15-20	4 Epiphany		B
26:1-11	1 Lent		C
26:1-11	Thanksgiving		C
30:9-14	S. btwn. July 10 and 16	Pr. 10	C
30:15-20	6 Epiphany		A
30:15-20	S. btwn. Sept. 4 and 10	Pr. 18	C
31:19-30	Vigil of Easter		A, B, C
32:1-4, 7, 36a, 43a	Vigil of Easter		A, B, C
34:1-12	S. btwn. Oct. 23 and 29*	Pr. 25	A

JOSHUA
3:7-17	S. btwn. Oct. 30 and Nov. 5*	Pr. 26	A
5:9-12	4 Lent		C
24:1-2a, 14-18	S. btwn. Aug. 21 and 27	Pr. 16	B
24:1-3a, 14-25	S. btwn. Nov. 6 and 12*	Pr. 27	A

JUDGES
4:1-7	S. btwn. Nov. 13 and 19*	Pr. 28	A

RUTH
1:1-18	S. btwn. Oct. 30 and Nov. 5*	Pr. 26	B
3:1-5; 4:13-17	S. btwn. Nov. 6 and 12*	Pr. 27	B

1 SAMUEL
1:4-20	S. btwn. Nov. 13 and 19*	Pr. 28	B
2:1-10	S. btwn. Nov. 13 and 19*	Pr. 28	B
2:1-10	Visitation of Mary to Elizabeth		A, B, C
2:18-20, 26	1 Christmas		C
3:1-10 [11-20]	2 Epiphany		B
3:1-10 [11-20]	S. btwn. May 29 and June 4*	Pr. 4	B
8:4-11 [12-15] 16-20 [11:14-15]	S. btwn. June 5 and 11*	Pr. 5	B
15:34—16:13	S. btwn. June 12 and 18*	Pr. 6	B
16:1-13	4 Lent		A
17:[1a, 4-11, 19-23] 32-49	S. btwn. June 19 and 25*	Pr. 7	B
17:57—18:5, 10-16	S. btwn. June 19 and 25*	Pr. 7	B

2 SAMUEL
1:1, 17-27	S. btwn. June 26 and July 2*	Pr. 8	B
5:1-5, 9-10	S. btwn. July 3 and 9*	Pr. 9	B
6:1-5, 12b-19	S. btwn. July 10 and 16*	Pr. 10	B
7:1-11, 16	4 Advent		B
7:1-14a	S. btwn. July 17 and 23*	Pr. 11	B
11:1-15	S. btwn. July 24 and 30*	Pr. 12	B
11:26—12:10, 13-15	S. btwn. June 12 and 18	Pr. 6	C
11:26—12:13a	S. btwn. July 31 and Aug. 6*	Pr. 13	B

2 SAMUEL (continued)
18:5-9, 15, 31-33	S. btwn. Aug. 7 and 13*	Pr. 14	B
23:1-7	Christ the King*		B

1 KINGS
2:10-12; 3:3-14	S. btwn. Aug. 14 and 20*	Pr. 15	B
3:5-12	S. btwn. July 24 and 30	Pr. 12	A
8:[1, 6, 10-11] 22-30, 41-43	S. btwn. Aug. 21 and 27*	Pr. 16	B
8:22-23, 41-43	S. btwn. May 29 and June 4	Pr. 4	C
17:8-16	S. btwn. Nov. 6 and 12	Pr. 27	B
17:8-16 [17-24]	S. btwn. June 5 and 11*	Pr. 5	C
17:17-24	S. btwn. June 5 and 11	Pr. 5	C
18:20-21 [22-29] 30-39	S. btwn. May 29 and June 4*	Pr. 4	C
19:1-4 [5-7] 8-15a	S. btwn. June 19 and 25*	Pr. 7	C
19:4-8	S. btwn. Aug. 7 and 13	Pr. 14	B
19:9-18	S. btwn. Aug. 7 and 13	Pr. 14	A
19:15-16, 19-21	S. btwn. June 26 and July 2	Pr. 8	C
21:1-10 [11-14] 15-21a	S. btwn. June 12 and 18*	Pr. 6	C

2 KINGS
2:1-12	Transfiguration of the Lord		B
2:1-2, 6-14	S. btwn. June 26 and July 2*	Pr. 8	C
4:42-44	S. btwn. July 24 and 30	Pr. 12	B
5:1-3, 7-15c	S. btwn. Oct. 9 and 15	Pr. 23	C
5:1-14	6 Epiphany		B
5:1-14	S. btwn. July 3 and 9*	Pr. 9	C

NEHEMIAH
8:1-3, 5-6, 8-10	3 Epiphany		C

ESTHER
7:1-6, 9-10; 9:20-22	S. btwn. Sept. 25 and Oct. 1*	Pr. 21	B

JOB
1:1; 2:1-10	S. btwn. Oct. 2 and 8*	Pr. 22	B
14:1-14	Saturday in Holy Week		A, B, C
19:23-27a	S. btwn. Nov. 6 and 12	Pr. 27	C
23:1-9, 16-17	S. btwn. Oct. 9 and 15*	Pr. 23	B
38:1-7 [34-41]	S. btwn. Oct. 16 and 22*	Pr. 24	B
38:1-11	S. btwn. June 19 and 25	Pr. 7	B
42:1-6, 10-17	S. btwn. Oct. 23 and 29*	Pr. 25	B

PSALMS
1	6 Epiphany		C
1	7 Easter		B
1	S. btwn. Sept. 4 and 10	Pr. 18	C
1	S. btwn. Sept. 18 and 24*	Pr. 20	B
1	S. btwn. Oct. 23 and 29	Pr. 25	A
2	Transfiguration of the Lord		A
4	3 Easter		B
5:1-8	S. btwn. June 12 and 18*	Pr. 6	C
8	Holy Trinity		A, C
8	New Year's Day		A, B, C
8	S. btwn. Oct. 2 and 8	Pr. 22	B
9:9-20	S. btwn. June 19 and 25*	Pr. 7	B
13	S. btwn. June 26 and July 2*	Pr. 8	A
14	S. btwn. July 24 and 30*	Pr. 12	B
14	S. btwn. Sept. 11 and 17*	Pr. 19	C
15	4 Epiphany		A
15	S. btwn. Aug. 28 and Sept. 3	Pr. 17	B
15	S. btwn. July 17 and 23	Pr. 11	C

16	2 Easter		A
16	S. btwn. June 26 and July 2	Pr. 8	C
16	S. btwn. Nov. 13 and 19	Pr. 28	B
16	Vigil of Easter		A, B, C
17:1-7, 15	S. btwn. July 31 and Aug. 6*	Pr. 13	A
17:1-9	S. btwn. Nov. 6 and 12	Pr. 27	A
19	3 Epiphany		C
19	3 Lent		B
19	S. btwn. Oct. 2 and 8*	Pr. 22	A
19	S. btwn. Sept. 11 and 17*	Pr. 19	B
19	Vigil of Easter		A, B, C
19:7-14	S. btwn. Sept. 25 and Oct. 1	Pr. 21	B
20	S. btwn. June 12 and 18*	Pr. 6	B
22	Good Friday		A, B, C
22:1-15	S. btwn. Oct. 9 and 15*	Pr. 23	B
22:19-28	S. btwn. June 19 and 25	Pr. 7	C
22:23-31	2 Lent		B
22:25-31	5 Easter		B
23	4 Easter		A, B, C
23	4 Lent		A
23	S. btwn. July 17 and 23	Pr. 11	B
23	S. btwn. Oct. 9 and 15	Pr. 23	A
24	All Saints		B
24	S. btwn. July 10 and 16*	Pr. 10	B
24:7-10	Presentation of the Lord		A, B, C
25:1-9	S. btwn. Sept. 25 and Oct. 1	Pr. 21	A
25:1-10	1 Advent		C
25:1-10	1 Lent		B
25:1-10	S. btwn. July 10 and 16	Pr. 10	C
26	S. btwn. Oct. 2 and 8*	Pr. 22	B
26:1-8	S. btwn. Aug. 28 and Sept. 3	Pr. 17	A
27	2 Lent		C
27:1, 4-9	3 Epiphany		A
29	Baptism of the Lord		A, B, C
29	Holy Trinity		B
30	3 Easter		C
30	6 Epiphany		B
30	S. btwn. July 3 and 9*	Pr. 9	C
30	S. btwn. June 26 and July 2	Pr. 8	B
30	S. btwn. June 5 and 11	Pr. 5	C
31:1-4, 15-16	Saturday in Holy Week		A, B, C
31:1-5, 15-16	5 Easter		A
31:1-5, 19-24	S. btwn. May 29 and June 4	Pr. 4	A
31:9-16	Sunday of the Passion		A, B, C
32	1 Lent		A
32	4 Lent		C
32	S. btwn. June 12 and 18	Pr. 6	C
32:1-7	S. btwn. Oct. 30 and Nov. 5	Pr. 26	C
33:1-12	S. btwn. June 5 and 11*	Pr. 5	A
33:12-22	S. btwn. Aug. 7 and 13	Pr. 14	C
33:12-22	Vigil of Pentecost		A, B, C
34:1-8	S. btwn. Aug. 7 and 13	Pr. 14	B
34:1-8 [19-22]	S. btwn. Oct. 23 and 29*	Pr. 25	B
34:1-10, 22	All Saints		A
34:9-14	S. btwn. Aug. 14 and 20	Pr. 15	B
34:15-22	S. btwn. Aug. 21 and 27	Pr. 16	B
36:5-10	2 Epiphany		C
36:5-11	Monday in Holy Week		A, B, C
37:1-9	S. btwn. Oct. 2 and 8	Pr. 22	C
37:1-11, 39-40	7 Epiphany		C
40:1-11	2 Epiphany		A

PSALMS *(continued)*

40:5-10	Annunciation of the Lord		A, B, C
41	7 Epiphany		B
42 and 43	S. btwn. June 19 and 25*	Pr. 7	C
42 and 43	Vigil of Easter		A, B, C
43	S. btwn. Oct. 30 and Nov. 5	Pr. 26	A
43	Vigil of Easter		C
45	Annunciation of the Lord		A, B, C
45:1-2, 6-9	S. btwn. Aug. 28 and Sept. 3*	Pr. 17	B
45:10-15	Mary, Mother of the Lord		A, B, C
45:10-17	S. btwn. July 3 and 9*	Pr. 9	A
46	Christ the King	Pr. 29	C
46	Reformation Day		A, B, C
46	S. btwn. May 29 and June 4*	Pr. 4	A
46	Vigil of Easter		A, B, C
47	Ascension of the Lord		A, B, C
48	S. btwn. July 3 and 9*	Pr. 9	B
49:1-12	S. btwn. July 31 and Aug. 6	Pr. 13	C
50:1-6	Transfiguration of the Lord		B
50:1-8, 22-23	S. btwn. Aug. 7 and 13*	Pr. 14	C
50:7-15	S. btwn. June 5 and 11	Pr. 5	A
51:1-10	S. btwn. Sept. 11 and 17	Pr. 19	C
51:1-12	5 Lent		B
51:1-12	S. btwn. July 31 and Aug. 6*	Pr. 13	B
51:1-17	Ash Wednesday		A, B, C
52	S. btwn. July 17 and 23*	Pr. 11	C
54	S. btwn. Sept. 18 and 24	Pr. 20	B
62:5-12	3 Epiphany		B
63:1-8	3 Lent		C
65	S. btwn. Oct. 23 and 29*	Pr. 25	C
65	Thanksgiving		A
65:[1-8] 9-13	S. btwn. July 10 and 16	Pr. 10	A
66:1-9	S. btwn. July 3 and 9	Pr. 9	C
66:1-12	S. btwn. Oct. 9 and 15*	Pr. 23	C
66:8-20	6 Easter		A
67	6 Easter		C
67	S. btwn. Aug. 14 and 20	Pr. 15	A
68:1-10, 32-35	7 Easter		A
69:7-10 [11-15] 16-18	S. btwn. June 19 and 25	Pr. 7	A
70	S. btwn. Nov. 6 and 12	Pr. 27	A
70	Wednesday in Holy Week		A, B, C
71:1-6	4 Epiphany		C
71:1-6	S. btwn. Aug. 21 and 27*	Pr. 16	C
71:1-14	Tuesday in Holy Week		A, B, C
72:1-7, 10-14	Epiphany of the Lord		A, B, C
72:1-7, 18-19	2 Advent		A
77:1-2, 11-20	S. btwn. June 26 and July 2*	Pr. 8	C
78:1-2, 34-38	Holy Cross		A, B, C
78:1-4, 12-16	S. btwn. Sept. 25 and Oct. 1*	Pr. 21	A
78:1-7	S. btwn. Nov. 6 and 12*	Pr. 27	A
78:23-29	S. btwn. July 31 and Aug. 6	Pr. 13	B
79:1-9	S. btwn. Sept. 18 and 24*	Pr. 20	C
80:1-2, 8-19	S. btwn. Aug. 14 and 20*	Pr. 15	C
80:1-7	4 Advent		C
80:1-7, 17-19	1 Advent		B
80:1-7, 17-19	4 Advent		A
80:7-15	S. btwn. Oct. 2 and 8	Pr. 22	A
81:1, 10-16	S. btwn. Aug. 28 and Sept. 3*	Pr. 17	C
81:1-10	S. btwn. May 29 and June 4	Pr. 4	B
82	S. btwn. Aug. 14 and 20	Pr. 15	C
82	S. btwn. July 10 and 16*	Pr. 10	C

146 / Index to the Revised Common Lectionary

84	Presentation of the Lord		A, B, C
84	S. btwn. Aug. 21 and 27*	Pr. 16	B
84:1-7	S. btwn. Oct. 23 and 29	Pr. 25	C
85	S. btwn. July 24 and 30*	Pr. 12	C
85:1-2, 8-13	2 Advent		B
85:8-13	S. btwn. Aug. 7 and 13	Pr. 14	A
85:8-13	S. btwn. July 10 and 16	Pr. 10	B
86:1-10, 16-17	S. btwn. June 19 and 25*	Pr. 7	A
86:11-17	S. btwn. July 17 and 23	Pr. 11	A
89:1-4, 15-18	S. btwn. June 26 and July 2	Pr. 8	A
89:1-4, 19-26	4 Advent		B
89:20-37	S. btwn. July 17 and 23*	Pr. 11	B
90:1-6, 13-17	S. btwn. Oct. 23 and 29*	Pr. 25	A
90:1-8 [9-11] 12	S. btwn. Nov. 13 and 19	Pr. 28	A
90:12-17	S. btwn. Oct. 9 and 15	Pr. 23	B
91:1-2, 9-16	1 Lent		C
91:1-6, 14-16	S. btwn. Sept. 25 and Oct. 1*	Pr. 21	C
91:9-16	S. btwn. Oct. 16 and 22	Pr. 24	B
92:1-4, 12-15	8 Epiphany		C
92:1-4, 12-15	S. btwn. June 12 and 18	Pr. 6	B
92:1-4, 12-15	S. btwn. May 24 and 28	Pr. 3	C
93	Ascension of the Lord		A, B, C
93	Christ the King	Pr. 29	B
95	3 Lent		A
95:1-7a	Christ the King	Pr. 29	A
96	Christmas Eve (I)		A, B, C
96	S. btwn. May 29 and June 4*	Pr. 4	C
96:1-9	S. btwn. May 29 and June 4	Pr. 4	C
96:1-9 [10-13]	S. btwn. Oct. 16 and 22	Pr. 24	A
97	7 Easter		C
97	Christmas Dawn (II)		A, B, C
98	6 Easter		B
98	Christmas Day (III)		A, B, C
98	S. btwn. Nov. 13 and 19	Pr. 28	C
98	S. btwn. Nov. 6 and 12*	Pr. 27	C
98	Vigil of Easter		A, B, C
98:1-5	Holy Cross		A, B, C
99	S. btwn. Oct. 16 and 22*	Pr. 24	A
99	Transfiguration of the Lord		A, C
100	Christ the King*	Pr. 29	A
100	S. btwn. June 12 and 18	Pr. 6	A
100	Thanksgiving		C
103:1-5, 20-22	St. Michael and All Angels		A, B, C
103:[1-7] 8-13	S. btwn. Sept. 11 and 17	Pr. 19	A
103:1-8	S. btwn. Aug. 21 and 27	Pr. 16	C
103:1-13, 22	8 Epiphany		B
103:1-13, 22	S. btwn. May 24 and 28	Pr. 3	B
104:1-9, 24, 35c	S. btwn. Oct. 16 and 22*	Pr. 24	B
104:24-34, 35b	Day of Pentecost		A, B, C
105:1-11, 45b	S. btwn. July 24 and 30*	Pr. 12	A
105:1-6, 16-22, 45b	S. btwn. Aug. 7 and 13*	Pr. 14	A
105:1-6, 23-26, 45c	S. btwn. Aug. 28 and Sept. 3*	Pr. 17	A
105:1-6, 37-45	S. btwn. Sept. 18 and 24*	Pr. 20	A
106:1-6, 19-23	S. btwn. Oct. 9 and 15*	Pr. 23	A
107:1-3, 17-22	4 Lent		B
107:1-3, 23-32	S. btwn. June 19 and 25	Pr. 7	B
107:1-7, 33-37	S. btwn. Oct. 30 and Nov. 5*	Pr. 26	A
107:1-9, 43	S. btwn. July 31 and Aug. 6*	Pr. 13	C
111	4 Epiphany		B
111	S. btwn. Aug. 14 and 20*	Pr. 15	B
111	S. btwn. Oct. 9 and 15	Pr. 23	C

PSALMS (continued)

112	S. btwn. Aug. 28 and Sept. 3	Pr. 17	C
112:1-9 [10]	5 Epiphany		A
113	S. btwn. Sept. 18 and 24	Pr. 20	C
113	Visitation of Mary to Elizabeth		A, B, C
114	Easter Evening		A, B, C
114	S. btwn. Sept. 11 and 17*	Pr. 19	A
114	Vigil of Easter		A, B, C
116:1-2, 12-19	Maundy Thursday		A, B, C
116:1-2, 12-19	S. btwn. June 12 and 18*	Pr. 6	A
116:1-4, 12-19	3 Easter		A
116:1-9	S. btwn. Sept. 11 and 17	Pr. 19	B
118:1-2, 14-24	Easter Day		A, B, C
118:1-2, 19-29	Sunday of the Passion (palms)		A, B, C
118:14-29	2 Easter		C
119:1-8	6 Epiphany		A
119:1-8	S. btwn. Oct. 30 and Nov. 5	Pr. 26	B
119:9-16	5 Lent		B
119:33-40	7 Epiphany		A
119:33-40	S. btwn. Sept. 4 and 10	Pr. 18	A
119:97-104	S. btwn. Oct. 16 and 22*	Pr. 24	C
119:105-112	S. btwn. July 10 and 16*	Pr. 10	A
119:129-136	S. btwn. July 24 and 30	Pr. 12	A
119:137-144	S. btwn. Oct. 30 and Nov. 5*	Pr. 26	C
121	2 Lent		A
121	S. btwn. Oct. 16 and 22	Pr. 24	C
122	1 Advent		A
123	S. btwn. July 3 and 9	Pr. 9	B
123	S. btwn. Nov. 13 and 19*	Pr. 28	A
124	S. btwn. Aug. 21 and 27*	Pr. 16	A
124	S. btwn. Sept. 25 and Oct. 1*	Pr. 21	B
125	S. btwn. Sept. 4 and 10*	Pr. 18	B
126	5 Lent		C
126	3 Advent		B
126	S. btwn. Oct. 23 and 29	Pr. 25	B
126	Thanksgiving		B
127	S. btwn. Nov. 6 and 12*	Pr. 27	B
128	S. btwn. July 24 and 30*	Pr. 12	A
130	5 Lent		A
130	S. btwn. Aug. 7 and 13*	Pr. 14	B
130	S. btwn. June 26 and July 2*	Pr. 8	B
130	S. btwn. June 5 and 11	Pr. 5	B
130	Vigil of Pentecost		A, B, C
131	8 Epiphany		A
131	S. btwn. May 24 and 28	Pr. 3	A
132:1-12 [13-18]	Christ the King*		B
133	2 Easter		B
133	S. btwn. Aug. 14 and 20*	Pr. 15	A
133	S. btwn. June 19 and 25*	Pr. 7	B
136:1-9, 23-26	Vigil of Easter		A, B, C
137	S. btwn. Oct. 2 and 8*	Pr. 22	C
138	5 Epiphany		C
138	S. btwn. Aug. 21 and 27	Pr. 16	A
138	S. btwn. July 24 and 30	Pr. 12	C
138	S. btwn. June 5 and 11*	Pr. 5	B
139:1-6, 13-18	S. btwn. Sept. 4 and 10*	Pr. 18	C
139:1-6, 13-18	2 Epiphany		B
139:1-6, 13-18	S. btwn. May 29 and June 4*	Pr. 4	B
139:1-12, 23-24	S. btwn. July 17 and 23*	Pr. 11	A
143	Vigil of Easter		A, B, C
145:1-5, 17-21	S. btwn. Nov. 6 and 12*	Pr. 27	C

145:1-8	S. btwn. Sept. 18 and 24	Pr. 20	A
145:8-14	S. btwn. July 3 and 9	Pr. 9	A
145:8-9, 14-21	S. btwn. July 31 and Aug. 6	Pr. 13	A
145:10-18	S. btwn. July 24 and 30	Pr. 12	B
146	S. btwn. June 5 and 11*	Pr. 5	C
146	S. btwn. Nov. 6 and 12	Pr. 27	B
146	S. btwn. Oct. 30 and Nov. 5*	Pr. 26	B
146	S. btwn. Sept. 25 and Oct. 1	Pr. 21	C
146	S. btwn. Sept. 4 and 10	Pr. 18	B
146:5-10	3 Advent		A
147:1-11, 20c	5 Epiphany		B
147:12-20	2 Christmas		A, B, C
148	1 Christmas		A, B, C
148	5 Easter		C
149	All Saints Day		C
149	S. btwn. Sept. 4 and 10*	Pr. 18	A
150	2 Easter		C

PROVERBS

1:20-33	S. btwn. Sept. 11 and 17*	Pr. 19	B
8:1-4, 22-31	Holy Trinity		C
8:1-8, 19-21; 9:4b-6	Vigil of Easter		A, B, C
9:1-6	S. btwn. Aug. 14 and 20	Pr. 15	B
22:1-2, 8-9, 22-23	S. btwn. Sept. 4 and 10*	Pr. 18	B
25:6-7	S. btwn. Aug. 28 and Sept. 3	Pr. 17	C
31:10-31	S. btwn. Sept. 18 and 24*	Pr. 20	B

ECCLESIASTES

1:2, 12-14; 2:18-23	S. btwn. July 31 and Aug. 6	Pr. 13	C
3:1-13	New Year's Day		A, B, C

SONG OF SOLOMON

2:8-13	S. btwn. Aug. 28 and Sept. 3*	Pr. 17	B
2:8-13	S. btwn. July 3 and 9*	Pr. 9	A

ISAIAH

1:1, 10-20	S. btwn. Aug. 7 and 13*	Pr. 14	C
1:10-18	S. btwn. Oct. 30 and Nov. 5	Pr. 26	C
2:1-5	1 Advent		A
5:1-7	S. btwn. Aug. 14 and 20*	Pr. 15	C
5:1-7	S. btwn. Oct. 2 and 8	Pr. 22	A
6:1-8	Holy Trinity		B
6:1-8 [9-13]	5 Epiphany		C
7:10-14	Annunciation of the Lord		A, B, C
7:10-16	4 Advent		A
9:1-4	3 Epiphany		A
9:2-7	Christmas Eve (I)		A, B, C
11:1-10	2 Advent		A
12	S. btwn. Nov. 13 and 19*	Pr. 28	C
12:2-6	3 Advent		C
12:2-6	Vigil of Easter		A, B, C
25:1-9	S. btwn. Oct. 9 and 15	Pr. 23	A
25:6-9	All Saints		B
25:6-9	Easter Day		B
25:6-9	Easter Evening		A, B, C
35:1-10	3 Advent		A
35:4-7a	S. btwn. Sept. 4 and 10	Pr. 18	B
40:1-11	2 Advent		B
40:21-31	5 Epiphany		B
42:1-9	Baptism of the Lord		A
42:1-9	Monday in Holy Week		A, B, C

ISAIAH *(continued)*

43:1-7	Baptism of the Lord		C
43:16-21	5 Lent		C
43:18-25	7 Epiphany		B
44:6-8	S. btwn. July 17 and 23	Pr. 11	A
45:1-7	S. btwn. Oct. 16 and 22	Pr. 24	A
49:1-7	2 Epiphany		A
49:1-7	Tuesday in Holy Week		A, B, C
49:8-16a	8 Epiphany		A
49:8-16a	S. btwn. May 24 and 28	Pr. 3	A
50:4-9a	S. btwn. Sept. 11 and 17	Pr. 19	B
50:4-9a	Sunday of the Passion		A, B, C
50:4-9a	Wednesday in Holy Week		A, B, C
51:1-6	S. btwn. Aug. 21 and 27	Pr. 16	A
52:7-10	Christmas Day (III)		A, B, C
52:13—53:12	Good Friday		A, B, C
53:4-12	S. btwn. Oct. 16 and 22	Pr. 24	B
55:1-5	S. btwn. July 31 and Aug. 6	Pr. 13	A
55:1-9	3 Lent		C
55:1-11	Vigil of Easter		A, B, C
55:10-13	S. btwn. July 10 and 16	Pr. 10	A
55:10-13	S. btwn. May 24 and 28	Pr. 3	C
55:10-13	8 Epiphany		C
56:1, 6-8	S. btwn. Aug. 14 and 20	Pr. 15	A
58:1-9a [9b-12]	5 Epiphany		A
58:1-12	Ash Wednesday		A, B, C
58:9b-14	S. btwn. Aug. 21 and 27	Pr. 16	C
60:1-6	Epiphany		A, B, C
61:1-4, 8-11	3 Advent		B
61:10—62:3	1 Christmas		B
61:7-11	Mary, Mother of the Lord		A, B, C
62:1-5	2 Epiphany		C
62:6-12	Christmas Dawn (II)		A, B, C
63:7-9	1 Christmas		A
64:1-9	1 Advent		B
65:1-9	S. btwn. June 19 and 25	Pr. 7	C
65:17-25	Easter Day		C
65:17-25	S. btwn. Nov. 13 and 19*	Pr. 28	C
66:10-14	S. btwn. July 3 and 9	Pr. 9	C

JEREMIAH

1:4-10	4 Epiphany		C
1:4-10	S. btwn. Aug. 21 and 27*	Pr. 16	C
2:4-13	S. btwn. Aug. 28 and Sept. 3*	Pr. 17	C
4:11-12, 22-28	S. btwn. Sept. 11 and 17*	Pr. 19	C
8:18—9:1	S. btwn. Sept. 18 and 24*	Pr. 20	C
11:18-20	S. btwn. Sept. 18 and 24	Pr. 20	B
14:7-10, 19-22	S. btwn. Oct. 23 and 29	Pr. 25	C
15:15-21	S. btwn. Aug. 28 and Sept. 3	Pr. 17	A
17:5-10	6 Epiphany		C
18:1-11	S. btwn. Sept. 4 and 10*	Pr. 18	C
20:7-13	S. btwn. June 19 and 25	Pr. 7	A
23:1-6	Christ the King	Pr. 29	C
23:1-6	Christ the King*	Pr. 29	C
23:1-6	S. btwn. July 17 and 23	Pr. 11	B
23:23-29	S. btwn. Aug. 14 and 20	Pr. 15	C
28:5-9	S. btwn. June 26 and July 2	Pr. 8	A
29:1, 4-7	S. btwn. Oct. 9 and 15*	Pr. 23	C
31:1-6	Easter Day		A
31:7-9	S. btwn. Oct. 23 and 29	Pr. 25	B
31:7-14	2 Christmas		A, B, C

31:27-34	S. btwn. Oct. 16 and 22*	Pr. 24	C
31:31-34	5 Lent		B
31:31-34	Reformation		A, B, C
32:1-3a, 6-15	S. btwn. Sept. 25 and Oct. 1*	Pr. 21	C
33:14-16	1 Advent		C

LAMENTATIONS

1:1-6	S. btwn. Oct. 2 and 8*	Pr. 22	C
3:1-9, 19-24	Saturday in Holy Week		A, B, C
3:19-26	S. btwn. Oct. 2 and 8*	Pr. 22	C
3:22-33	S. btwn. June 26 and July 2	Pr. 8	B

EZEKIEL

2:1-5	S. btwn. July 3 and 9	Pr. 9	B
17:22-24	S. btwn. June 12 and 18	Pr. 6	B
18:1-4, 25-32	S. btwn. Sept. 25 and Oct. 1	Pr. 21	A
33:7-11	S. btwn. Sept. 4 and 10	Pr. 18	A
34:11-16, 20-24	Christ the King	Pr. 29	A
36:24-28	Vigil of Easter		A, B, C
37:1-14	5 Lent		A
37:1-14	Day of Pentecost		B
37:1-14	Vigil of Easter		A, B, C

DANIEL

3:1-29	Vigil of Easter		A, B, C
7:1-3, 15-18	All Saints Day		C
7:9-10, 13-14	Christ the King	Pr. 29	B
10:10-14; 12:1-3	St. Michael and All Angels		A, B, C
12:1-3	S. btwn. Nov. 13 and 19	Pr. 28	B

HOSEA

1:2-10	S. btwn. July 24 and 30*	Pr. 12	C
2:14-20	8 Epiphany		B
2:14-20	S. btwn. May 24 and 28	Pr. 3	B
5:15—6:6	S. btwn. June 5 and 11	Pr. 5	A
11:1-11	S. btwn. July 31 and Aug. 6*	Pr. 13	C

JOEL

2:1-2, 12-17	Ash Wednesday		A, B, C
2:21-27	Thanksgiving		B
2:23-32	S. btwn. Oct. 23 and 29*	Pr. 25	C

AMOS

5:6-7, 10-15	S. btwn. Oct. 9 and 15	Pr. 23	B
5:18-24	S. btwn. Nov. 6 and 12	Pr. 27	A
6:1a, 4-7	S. btwn. Sept. 25 and Oct. 1	Pr. 21	C
7:7-15	S. btwn. July 10 and 16	Pr. 10	B
7:7-17	S. btwn. July 10 and 16*	Pr. 10	C
8:1-12	S. btwn. July 17 and 23*	Pr. 11	C
8:4-7	S. btwn. Sept. 18 and 24	Pr. 20	C

JONAH

2:1-3 [4-6] 7-9	Vigil of Easter		A, B, C
3:1-5, 10	3 Epiphany		B
3:1-10	Vigil of Easter		A, B, C
3:10—4:11	S. btwn. Sept. 18 and 24	Pr. 20	A

MICAH

3:5-12	S. btwn. Oct. 30 and Nov. 5	Pr. 26	A
5:2-5a	4 Advent		C
6:1-8	4 Epiphany		A

HABAKKUK
1:1-4; 2:1-4	S. btwn. Oct. 2 and 8	Pr. 22	C
1:1-4; 2:1-4	S. btwn. Oct. 30 and Nov. 5*	Pr. 26	C

ZEPHANIAH
1:7, 12-18	S. btwn. Nov. 13 and 19	Pr. 28	A
3:14-20	3 Advent		C
3:14-20	Vigil of Easter		A, B, C

HAGGAI
1:15b—2:9	S. btwn. Nov. 6 and 12*	Pr. 27	C

ZECHARIAH
9:9-12	S. btwn. July 3 and 9	Pr. 9	A

MALACHI
3:1-4	Presentation of the Lord		A, B, C
3:1-4	2 Advent		C
4:1-2a	S. btwn. Nov. 13 and 19	Pr. 28	C

WISDOM OF SOLOMON
1:13-15; 2:23-24	S. btwn. June 26 and July 2	Pr. 8	B
1:16—2:1, 12-22	S. btwn. Sept. 18 and 24	Pr. 20	B
3:1-9	All Saints		B
6:12-16	S. btwn. Nov. 6 and 12	Pr. 27	A
6:17-20	S. btwn. Nov. 6 and 12	Pr. 27	A
7:26—8:1	S. btwn. Sept. 11 and 17*	Pr. 19	B
10:15-21	2 Christmas		A, B, C
12:13, 16-19	S. btwn. July 17 and 23	Pr. 11	A

SIRACH
10:12-18	S. btwn. Aug. 28 and Sept. 3	Pr. 17	C
15:15-20	6 Epiphany		A
24:1-12	2 Christmas		A, B, C
27:4-7	S. btwn. May 24 and 28	Pr. 3	C
27:4-7	8 Epiphany		C
35:12-17	S. btwn. Oct. 23 and 29	Pr. 25	C

BARUCH
3:9-15, 32—4:4	Vigil of Easter		A, B, C
5:1-9	2 Advent		C

SONG OF THREE YOUNG MEN
35–65	Vigil of Easter		A, B, C

MATTHEW
1:18-25	4 Advent		A
2:1-12	Epiphany		A, B, C
2:13-23	1 Christmas		A
3:1-12	2 Advent		A
3:13-17	Baptism of the Lord		A
4:1-11	1 Lent		A
4:12-23	3 Epiphany		A
5:1-12	4 Epiphany		A
5:1-12	All Saints		A
5:13-20	5 Epiphany		A
5:21-37	6 Epiphany		A
5:38-48	7 Epiphany		A
6:1-6, 16-21	Ash Wednesday		A, B, C
6:24-34	8 Epiphany		A
6:24-34	S. btwn. May 24 and 28	Pr. 3	A

6:25-33	Thanksgiving		B
7:21-29	S. btwn. May 29 and June 4	Pr. 4	A
9:9-13, 18-26	S. btwn. June 5 and 11	Pr. 5	A
9:35—10:8 [9-23]	S. btwn. June 12 and 18	Pr. 6	A
10:24-39	S. btwn. June 19 and 25	Pr. 7	A
10:40-42	S. btwn. June 26 and July 2	Pr. 8	A
11:2-11	3 Advent		A
11:16-19, 25-30	S. btwn. July 3 and 9	Pr. 9	A
13:1-9, 18-23	S. btwn. July 10 and 16	Pr. 10	A
13:24-30, 36-43	S. btwn. July 17 and 23	Pr. 11	A
13:31-33, 44-52	S. btwn. July 24 and 30	Pr. 12	A
14:13-21	S. btwn. July 31 and Aug. 6	Pr. 13	A
14:22-33	S. btwn. Aug. 7 and 13	Pr. 14	A
15:[10-20] 21-28	S. btwn. Aug. 14 and 20	Pr. 15	A
16:13-20	S. btwn. Aug. 21 and 27	Pr. 16	A
16:21-28	S. btwn. Aug. 28 and Sept. 3	Pr. 17	A
17:1-9	Transfiguration of the Lord		A
18:15-20	S. btwn. Sept. 4 and 10	Pr. 18	A
18:21-35	S. btwn. Sept. 11 and 17	Pr. 19	A
20:1-16	S. btwn. Sept. 18 and 24	Pr. 20	A
21:1-11	Sunday of the Passion (palms)		A
21:23-32	S. btwn. Sept. 25 and Oct. 1	Pr. 21	A
21:33-46	S. btwn. Oct. 2 and 8	Pr. 22	A
22:1-14	S. btwn. Oct. 9 and 15	Pr. 23	A
22:15-22	S. btwn. Oct. 16 and 22	Pr. 24	A
22:34-46	S. btwn. Oct. 23 and 29	Pr. 25	A
23:1-12	S. btwn. Oct. 30 and Nov. 5	Pr. 26	A
24:36-44	1 Advent		A
25:1-13	S. btwn. Nov. 6 and 12	Pr. 27	A
25:14-30	S. btwn. Nov. 13 and 19	Pr. 28	A
25:31-46	Christ the King	Pr. 29	A
25:31-46	New Year's Day		A, B, C
26:14—27:66	Sunday of the Passion		A
27:11-54	Sunday of the Passion		A
27:57-66	Saturday in Holy Week		A, B, C
28:1-10	Easter Day		A
28:1-10	Vigil of Easter		A
28:16-20	Holy Trinity		A

MARK

1:1-8	2 Advent		B
1:4-11	Baptism of the Lord		B
1:9-15	1 Lent		B
1:14-20	3 Epiphany		B
1:21-28	4 Epiphany		B
1:29-39	5 Epiphany		B
1:40-45	6 Epiphany		B
2:1-12	7 Epiphany		B
2:13-22	8 Epiphany		B
2:13-22	S. btwn. May 24 and 28	Pr. 3	B
2:23—3:6	S. btwn. May 29 and June 4	Pr. 4	B
3:20-35	S. btwn. June 5 and 11	Pr. 5	B
4:26-34	S. btwn. June 12 and 18	Pr. 6	B
4:35-41	S. btwn. June 19 and 25	Pr. 7	B
5:21-43	S. btwn. June 26 and July 2	Pr. 8	B
6:1-13	S. btwn. July 3 and 9	Pr. 9	B
6:14-29	S. btwn. July 10 and 16	Pr. 10	B
6:30-34, 53-56	S. btwn. July 17 and 23	Pr. 11	B
7:1-8, 14-15, 21-23	S. btwn. Aug. 28 and Sept. 3	Pr. 17	B
7:24-37	S. btwn. Sept. 4 and 10	Pr. 18	B
8:27-38	S. btwn. Sept. 11 and 17	Pr. 19	B

MARK (continued)

8:31-38	2 Lent		B
9:2-9	Transfiguration of the Lord		B
9:30-37	S. btwn. Sept. 18 and 24	Pr. 20	B
9:38-50	S. btwn. Sept. 25 and Oct. 1	Pr. 21	B
10:2-16	S. btwn. Oct. 2 and 8	Pr. 22	B
10:17-31	S. btwn. Oct. 9 and 15	Pr. 23	B
10:35-45	S. btwn. Oct. 16 and 22	Pr. 24	B
10:46-52	S. btwn. Oct. 23 and 29	Pr. 25	B
11:1-11	Sunday of the Passion (palms)		B
12:28-34	S. btwn. Oct. 30 and Nov. 5	Pr. 26	B
12:38-44	S. btwn. Nov. 6 and 12	Pr. 27	B
13:1-8	S. btwn. Nov. 13 and 19	Pr. 28	B
13:24-37	1 Advent		B
14:1—15:47	Sunday of the Passion		B
15:1-39 [40-47]	Sunday of the Passion		B
16:1-8	Easter Day		B
16:1-8	Vigil of Easter		B

LUKE

1:26-38	4 Advent		B
1:26-38	Annunciation of the Lord		A, B, C
1:39-45 [46-55]	4 Advent		C
1:39-57	Visitation of Mary to Elizabeth		A, B, C
1:46-55	Mary, Mother of the Lord		A, B, C
1:47-55	3 Advent		A, B
1:47-55	4 Advent		B, C
1:68-79	2 Advent		C
1:68-79	Christ the King*	Pr. 29	C
2:[1-7] 8-20	Christmas Dawn (II)		A, B, C
2:1-14 [15-20]	Christmas Eve (I)		A, B, C
2:22-40	1 Christmas		B
2:22-40	Presentation of the Lord		A, B, C
2:41-52	1 Christmas		C
3:1-6	2 Advent		C
3:7-18	3 Advent		C
3:15-17, 21-22	Baptism of the Lord		C
4:1-13	1 Lent		C
4:14-21	3 Epiphany		C
4:21-30	4 Epiphany		C
5:1-11	5 Epiphany		C
6:17-26	6 Epiphany		C
6:20-31	All Saints Day		C
6:27-38	7 Epiphany		C
6:39-49	8 Epiphany		C
6:39-49	S. btwn. May 24 and 28	Pr. 3	C
7:1-10	S. btwn. May 29 and June 4	Pr. 4	C
7:11-17	S. btwn. June 5 and 11	Pr. 5	C
7:36—8:3	S. btwn. June 12 and 18	Pr. 6	C
8:26-39	S. btwn. June 19 and 25	Pr. 7	C
9:28-36 [37-43]	Transfiguration of the Lord		C
9:51-62	S. btwn. June 26 and July 2	Pr. 8	C
10:1-11, 16-20	S. btwn. July 3 and 9	Pr. 9	C
10:17-20	St. Michael and All Angels		A, B, C
10:25-37	S. btwn. July 10 and 16	Pr. 10	C
10:38-42	S. btwn. July 17 and 23	Pr. 11	C
11:1-13	S. btwn. July 24 and 30	Pr. 12	C
12:13-21	S. btwn. July 31 and Aug. 6	Pr. 13	C
12:32-40	S. btwn. Aug. 7 and 13	Pr. 14	C
12:49-56	S. btwn. Aug. 14 and 20	Pr. 15	C
13:1-9	3 Lent		C

13:10-17	S. btwn. Aug. 21 and 27	Pr. 16	C
13:31-35	2 Lent		C
14:1, 7-14	S. btwn. Aug. 28 and Sept. 3	Pr. 17	C
14:25-33	S. btwn. Sept. 4 and 10	Pr. 18	C
15:1-3, 11b-32	4 Lent		C
15:1-10	S. btwn. Sept. 11 and 17	Pr. 19	C
16:1-13	S. btwn. Sept. 18 and 24	Pr. 20	C
16:19-31	S. btwn. Sept. 25 and Oct. 1	Pr. 21	C
17:5-10	S. btwn. Oct. 2 and 8	Pr. 22	C
17:11-19	S. btwn. Oct. 9 and 15	Pr. 23	C
17:11-19	Thanksgiving		A
18:1-8	S. btwn. Oct. 16 and 22	Pr. 24	C
18:9-14	S. btwn. Oct. 23 and 29	Pr. 25	C
19:1-10	S. btwn. Oct. 30 and Nov. 5	Pr. 26	C
19:28-40	Sunday of the Passion		C
20:27-38	S. btwn. Nov. 6 and 12	Pr. 27	C
21:5-19	S. btwn. Nov. 13 and 19	Pr. 28	C
21:25-36	1 Advent		C
22:14—23:56	Sunday of the Passion		C
23:1-49	Sunday of the Passion		C
23:33-43	Christ the King	Pr. 29	C
24:1-12	Vigil of Easter		C
24:1-12	Easter Day		C
24:13-35	3 Easter		A
24:13-49	Easter Evening		A, B, C
24:36b-48	3 Easter		B
24:44-53	Ascension of the Lord		A, B, C

JOHN

1:[1-9] 10-18	2 Christmas		A, B, C
1:1-14	Christmas Day (III)		A, B, C
1:6-8, 19-28	3 Advent		B
1:29-42	2 Epiphany		A
1:43-51	2 Epiphany		B
2:1-11	2 Epiphany		C
2:13-22	3 Lent		B
3:1-17	2 Lent		A
3:1-17	Holy Trinity		B
3:13-17	Holy Cross		A, B, C
3:14-21	4 Lent		B
4:5-42	3 Lent		A
5:1-9	6 Easter		C
6:1-21	S. btwn. July 24 and 30	Pr. 12	B
6:24-35	S. btwn. July 31 and Aug. 6	Pr. 13	B
6:25-35	Thanksgiving		C
6:35, 41-51	S. btwn. Aug. 7 and 13	Pr. 14	B
6:51-58	S. btwn. Aug. 14 and 20	Pr. 15	B
6:56-69	S. btwn. Aug. 21 and 27	Pr. 16	B
7:37-39	Day of Pentecost		A
7:37-39	Vigil of Pentecost		A, B, C
8:31-36	Reformation		A, B, C
9:1-41	4 Lent		A
10:1-10	4 Easter		A
10:11-18	4 Easter		B
10:22-30	4 Easter		C
11:1-45	5 Lent		A
11:32-44	All Saints		B
12:1-8	5 Lent		C
12:1-11	Monday in Holy Week		A, B, C
12:12-16	Sunday of the Passion (palms)		B
12:20-33	5 Lent		B

JOHN (continued)

12:20-36	Tuesday in Holy Week		A, B, C
13:1-17, 31b-35	Maundy Thursday		A, B, C
13:21-32	Wednesday in Holy Week		A, B, C
13:31-35	5 Easter		C
14:1-14	5 Easter		A
14:8-17 [25-27]	Day of Pentecost		C
14:15-21	6 Easter		A
14:23-29	6 Easter		C
15:1-8	5 Easter		B
15:9-17	6 Easter		B
15:26-27; 16:4b-15	Day of Pentecost		B
16:12-15	Holy Trinity		C
17:1-11	7 Easter		A
17:6-19	7 Easter		B
17:20-26	7 Easter		C
18:1—19:42	Good Friday		A, B, C
18:33-37	Christ the King	Pr. 29	B
19:38-42	Saturday in Holy Week		A, B, C
20:1-18	Easter Day		A, B, C
20:19-23	Day of Pentecost		A
20:19-31	2 Easter		A, B, C
21:1-19	3 Easter		C

ACTS

1:1-11	Ascension of the Lord		A, B, C
1:6-14	7 Easter		A
1:15-17, 21-26	7 Easter		B
2:1-11	Vigil of Pentecost		A, B, C
2:1-21	Day of Pentecost		A, B, C
2:14a, 22-32	2 Easter		A
2:14a, 36-41	3 Easter		A
2:42-47	4 Easter		A
3:12-19	3 Easter		B
4:5-12	4 Easter		B
4:32-35	2 Easter		B
5:27-32	2 Easter		C
7:55-60	5 Easter		A
8:14-17	Baptism of the Lord		C
8:26-40	5 Easter		B
9:1-6 [7-20]	3 Easter		C
9:36-43	4 Easter		C
10:34-43	Baptism of the Lord		A
10:34-43	Easter Day		A, B, C
10:44-48	6 Easter		B
11:1-18	5 Easter		C
16:9-15	6 Easter		C
16:16-34	7 Easter		C
17:22-31	6 Easter		A
19:1-7	Baptism of the Lord		B

ROMANS

1:1-7	4 Advent		A
1:16-17; 3:22b-28 [29-31]	S. btwn. May 29 and June 4	Pr. 4	A
3:19-28	Reformation		A, B, C
4:1-5, 13-17	2 Lent		A
4:13-25	2 Lent		B
4:13-25	S. btwn. June 5 and 11	Pr. 5	A
5:1-5	Holy Trinity		C
5:1-8	S. btwn. June 12 and 18	Pr. 6	A
5:1-11	3 Lent		A

5:12-19	1 Lent		A
6:1b-11	S. btwn. June 19 and 25	Pr. 7	A
6:12-23	S. btwn. June 26 and July 2	Pr. 8	A
6:3-11	Vigil of Easter		A, B, C
7:15-25a	S. btwn. July 3 and 9	Pr. 9	A
8:1-11	S. btwn. July 10 and 16	Pr. 10	A
8:6-11	5 Lent		A
8:12-17	Holy Trinity		B
8:12-25	S. btwn. July 17 and 23	Pr. 11	A
8:14-17	Day of Pentecost		C
8:14-17, 22-27	Vigil of Pentecost		A, B, C
8:22-27	Day of Pentecost		B
8:26-39	S. btwn. July 24 and 30	Pr. 12	A
9:1-5	S. btwn. July 31 and Aug. 6	Pr. 13	A
10:5-15	S. btwn. Aug. 7 and 13	Pr. 14	A
10:8b-13	1 Lent		C
11:1-2a, 29-32	S. btwn. Aug. 14 and 20	Pr. 15	A
12:1-8	S. btwn. Aug. 21 and 27	Pr. 16	A
12:9-16b	Visitation of Mary to Elizabeth		A, B, C
12:9-21	S. btwn. Aug. 28 and Sept. 3	Pr. 17	A
13:8-14	S. btwn. Sept. 4 and 10	Pr. 18	A
13:11-14	1 Advent		A
14:1-12	S. btwn. Sept. 11 and 17	Pr. 19	A
15:4-13	2 Advent		A
16:25-27	4 Advent		B

1 CORINTHIANS

1:1-9	2 Epiphany		A
1:3-9	1 Advent		B
1:10-18	3 Epiphany		A
1:18-24	Holy Cross		A, B, C
1:18-25	3 Lent		B
1:18-31	4 Epiphany		A
1:18-31	Tuesday in Holy Week		A, B, C
2:1-12 [13-16]	5 Epiphany		A
3:1-9	6 Epiphany		A
3:10-11, 16-23	7 Epiphany		A
4:1-5	8 Epiphany		A
4:1-5	S. btwn. May 24 and 28	Pr. 3	A
5:6b-8	Easter Evening		A, B, C
6:12-20	2 Epiphany		B
7:29-31	3 Epiphany		B
8:1-13	4 Epiphany		B
9:16-23	5 Epiphany		B
9:24-27	6 Epiphany		B
10:1-13	3 Lent		C
11:23-26	Maundy Thursday		A, B, C
12:1-11	2 Epiphany		C
12:3b-13	Day of Pentecost		A
12:12-31a	3 Epiphany		C
13:1-13	4 Epiphany		C
15:1-11	5 Epiphany		C
15:1-11	Easter Day		B
15:12-20	6 Epiphany		C
15:19-26	Easter Day		C
15:35-38, 42-50	7 Epiphany		C
15:51-58	8 Epiphany		C
15:51-58	S. btwn. May 24 and 28	Pr. 3	C

2 CORINTHIANS

1:18-22	7 Epiphany		B
3:1-6	8 Epiphany		B
3:1-6	S. btwn. May 24 and 28	Pr. 3	B
3:12—4:2	Transfiguration of the Lord		C
4:3-6	Transfiguration of the Lord		B
4:5-12	S. btwn. May 29 and June 4	Pr. 4	B
4:13—5:1	S. btwn. June 5 and 11	Pr. 5	B
5:6-10 [11-13] 14-17	S. btwn. June 12 and 18	Pr. 6	B
5:16-21	4 Lent		C
5:20b—6:10	Ash Wednesday		A, B, C
6:1-13	S. btwn. June 19 and 25	Pr. 7	B
8:7-15	S. btwn. June 26 and July 2	Pr. 8	B
9:6-15	Thanksgiving		A
12:2-10	S. btwn. July 3 and 9	Pr. 9	B
13:11-13	Holy Trinity		A

GALATIANS

1:1-12	S. btwn. May 29 and June 4	Pr. 4	C
1:11-24	S. btwn. June 5 and 11	Pr. 5	C
2:15-21	S. btwn. June 12 and 18	Pr. 6	C
3:23-29	S. btwn. June 19 and 25	Pr. 7	C
4:4-7	1 Christmas		B
4:4-7	Mary, Mother of the Lord		A, B, C
5:1, 13-25	S. btwn. June 26 and July 2	Pr. 8	C
6:[1-6] 7-16	S. btwn. July 3 and 9	Pr. 9	C

EPHESIANS

1:3-14	2 Christmas		A, B, C
1:3-14	S. btwn. July 10 and 16	Pr. 10	B
1:11-23	All Saints Day		C
1:15-23	Ascension of the Lord		A, B, C
1:15-23	Christ the King	Pr. 29	A
2:1-10	4 Lent		B
2:11-22	S. btwn. July 17 and 23	Pr. 11	B
3:1-12	Epiphany of the Lord		A, B, C
3:14-21	S. btwn. July 24 and 30	Pr. 12	B
4:1-16	S. btwn. July 31 and Aug. 6	Pr. 13	B
4:25—5:2	S. btwn. Aug. 7 and 13	Pr. 14	B
5:8-14	4 Lent		A
5:15-20	S. btwn. Aug. 14 and 20	Pr. 15	B
6:10-20	S. btwn. Aug. 21 and 27	Pr. 16	B

PHILIPPIANS

1:3-11	2 Advent		C
1:21-30	S. btwn. Sept. 18 and 24	Pr. 20	A
2:1-13	S. btwn. Sept. 25 and Oct. 1	Pr. 21	A
2:5-11	Sunday of the Passion		A, B, C
3:4b-14	5 Lent		C
3:4b-14	S. btwn. Oct. 2 and 8	Pr. 22	A
3:17—4:1	2 Lent		C
4:1-9	S. btwn. Oct. 9 and 15	Pr. 23	A
4:4-7	3 Advent		C
4:4-9	Thanksgiving		C

COLOSSIANS

1:1-14	S. btwn. July 10 and 16	Pr. 10	C
1:11-20	Christ the King	Pr. 29	C
1:15-28	S. btwn. July 17 and 23	Pr. 11	C
2:6-15 [16-19]	S. btwn. July 24 and 30	Pr. 12	C
3:1-4	Easter Day		A

3:1-11	S. btwn. July 31 and Aug. 6	Pr. 13	C
3:12-17	1 Christmas		C

1 THESSALONIANS

1:1-10	S. btwn. Oct. 16 and 22	Pr. 24	A
2:1-8	S. btwn. Oct. 23 and 29	Pr. 25	A
2:9-13	S. btwn. Oct. 30 and Nov. 5	Pr. 26	A
3:9-13	1 Advent		C
4:13-18	S. btwn. Nov. 6 and 12	Pr. 27	A
5:1-11	S. btwn. Nov. 13 and 19	Pr. 28	A
5:16-24	3 Advent		B

2 THESSALONIANS

1:1-4, 11-12	S. btwn. Oct. 30 and Nov. 5	Pr. 26	C
2:1-5, 13-17	S. btwn. Nov. 6 and 12	Pr. 27	C
3:6-13	S. btwn. Nov. 13 and 19	Pr. 28	C

1 TIMOTHY

1:12-17	S. btwn. Sept. 11 and 17	Pr. 19	C
2:1-7	S. btwn. Sept. 18 and 24	Pr. 20	C
2:1-7	Thanksgiving		B
6:6-19	S. btwn. Sept. 25 and Oct. 1	Pr. 21	C

2 TIMOTHY

1:1-14	S. btwn. Oct. 2 and 8	Pr. 22	C
2:8-15	S. btwn. Oct. 9 and 15	Pr. 23	C
3:14—4:5	S. btwn. Oct. 16 and 22	Pr. 24	C
4:6-8, 16-18	S. btwn. Oct. 23 and 29	Pr. 25	C

TITUS

2:11-14	Christmas Eve (I)		A, B, C
3:4-7	Christmas Dawn (II)		A, B, C

PHILEMON

1–21	S. btwn. Sept. 4 and 10	Pr. 18	C

HEBREWS

1:1-4 [5-12]	Christmas Day (III)		A, B, C
1:1-4; 2:5-12	S. btwn. Oct. 2 and 8	Pr. 22	B
2:10-18	1 Christmas		A
2:14-18	Presentation of the Lord		A, B, C
4:12-16	S. btwn. Oct. 9 and 15	Pr. 23	B
4:14-16; 5:7-9	Good Friday		A, B, C
5:1-10	S. btwn. Oct. 16 and 22	Pr. 24	B
5:5-10	5 Lent		B
7:23-28	S. btwn. Oct. 23 and 29	Pr. 25	B
9:11-14	S. btwn. Oct. 30 and Nov. 5	Pr. 26	B
9:11-15	Monday in Holy Week		A, B, C
9:24-28	S. btwn. Nov. 6 and 12	Pr. 27	B
10:4-10	Annunciation of the Lord		A, B, C
10:5-10	4 Advent		C
10:11-14 [15-18] 19-25	S. btwn. Nov. 13 and 19	Pr. 28	B
10:16-25	Good Friday		A, B, C
11:1-3, 8-16	S. btwn. Aug. 7 and 13	Pr. 14	C
11:29—12:2	S. btwn. Aug. 14 and 20	Pr. 15	C
12:1-3	Wednesday in Holy Week		A, B, C
12:18-29	S. btwn. Aug. 21 and 27	Pr. 16	C
13:1-8, 15-16	S. btwn. Aug. 28 and Sept. 3	Pr. 17	C

JAMES

1:17-27	S. btwn. Aug. 28 and Sept. 3	Pr. 17	B
2:1-10 [11-13] 14-17	S. btwn. Sept. 4 and 10	Pr. 18	B
3:1-12	S. btwn. Sept. 11 and 17	Pr. 19	B
3:13—4:3, 7-8a	S. btwn. Sept. 18 and 24	Pr. 20	B
5:7-10	3 Advent		A
5:13-20	S. btwn. Sept. 25 and Oct. 1	Pr. 21	B

1 PETER

1:3-9	2 Easter	A
1:17-23	3 Easter	A
2:2-10	5 Easter	A
2:19-25	4 Easter	A
3:13-22	6 Easter	A
3:18-22	1 Lent	B
4:1-8	Saturday in Holy Week	A, B, C
4:12-14; 5:6-11	7 Easter	A

2 PETER

1:16-21	Transfiguration of the Lord	A
3:8-15a	2 Advent	B

1 JOHN

1:1—2:2	2 Easter	B
3:1-3	All Saints	A
3:1-7	3 Easter	B
3:16-24	4 Easter	B
4:7-21	5 Easter	B
5:1-6	6 Easter	B
5:9-13	7 Easter	B

REVELATION

1:4-8	2 Easter		C
1:4b-8	Christ the King	Pr. 29	B
5:11-14	3 Easter		C
7:9-17	4 Easter		C
7:9-17	All Saints		A
12:7-12	St. Michael and All Angels		A, B, C
21:1-6	5 Easter		C
21:1-6a	All Saints		B
21:1-6a	New Year's Day		A, B, C
21:10, 22—22:5	6 Easter		C
22:12-14, 16-17, 20-21	7 Easter		C

Index of Composers

Adams, Stephen
: The Holy City
    Passion/Palm Sunday B
Adler, Samuel
: God's Promise
    2 Lent A
: Mizmor shir l'yom ha-Shabat
    Sun btwn May 24 and 28 C
    Sun btwn Jun 12 and 18 B
Aguiar, Ernani
: Psalm 150/Salmo 150
    2 Easter C
    Day of Thanksgiving B
Åhlén, Waldemar
: The Earth Adorned/Sommersalm
    6 Easter C
    Sun btwn Jun 19 and 25 A
    Sun btwn Aug 14 and 20 C
Allegri, Gregorio
: Miserere mei, Deus
    Ash Wednesday A, B, C
    5 Lent B
Anerio, Felice
: Angelus autem Domini
    Easter Vigil A, B, C
    Easter Day A
Anerio, Felice/ed. Walter Ehret
: Christ Became Obedient for Us unto Death
    Sun btwn Sep 25 and Oct 1 A
Anonymous sixteenth century/arr. John Redford
: Rejoice in the Lord Always
    3 Advent C
    Sun btwn Oct 9 and 15 A
Archer, Malcolm
: Author of Life Divine
    Sun btwn Jun 19 and 25 B
: Christ, Whose Glory
    2 Epiphany B
: The Lord's My Shepherd
    4 Easter A
Arnatt, Ronald
: Holy God, We Praise Thy Name
    Holy Trinity A
: When the Morning Stars Together
    Holy Trinity A
Ashdown, Franklin D.
: Jesus, the Very Thought of Thee
    4 Epiphany A
    6 Epiphany C
    5 Lent C
    Sun btwn Aug 28 and Sep 3 A
    Sun btwn Sep 25 and Oct 1 B
    Sun btwn Oct 2 and 8 A
    Sun btwn Nov 6 and 12 B
    Name of Jesus A, B, C
Aston, Peter
: God Be Merciful unto Us
    Sun btwn Aug 14 and 20 A
: I Give You a New Commandment
    Maundy Thursday A, B, C
    5 Easter C
Attwood, Thomas
: Come, Holy Ghost
    Vigil of Pentecost A, B, C
    Day of Pentecost A
    Sun btwn Aug 14 and 20 C
: Teach Me, O Lord
    7 Epiphany A
    Sun btwn Jul 10 and 16 C
    Sun btwn Sep 4 and 10 A
    Sun btwn Oct 16 and 22 C

(Attwood, Thomas)
    Turn Thee Again, O Lord
        Sun btwn Nov 13 and 19 A
    Turn Thy Face from My Sins
        Ash Wednesday A, B, C

Averitt, William
    He Is Born the Divine Christ Child
        1 Christmas C

Bach, Johann Christoph Friedrich
    In the Resurrection Glorious
        Sun btwn Jul 17 and 23 A
        Sun btwn Nov 6 and 12 C
        All Saints Day A, C

Bach, Johann Sebastian
    All Who Believe and Are Baptized
        3 Epiphany C
        Sun btwn May 29 and Jun 4 A
        Sun btwn Jun 12 and 18 B
        Sun btwn Jun 19 and 25 C
    Alleluia
        Transfiguration of Our Lord A
        6 Easter B
    Alles was Odem hat
        Day of Thanksgiving B
    Awake, Thou Wintry Earth
        Easter Day B
    Bist du bei mir
        Sun btwn Sep 18 and 24 A
    Break Forth, O Beauteous Heavenly Light
        Christmas Dawn (II) A, B, C
        1 Christmas A
    Bridegroom of My Soul
        Sun btwn May 24 and 28 B
    Bring Low Our Ancient Adam
        4 Epiphany B
        Ash Wednesday A, B, C
        Sun btwn Oct 30 and Nov 5 A
    Christ Is Arisen
        3 Easter A
    Christ unser Herr zum Jordan kam
        Baptism of Our Lord B
    Come, Holy Ghost, God and Lord
        Vigil of Pentecost A, B, C
    Come, Holy, Quickening Spirit
        Day of Pentecost A, B
    Comfort, Comfort Ye My People
        2 Advent A
    Crucifixus
        Passion/Palm Sunday A
        Good Friday A, B, C
    Dedication Prayer/Bist du bei mir
        3 Epiphany B
    Domine Deus
        Sun btwn Oct 16 and 22 B
    Dona nobis pacem
        Day of Pentecost A
    Ein feste Burg/A Mighty Fortress
        Reformation Day A, B, C
    Flocks in Pastures Green Abiding
        4 Easter C
    For There Is Now No Condemnation
        Sun btwn Jul 10 and 16 A
    From Heaven Above
        Christmas Eve (I) A, B, C

From Heaven Above to Earth I Come
    Christmas Eve (I) A, B, C
    Christmas Dawn (II) A, B, C
    Name of Jesus A, B, C
Gloria in excelsis Deo
    Christmas Eve (I) A, B, C
    Christmas Day (III) A, B, C
God, the Lord Is Sun and Shield/Gott, der Herr, ist Sonn' und Schild
    Sun btwn Oct 23 and 29 B
He Who Would Be Called
    Sun btwn Aug 28 and Sep 3 C
Jesu, Joy—My Joy Forever
    6 Epiphany B
    Sun btwn Aug 21 and 27 B
Jesus Is My Joy, My All
    Sun btwn Jun 5 and 11 A
Jesus, My Sweet Pleasure/Jesu, meine Freude
    8 Epiphany A, B
    Ash Wednesday A, B, C
    5 Lent B
    Sun btwn Jul 24 and 30 A, B
    Sun btwn Jul 31 and Aug 6 C
    Sun btwn Aug 7 and 13 C
    Sun btwn Sep 18 and 24 C
Lord Jesus Christ, God's Only Son
    1 Lent B
    Easter Vigil A, B, C
Lord Jesus Christ, Thou Prince of Peace
    Sun btwn Oct 30 and Nov 5 A
Lord, Keep Us Steadfast
    1 Lent A
Lord, Thee I Love with All My Heart
    2 Lent B, C
    Sun btwn Jul 17 and 23 C
    Sun btwn Sep 25 and Oct 1 C
    Sun btwn Oct 23 and 29 A
    Sun btwn Oct 30 and Nov 5 B
    Sun btwn Nov 13 and 19 C
Magnificat anima mea
    4 Advent C
Nations, Listen to God's Calling
    Sun btwn Jul 3 and 9 B
Now Thank We All Our God
    Sun btwn Oct 9 and 15 C
    Day of Thanksgiving A, B, C
Nun lob, mein Seel
    Sun btwn Aug 21 and 27 C
O Bread of Life from Heaven
    3 Lent C
    Sun btwn Jul 31 and Aug 6 B
O God, You Are My Refuge
    4 Epiphany C
O Jesus Christ, My Life, My Light/O Jesu Christ, meins Lebens Licht
    2 Christmas A, B, C
    Sun btwn Nov 13 and 19 B
O Little One, Sweet
    Christmas Day (III) A, B, C
O Morning Star, How Fair and Bright
    Epiphany of Our Lord A, B, C
O Mortal World
    Sun btwn Jul 17 and 23 A
    Sun btwn Jul 31 and Aug 6 C

(Bach, Johann Sebastian)	O Thou Sweetest Source of Gladness
	Sun btwn Sep 25 and Oct 1 A
	Salvation unto Us Has Come
	8 Epiphany B
	Sun btwn May 29 and Jun 4 A
	Sun btwn Jun 5 and 11 C
	Sun btwn Jun 19 and 25 C
	Sun btwn Sep 18 and 24 A
	Reformation Day A, B, C
	Savior of the Nations, Come
	1 Advent B, C
	Sheep May Safely Graze
	4 Easter A
	Sing Praise to Christ
	3 Easter A
	Sun btwn Sep 4 and 10 A
	Take Heart, Contented Be, and Restful
	Sun btwn Jun 5 and 11 C
	The Only Son from Heaven
	Epiphany of Our Lord A, B, C
	Baptism of Our Lord A, C
	2 Epiphany A
	The Savior of the World Is Born
	Christmas Dawn (II) A, B, C
	The Wise Confine Their Choice in Friends
	Sun btwn Jun 12 and 18 C
	'Tis Well with Me, for by Thy Might
	Sun btwn May 29 and Jun 4 B
	Transcendent, Holy God
	Transfiguration of Our Lord C
	Wake, Awake, for Night Is Flying
	1 Advent B, C
	Sun btwn Nov 6 and 12 A
	What God Ordains Is Good Indeed
	Sun btwn Jul 17 and 23 B
	Who Himself Exalteth
	Sun btwn Aug 28 and Sep 3 C
	Ye Are Not of the Flesh
	5 Lent A
	Sun btwn Jul 10 and 16 A
	Zion Hears the Watchmen Singing
	1 Advent A
	3 Advent C
	Sun btwn Aug 7 and 13 C
Bach, Johann Sebastian/arr. Hal H. Hopson	The Lord Will Soon Appear
	2 Advent B
Bach, Johann Sebastian/arr. Michael Burkhardt	Christ Jesus Lay in Death's Strong Bands
	Easter Day A
	Prepare Thyself, Zion
	3 Advent C
Bainton, Edgar L.	And I Saw a New Heaven
	5 Easter C
	Christ the King C
	All Saints Day B
Bairstow, Edward C.	I Sat Down under His Shadow
	4 Epiphany C
	Sun btwn Aug 14 and 20 B
	I Will Wash My Hands in Innocency
	Sun btwn Jul 17 and 23 A
	Jesus, the Very Thought of Thee
	Transfiguration of Our Lord A
	Sun btwn Sep 25 and Oct 1 A

	Let All Mortal Flesh Keep Silence
	4 Advent A
	5 Epiphany C
	Transfiguration of Our Lord B
	Sun btwn May 29 and Jun 4 B
	Lord, Thou Hast Been Our Refuge
	Sun btwn Nov 13 and 19 A
	Sing Ye to the Lord
	Easter Vigil A, B, C
	The Day Draws on the Golden Light
	Easter Day A
	The King of Love My Shepherd Is
	4 Easter A
Baldwin, Anthony	Holy Spirit, Ever Dwelling
	Vigil of Pentecost A, B, C
Barker, Michael	Miriam's Song
	Easter Vigil A, B, C
Barnett, Steve	Go! Tell It On the Mountain
	Christmas Dawn (II) A, B, C
Basler, Paul	Agnus Dei
	2 Epiphany A
	Alleluia
	5 Easter B
	Ubi caritas
	Maundy Thursday A, B, C
Bass, Claude L.	At Bethlehem
	1 Christmas B
Batastini, Robert J.	Exsultet/Easter Proclamation
	Easter Vigil A, B, C
	Gaudete
	Christmas Dawn (II) A, B, C
Beck, Theodore	I Know That My Redeemer Lives
	Sun btwn Nov 6 and 12 C
	Jesus, Priceless Treasure
	Sun btwn Jul 24 and 30 B
Beethoven, Ludwig van	A Contrite Heart
	5 Lent B
	Hallelujah
	Transfiguration of Our Lord B
	Prayer
	Sun btwn Jun 26 and Jul 2 A, B
	Sun btwn Jul 24 and 30 B
	The Heavens Sing Praises
	Sun btwn Jun 5 and 11 A
	Sun btwn Aug 21 and 27 C
Beethoven, Ludwig van/arr. Richard Proulx	Give Thanks to God
	5 Epiphany A
	4 Lent B
	Sun btwn Jun 19 and 25 B
	Sun btwn Nov 6 and 12 B
Behnke, John	I Know That My Redeemer Lives
	Sun btwn Nov 6 and 12 C
	Of the Father's Love Begotten
	2 Christmas A, B, C
	The Head That Once Was Crowned
	Christ the King A
Bell, John L.	O the Lamb
	Passion/Palm Sunday B
	Sing a New Song to the Lord/Psalm 98
	Christmas Day (III) A, B, C
	Will You Come and Follow Me
	Sun btwn Jul 3 and 9 B

Below, Robert	The Glory of These Forty Days
	1 Lent A
Bender, Jan	Begone, Satan
	1 Lent A
	I Am the Good Shepherd
	4 Easter A
	Lord, Lord, Open to Us
	Sun btwn Nov 6 and 12 A
	O God, O Lord of Heaven and Earth
	3 Epiphany C
	7 Epiphany C
	Sun btwn Jun 12 and 18 A
	Sun btwn Jul 3 and 9 B
	Sun btwn Oct 16 and 22 A
Bender, Mark	Hail to the Lord's Anointed
	2 Epiphany A
	3 Epiphany C
	O Lord, I Love the Habitation of Your House
	Sun btwn Aug 28 and Sep 3 A
Bengtson, Bruce	Behold My Servant
	2 Christmas A, B, C
	O Sing to the Lord a New Song
	6 Easter B
	Sun btwn Nov 13 and 19 C
Benson, Robert A.	Good Christians All, Rejoice and Sing
	Easter Day B
	O Lord Most High, Eternal King
	Ascension of Our Lord A, B, C
	On Earth Has Dawned This Day of Days
	Easter Day A
	Ride On! Ride On in Majesty!
	Passion/Palm Sunday A, C
	Wondrous Love
	Maundy Thursday A, B, C
Berger, Jean	A Rose Touched by the Sun's Warm Rays
	7 Easter A
	Behold, the Lord Hath Proclaimed
	Christmas Dawn (II) A, B, C
	I to the Hills Lift Up Mine Eyes
	2 Lent A
	Sun btwn Oct 16 and 22 C
	The Eyes of All Wait upon Thee
	Day of Pentecost A, C
	Sun btwn Jun 19 and 25 C
	Sun btwn Jul 24 and 30 B
	Sun btwn Jul 31 and Aug 6 A
	Sun btwn Oct 2 and 8 C
	Day of Thanksgiving C
Bernstein, Leonard	Sanctus
	Holy Trinity B
Bertalot, John	Abide with Me
	Easter Evening A, B, C
	Amazing Grace
	7 Epiphany B
	3 Lent A, B
	4 Lent B, C
	Sun btwn Sep 11 and 17 C
	Sun btwn Oct 23 and 29 B
	Christ upon the Mountain Peak
	Transfiguration of Our Lord A
	Come, Risen Lord
	3 Easter A, B, C

	Passion of Our Lord According to St. Luke
	Passion/Palm Sunday C
	Passion of Our Lord According to St. Matthew
	Passion/Palm Sunday A
	See Amid the Winter's Snow
	Christmas Day (III) A, B, C
	Thy Word Is a Lantern
	Sun btwn May 29 and Jun 4 A
	Sun btwn Jul 10 and 16 A
	Reformation Day A, B, C
Berthier, Jacques	Eat This Bread
	Sun btwn Jul 31 and Aug 6 A
	Magnificat
	3 Advent A
	Surrexit Christus
	Easter Vigil A, B, C
Biebl, Franz	Ave Maria
	4 Advent B
Biery, James	Easter Sequence
	Easter Vigil A, B, C
	Now Join We to Praise the Creator
	Day of Thanksgiving A, C
	O sacrum convivium
	Easter Vigil A, B, C
	The Waters of Life
	Baptism of Our Lord A, C
	7 Easter A
	Vigil of Pentecost A, B, C
	Sun btwn Aug 7 and 13 A
Billings, William	Easter Anthem
	Easter Day A, B
	Rejoice Ye Shining Worlds on High
	2 Advent A
	Ascension of Our Lord A, B, C
	The Lord Is Risen Indeed
	2 Easter B
	Universal Praise
	All Saints Day C
Binkerd, Gordon	Third Mass of Christmas
	Christmas Dawn (II) A, B, C
Bisbee, B. Wayne	O Splendor of God's Glory Bright
	2 Christmas A, B, C
	7 Epiphany A
	Transfiguration of Our Lord C
	Teach Me Your Way, O Lord
	Sun btwn Jun 5 and 11 A
	Sun btwn Jun 19 and 25 A, B
	Sun btwn Jul 3 and 9 B
	Sun btwn Jul 17 and 23 A, B
	Sun btwn Aug 28 and Sep 3 B
	Sun btwn Sep 4 and 10 A
	Sun btwn Oct 30 and Nov 5 B
Blake, Leonard	Sing to the Lord of Harvest
	Day of Thanksgiving A
Boatner, Edward	Wade in the Water
	Sun btwn Aug 7 and 13 A
Bonnemère, Edward V.	I'm Going on a Journey
	Sun btwn Jun 12 and 18 B
Bortniansky, Dmitri	We Thank Thee, Lord
	Sun btwn Aug 21 and 27 A
Boulanger, Lili	Psalm XXIV/Psaume XXIV
	Christ the King B

Bouman, Paul
    A Babe Is Born
        Christmas Day (III) A, B, C
    Behold the Lamb of God
        2 Epiphany A
        Good Friday A, B, C
    Blest Are They
        Sun btwn Jul 10 and 16 B
    Christ upon the Mountain Peak
        Transfiguration of Our Lord A, B, C
    Create in Me a Clean Heart, O God
        Sun btwn Sep 11 and 17 C
    God Be Merciful
        Sun btwn Aug 14 and 20 A
    God Be Merciful unto Us
        Sun btwn Aug 14 and 20 A
    God Is Light
        2 Christmas A, B, C
        2 Easter B
    I Lift Up My Eyes to the Hills
        2 Lent A
        Sun btwn Jul 3 and 9 B
    Lord of Lords, Adored by Angels
        Maundy Thursday A, B, C
    O God of Mercy
        Sun btwn Jul 10 and 16 C
        Sun btwn Sep 11 and 17 B
    Rejoice, Rejoice Believers
        Sun btwn Nov 6 and 12 A
    Son of God, Eternal Savior
        Sun btwn Oct 9 and 15 B
    Take Up Your Cross, the Savior Said
        Sun btwn Aug 28 and Sep 3 A
        Sun btwn Sep 4 and 10 C
    The Lord Is My Shepherd
        4 Easter C
        Sun btwn Oct 9 and 15 A

Boyce, William
    I Was Glad
        1 Advent A

Boyle, Malcolm
    Thou O God Art Praised in Zion
        6 Easter C

Brahms, Johannes
    A Dove Flew Down from Heaven
        4 Advent B, C
    Ah Thou Poor World
        Sun btwn Jul 31 and Aug 6 C
        Sun btwn Aug 7 and 13 C
    Create in Me, O God
        Ash Wednesday A, B, C
        5 Lent B
        Sun btwn Sep 11 and 17 C
    How Lovely Is Thy Dwellingplace
        Sun btwn Oct 23 and 29 C
        Presentation of Our Lord A, B, C
    Let Grief Not Overwhelm You
        Sun btwn Sep 4 and 10 B
    Magdalena
        Easter Day A
    O Savior Rend the Heavens Wide/O Heiland, reiss die Himmel auf
        1 Advent B
    O World So Vain
        Ash Wednesday A, B, C

Britten, Benjamin
  A Boy Was Born
    Christmas Eve (I) A, B, C
    1 Christmas C
  A New Year's Carol
    2 Advent B
  Canticle II: Abraham and Isaac
    Vigil of Easter A, B, C
  Festival Te Deum
    Christ the King C
  Jubilate Deo
    7 Epiphany B
    Sun btwn Jun 12 and 18 A
    Sun btwn Aug 21 and 27 B
    Day of Thanksgiving A
  Te Deum in C
    Holy Trinity C
  This Little Babe
    1 Christmas B

Bruckner, Anton
  Christus factus est
    3 Lent B
    Passion/Palm Sunday A, B
    Sun btwn Sep 25 and Oct 1 A
  God So Loved the World
    2 Lent A
  Locus iste
    Sun btwn Aug 14 and 20 A

Bunjes, Paul
  Comfort, Comfort Ye My People
    2 Advent A
  I Know That My Redeemer Lives
    Sun btwn Nov 6 and 12 C

Burkhardt, Michael
  Built on the Rock
    Sun btwn Aug 21 and 27 A
  Christ the Lord Is Risen Again
    Easter Day A
  Come, Holy Ghost, Our Souls Inspire
    Day of Pentecost B
  Filled with the Spirit
    Vigil of Pentecost A, B, C
    Sun btwn Aug 14 and 20 B
  From Heaven Above to Earth I Come
    Christmas Eve (I) A, B, C
  Go, My Children, with My Blessing
    7 Epiphany B
  Hymn to the Trinity
    Holy Trinity A
  Lift High the Cross
    Sun btwn Sep 11 and 17 B
  Praise the Lord! O Heavens Adore Him
    5 Easter C

Burleigh, Harry T.
  Balm in Gilead
    6 Epiphany B
  Every Time I Feel the Spirit
    Day of Pentecost C
  I Know De Lord's Laid His Hands On Me
    Sun btwn Jun 5 and 11 C
  My Lord What a Mornin'
    1 Advent B, C
  Nobody Knows the Trouble I've Seen
    Sun btwn Aug 21 and 27 C
  Were You There
    Good Friday A, B, C

Burt, Alfred   All on a Christmas Morning
         Christmas Dawn (II) A, B, C

Busarow, Donald   A Mighty Fortress
         1 Lent A
         Sun btwn Jun 5 and 11 B
    A Nobler Life
         Sun btwn Oct 2 and 8 C
    All Creatures of Our God and King
         6 Easter B
         Ascension of Our Lord A, B, C
    At the Lamb's High Feast We Sing
         Easter Day A
    Come Down, O Love Divine
         Sun btwn Aug 28 and Sep 3 C
    Day by Day
         8 Epiphany B
    Eternal Ruler of the Ceaseless Round
         Sun btwn Aug 21 and 27 B
         Sun btwn Oct 16 and 22 A
    Farewell to Alleluia
         Transfiguration of Our Lord B
    Holy God, We Praise Your Name
         Holy Trinity A
    How Firm a Foundation
         Sun btwn Jun 19 and 25 B
    I Heard the Voice of Jesus Say
         3 Lent A
    Jesus Has Come and Brings Pleasure
         5 Epiphany B
    Lift High the Cross
         Sun btwn Sep 11 and 17 B
    Lord Keep Us Steadfast in Your Word
         1 Lent B
         Sun btwn Sep 25 and Oct 1 A
    Lord, Thee I Love with All My Heart
         Sun btwn Oct 30 and Nov 5 B
    Love Divine, All Loves Excelling
         Ascension of Our Lord A, B, C
    O Lord, You Are My God and King
         Ascension of Our Lord A, B, C
         Christ the King A, B
    O Morning Star, How Fair and Bright
         Epiphany of Our Lord A, B, C
         7 Easter C
    On Jordan's Banks the Baptist's Cry
         2 Advent A
    Our Father, by Whose Name
         Sun btwn Oct 2 and 8 B
    Proclaim with Me
         Sun btwn Aug 14 and 20 B
    The Baptism Carol
         Baptism of Our Lord B, C
    The Church of Christ in Every Age
         Sun btwn Oct 16 and 22 B
    The Days of Summer
         Sun btwn Jul 17 and 23 B
    Thy Strong Word
         3 Epiphany A

Buszin, Walter   Jesus Is Our Joy, Our Treasure
         5 Easter A

Buxtehude, Dietrich	Everything You Do
	6 Epiphany A
	5 Easter B
	Sun btwn Oct 9 and 15 B, C
	God Shall Do My Advising
	5 Epiphany A
	In God, My Faithful God
	Sun btwn Aug 28 and Sep 3 A
	My Jesus Is My Lasting Joy
	Sun btwn Jul 10 and 16 B
Byrd, William	Cognoverunt discipuli/The Disciples with Wondering Eyes
	3 Easter A
	Ego sum panis vivus
	Sun btwn Jul 31 and Aug 6 B
	Haec dies
	Easter Day C
	I Will Not Leave You Comfortless
	6 Easter A
	Laetentur coeli
	3 Advent C
	Miserere mei/Mercy Grant unto Me
	Ash Wednesday A, B, C
	Sing Praise to God This Holy Day
	Easter Day B
	Surge illuminare
	2 Epiphany C
	Teach Me, O Lord
	7 Epiphany A
	The Passion According to St. John
	Good Friday A, B, C
Byrd, William/arr. Austin Lovelace	Lord, Make Me to Know Thy Ways
	2 Epiphany B
	Sun btwn Sep 18 and 24 B
Cain, Noble	In the Night, Christ Came Walking
	Sun btwn Aug 7 and 13 A
Caldwell, Paul/arr. Sean Ivory	Hope for Resolution
	Christmas Day (III) A, B, C
Callahan, Charles	In Your Mercy, Lord, You Called Me
	Sun btwn Jun 26 and Jul 2 C
	The Baptism of Our Lord
	Baptism of Our Lord A, B
Campbell, Sidney	Sing We Merrily Unto God Our Strength
	Sun btwn Oct 23 and 29 B
Carnahan, Craig	The Christ-Child Lay on Mary's Lap
	1 Christmas C
Carter, Andrew	Come, Holy Ghost, Creator Blest
	Day of Pentecost B
	Deep Peace
	8 Epiphany A
	For the Beauty of the Earth
	Sun btwn May 29 and Jun 4 C
	God Be in My Head
	Sun btwn Aug 28 and Sep 3 B
	Hodie Christus natus est
	Christmas Day (III) A, B, C
	Love One Another
	3 Easter A
	Mary's Magnificat
	4 Advent C
	The Light of the World
	5 Epiphany A
	5 Easter A

(Carter, Andrew)   Thou Art the Vine
    5 Easter B
    Sun btwn Sep 18 and 24 A

Casals, Pablo   O vos omnes
    Passion/Palm Sunday C
    Good Friday A, B, C

Chemin-Petit, Hans   Salvation unto Us Has Come
    Sun btwn May 29 and Jun 4 A

Cherubini, Luigi   Come Unto Me, All Ye Heavy Laden
    Sun btwn Jul 3 and 9 A

Cherubini, Luigi/arr. Austin Lovelace   Like as a Father
    8 Epiphany B

Cherwien, David   At the Lamb's High Feast We Sing
    Easter Vigil A, B, C
    Easter Day A, B
    Beautiful Savior
    Transfiguration of Our Lord B, C
    Christ the King C
    Go Down, Moses
    Easter Vigil A, B, C
    God Is Our Refuge and Strength
    Easter Vigil A, B, C
    Healing River
    Sun btwn Jun 26 and Jul 2 B
    My Song Is Love Unknown
    4 Lent B
    On Jordan's Banks
    2 Advent A
    Our Father, by Whose Name
    Sun btwn Oct 2 and 8 B
    Psalm 22
    Maundy Thursday A, B, C
    Psalm 23/The Lord Is My Shepherd
    4 Easter B, C
    Up Through Endless Ranks of Angels
    Ascension of Our Lord A, B, C

Cherwien, David/Susan Palo Cherwien   Life Tree
    Easter Vigil A, B, C

Chilcott, Bob   Just As I Am
    Sun btwn May 24 and 28 B
    Shepherd's Carol
    Christmas Dawn (II) A, B, C
    Were You There
    Good Friday A, B, C

Christiansen, F. Melius   Wake, Awake
    1 Advent C
    Beautiful Savior
    Epiphany of Our Lord A, B, C
    Transfiguration of Our Lord A, B
    Built on the Rock
    Sun btwn Aug 21 and 27 A
    Lamb of God
    2 Epiphany A
    5 Lent B
    Maundy Thursday A, B, C
    Good Friday A, B, C
    Lullaby on Christmas Eve
    Christmas Eve (I) A, B, C
    My God, How Wonderful Thou Art
    Sun btwn Oct 23 and 29 A

	O Day Full of Grace
	3 Epiphany B
	Vigil of Pentecost A, B, C
	Day of Pentecost A, B
	Praise to the Lord
	Sun btwn Jun 19 and 25 B
	Psalm 50/Offer unto God
	Sun btwn Aug 21 and 27 C
	Sun btwn Nov 6 and 12 B
	Wake, Awake
	Sun btwn Nov 6 and 12 A
Christiansen, Olaf C.	Light Everlasting
	2 Epiphany A
	3 Epiphany A
Christiansen, Paul J.	Create in Me a Clean Heart
	Ash Wednesday A, B, C
	Sun btwn Sep 11 and 17 C
	Easter Morning
	Easter Day A
	2 Easter A, B, C
	Wondrous Love
	3 Lent A, B
	4 Lent B
Clausen, René	A New Creation
	4 Lent C
	All That Hath Life and Breath, Praise Ye the Lord
	2 Easter C
	Sun btwn Oct 16 and 22 A
	At the Name of Jesus
	Easter Day B
	Christ the King B
	My God, How Wonderful Thou Art
	5 Epiphany A
	Nunc dimittis
	1 Christmas B
	Presentation of Our Lord A, B, C
	Peace I Leave with You
	6 Easter C
	Seek the Lord
	Sun btwn Jul 10 and 16 A
	Set Me As a Seal
	2 Epiphany C
	Thank the Lord
	Sun btwn Oct 30 and Nov 5 C
	The Greatest of These Is Love
	4 Epiphany C
Cleobury, Stephen	Joys Seven
	Baptism of Our Lord A
Conlon, Joan	Come, Enjoy God's Festive Springtime
	2 Easter A
Copland, Aaron	Help Us, O Lord
	Wednesday in Holy Week A, B, C
	Sun btwn Jun 19 and 25 C
	Sun btwn Oct 23 and 29 B
	In the Beginning
	Holy Trinity A
	Sing Ye Praises to Our King
	Sun btwn Jul 3 and 9 C
	Christ the King A
	Zion's Walls
	Sun btwn Jul 3 and 9 C

Copley, R. Evan — Surely He Has Borne Our Griefs
    Good Friday A, B, C

Corfe, Joseph — I Will Magnify Thee, O Lord
    Sun btwn Jun 26 and Jul 2 B

Croft, William — God Is Gone Up with a Merry Noise
    Ascension of Our Lord A, B, C
— O Give Thanks unto the Lord
    Sun btwn Sep 18 and 24 A

Crotch, William — Be Peace on Earth
    3 Advent C

Crouch, Andraé/Jack Schrader — Soon and Very Soon
    Sun btwn Nov 13 and 19 B

Crüger, Johann — Awake, My Heart, with Gladness
    Easter Day A
    2 Easter B
    3 Easter A, B

Darst, W. Glen — Walk Humbly with Thy God
    Sun btwn Nov 6 and 12 A

Davies, H. Walford — Blessed Are the Pure in Heart
    4 Epiphany A
— God Be in My Head
    7 Easter B
— O Sons and Daughters
    2 Easter A

Davis, Katherine — Who Was the Man
    Sun btwn Aug 7 and 13 A

Dawson, William — Ain'a That Good News
    Sun btwn Sep 18 and 24 C
    Christ the King C
— Ev'ry Time I Feel the Spirit
    Day of Pentecost A, C
— Mary Had a Baby
    4 Advent A
— There Is a Balm in Gilead
    6 Epiphany B
    7 Epiphany B
    Sun btwn Jul 3 and 9 C
    Sun btwn Jul 17 and 23 C

Decastre, Richard — Richard de Castre's Prayer to Jesus
    Sun btwn Sep 11 and 17 C

DeLienas, Juan — Coenantibus autem illis/As They Were Eating
    Maundy Thursday A, B, C

DeLong, Richard P. — Almighty God, Your Word Is Cast
    Sun btwn Jul 10 and 16 A
— Loving Shepherd of Thy Sheep
    4 Easter A
— Seek Ye the Lord
    Easter Vigil A, B, C
— This Is the Hour of Banquet and of Song
    Sun btwn Aug 14 and 20 B

Dengler, Lee — Look at the Birds of the Air
    Sun btwn Oct 2 and 8 C
— O Clap Your Hands
    Ascension of Our Lord A, B, C
— Sing unto the Lord
    Sun btwn Jun 12 and 18 C
    Sun btwn Jun 19 and 25 B

Dering, Richard — O vos omnes
    Passion/Palm Sunday C

Desamours, Emile — Noel Ayisyen
    1 Christmas B

Diemer, Emma Lou	Blessed Are You
	All Saints Day C
	I Will Extol You
	Sun btwn Sep 18 and 24 A
	Praise Ye the Lord
	Sun btwn Sep 4 and 10 B
	Sing, O Heavens
	2 Epiphany A
Dietterich, Philip R.	Carol of the Advent
	2 Advent C
Dirksen, Richard	Christ, Our Passover
	Easter Evening A, B, C
Distler, Hugo	A Lamb Goes Uncomplaining Forth
	2 Lent B
	Passion/Palm Sunday B
	Good Friday A, B, C
	A Little Advent Music
	1 Advent A
	Come Holy Ghost, God and Lord
	Day of Pentecost A, C
	Creator Spirit, Heavenly Dove
	Day of Pentecost A, B
	Dear Christians, One and All Rejoice
	5 Easter B
	For God So Loved the World/Also hat Gott die Welt geliebet
	2 Lent A, C
	4 Lent B
	Holy Trinity B
	Lo! How a Rose E'er Blooming
	1 Advent C
	2 Advent A
	3 Advent A
	4 Advent B
	Christmas Day (III) A, B, C
	Maria Walks amid the Thorn
	3 Advent A
	4 Advent A, B
	O Savior, Rend the Heavens Wide
	1 Advent A
	Praise to the Lord
	Sun btwn Oct 9 and 15 C
	Salvation unto Us Has Come
	8 Epiphany B
	Sun btwn May 29 and Jun 4 C
	Sun btwn Sep 18 and 24 A
	Sun btwn Oct 30 and Nov 5 C
	Reformation Day A, B, C
Dowland, John	He That Is Down Need Fear No Fall
	3 Lent C
	Sun btwn Aug 21 and 27 C
	Sun btwn Oct 23 and 29 C
Dressler, Gallus	I Am the Resurrection
	5 Lent A
	Sun btwn Nov 6 and 12 C
Dupré, Marcel	O salutaris
	Sun btwn Nov 13 and 19 C
Duruflé, Maurice	Notre Pére
	Sun btwn Jul 24 and 30 C
	Sanctus
	5 Epiphany C

(Duruflé, Maurice) Tantum ergo
    Sun btwn Nov 13 and 19 B
Tu es Petrus
    Sun btwn Aug 21 and 27 A
Ubi caritas
    4 Epiphany C
    Maundy Thursday A, B, C
    5 Easter C
    6 Easter B
    Sun btwn Jun 26 and Jul 2 C
    Sun btwn Sep 11 and 17 A

Dvořák, Antonín God Is My Shepherd
    Sun btwn Jul 17 and 23 B
I Will Sing New Songs of Gladness
    Sun btwn Jun 12 and 18 A
Search Me, O God
    Sun btwn Jul 17 and 23 A, C
Songs of Gladness I Will Sing Thee
    Sun btwn Jun 5 and 11 A

Ebeling, Johann Georg All My Heart This Night Rejoices: Be Glad and Sing
    Christmas Eve (I) A, B, C

Eccard, Johannes Over the Hills Maria Went
    4 Advent C
Raise a Song, Let Praise Abound
    1 Christmas A

Edwards, Paul Thy Mercy, O Lord, Reacheth unto the Heavens
    2 Epiphany C

Ehret, Walter O My Soul, Bless God the Father
    Sun btwn Sep 11 and 17 A

Elgar, Edward Ave verum corpus
    3 Lent B
    Maundy Thursday A, B, C
    Sun btwn Oct 16 and 22 B
The Spirit of the Lord Is upon Me
    3 Epiphany C

Ellen, Jane Love One Another
    7 Epiphany C

Ellingboe, Bradley For the Beauty of the Earth
    Sun btwn Aug 21 and 27 B
How Can I Keep from Singing?
    5 Epiphany B
    Sun btwn Jun 19 and 25 B
Jesus, Good Shepherd
    4 Lent A
    4 Easter A, B
    Sun btwn Jul 17 and 23 B
    Sun btwn Oct 9 and 15 A
Jesus, Jesus, Rest Your Head
    Christmas Eve (I) A, B, C
    Christmas Dawn (II) A, B, C
Let Us Talents and Tongues Employ
    3 Epiphany A
Magnificat
    4 Advent B
Mary at the Tomb
    Easter Day A
    2 Easter A, B, C
Simeon's Song
    1 Christmas B
    Presentation of Our Lord A, B, C

Soul Adorn Yourself with Gladness/Vengo a ti, Jesús amado
    2 Advent B, C
    2 Epiphany C
    Sun btwn Aug 7 and 13 B
    Sun btwn Nov 6 and 12 A
    Sun btwn Nov 13 and 19 C
Spirit of God, Descend upon My Heart
    Baptism of Our Lord A
Teach Each Other in Wisdom
    1 Christmas C
The Chief Cornerstone
    8 Epiphany C
    Tuesday in Holy Week A, B, C
    Easter Day A
    3 Easter C
    5 Easter A
    Sun btwn May 24 and 28 C
The Food of Life
    Sun btwn Jul 31 and Aug 6 C
The Holy Trinity
    Holy Trinity A, C
The Lord's My Shepherd
    4 Easter A
    Sun btwn Oct 9 and 15 A
The Lord's Prayer
    Sun btwn Jul 24 and 30 C
The Prayer of St. Francis
    Sun btwn Jul 10 and 16 B
There Is a Green Hill Far Away
    4 Lent B
    Good Friday A, B, C
There's a Wideness in God's Mercy
    3 Epiphany B
    8 Epiphany B
    2 Lent A
    Sun btwn May 24 and 28 B
    Sun btwn Jun 5 and 11 A
    Sun btwn Sep 18 and 24 A
Thy Holy Wings
    2 Lent C
    Monday in Holy Week A, B, C
You Are Peter!
    Sun btwn Aug 21 and 27 A

Erickson, Karle
Thy Holy Wings
    1 Lent B
    Monday in Holy Week A, B, C

Erickson, Richard
Come Away to the Skies
    Ascension of Our Lord A, B, C
    Easter Vigil A, B, C
    Easter Day A
    6 Easter C
    Sun btwn Jul 31 and Aug 6 C
I Want to Walk as a Child of the Light
    Epiphany of Our Lord A, B, C
    3 Epiphany B
    Presentation of Our Lord A, B, C
Light One Candle to Watch for Messiah
    3 Advent C
When Long Before Time
    Easter Vigil A, B, C
    Holy Trinity C

Farlee, Robert Buckley	Christ Is Living!/Cristo vive
	Easter Day C
	3 Easter B
	Christmas Day
	Christmas Day (III) A, B, C
	Farewell to Alleluia
	Transfiguration of Our Lord A, C
	Holy God
	Sun btwn Sep 11 and 17 C
	Mandatum
	Maundy Thursday A, B, C
	5 Easter C
	O Blessed Spring
	3 Lent A
	Easter Vigil A, B, C
	5 Easter B
	7 Easter C
	Day of Pentecost A
	Sun btwn Sep 25 and Oct 1 A
	Sun btwn Oct 9 and 15 C
	O My People, Turn to Me
	Sun btwn Jul 10 and 16 A
	Solemn Reproaches of the Cross
	Passion/Palm Sunday B
	Good Friday A, B, C
	The Lightener of the Stars
	Transfiguration of Our Lord A
	Ascension of Our Lord A, B, C
	This Is the Night
	Christmas Eve (I) A, B, C
	We Are a Garden Walled Around
	Easter Evening A, B, C
	Sun btwn Jul 31 and Aug 6 B
	When Twilight Comes
	2 Lent C
	Maundy Thursday A, B, C
Farrant, Richard	Call to Remembrance
	1 Lent B
	Sun btwn Jul 10 and 16 C
	Sun btwn Sep 25 and Oct 1 A
	Hide Not Thou Thy Face
	Sun btwn Jun 26 and Jul 2 A
Farrant, Richard or John Hilton	Lord, for Thy Tender Mercy's Sake
	3 Epiphany B
	7 Epiphany A, C
	Ash Wednesday A, B, C
	2 Lent B
	3 Lent A
Farrar, Sue	As Long as I Have Breath
	Sun btwn Jul 17 and 23 C
Farrell, Bernadette	Bread of Life
	Sun btwn Jul 31 and Aug 6 B
Fauré, Gabriel	Agnus Dei
	Sun btwn Nov 6 and 12 B
	Benedictus
	Sun btwn Aug 14 and 20 B
	Cantique de Jean Racine
	3 Epiphany C
	Sun btwn Oct 23 and 29 C
	In paradisum
	Sun btwn Sep 25 and Oct 1 C
	Christ the King C

Fay, Peter O Sacred and Blessed Feast/O sacrum convivium
            Sun btwn Jul 31 and Aug 6 B

Fedak, Alfred V. Begin the Song of Glory Now
            Easter Day B
        Christus Paradox
            Christ the King C
        This Touch of Love
            Sun btwn Aug 28 and Sep 3 C

Ferguson, John A Mighty Fortress
            1 Lent A, B
            Reformation Day A, B, C
        A Song of Thanksgiving/Psalm 90
            Sun btwn Oct 9 and 15 B, C
            Sun btwn Nov 13 and 19 A
            Day of Thanksgiving B, C
        Advent Processional
            2 Advent C
            3 Advent A
            4 Advent B
        Ah, Holy Jesus
            Passion/Palm Sunday A, B
            Wednesday in Holy Week A, B, C
            Good Friday A, B, C
        Be Thou My Vision
            4 Epiphany A
            Sun btwn Jul 31 and Aug 6 C
            Sun btwn Sep 18 and 24 B, C
            Sun btwn Oct 9 and 15 B
        By Gracious Powers
            Sun btwn Jun 19 and 25 C
            Sun btwn Oct 16 and 22 C
        Children of the Heavenly Father
            Sun btwn May 24 and 28 B
        Christ the Lord Is Risen Today!
            Easter Day A
        Come, Labor On
            7 Easter B
        Comfort, Comfort
            2 Advent A, B, C
        God Is Here
            Sun btwn Sep 4 and 10 B
        Good Christian Friends, Rejoice
            Christmas Dawn (II) A, B, C
            1 Christmas A
        He Comes to Us as One Unknown
            3 Advent A
            4 Advent A
            2 Epiphany B
            3 Epiphany A
            4 Epiphany C
            Sun btwn May 29 and Jun 4 B
        Holy God, We Praise Thy Name
            Holy Trinity A
            All Saints Day A
        In the Beginning
            Christmas Day (III) A, B, C
        Jesus Loves Me
            Sun btwn Sep 25 and Oct 1 A
        Jesus, My Lord and God
            5 Easter A
            7 Easter B
            Sun btwn Jul 10 and 16 B

(Ferguson, John)   Let All Mortal Flesh
        Transfiguration of Our Lord B
    Lord, in All Love
        2 Lent B
        5 Lent C
        Sun btwn Jul 17 and 23 C
        Sun btwn Sep 25 and Oct 1 C
    New Songs of Celebration Render
        Sun btwn Nov 13 and 19 C
    O Come, O Come, Emmanuel
        4 Advent A
    O God, Our Help in Ages Past
        Sun btwn Jun 5 and 11 B
        Sun btwn Nov 13 and 19 A
    Psalm 46/The Lord of Hosts
        Christ the King C
    Psalm 130/Out of the Depths
        Ash Wednesday A, B, C
        5 Lent A
    Rejoice, Rejoice, This Happy Morn
        Christmas Day (III) A, B, C
    St. John Passion
        Good Friday A, B, C
    The Church's One Foundation
        Sun btwn Jun 19 and 25 A
        Reformation Day A, B, C
    The Head That Once Was Crowned with Thorns
        7 Easter A
        Sun btwn Jun 12 and 18 B
        Christ the King A
    Thy Holy Wings
        Sun btwn May 24 and 28 A
    Unto Us Is Born God's Son
        Christmas Dawn (II) A, B, C
        2 Christmas A, B, C
    What Then
        8 Epiphany C
        Sun btwn May 24 and 28 C
    When I Survey the Wondrous Cross
        2 Lent B
    Word of God Come Down on Earth
        Sun btwn May 29 and Jun 4 A
        Sun btwn Jul 10 and 16 A

Ferko, Frank   Motet for Passion Sunday
        Passion/Palm Sunday A

Fetler, Paul   Sing unto God
        7 Easter A

Finzi, Gerald   Lo, the Full Final Sacrifice
        Christ the King C

Fleming, Larry L.   Blessed Are They
        Sun btwn Nov 13 and 19 B
        All Saints Day C
    Give Me Jesus
        3 Lent B
        Sun btwn Jun 26 and Jul 2 C
        Sun btwn Aug 21 and 27 B
    Go and Tell John
        3 Advent A
    His Voice
        2 Advent B
        Sun btwn Aug 28 and Sep 3 B

	Humble Service
	7 Epiphany A, B, C
	5 Lent C
	Sun btwn May 29 and Jun 4 C
	Sun btwn Sep 4 and 10 B
	Sun btwn Sep 18 and 24 B
	Sun btwn Oct 16 and 22 B
	Sun btwn Oct 30 and Nov 5 A
	Lord of the Dance
	Epiphany of Our Lord A, B, C
	Ascension of Our Lord A, B, C
	Sun btwn Nov 6 and 12 B
	Ride On, King Jesus
	Passion/Palm Sunday A, B
	Sing and Ponder
	Maundy Thursday A, B, C
	Good Friday A, B, C
Folkening, John	Psalm 147
	2 Christmas A, B, C
Forsberg, Charles	Fairest Lord Jesus
	Epiphany of Our Lord A, B, C
	Transfiguration of Our Lord A, B, C
Frahm, Frederick	How Sweet the Name of Jesus Sounds
	Name of Jesus A, B, C
Franck, César	Nativity Carol
	Christmas Dawn (II) A, B, C
	O Bread of Heaven
	Sun btwn Jul 24 and 30 B
	O Bread of Life/Panis angelicus
	Sun btwn Jul 31 and Aug 6 A
Franck, Melchior	Come, O Blessed of My Father
	Sun btwn Sep 18 and 24 B
	Our Father, Thou in Heaven Above
	Sun btwn Jul 24 and 30 C
Friedell, Harold	Draw Us in the Spirit's Tether
	Holy Trinity A
	Sun btwn Jun 19 and 25 C
	Sun btwn Jun 26 and Jul 2 C
	Sun btwn Jul 3 and 9 B
	Sun btwn Sep 4 and 10 A
	Sun btwn Oct 2 and 8 B
	The Way to Jerusalem
	Sun btwn Jun 26 and Jul 2 C
Gabrieli, Giovanni	O Bless the Lord
	Sun btwn Aug 21 and 27 C
Gallus, Jacobus (Handl)	Ascendit Deus
	Ascension of Our Lord A, B, C
	Enredietur virga
	2 Advent A
	Repleti sunt omnes/And They All Were Filled
	Day of Pentecost B, C
	Stetit Iesus/There Came Jesus
	2 Easter B
	This Is the Day
	Easter Day A, C
Gardner, John	Fight the Good Fight
	6 Epiphany B
	Sun btwn Aug 14 and 20 C
	Sun btwn Sep 25 and Oct 1 A, C
	Sun btwn Oct 23 and 29 C

(Gardner, John)	Tomorrow Shall Be My Dancing Day
	Christmas Eve (I) A, B, C
	2 Christmas A, B, C
Gastoldi, Giovanni	In You Is Gladness
	Transfiguration of Our Lord A
Gehring, Philip	Taste and See
	Sun btwn Oct 2 and 8 B
	The Cup of Blessing
	Sun btwn Oct 16 and 22 B
Gerike, Henry V.	Create in Me
	Ash Wednesday A, B, C
	Sing with All the Saints in Glory
	Sun btwn Nov 6 and 12 C
	The Strife Is O'er, the Battle Done
	Easter Vigil A, B, C
	3 Easter B
	Up through Endless Ranks of Angels
	Ascension of Our Lord A, B, C
Gesius, Bartholomäus	Hosanna to the Son of David
	Passion/Palm Sunday C
	Sing Hosanna to the Son of David
	Passion/Palm Sunday B
	Today in Triumph Christ Arose
	Easter Day C
Gibbons, Orlando	Almighty and Everlasting God
	1 Lent C
	Sun btwn Jun 19 and 25 B
	Sun btwn Sep 25 and Oct 1 C
	Come, Holy Spirit
	Day of Pentecost A
	Hosanna to the Son of David
	Passion/Palm Sunday B, C
	O Clap Your Hands
	Ascension of Our Lord A, B, C
	O Lord, Increase My Faith
	Sun btwn Oct 2 and 8 C
	This Is the Record of John
	3 Advent B
Gibbs, Armstrong C.	Bless the Lord, O My Soul
	3 Advent A
	5 Lent C
Gieschen, Thomas	Of the Father's Love Begotten
	Christmas Day (III) A, B, C
Gieseke, Richard	Lift Up Your Heads
	1 Advent B
Glarum, L. Stanley	Seek Ye First the Kingdom of God
	Sun btwn May 24 and 28 A
	Sing Praises
	8 Epiphany A
Glinka, Mikhail	Cherubic Hymn
	Holy Trinity A
Goemanne, Noël	Fanfare for Festivals
	Easter Day A
	Holy God, We Praise Thy Name
	Holy Trinity A
	Hymns of Thanks
	Day of Thanksgiving A
Goetze, Mary	The Angel Gabriel
	4 Advent C
Goodall, Howard	The Lord Is My Shepherd
	4 Easter C

Goss, John	God So Loved the World
	2 Lent A
	These Are They Which Follow the Lamb
	2 Epiphany A
Goudimel, Claude	As the Deer, for Water Yearning
	3 Lent C
	Easter Vigil A, B, C
	Comfort, Comfort Ye My People
	2 Advent C
	Psalm 1
	Sun btwn Oct 23 and 29 A
Gounod, Charles	Blessed Is He Who Cometh
	Passion/Palm Sunday A
Greene, Maurice	You Visit the Earth
	Sun btwn Jul 10 and 16 A
	Day of Thanksgiving A
Grieg, Edvard	God's Son Has Made Me Free
	Sun btwn Jun 19 and 25 C
	Sun btwn Jun 26 and Jul 2 A
	Reformation Day A, B, C
	Pentecost Hymn
	Day of Pentecost B
Grundahl, Nancy	The Best of Rooms
	Sun btwn Oct 30 and Nov 5 C
Haan, Raymond H.	I Want Jesus to Walk with Me
	4 Epiphany B
	1 Lent A, C
	They Shall Shine as the Stars
	Sun btwn Nov 13 and 19 B
Haas, David	Blest Are They
	6 Epiphany C
	All Saints Day C
	Dust and Ashes
	Ash Wednesday A, B, C
	I Am the Living Bread
	Sun btwn Aug 7 and 13 B
	Sun btwn Aug 14 and 20 B
Hairston, Jester	Poor Man Laz'rus
	Sun btwn Sep 25 and Oct 1 C
Hallock, Peter	I Will Exalt You
	Sun btwn Sep 18 and 24 A
	The Baptism of Christ
	Baptism of Our Lord A
	The 'O' Antiphons
	4 Advent A
	Wash Me Through and Through
	Ash Wednesday A, B, C
	Your Love, O Lord, For Ever I Will Sing
	Sun btwn Jun 26 and Jul 2 A
Halloran, Jack	Witness
	3 Lent C
	Sun btwn Aug 28 and Sep 3 B
Hammerschmidt, Andreas	Heilig ist der Herr/Holy Is the Lord
	5 Epiphany C
	Let the People Praise Thee, O God
	Sun btwn Aug 14 and 20 A
Hampton, Calvin	Fairest Lord Jesus
	Sun btwn Jul 10 and 16 B
Hampton, Keith	Give Me Jesus
	1 Lent B
	He's Got the Whole World
	7 Epiphany B

Hancock, Gerre

Hancock, Gerre/arr. Paul Bouman

Handel, George Frideric

Christ Our Passover/Pascha nostrum
    Easter Day B
O God of Mercy
    Sun btwn Aug 28 and Sep 3 C
All My Spirit Longs to Savor
    2 Epiphany C
    7 Easter B
    Sun btwn Jul 10 and 16 B
All We Like Sheep Have Gone Astray
    4 Easter A
Alleluia
    Easter Day A
And He Shall Purify
    2 Advent C
    2 Epiphany A
And the Glory of the Lord
    2 Advent B, C
And with His Stripes We Are Healed
    4 Easter A
Behold, a Virgin Shall Conceive
    4 Advent A
But Thanks Be to God
    Sun btwn Jun 26 and Jul 2 A
But Who May Abide
    2 Advent C
    Sun btwn Aug 21 and 27 C
Come unto Him
    Sun btwn Jul 3 and 9 A
Deck Thyself, My Soul, with Gladness
    Sun btwn Jul 31 and Aug 6 A
    Sun btwn Nov 6 and 12 A
Ev'ry Valley
    8 Epiphany A
    Sun btwn Oct 23 and 29 C
    Sun btwn Oct 30 and Nov 5 A
Exceeding Glad
    4 Epiphany A
For Unto Us a Child Is Born
    Christmas Eve (I) A, B, C
    2 Epiphany B
Glory and Worship
    7 Easter A
    Sun btwn Oct 2 and 8 A
    Christ the King A
He Shall Feed His Flock
    4 Easter A
    Christ the King A
He Was Despised
    Passion/Palm Sunday A
    Wednesday in Holy Week A, B, C
His Yoke Is Easy
    3 Epiphany A
    Sun btwn Jul 3 and 9 A
How Beautiful Are the Feet
    Sun btwn Aug 7 and 13 A
How Excellent Thy Name
    Holy Trinity C
I Know that My Redeemer Liveth
    6 Epiphany C
    Easter Day C
    Sun btwn Jun 5 and 11 B
    Sun btwn Nov 6 and 12 C

  If God Is for Us, Who Is against Us
    Sun btwn Jul 24 and 30 A
  Jesu, Thou Art Watching Ever
    Sun btwn Jul 31 and Aug 6 B
  Jesus, Sun of Life, My Splendor
    Sun btwn Jun 26 and Jul 2 C
  Keep Me Faithfully in Thy Paths
    Sun btwn Jun 5 and 11 A
    Sun btwn Sep 4 and 10 A
  Laudate pueri Dominum
    Sun btwn Sep 18 and 24 C
  Let All the Angels of God Worship Him
    Christmas Day (III) A, B, C
  Let Justice and Judgment
    Sun btwn Oct 16 and 22 C
  Let Thy Hand Be Strengthened
    Sun btwn Sep 25 and Oct 1 A
  Lord, I Trust Thee
    Sun btwn Aug 28 and Sep 3 A
  My Heart Is Inditing
    Christ the King A
  O Death, Where Is Thy Sting?
    Sun btwn Jun 26 and Jul 2 A
  O Thou That Tellest
    4 Advent A
  O Zion, Herald of Good News
    Sun btwn Jun 12 and 18 C
  Rejoice Greatly, O Daughter of Zion
    Sun btwn Jul 3 and 9 A, C
  Since by Man Came Death
    1 Lent A
    Easter Vigil A, B, C
    Easter Day C
    Sun btwn Jun 19 and 25 A
    Sun btwn Oct 2 and 8 A
    Sun btwn Oct 9 and 15 C
    Sun btwn Nov 6 and 12 C
  Surely He Hath Borne Our Griefs
    3 Lent A
    Good Friday A, B, C
    Sun btwn Oct 16 and 22 B
  The King Shall Rejoice
    Christ the King A, C
  The People That Walked in Darkness
    3 Epiphany A
  Thine Is the Glory
    2 Easter C
  Why Do the Nations So Furiously Rage?
    Sun btwn Aug 14 and 20 C
    Sun btwn Nov 13 and 19 C
  Worthy Is the Lamb
    3 Easter C

Handel, George Frideric/arr. Andrews, Stephen
  I Will Praise Forever
    Sun btwn Oct 2 and 8 B

Handl, Jakob
  Ascendit Deus
    Ascension of Our Lord A, B, C
  Enredietur virga
    2 Advent A
  Repleti sunt omnes/And They All Were Filled
    Day of Pentecost B, C
  Stetit Iesus/There Came Jesus
    2 Easter B

(Handl, Jakob)	This Is the Day
	Easter Day A, C
Hanson, Howard	God Is Our Refuge and Strength
	Sun btwn May 29 and Jun 4 A
	O Lord Our Lord, How Excellent Thy Name
	Holy Trinity A, C
Harris, David S.	Come, and Let Us Return unto the Lord
	Sun btwn Jun 5 and 11 A
Harris, William H.	Come Down, O Love Divine
	6 Easter C
	Sun btwn Oct 30 and Nov 5 A
	Faire Is the Heaven
	6 Easter C
	All Saints Day A, C
	This Joyful Eastertide
	Easter Day B
Harrison, Benjamin	Alleluia! Sing to Jesus
	7 Easter B
Harwood, Basil	I Am the Living Bread
	Sun btwn Aug 28 and Sep 3 B
Hassler, Hans Leo	A Mighty Fortress Is Our God/Ein feste Burg ist unser Gott
	1 Lent A, C
	Reformation Day A, B, C
	Agnus Dei
	Sun btwn Sep 11 and 17 B
	Because You Have Seen Me, Thomas
	2 Easter A
	Cantate Domino
	Sun btwn Sep 25 and Oct 1 B
	Sun btwn Oct 16 and 22 A
	God Now Dwells among Us
	Christmas Day (III) A, B, C
	Lord, Let at Last Thine Angels Come
	5 Lent A
	My Soul Proclaims the Greatness of the Lord
	3 Advent A
	O Sing unto the Lord
	Christmas Eve (I) A, B, C
	Then Mary Said to the Angel
	4 Advent C
Hassler, Hans Leo/Hugo Distler	Dear Christians, One and All, Rejoice
	6 Easter A
Haugen, Marty	Bread to Share
	Sun btwn Jul 24 and 30 B
	Come to the Feast
	Sun btwn Jul 10 and 16 A
	Healer of Our Every Ill
	Sun btwn Sep 4 and 10 B
	Sun btwn Oct 23 and 29 B
	Shepherd Me, O God
	4 Easter B
	Taste and See
	Sun btwn Aug 14 and 20 B
	Triduum Hymn: Wondrous Love
	Maundy Thursday A, B, C
Haydn, Franz Joseph	Achieved Is the Glorious Work
	Ascension of Our Lord A, B, C
	Holy Trinity C
	In Thee, O Lord
	5 Easter A
	Sun btwn May 29 and Jun 4 A

	Lo, My Shepherd's Hand Divine
	4 Lent A
	Sun btwn Jul 17 and 23 B
	Rolling in Foaming Billows
	Sun btwn Jun 19 and 25 B
	Show Me Your Ways, O Lord
	Sun btwn Jul 10 and 16 C
	The Heavens Are Telling
	Sun btwn Sep 25 and Oct 1 B
Haydn, Franz Joseph/arr. Robert Scholz	God of Life
	Sun btwn Aug 21 and 27 B
Hayes, Mark	Alleluia, Christ Is Risen
	Easter Day C
	Day by Day
	6 Epiphany A
	Sun btwn Jul 17 and 23 C
	Sun btwn Sep 4 and 10 C
	Sun btwn Oct 2 and 8 B
	Sun btwn Nov 6 and 12 B
	Let the Word Go Forth
	Sun btwn Jul 24 and 30 A
Head, Michael	Make a Joyful Noise unto the Lord
	Sun btwn Jun 12 and 18 A
	Day of Thanksgiving A
Heim, Bret	All Glory Be to God Alone
	1 Christmas C
	Lord of Lords Adored by Angels
	Maundy Thursday A, B, C
Helgen, John	Breath of God
	Vigil of Pentecost A, B, C
	In God's Presence
	Sun btwn Jul 31 and Aug 6 B
	Keep Silence
	1 Advent B
	5 Epiphany C
	Praise the Living God Who Sings
	Day of Pentecost B
	Sun btwn May 24 and 28 A
	Sun btwn Oct 9 and 15 C
	Spirit of God, Descend
	Vigil of Pentecost A, B, C
	Sun btwn Jul 10 and 16 C
	Sun btwn Sep 4 and 10 C
	That Priceless Grace
	2 Lent C
	Sun btwn May 24 and 28 B
	Sun btwn Sep 25 and Oct 1 C
Hellerman, Fred, and Fran Minkoff /arr. David Cherwien	O Healing River
	Sun btwn Jun 26 and Jul 2 B
	Sun btwn Aug 14 and 20 A
Helman, Michael	Christ, When for Us You Were Baptized
	Baptism of Our Lord C
	Go Up to the Mountain of God
	Transfiguration of Our Lord A, B, C
	We Walk by Faith
	2 Easter B
Henderson, Ruth Watson	Bless the Lord, O My Soul
	Sun btwn Sep 11 and 17 A
Hewitt-Jones, Tony	Thou Art Peter
	Sun btwn Aug 21 and 27 A

Hillert, Richard
    Alleluia! Voices Raise!
        7 Easter A
    Amid the World's Bleak Wilderness
        Sun btwn Oct 2 and 8 A
    Come, Thou Long-Expected Jesus
        4 Advent A
    Festival Canticle
        Sun btwn Nov 13 and 19 A
    God Whose Giving Knows No Ending
        Sun btwn Oct 16 and 22 A
    Happy Are Those Who Delight
        Sun btwn Oct 23 and 29 A
    He Shall Give His Angels Charge
        1 Lent C
    How Great Is Your Name
        Sun btwn Oct 2 and 8 B
    Image of the Unseen God
        2 Easter A
        Sun btwn Jul 17 and 23 A
    O Sons and Daughters of the King
        2 Easter B
    On This Day Earth Shall Ring
        Christmas Dawn (II) A, B, C
    Surely He Hath Borne Our Griefs
        Good Friday A, B, C
    The Lord Is My Light and My Salvation
        Sun btwn Aug 21 and 27 A
    You Are the Light of the World
        4 Epiphany A

Hilton, John
    Wilt Thou Forgive?/A Hymn to God the Father
        1 Lent A
        Sun btwn May 24 and 28 B

Hirten, John Karl
    For Glory Dawns upon You
        Epiphany of Our Lord A, B, C

Hobby, Robert A.
    Beloved, God's Chosen
        Sun btwn Jun 26 and Jul 2 C
        Sun btwn Jul 3 and 9 B
    Forgive Our Sins as We Forgive
        7 Epiphany C
    Glorious Things of You Are Spoken
        Sun btwn Jul 31 and Aug 6 B
    I Lift My Soul
        Sun btwn Jun 26 and Jul 2 B
    I Will Bless the Lord
        All Saints Day A
    Immortal, Invisible, God Only Wise
        Sun btwn Jul 17 and 23 C
    Now All the Vault of Heaven Resounds/Ye Watchers and Ye Holy Ones
        Easter Vigil A, B, C
        6 Easter B
    O Christ, Our Light, O Radiance True/
      Jesus, Thy Church with Longing Eyes
        Sun btwn Jul 3 and 9 B
    O God of Light
        4 Epiphany C
    O Morning Star, How Fair and Bright
        Epiphany of Our Lord A, B, C
    Offertory for All Saints Day
        All Saints Day C
    Offertory for the Transfiguration of Our Lord
        Transfiguration of Our Lord A, C

	Psalm 150
	2 Easter C
	Take My Life, That I May Be
	Sun btwn Sep 11 and 17 B
	Sun btwn Oct 9 and 15 B
Hogan, David	O Jesus, King Most Wonderful
	Sun btwn Oct 23 and 29 A
Hogan, Moses	I'm Gonna Sing 'til the Spirit Moves in My Heart
	Baptism of Our Lord C
	Day of Pentecost A
	Lord, I Want to Be a Christian
	5 Lent B
Holst, Gustav	Christmas Day
	Christmas Day (III) A, B, C
	In the Bleak Midwinter
	Christmas Dawn (II) A, B, C
	Let All Mortal Flesh
	5 Epiphany C
	Sun btwn Aug 14 and 20 B
	Psalm 148
	5 Easter C
	Turn Back O Man
	Sun btwn Sep 4 and 10 A
Holst, Gustav/arr. Brad Printz	In the Bleak Midwinter
	Christmas Dawn (II) A, B, C
Hopp, Roy H.	From the Apple in the Garden
	Sun btwn Nov 6 and 12 C
	God of Grace and God of Laughter
	4 Epiphany C
	7 Epiphany B
	May I Love You, Lord
	2 Lent C
	Not for Tongues of Heaven's Angels
	4 Epiphany C
Hopson, Hal H.	A Lenten Walk
	1 Lent B, C
	A Mighty Fortress Is Our God
	1 Lent A
	A Psalm of Confession
	Ash Wednesday A, B, C
	Advent Prayer
	1 Advent C
	For as the Rain and Snow Come Down
	Easter Vigil A, B, C
	Sun btwn Jul 10 and 16 A
	God Has Gone Up with a Shout
	Ascension of Our Lord A, B, C
	O Day of Peace
	3 Advent B
	O Praise the Lord Who Made All Beauty
	Easter Vigil A, B, C
	Sing Aloud to God
	Sun btwn Oct 23 and 29 B
	Sing Praise to the Lord
	Sun btwn Oct 9 and 15 C
	The Gift of Love
	Sun btwn Oct 2 and 8 B
	We Know That Christ Is Raised
	Sun btwn Jun 12 and 18 B
Hovhaness, Alan	Make Haste
	Sun btwn Nov 6 and 12 A

(Hovhaness, Alan) — Watchman, Tell Us of the Night
    1 Advent A
Jesus Christ Is Risen Today
    Easter Day B

Hovland, Egil — Saul
    3 Easter C
Stay with Us
    Easter Evening A, B, C
    3 Easter A
The Glory of the Father
    Christmas Day (III) A, B, C
    2 Christmas A, B, C
    3 Epiphany B

How, Martin — Advent Message
    1 Advent B
    3 Advent B
An Easter Greeting
    5 Easter A
Arise, Shine, for Your Light Has Come
    Epiphany of Our Lord A, B, C
Day by Day
    6 Epiphany A
    Sun btwn Jun 19 and 25 B
    Sun btwn Jul 10 and 16 C
    Sun btwn Aug 21 and 27 B
Lenten Litany
    5 Lent B
O Come, Let Us Sing Unto the Lord
    3 Lent A
O Holy Spirit, Lord of Grace
    Day of Pentecost A
Praise, O Praise
    Day of Thanksgiving B
Psalm 23
    4 Lent A
    4 Easter A
    Sun btwn Oct 9 and 15 A

Howells, Herbert — A Spotless Rose
    1 Advent C
    2 Advent A
Coventry Antiphon
    Sun btwn Aug 14 and 20 A
Here Is the Little Door
    1 Christmas A
Like As the Hart
    3 Lent C
    Easter Vigil A, B, C
My Eyes for Beauty Pine
    7 Epiphany C
    Sun btwn Aug 21 and 27 B
O Pray for the Peace of Jerusalem
    1 Advent A
    Sun btwn Jul 3 and 9 A

Hurd, David — Alleluia for a Festival
    5 Easter A
Cantate Domino/Psalm 98
    Christmas Day (III) A, B, C
Creating God
    Holy Trinity A
Love Bade Me Welcome
    8 Epiphany B
    Sun btwn Nov 13 and 19 B

	Psalm 96: Sing to the Lord a New Song
	Sun btwn Oct 16 and 22 A
	Show Us Your Kindness
	Sun btwn Aug 7 and 13 A
	Teach Me, O Lord
	Sun btwn Sep 4 and 10 A
	The Lord Shall Reign
	Ascension of Our Lord A, B, C
Hurford, Peter	Litany to the Holy Spirit
	7 Epiphany B
	Day of Pentecost A
Hutchings, Arthur	God Is Gone Up with a Merry Noise
	Ascension of Our Lord A, B, C
Ippolitof-Ivanov, Mikhail	Bless the Lord, O My Soul
	Sun btwn Aug 21 and 27 C
Ireland, John	Greater Love Hath No Man
	4 Easter A
	6 Easter B
Isaac, Heinrich	O Bread of Life from Heaven/O esca viatorum
	Sun btwn Jul 31 and Aug 6 B
	Sun btwn Aug 7 and 13 B
	Sun btwn Oct 2 and 8 A
	O World, I Must Be Parting
	Sun btwn Nov 13 and 19 A
	Upon the Cross Extended
	Good Friday A, B, C
Isaac, Heinrich/arr. Anthony G. Petti	Ecce virgo concipies
	4 Advent A
Isom, Paul	King of All Ages, Throned on High
	Christ the King B
Ives, Charles	Hymn
	Sun btwn Jun 5 and 11 C
Jacob, Gordon	Brother James's Air
	Sun btwn Oct 9 and 15 A
	O Lord I Will Praise Thee
	3 Advent C
Jean, Martin	Advent Hymn
	2 Advent A
	3 Advent B, C
Jennings, Arthur	Springs in the Desert
	3 Advent A
Jennings, Carolyn	A New Magnificat
	3 Advent A
	4 Advent B, C
	Ah, Holy Jesus
	Passion/Palm Sunday B
	Good Friday A, B, C
	Climb to the Top of the Highest Mountain
	2 Advent B
	3 Advent C
	Sun btwn Oct 2 and 8 C
	Creator Spirit, by Whose Aid
	Day of Pentecost A, C
	God's Word Is Our Great Heritage
	Sun btwn Oct 16 and 22 A
	My Song Is Love Unknown
	Passion/Palm Sunday A
	Praise, My Soul, the God of Heaven
	Sun btwn Oct 9 and 15 C
	The Kingdom of God
	Sun btwn Sep 11 and 17 B

(Jennings, Carolyn)	We Praise You, O God
	Day of Thanksgiving A, B, C
Jennings, Kenneth	All You Works of the Lord, Bless the Lord
	Easter Vigil A, B, C
	Arise, O Zion
	2 Epiphany C
	Arise, Shine, for Thy Light Has Come
	Epiphany of Our Lord A, B, C
	If Ye Be Risen Again with Christ
	Sun btwn Jul 31 and Aug 6 C
	Thee Will I Love
	7 Easter B
	Sun btwn Jun 12 and 18 C
	Sun btwn Jul 10 and 16 C
	With a Voice of Singing
	5 Easter A
	6 Easter B
	7 Easter A
	Sun btwn Jul 3 and 9 C
Johnson, Carolyn	Now the Green Blade Rises
	3 Easter C
Johnson, David N.	O Dearest Lord, Thy Sacred Head
	Passion/Palm Sunday B
	Good Friday A, B, C
	Souls of the Righteous
	All Saints Day A
	The Lone, Wild Bird
	7 Easter A
Johnson, Hall	Ev'ry Time I Feel de Spirit
	Holy Trinity B
	This Is de Healin' Water
	Sun btwn Jun 19 and 25 A
	Witness
	Sun btwn Jun 19 and 25 B
Johnson, J. Rosamond	Little David Play On Your Harp
	Sun btwn Jun 5 and 11 A
Johnson, Ralph M.	Be Thou a Smooth Way
	Sun btwn Nov 6 and 12 A
Jordan, Alice	See the Land, Her Easter Keeping
	Easter Evening A, B, C
Josquin Desprez	Come, O Creator Spirit, Come
	Day of Pentecost A
	God, the Lord, Now Reigneth
	Ascension of Our Lord A, B, C
	Christ the King A
	O Jesu, fili David
	Sun btwn Aug 14 and 20 A
	O Mighty Word from God Come Down
	3 Easter C
Joubert, John	Torches
	1 Christmas C
Kallman, Daniel	Amazing Grace
	Sun btwn Jun 26 and Jul 2 B
	Sun btwn Sep 11 and 17 C
	In Thee Is Gladness
	8 Epiphany C
	Sun btwn May 24 and 28 A
	Name of Jesus A, B, C
	Just a Closer Walk
	4 Epiphany B
	Lord of All Hopefulness
	Sun btwn Jul 3 and 9 A

	Lord, Whose Love in Humble Service
	Sun btwn Sep 25 and Oct 1 B
Kemp, Helen	A Lenten Love Song
	Maundy Thursday A, B, C
	A Waiting Carol
	4 Advent A
Kern, Jan	Chants of the Passion
	Passion/Palm Sunday A
	Good Friday A, B, C
Kitson, C. H.	Jesu, Grant Me This, I Pray
	1 Lent C
	Sun btwn Jul 17 and 23 B
Kodály, Zoltán	Jesus and the Traders
	3 Lent B
Kopylow, Alexander/arr. Peter Wilhousky	Heavenly Light
	3 Epiphany A, B
Kosche, Kenneth T.	Come, Thou Fount of Every Blessing
	Sun btwn Sep 11 and 17 C
	If You Will Trust the Lord to Guide You
	Sun btwn Sep 25 and Oct 1 B
Krapf, Gerhard	The King of Love My Shepherd Is
	4 Easter A, C
Kremser, Eduard	Prayer of Thanksgiving
	Day of Thanksgiving A
Kreutz, Robert	Jesu dulcis/The Taste of Goodness
	All Saints Day A
Lallouette, Jean François/arr. Richard Proulx	Christ the Glory
	Transfiguration of Our Lord B
Lamberton, Dodd	I Want to Walk as a Child of the Light
	Sun btwn Jun 26 and Jul 2 A
Larkin, Michael	O Child of Promise Come
	2 Advent B
	The Eyes of All
	Sun btwn Jul 31 and Aug 6 A
Lassus, Orlande de	Adoramus te
	Sun btwn Jul 17 and 23 C
	Christ Has Arisen/Christ ist erstanden
	3 Easter B
Lassus, Rudolph de/arr. Richard Proulx	Stars in the Sky Proclaim
	Epiphany of Our Lord A, B, C
Laster, James	Forgive Our Sins as We Forgive
	Sun btwn Jun 12 and 18 A
	Sing of Mary, Pure and Lowly
	1 Christmas C
	Presentation of Our Lord A, B, C
Lau, Robert	Christ Is Risen! Alleluia!
	3 Easter B
Lauridsen, Morten	O nata lux
	Epiphany of Our Lord A, B, C
Leaf, Robert	Come with Rejoicing
	Sun btwn Jul 3 and 9 A
	O Sacred Head, Now Wounded
	Passion/Palm Sunday B
	Good Friday A, B, C
Leavitt, John	An Easter Gloria!
	2 Easter B
	At the Lamb's High Feast
	Easter Vigil A, B, C
	Come, Follow Me
	Sun btwn Aug 28 and Sep 3 A
	Easter
	Easter Day B

(Leavitt, John)	Festival Sanctus
	Holy Trinity A
Leighton, Kenneth	Solus ad victimam/Alone to Sacrifice
	Maundy Thursday A, B, C
	Good Friday A, B, C
Lekberg, Sven	For as the Rain Cometh Down
	Sun btwn May 24 and 28 C
	Sun btwn Jul 10 and 16 A
Lenel, Ludwig	When I Survey the Wondrous Cross
	Sun btwn Oct 2 and 8 A
Ley, Henry G.	The Strife Is O'er
	Easter Vigil A, B, C
Liddle, Samuel	The Lord Is My Shepherd
	Sun btwn Jul 17 and 23 B
Lienas, Juan de	Coenantibus autem illis
	Maundy Thursday A, B, C
Lindley, Simon	O God, My Heart Is Ready
	Sun btwn Aug 28 and Sep 3 A
Loosemore, Henry	O Lord, Increase Our Faith
	Sun btwn Sep 4 and 10 C
Lovelace, Austin	Hope of the World
	4 Epiphany B
	5 Epiphany B
Lowenberg, Kenneth	Blessed Are the Pure in Spirit
	4 Lent A
Lynn, George	I Want Jesus to Walk with Me
	Sun btwn Jun 26 and Jul 2 A
Maddux, David	O Sifuni Mungu
	Day of Pentecost B
Manz, Paul	E'en So, Lord Jesus, Quickly Come
	1 Advent A, C
	3 Advent B
	2 Easter C
	6 Easter C
	7 Easter C
	Sun btwn Nov 13 and 19 A, C
	Christ the King B
	I Caused Thy Grief
	Good Friday A, B, C
	I Want to Walk as a Child of the Light
	3 Epiphany A
	Let Us Ever Walk with Jesus
	Sun btwn Jun 26 and Jul 2 A, B
	Sun btwn Aug 7 and 13 A
	On My Heart Imprint Thine Image
	4 Lent A
	Peace Came to Earth
	Christmas Day (III) A, B, C
Marcello, Benedetto	Give Ear unto Me
	2 Lent C
	Sun btwn Jul 31 and Aug 6 A
	O Lord, Our Governor
	Holy Trinity C
	Oh, Hold Thou Me Up
	Sun btwn Jun 5 and 11 A
	Sun btwn Jul 3 and 9 B
Marcello, Benedetto/arr. Dale Grotenhuis	Teach Me Now, O Lord
	Sun btwn Jul 17 and 23 A, B
	Sun btwn Sep 4 and 10 A
	Sun btwn Oct 30 and Nov 5 B

Marchant, Stanley The Souls of the Righteous
  All Saints Day C

Marenzio, Luca Quia vidisti me, Thomas/Because You Have Seen Me, Thomas
  2 Easter A, B, C

Marshall, Jane A Joyful Psalm
  Sun btwn Sep 25 and Oct 1 C
 Bless the Lord, My Soul
  Sun btwn Sep 11 and 17 A
 Create in Me, O God
  Sun btwn Sep 25 and Oct 1 A
 How Lovely Is Your Dwelling Place
  Sun btwn Oct 23 and 29 C
  Christ the King B
  Presentation of Our Lord A, B, C
 Psalm 98
  Easter Vigil A, B, C
 Sing to God
  2 Christmas A, B, C
 Song of Simeon
  1 Christmas B

Martin, Gilbert When I Survey the Wondrous Cross
  5 Lent C
  Tuesday in Holy Week A, B, C

Martini, Giovanni Battista Lord, My God, Assist Me Now
  Sun btwn Nov 6 and 12 A

Martinson, Joel And the Word Became Flesh
  2 Christmas A, B, C
 Arise, Shine!
  Epiphany of Our Lord A, B, C
 Awake, Arise!
  3 Easter B
 God So Loved the World
  2 Lent A, B
 Psalm 15
  4 Epiphany A
 Psalm 98
  Sun btwn Nov 13 and 19 C
 Three Days Had Passed
  Easter Day A
 Transfiguration
  Transfiguration of Our Lord A, B

Mathews, Peter Blest Be the King
  2 Advent C
 The Prayer of St. Francis
  Sun btwn Jul 10 and 16 B

Mathias, William H. A Babe Is Born
  Christmas Eve (I) A, B, C
 Ah, Holy Jesus
  Good Friday A, B, C
 Alleluia! Christ Is Risen
  Easter Day B
 Arise, Shine, for Your Light Has Come
  Baptism of Our Lord A
 Hear, O Thou Shepherd of Israel
  4 Advent A, C
  Sun btwn Oct 2 and 8 A
 Hodie Christus natus est
  Christmas Dawn (II) A, B, C
 In excelsis gloria
  Christmas Eve (I) A, B, C
 Let All the World in Every Corner Sing
  Christ the King A

(Mathias, William H.)	Let the People Praise Thee, O God
	6 Easter C
	Sun btwn Aug 14 and 20 A
	Lift Up Your Heads, O Ye Gates
	Passion/Palm Sunday A, C
	Ascension of Our Lord A, B, C
	O Clap Your Hands
	Ascension of Our Lord A, B, C
	Rejoice in the Lord
	Sun btwn Sep 25 and Oct 1 B
Mathias, William H./arr. Donald D. Livingston	Come Down, O Love Divine
	Vigil of Pentecost A, C
	Day of Pentecost C
McCabe, Michael	I Am the Living Bread
	Sun btwn Aug 7 and 13 B
McFerrin, Bobby	The 23rd Psalm
	4 Easter A
McKie, William	We Wait for Thy Loving Kindness, O God
	4 Epiphany C
Mendelssohn, Felix	Above All Praise and All Majesty
	Ascension of Our Lord A, B, C
	Sun btwn Oct 9 and 15 C
	All Ye That Cried unto the Lord
	6 Epiphany B
	And Then Shall Your Light Break Forth
	Transfiguration of Our Lord C
	Be Thou Faithful to the Truth
	Sun btwn Jun 5 and 11 B
	Cast Thy Burden upon the Lord
	Sun btwn Jun 19 and 25 A
	For God Commanded Angels to Watch Over You
	Sun btwn Oct 16 and 22 B
	For He Shall Give His Angels Charge Over Thee
	1 Lent C
	For the Lord Will Lead
	6 Epiphany B
	Sun btwn Jun 19 and 25 A, B
	Sun btwn Jul 3 and 9 C
	Sun btwn Aug 21 and 27 C
	Grant Peace We Pray/Verleih uns Frieden
	7 Epiphany C
	He That Shall Endure
	Sun btwn Nov 13 and 19 B
	He, Watching Over Israel
	Sun btwn Oct 16 and 22 C
	Heilig/Holy
	5 Epiphany C
	How Lovely Are the Messengers
	4 Epiphany B
	I Praise Thee
	Sun btwn Oct 9 and 15 A
	I Will Sing of Thy Great Mercies
	Sun btwn Jun 5 and 11 A, C
	Sun btwn Jul 10 and 16 A
	Sun btwn Aug 14 and 20 A
	Jerusalem, Jerusalem
	2 Lent C
	Jerusalem, Thou That Killest the Prophets
	Sun btwn Jun 12 and 18 A
	Jesus Christ, My Sure Defense—Alleluia
	Easter Day A
	5 Easter A

	Lift Thine Eyes
	  2 Lent A
	  Sun btwn Oct 16 and 22 C
	Lord, God of Abraham
	  Sun btwn May 29 and Jun 4 C
	Not unto Him
	  Sun btwn Sep 11 and 17 A
	O Come, Every One that Thirsteth
	  3 Lent A, C
	  Sun btwn Jul 31 and Aug 6 A
	O Rest in the Lord
	  Sun btwn Aug 7 and 13 C
	On God Alone My Hope I Build
	  4 Epiphany B
	  Sun btwn May 29 and Jun 4 A
	  Sun btwn Aug 21 and 27 A
	  Sun btwn Sep 11 and 17 B
	  Sun btwn Oct 2 and 8 A
	See What Love
	  4 Epiphany C
	  Maundy Thursday A, B, C
	  3 Easter B
	Sleeper Wake
	  Sun btwn Nov 6 and 12 A
	The Lord Is Ever Watchful
	  Sun btwn Aug 7 and 13 A
	There Shall a Star Come Out of Jacob
	  2 Christmas A, B, C
	  Epiphany of Our Lord A, B, C
	They That Shall Endure to the End
	  Sun btwn Jun 12 and 18 A

Mendelssohn, Felix/arr. Olaf C. Christiansen	The Lord Is a Mighty God Christ the King A
Mendelssohn, Felix/arr. Wilbur Held	Then Shall the Righteous Shine Forth Sun btwn Jul 17 and 23 A
Messiaen, Olivier	O sacrum convivium Maundy Thursday A, B, C
Mezzogorri, Giovanni Nicolò	Jubilate Deo Sun btwn Jun 12 and 18 A
Monteverdi, Claudio	Christe, adoramus te 5 Lent B
Moore, Bob	Have Mercy, O Lord: Music for the Imposition of Ashes Ash Wednesday A, B, C
Moore, Don Andrew	O Holy Spirit Sun btwn Aug 28 and Sep 3 B
Moore, James	Taste and See Sun btwn Aug 7 and 13 B

Moore, Philip	He That Is Down Need Fear No Fall
	  3 Lent C
	  Sun btwn Aug 21 and 27 C
	  Sun btwn Oct 23 and 29 C
	O sacrum convivium
	  Maundy Thursday A, B, C
	The Ascension/Lift Up Your Heads
	  Ascension of Our Lord A, B, C

Moore, Undine Smith	I Will Trust in the Lord
	  Sun btwn Oct 2 and 8 A
	Oh, That Bleeding Lamb
	  Good Friday A, B, C

Moore, Undine Smith/arr. Kenneth Jennings	I Believe This Is Jesus 2 Epiphany A, B

Morales, Cristóbal de
    Simile est regnum
        Sun btwn Sep 18 and 24 A
    Tu es Petrus
        Sun btwn Aug 21 and 27 A

Morgan, David C.
    A Palm Sunday Antiphon/Hosanna to the Son of David
        Passion/Palm Sunday A

Morley, Thomas
    Agnus Dei
        2 Epiphany A
    Lamb of God
        Sun btwn Nov 6 and 12 C

Morton, Graeme
    In the Splendor of the Dawn
        Christmas Dawn (II) A, B, C
    Ring Glad Bells
        Christmas Dawn (II) A, B, C
        Christmas Day (III) A, B, C

Mozart, Wolfgang Amadeus
    Adoramus te
        5 Lent C
    Agnus Dei
        Good Friday A, B, C
    Ave verum corpus
        Maundy Thursday A, B, C
        Sun btwn Jul 31 and Aug 6 A
    De profundis clamavi/From the Depths I Have Called unto Thee
        3 Lent B
    God Is Our Refuge
        Sun btwn Aug 7 and 13 C
    Laudate Dominum
        2 Epiphany C
        Day of Thanksgiving B
    Laudate pueri
        Sun btwn Sep 18 and 24 C
    Mighty Are Your Works, O God
        Holy Trinity C
    Quaerite primum regnum Dei/Seek Ye First
        Sun btwn May 24 and 28 A

Mueller, Carl F.
    An Anthem of Faith
        Sun btwn Oct 2 and 8 C
    The New Covenant
        Sun btwn Oct 16 and 22 C

Mueller, Jonathan R.
    For All the Saints
        All Saints Day A

Near, Gerald
    A Lenten Prayer
        1 Lent C
    Arise, My Love, My Fair One
        Easter Day C
    Awake, O Sleeper, Rise from Death
        6 Easter A
    Christ for Us Became Obedient unto Death
        Passion/Palm Sunday A
        Maundy Thursday A, B, C
    O magnum mysterium
        Christmas Eve (I) A, B, C
    The Best of Rooms
        Sun btwn Oct 30 and Nov 5 C
    They That Wait upon the Lord
        Sun btwn Oct 2 and 8 C

Nelson, Eric
    How Can I Keep from Singing?
        5 Epiphany B
        Sun btwn Jun 19 and 25 B
        Sun btwn Oct 30 and Nov 5 C

Nelson, Ronald A.
    Choral Fanfare for Christmas
        Christmas Dawn (II) A, B, C

	Create in Me a Clean Heart
	Ash Wednesday A, B, C
	4 Lent C
	He Rose
	Easter Day B
	I Will Not Leave You Comfortless
	7 Easter B
	If You Love One Another
	Maundy Thursday A, B, C
	6 Easter C
	The Vision of John
	All Saints Day C
	Whoever Would Be Great among You
	5 Epiphany C
	Sun btwn Sep 18 and 24 A, B
	Sun btwn Oct 16 and 22 B
	Sun btwn Oct 30 and Nov 5 A
Nester, Leo	Magnificat
	4 Advent A
	A Child Is Born
	Christmas Dawn (II) A, B, C
Neswick, Bruce	Epiphany Carol
	Epiphany of Our Lord A, B, C
	Baptism of Our Lord B
	Hearken to My Voice, O Lord, When I Call
	2 Lent B
	Jesus Came from Nazareth
	Baptism of Our Lord A
	Let the Peoples Praise You, O God
	Sun btwn Aug 14 and 20 A
	Magna et mirabilia
	Holy Trinity A
	O Taste and See
	Easter Vigil A, B, C
	Sun btwn Aug 7 and 13 B
	Sun btwn Oct 2 and 8 A, C
	Sun btwn Oct 16 and 22 A
	All Saints Day A
	The Blessed Son of God
	2 Christmas A, B, C
Nicholson, Sydney	O salutaris hostia
	Sun btwn Nov 13 and 19 C
Niedmann, Peter	Lift Up Your Heads, Ye Mighty Gates
	2 Advent C
	Passion/Palm Sunday C
Noble, T. Tertius	Grieve Not the Holy Spirit
	2 Easter C
	The Risen Christ
	6 Epiphany C
Nystedt, Knut	Get You Up
	5 Epiphany B
	I Will Greatly Rejoice
	3 Advent B
	Now Is Christ Risen
	Easter Day C
	Peace I Leave with You
	2 Easter A
	6 Easter C
	Day of Pentecost A

(Nystedt, Knut)   Teach Me, O Lord
- Sun btwn Jul 17 and 23 A
- Sun btwn Sep 4 and 10 A
- Sun btwn Oct 16 and 22 B

This Is My Beloved Son
- Baptism of Our Lord C
- Transfiguration of Our Lord A

Your Savior Comes
- Christmas Dawn (II) A, B, C

Oldham, Kevin   Out of the Depths Have I Cried to Thee
- Ash Wednesday A, B, C

Oldroyd, George   Prayer to Jesus
- Sun btwn Sep 11 and 17 A

Ore, Charles W.   This Is My Son
- Baptism of Our Lord B

Organ, Anne Krentz   Come and Find the Quiet Center
- Sun btwn Jul 24 and 30 C

Come My Light
- 3 Advent C

Love One Another
- Maundy Thursday A, B, C
- Sun btwn Sep 11 and 17 A

Owens, Sam Batt   O Paschal Lamp of Radiant Light
- Easter Evening A, B, C

Pachelbel, Johann   Canon of Praise
- Sun btwn Aug 21 and 27 C

Der Herr ist König/The Lord God Reigneth (Psalm 99)
- Transfiguration of Our Lord A

Now Thank We All Our God/Nun danket alle Gott
- Day of Thanksgiving A, B, C

On God and Not on Human Trust
- Sun btwn Sep 18 and 24 A

Sing to the Lord a New Song
- 6 Easter B

Palestrina, Giovanni Pierluigi da   Adoramus te Christe
- Good Friday A, B, C

Exultate jubilate
- Day of Thanksgiving B

Jesu! Rex admirabilis/Jesus, Thou Wondrous King
- Sun btwn Jun 26 and Jul 2 B

O Holy and Glorious Trinity
- Holy Trinity B

Tu es Petrus
- Sun btwn Aug 21 and 27 A

When Fully Came the Day of Pentecost
- Day of Pentecost A

Parker, Alice   Be Thou My Vision
- Sun btwn Jul 31 and Aug 6 C

I Know the Lord
- Sun btwn Jun 5 and 11 A

Pues si vivimos/While We Are Living
- Sun btwn Sep 11 and 17 A

Take Me to the Water
- 1 Lent B

The Wells of Salvation
- 5 Easter A

We Will March thro' the Valley
- 1 Lent B

Parker, Alice/Robert Shaw   Amazing Grace
- 4 Lent C

	Hark! I Hear the Harps Eternal
	All Saints Day B
	John Saw Duh Numbuh
	3 Easter C
	On Easter Morn
	Easter Day A
Parry, Charles Hubert H.	Dear Lord and Father
	Sun btwn Aug 28 and Sep 3 A
	Sun btwn Sep 25 and Oct 1 B
	I Was Glad When They Said unto Me
	1 Advent A
	O Day of Peace
	Sun btwn Nov 6 and 12 A
Paulus, Stephen	Built on a Rock
	3 Lent C
	Carol of the Hill
	Good Friday A, B, C
Pavlechko, Thomas	The Souls of the Righteous
	All Saints Day B, C
Paynter, John	The Call
	5 Easter A
Pearce, Thomas	Son of God, Eternal Savior
	Sun btwn Aug 28 and Sep 3 A
Peeters, Flor	Entrata Festiva
	Easter Day C
	The Lord's Prayer
	Sun btwn Jul 24 and 30 C
Peloquin, Alexander	A Great Harvest
	7 Easter A
	Psalm for Holy Week
	Maundy Thursday A, B, C
Pelz, Walter L.	Alleluia! Sing to Jesus
	7 Easter B
	Coventry Carol
	1 Christmas A
	Crown Him with Many Crowns
	Christ the King A
	Have No Fear, Little Flock
	Sun btwn Jun 5 and 11 A
	O Morning Star, How Fair and Bright
	7 Easter C
	Peace I Leave with You
	2 Easter A, B, C
	5 Easter A
	6 Easter A
	7 Easter B
	Psalm 23
	Sun btwn Oct 9 and 15 A
	Show Me Thy Ways
	1 Advent C
	1 Lent B
	Sun btwn Jul 10 and 16 C
	Sun btwn Sep 4 and 10 C
	Sun btwn Sep 25 and Oct 1 A
	Stay with Us
	Easter Evening A, B, C
	3 Easter A, B
	The King of Love My Shepherd Is
	4 Easter A, C
	Sun btwn Jul 17 and 23 B

(Pelz, Walter L.)	Up through Endless Ranks of Angels
	Ascension of Our Lord A, B, C
	Who Shall Abide
	4 Epiphany A
	With High Delight Let Us Unite
	3 Easter A
Pergolesi, Giovanni	Glory to God in the Highest
	Christmas Dawn (II) A, B, C
Peter, Johann F.	Adorn Yourself, My Soul
	Sun btwn Aug 21 and 27 B
	Praise the Lord, O My Soul
	Sun btwn Sep 11 and 17 A
Petker, Allan	Grace Above All
	Sun btwn May 29 and Jun 4 B
Petrich, Robert	Alleluia! Risen Indeed
	3 Easter A
Petrich, Roger	Ah, Holy Jesus
	Passion/Palm Sunday C
Philips, Craig	On This Bright Easter Morn
	Easter Evening A, B, C
Philips, Peter	Surgens Jesus/He Is Risen
	3 Easter B
Piccolo, Anthony	O Come, Let Us Sing unto the Lord
	Sun btwn May 29 and Jun 4 B
	Christ the King A
Pinkham, Daniel	Christmas Cantata
	Christmas Eve (I) A, B, C
	De profundis
	5 Lent A
	For the Gift of Water
	Baptism of Our Lord A
	Hosanna to the Son of David
	Passion/Palm Sunday C
	In the Beginning of Creation
	Holy Trinity A
	Let All His Saints Rejoice
	All Saints Day C
	Let the Word of Christ Dwell in You
	1 Christmas C
	Near the Cross of Jesus/Stabat mater
	Good Friday A, B, C
	This Is the Bread
	Sun btwn Aug 7 and 13 B
	Thou Art Ascended Up on High
	7 Easter A
	Wash Yourself in the Jordan
	6 Epiphany B
	Who Shall Separate Us from the Love of Christ
	Sun btwn Jul 24 and 30 A
Plag, Johannes/arr. Richard Proulx	Jesus Went to Jordan's Stream
	Baptism of Our Lord B, C
Popora, Niccolo/arr. E. Hyde	Credidi
	3 Easter A
Poston, Elizabeth	Jesus Christ the Apple Tree
	5 Easter B
	The Apple Tree
	4 Epiphany B
Pote, Allen	A Song of Joy
	5 Epiphany B
	God Is Our Refuge
	Reformation Day A, B, C

	Many Gifts, One Spirit
	Sun btwn Aug 21 and 27 A
	On the Third Day
	Easter Day A
	The Last Supper
	Sun btwn Aug 7 and 13 A
	The Lord Is My Shepherd
	4 Easter A, B
	Sun btwn Jul 17 and 23 B
	Sun btwn Oct 9 and 15 A
Poulenc, Francis	O magnum mysterium
	Christmas Eve (I) A, B, C
Powell, Robert J.	Jesu, the Very Thought of Thee
	4 Epiphany A
	The Church's One Foundation
	Reformation Day A, B, C
	The Great Creator of the Worlds
	5 Epiphany B
	7 Epiphany B
	The Lord Will Guide Our Ways
	6 Epiphany A
	Sun btwn Oct 9 and 15 B
	The Wisdom, Riches, and Knowledge of God
	Sun btwn Jul 3 and 9 B
	Ye Watchers and Ye Holy Ones
	Ascension of Our Lord A, B, C
Powell, Rosephanye	I Wanna Be Ready
	Sun btwn Aug 7 and 13 C
	The Word Was God
	2 Christmas A, B, C
Praetorius, Michael	Christ Jesus Lord, Thy Name Adored
	Sun btwn Sep 25 and Oct 1 A
	Jubilate Deo
	Sun btwn Jul 24 and 30 B
	Let All Together Praise Our God
	Christmas Day (III) A, B, C
	Lo, How a Rose E'er Blooming
	2 Advent A
	O Lord, We Praise Thee
	Maundy Thursday A, B, C
	O Morning Star, How Fair and Bright!
	Epiphany of Our Lord A, B, C
	Transfiguration of Our Lord A
	Praise the Lord
	Holy Trinity A
	Psallite
	Christmas Eve (I) A, B, C
	Christmas Dawn (II) A, B, C
	Stay with Us, Lord/Bleib bei uns, Herr
	Easter Evening A, B, C
	3 Easter A
	The Strife Is O'er, the Battle Done
	Easter Day A
	To Us Is Born Emmanuel/Enatus est Emanuel
	Christmas Dawn (II) A, B, C
	Christmas Day (III) A, B, C
	1 Christmas A
Proulx, Richard	A Child Is Born in Bethlehem
	Christmas Dawn (II) A, B, C
	Alleluia, Song of Gladness
	Transfiguration of Our Lord A

(Proulx, Richard)

Christ Sends the Spirit
    Day of Pentecost A, B
    Vigil of Pentecost A, B, C

Easter Carol
    2 Easter B, C

Entrance into Jersualem and Hymn
    Passion/Palm Sunday A, C

Festival Magnificat
    4 Advent B

God Is Love
    Maundy Thursday A, B, C

How Blest Are They
    Sun btwn Oct 23 and 29 A

I Rejoiced When I Heard Them Say
    1 Advent A

Immortal, Invisible
    Sun btwn Nov 6 and 12 A

It Came upon the Midnight Clear
    Christmas Eve (I) A, B, C

O God Beyond All Praising
    Day of Thanksgiving C

Once in Royal David's City
    Christmas Dawn (II) A, B, C

Our Paschal Lamb, That Sets Us Free
    Easter Vigil A, B, C
    Easter Day C
    3 Easter C
    6 Easter C

Psalm 133
    7 Epiphany C

Sing We Merrily
    Sun btwn May 29 and Jun 4 B

Song of the Three Children
    Easter Vigil A, B, C

Strengthen for Service
    6 Epiphany A
    Sun btwn Jun 5 and 11 B
    Sun btwn Jun 19 and 25 A
    Sun btwn Aug 21 and 27 B
    Sun btwn Sep 25 and Oct 1 B

The Eyes of All
    Sun btwn Jul 24 and 30 B, C
    Sun btwn Jul 31 and Aug 6 A
    Day of Thanksgiving C

Though We Are Many, in Christ We Are One
    4 Easter A

Ubi caritas et amor
    Maundy Thursday A, B, C

We Adore You O Christ
    Passion/Palm Sunday C

Weary of All Trumpeting
    5 Lent C
    Sun btwn Jun 19 and 25 A
    Sun btwn Oct 9 and 15 B
    Sun btwn Oct 16 and 22 B
    Sun btwn Oct 23 and 29 B

Were You There
    Passion/Palm Sunday A
    Good Friday A, B, C

What Shall We Offer
    Day of Thanksgiving C

	You Are God: We Praise You
	Holy Trinity C
Proulx, Richard, ed.	Verbum caro factum est
	2 Christmas A, B, C
Prower, Anthony	For the Fruits of All Creation
	Day of Thanksgiving A
	The Angel Gabriel from Heaven Came
	4 Advent C
Purcell, Henry	O God the King of Glory
	7 Easter A
	O God, Thou Art My God
	3 Lent C
	O Sing unto the Lord
	Christmas Eve (I) A, B, C
	Sun btwn Oct 16 and 22 A
	Rejoice in the Lord Always
	3 Advent C
	Sun btwn Sep 4 and 10 B
	Sun btwn Oct 9 and 15 A
	Thou Knowest, Lord, the Secrets of Our Hearts
	3 Advent A
	4 Lent C
	Sun btwn Jul 10 and 16 C
	Sun btwn Jul 17 and 23 A
	Sun btwn Nov 6 and 12 A
	Thy Word Is a Lantern
	Sun btwn Oct 9 and 15 B
	We Sing to Him
	Holy Trinity C
Rachmaninoff, Sergei	Blessed Is the Man
	6 Epiphany C
	All Saints Day A, C
	Magnificat
	4 Advent C
	O Come Let Us Worship
	3 Lent A
	Christ the King A
	To Thee We Sing
	Sun btwn Aug 28 and Sep 3 B
	Today Hath Salvation Come
	Easter Vigil A, B, C
	Easter Day C
	Sun btwn Oct 9 and 15 A
	To Thee O Lord
	Sun btwn Sep 25 and Oct 1 A
Rameau, Jean Philippe	Come, Thou Long-Expected Jesus
	1 Advent A
	Christ the King B
	Wake, O Shepherds
	Christmas Eve (I) A, B, C
Raminsh, Imant	Ubi caritas
	Maundy Thursday A, B, C
Ratcliff, Cary	Come to the Waters
	Sun btwn Oct 30 and Nov 5 C
Ray, Robert	He Never Failed Me Yet
	4 Easter A
	Sun btwn Aug 7 and 13 A
Reger, Max	Meinen Jesum lass ich nicht/I Stand Fast with Jesus Christ
	2 Lent B
	Our Lady's Vision
	Sun btwn Oct 23 and 29 B

(Reger, Max)	The Virgin's Slumber Song
	Christmas Eve (I) A, B, C
	We Bless the Father and the Son and the Holy Ghost
	Holy Trinity A
Repulski, John	Exsultet
	Easter Vigil A, B, C
Rickard, Jeffrey H.	Let Thy Blood in Mercy Poured
	Good Friday A, B, C
Riegal, Friedrich Samuel	See God to Heaven Ascending
	Ascension of Our Lord A, B, C
Roberts, Paul	The Word Became Flesh
	2 Christmas A, B, C
Roberts, William Bradley	In All These You Welcomed Me
	2 Easter B
	Ascension of Our Lord A, B, C
	Sun btwn Jun 26 and Jul 2 B
	Sun btwn Aug 28 and Sep 3 C
	Sun btwn Sep 18 and 24 B
	Savior, Like a Shepherd Lead Us
	4 Easter A, B, C
Roff, Joseph	Put Ye on the Lord Jesus
	Sun btwn Sep 4 and 10 A
Rorem, Ned	Breathe on Me, Breath of God
	Vigil of Pentecost A, B, C
	God Is Gone Up
	7 Easter A
	Lay Up for Yourselves
	Ash Wednesday A, B, C
	Love Divine, All Loves Excelling
	Sun btwn Jul 10 and 16 C
	Praise the Lord, O My Soul/Psalm 146
	Sun btwn Sep 4 and 10 B
	Sun btwn Sep 25 and Oct 1 C
	Psalm 148
	1 Christmas A
	Sing, My Soul, His Wondrous Love
	3 Lent A
	6 Easter B
	Sun btwn Jul 10 and 16 C
	Christ the King B
Rose, Michael	Ye Choirs of New Jerusalem
	Ascension of Our Lord A, B, C
Rossi, Richard Robert	Conditor alme siderum
	1 Advent C
Rotermund, Melvin	O God of Light
	3 Epiphany C
Routley, Erik	Light and Salt
	5 Epiphany A
Routley, Erik/arr. John Hakes	What Does the Lord Require?
	4 Epiphany A
Rowan, William P.	With the Lord, There Is Mercy
	1 Lent C
	5 Lent A
	Woman in the Night
	Sun btwn Aug 14 and 20 A
Rudolph, Glen	Arise, Shine
	5 Epiphany A
Rutter, John	Agnus Dei
	5 Lent A

	All Things Bright and Beautiful
	6 Easter B
	Sun btwn Oct 9 and 15 B
	Day of Thanksgiving B
	Christ the Lord Is Risen Again
	Easter Day A
	5 Easter B
	Christmas Night
	Christmas Eve (I) A, B, C
	For the Beauty of the Earth
	Sun btwn Jul 10 and 16 A
	Sun btwn Aug 14 and 20 A
	Sun btwn Aug 21 and 27 B
	Sun btwn Oct 2 and 8 B
	Presentation of Our Lord A, B, C
	God Be in My Head
	Sun btwn Jul 31 and Aug 6 C
	I Will Lift Up Mine Eyes
	2 Lent A
	O Be Joyful in the Lord
	Sun btwn Nov 6 and 12 B
	O Clap Your Hands
	Ascension of Our Lord A, B, C
	Open Thou Mine Eyes
	4 Lent A
	Sun btwn Jun 26 and Jul 2 C
	Sun btwn Sep 18 and 24 B
	Sun btwn Sep 25 and Oct 1 B
	Praise the Lord, O My Soul
	Sun btwn Sep 25 and Oct 1 C
	Praise Ye the Lord
	Sun btwn Jul 3 and 9 C
	The Lord Is My Shepherd
	4 Lent A
	4 Easter C
	Sun btwn Oct 9 and 15 A
	The Peace of God
	Sun btwn Oct 9 and 15 A
	Thy Perfect Love
	Sun btwn Jun 12 and 18 C
	Sun btwn Sep 18 and 24 C
	What Sweeter Music
	2 Advent B
Ryan-Wenger, Michael	In the Beginning Was the Word
	Christmas Day (III) A, B, C
	2 Christmas A, B, C
Saint-Saëns, Camille	A Christmas Alleluia
	2 Christmas A, B, C
	Ave verum corpus
	Maundy Thursday A, B, C
Sampson, Godfrey	My Song Shall Be Alway of the Lovingkindness
	Sun btwn Jun 26 and Jul 2 A
Sateren, Leland	O Lord, Thou Art My God and King
	Sun btwn Sep 18 and 24 A
Satie, Erik/Luigi Zaninelli	Give Thanks to the Lord
	Sun btwn Oct 30 and Nov 5 C
Saylor, Bruce	When I Survey the Wondrous Cross
	5 Lent C
Scarlatti, Alessandro	Exsultate Deo
	Sun btwn Oct 9 and 15 C
Schalk, Carl	A Mighty Fortress
	Sun btwn Jun 5 and 11 B

(Schalk, Carl)

A Parish Magnificat
    3 Advent A
All the Ends of the Earth
    2 Lent B
All Things Are Yours, My God
    Sun btwn Sep 25 and Oct 1 C
As the Dark Awaits the Dawn
    1 Advent C
    3 Advent A, B
Be Known to Us, Lord Jesus
    Sun btwn Aug 14 and 20 B
Before the Marvel of This Night
    Christmas Eve (I) A, B, C
Blessed Are the Dead Who Die in the Lord
    All Saints Day A, B
Chorales for Advent
    1 Advent A
Christ Be Our Seed
    Sun btwn Jul 10 and 16 B
Christ Goes Before
    5 Easter A
    Sun btwn Oct 9 and 15 B
Christ Is Made the Sure Foundation
    7 Easter B
    Sun btwn Aug 21 and 27 A
Creator Spirit, Heavenly Dove
    Vigil of Pentecost A, B, C
    Day of Pentecost C
Day of Arising
    3 Easter A
Evening and Morning
    Sun btwn Jun 19 and 25 B
    Sun btwn Oct 16 and 22 A
Gather Your Children, Dear Savior, in Peace
    Sun btwn Jul 3 and 9 A
Go Therefore and Make Disciples of All Nations
    Holy Trinity A
Hail, O Favored One
    3 Advent A
Have Mercy on Me, O God
    Ash Wednesday A, B, C
    5 Lent B
Here, O My Lord, I See Thee
    Sun btwn Aug 28 and Sep 3 C
How Lovely Shines the Morning Star
    Epiphany of Our Lord A, B, C
I Have Set the Lord Always Before Me
    2 Easter A
I Saw a New Heaven and a New Earth
    5 Easter C
    Sun btwn Oct 23 and 29 B
Jesus, Take Us to the Mountain
    Transfiguration of Our Lord A, B, C
Let Our Gladness Have No End
    Christmas Day (III) A, B, C
    2 Christmas A, B, C
Lift High the Cross
    Sun btwn Sep 11 and 17 B
Lo! He Comes with Clouds Descending
    Christ the King A
Lord God, the Holy Ghost
    Day of Pentecost A

Lord, It Belongs Not to My Care
   3 Lent B
   5 Lent A
   Sun btwn Nov 6 and 12 B
Lord of Feasting and of Hunger
   Sun btwn Jun 19 and 25 A
   Sun btwn Sep 25 and Oct 1 C
Mary Went Up to Hill Country
   4 Advent C
My Soul Gives Glory to the Lord
   4 Advent B, C
O Day Full of Grace
   Vigil of Pentecost A, B, C
   Day of Pentecost A, B
O Lord, Thou Hast Been Our Dwelling Place
   Sun btwn Nov 13 and 19 A
O Love, How Deep, How Broad, How High
   7 Easter A
Oh, Wondrous Type, Oh, Vision Fair
   Transfiguration of Our Lord B
Our Soul Waits for the Lord
   Sun btwn Aug 7 and 13 C
   Sun btwn Oct 2 and 8 C
Out of the Depths
   Ash Wednesday A, B, C
   5 Lent A
Show Me Your Ways, O Lord
   1 Lent B
   Sun btwn Jul 10 and 16 C
The Church's One Foundation
   Reformation Day A, B, C
The God of Love My Shepherd Is
   4 Easter B
   Sun btwn Oct 9 and 15 A
Thine the Amen, Thine the Praise
   4 Easter C
   6 Easter C
   7 Easter A, C
   Sun btwn Nov 6 and 12 A
   Christ the King C
This Touch of Love
   2 Epiphany C
Thy Strong Word
   3 Epiphany A
Where Charity and Love Prevail
   Maundy Thursday A, B, C
   Sun btwn Sep 11 and 17 A
Who Is the One We Love the Most
   7 Epiphany B

Scheidt, Samuel
My Inmost Heart Now Raises
   Sun btwn Jun 19 and 25 A
Sing, Rejoice/Psallite unigenito
   Christmas Day (III) A, B, C

Schein, Johann H.
Come, Holy Ghost, God and Lord
   Day of Pentecost A
Christ Lay in Death's Dark Tomb
   Easter Vigil A, B, C
From Heaven Above
   Christmas Eve (I) A, B, C
Sing to the Lord
   Sun btwn Oct 16 and 22 A

Schickele, Peter — Amazing Grace
    Sun btwn Jun 26 and Jul 2 A

Scholz, Robert — Children of the Heavenly Father
    8 Epiphany A
    6 Easter A
    Sun btwn May 24 and 28 A
    Sun btwn Jun 26 and Jul 2 B
    Sun btwn Sep 18 and 24 B

Nunc dimittis
    1 Christmas B

Oh, Wondrous Type! Oh, Vision Fair
    Transfiguration of Our Lord C

What Wondrous Love
    4 Lent B

Schroeder, Hermann — In Bethlehem a Wonder
    Christmas Eve (I) A, B, C

The Angel Gabriel
    4 Advent B

Schubert, Franz — Lord, to Whom Our Prayers Ascend
    Sun btwn Jul 24 and 30 C

O Jesus, Crucified for Man/Begrabt dem Leib in seinen Gruft
    Sun btwn Sep 11 and 17 B

The Lord Is My Shepherd
    4 Easter B

Schultz, Donna Gartman — Shall We Gather at the River
    All Saints Day A

Schulz-Widmar, Russell — Give Rest, O Christ
    All Saints Day C

God Remembers
    4 Epiphany B
    Sun btwn Oct 23 and 29 A

Jerusalem, Jerusalem
    All Saints Day B
    Sun btwn Nov 6 and 12 C

Midnight Clear
    Christmas Day (III) A, B, C

We Are Not Our Own
    7 Epiphany C

Schumann, Georg — Yea Though I Wander
    4 Easter C

Schutte, Daniel L./arr. Ovid Young — Here I Am, Lord
    2 Epiphany B
    3 Epiphany A
    5 Epiphany C

Schütz, Heinrich — A Song of Praise to the Holy Trinity
    Holy Trinity A

Father Abraham, Have Mercy on Me
    Sun btwn Sep 25 and Oct 1 C

God So Loved the World/Also hat Gott die Welt geliebet
    2 Lent A, C
    4 Lent B

Herr, ich hoffe darauf/Lord, My Hope Is in Thee
    Sun btwn Jun 26 and Jul 2 B

I Am the Resurrection
    5 Lent A

I Go My Way to Jesus Christ/So fahr ich hin zu Jesu Christ
    Sun btwn Nov 13 and 19 B

In Thee, O Lord, Do I Put My Trust
    5 Easter A

Lift Up Your Voice
    Sun btwn Jun 26 and Jul 2 B
    Sun btwn Aug 14 and 20 A

	My God, My God
	Maundy Thursday A, B, C
	No Man Liveth to Himself
	Sun btwn Sep 11 and 17 A
	O Gracious Lord, Our God
	4 Advent A
	O Lord, I Trust Your Shepherd Care
	4 Lent A
	4 Easter B, C
	Sun btwn Oct 9 and 15 A
	Our Father
	Sun btwn Jul 24 and 30 C
	Praise God in Heaven
	Sun btwn Jul 3 and 9 B
	Praise God, Ye Lands
	Sun btwn Jul 3 and 9 C
	Praise to You, Lord Jesus
	3 Lent B
	5 Lent C
	Good Friday A, B, C
	Psalm 29
	Baptism of Our Lord C
	Psalm 97
	7 Easter C
	St. Matthew Passion
	Passion/Palm Sunday A
	Sing to the Lord
	Sun btwn Jul 24 and 30 A
	Sun btwn Nov 13 and 19 C
	The Pharisee and the Publican
	Sun btwn Oct 23 and 29 C
	The Voice of the Lord Sounds upon the Waters
	Baptism of Our Lord A
	To Thee We Turn Our Eyes
	Sun btwn Jul 3 and 9 A
	We Offer Our Thanks and Praise
	Sun btwn Sep 25 and Oct 1 B
	Sun btwn Nov 6 and 12 C
	Day of Thanksgiving C
	Who Shall Separate Us
	Sun btwn Jul 24 and 30 A
Schütz, Heinrich/arr. George Lynn	Psalm 1
	Sun btwn Sep 4 and 10 C
Schütz, Heinrich/arr. Nancy Grundahl	Rejoice in God
	Sun btwn Oct 9 and 15 A
Schütz, Heinrich/arr. Robert Buckley Farlee	My Soul Exalts Your Name, O Lord
	4 Advent B, C
	Sun btwn Oct 30 and Nov 5 A
Scott, K. Lee	A Song of Trust
	Sun btwn Jul 3 and 9 A
	A Vineyard Grows
	Sun btwn Oct 2 and 8 A
	Blessed Lamb, on Calvary's Mountain
	Good Friday A, B, C
	Come, O Thou Traveler Unknown
	Sun btwn Jun 12 and 18 A
	Sun btwn Oct 16 and 22 C
	Giver of Every Perfect Gift
	Sun btwn Sep 4 and 10 B

(Scott, K. Lee)

God Shall the Broken Heart Repair
    5 Easter B
    Sun btwn Jun 5 and 11 A
    Sun btwn Jul 3 and 9 C

Gracious Spirit, Dwell with Me
    Vigil of Pentecost A, B, C
    Day of Pentecost A
    Sun btwn Jun 5 and 11 A
    Sun btwn Jun 12 and 18 C
    Sun btwn Jun 26 and Jul 2 A
    Sun btwn Sep 4 and 10 B
    Sun btwn Sep 18 and 24 C

Holy, Holy, Holy
    Holy Trinity B

I Will Sing of Thy Great Mercies
    Sun btwn Jun 26 and Jul 2 A

Infant Holy, Infant Lowly
    Christmas Eve (I) A, B, C

Jesu, Our Hope, Our Heart's Desire
    5 Lent C

Jesus, My All, to Heaven Is Gone
    Ascension of Our Lord A, B, C

Jesus, Thou Joy of Loving Hearts
    2 Lent A

Keep Your Lamps Trimmed and Burning
    Sun btwn Aug 7 and 13 C

King of Glory, King of Peace
    Sun btwn Aug 21 and 27 A

Nobody Knows the Trouble I See
    Sun btwn Oct 9 and 15 B

Open My Eyes
    Sun btwn Jul 24 and 30 A
    Sun btwn Oct 2 and 8 B

Out of the Depths I Cry to Thee
    Ash Wednesday A, B, C
    5 Lent A
    Sun btwn Jun 5 and 11 B

Peace Came to Earth
    4 Advent A

Redeeming Grace
    1 Lent B
    Sun btwn Jun 19 and 25 C
    Sun btwn Jul 17 and 23 C
    Sun btwn Jul 24 and 30 A
    Sun btwn Aug 14 and 20 C

Sing a Song of Joy
    Sun btwn Jul 31 and Aug 6 C

Sing Aloud to God Our Strength
    Sun btwn Oct 16 and 22 A
    Reformation Day A, B, C

So Art Thou to Me
    6 Easter A
    Sun btwn Jun 12 and 18 B
    Sun btwn Jul 24 and 30 A
    Sun btwn Aug 7 and 13 B
    Sun btwn Aug 28 and Sep 3 A, B

Teach Me, My God and King
    Sun btwn Jul 24 and 30 A
    Sun btwn Sep 4 and 10 A

	The Call
	5 Easter A
	Sun btwn Jul 17 and 23 A
	Sun btwn Aug 14 and 20 B
	Sun btwn Oct 30 and Nov 5 B
	Thy Perfect Love
	7 Easter C
	Sun btwn May 29 and Jun 4 B
	Sun btwn Jun 26 and Jul 2 A
	Trinitarian Blessings
	Holy Trinity A, B, C
	When Christmas Morn Is Dawning
	Christmas Dawn (II) A, B, C
Sedio, Mark	Once He Came in Blessing
	Sun btwn Jun 19 and 25 A
	Sun btwn Sep 11 and 17 B
	Sun btwn Nov 13 and 19 A
	Take My Life, That I May Be/Toma, oh Dios, mi voluntad
	2 Epiphany B, C
	Sun btwn Oct 9 and 15 B
	Sun btwn Nov 6 and 12 B
	Teach Me Your Way, O Lord
	Sun btwn Jul 3 and 9 B
	There Is No Rose of Such Vertu
	Christmas Day (III) A, B, C
	The Thirsty Fields Drink In the Rain
	Sun btwn Jul 10 and 16 A, B
	Wexford Carol
	2 Christmas A, B, C
Shaw, Martin	Coventry Carol
	1 Christmas A
	Fanfare for Christmas Day
	Christmas Dawn (II) A, B, C
	With a Voice of Singing
	5 Easter A
Shaw, Robert/Alice Parker	'Tis Finished
	Good Friday A, B, C
Shepperd, Mark	Balm in Gilead
	6 Epiphany B
	7 Epiphany B
Sirett, Mark G.	Thou Shalt Know Him When He Comes
	1 Advent B, C
	Easter Evening A, B, C
	Sun btwn Nov 13 and 19 B
	Christ the King B
	What Sweeter Music
	Christmas Dawn (II) A, B, C
Sitton, Michael	Tantum ergo
	1 Lent C
Sjolund, Paul	Children of the Heavenly Father
	6 Easter A
	Sun btwn Sep 18 and 24 B
Smith, Byron J.	Worthy to Be Praised
	Easter Vigil A, B, C
	Sun btwn Sep 18 and 24 A
Smith, Carl	Trinity Sunday
	Holy Trinity B
Smith, Gregg	The Lord Is My Shepherd
	4 Lent A
Sowerby, Leo	All Hail, Adored Trinity
	Holy Trinity A, C

(Sowerby, Leo)	O Be Joyful in the Lord
	Sun btwn Jun 12 and 18 A
	O God of Light
	Sun btwn Jun 19 and 25 C
	Thou Art My Strength
	Sun btwn May 29 and Jun 4 A
Stainer, John	God So Loved the World
	2 Lent A, C
	4 Lent B
	Holy Trinity B
	How Beautiful upon the Mountains
	Christmas Day (III) A, B, C
Stanford, Charles Villiers	Beati quorum via
	Sun btwn Oct 30 and Nov 5 B
	Benedictus
	2 Advent C
	Glorious and Powerful God
	Christ the King C
	If Thou Shalt Confess with Thy Mouth
	Sun btwn Aug 7 and 13 A
	O for a Closer Walk with God
	Sun btwn Sep 4 and 10 C
	Sun btwn Oct 23 and 29 A
	We Know That Christ Is Raised
	Easter Vigil A, B, C
	Ye Choirs of New Jerusalem
	Easter Day A
Statham, Heathcoat	Drop Down, Ye Heavens
	Sun btwn Aug 7 and 13 A
Stearns, Peter Pindar	Your Love, O Lord, Reaches to the Heavens
	2 Epiphany C
Stevens, Halsey	In Thee, O Lord, Have I Put My Trust
	Sun btwn May 29 and Jun 4 A
	Psalm 148/Praise Ye the Lord
	1 Christmas A
Stout, Alan	The Great Day of the Lord
	Sun btwn Nov 13 and 19 A
Susa, Conrad	El Desembre Congelat/On December's Frozen Ground
	3 Advent B
Sutcliffe, James	What Child Is This?
	1 Christmas C
	Presentation of Our Lord A, B, C
Svedlund, Karl-Erik/arr. Bruce Bengtson	There'll Be Something In Heaven
	Sun btwn Nov 6 and 12 B, C
	All Saints Day A
Sweelinck, Jan Pieterszoon	Hodie Christus natus est
	Christmas Eve (I) A, B, C
	Christmas Day (III) A, B, C
	Psalm 100
	Sun btwn Jun 12 and 18 A
	Sing to the Lord, New Songs Be Raising
	3 Easter C
	Sun btwn May 29 and Jun 4 C
	Sun btwn Oct 16 and 22 A
	Christ the King C
	Day of Thanksgiving A, C
Tallis, Thomas	Audivi, media nocte
	Sun btwn Nov 6 and 12 A
	All People That on Earth Do Dwell
	Sun btwn Jun 12 and 18 A

	If Ye Love Me
	5 Easter C
	6 Easter A, B
	Vigil of Pentecost A, B, C
	Day of Pentecost C
	O Lord, Give Thy Holy Spirit
	Vigil of Pentecost A, B, C
	Holy Trinity B
	O nata lux
	Epiphany of Our Lord A, B, C
	Transfiguration of Our Lord C
	O sacrum convivium
	Maundy Thursday A, B, C
	Purge Me, O Lord
	Ash Wednesday A, B, C
	Verily, Verily I Say unto You
	Sun btwn Aug 14 and 20 B
Taranto, Steven	Into Jerusalem
	Passion/Palm Sunday C
Tavener, John	The Lamb
	4 Easter A
	Sun btwn Sep 18 and 24 B
Taverner, John	Audivi
	Sun btwn Nov 6 and 12 A
Tchaikovsky, Pyotr Il'yich	Holy, Holy, Holy
	Holy Trinity B
	The Crown of Roses
	Passion/Palm Sunday A
Tchesnokov, Pavel	Salvation Is Created
	5 Lent B
Telemann, Georg Philipp	Halleluja
	Easter Day B
	3 Easter A
	I Want to Praise the Lord All of My Life
	Sun btwn Aug 7 and 13 B
	Make Me Pure, O Sacred Spirit
	Ash Wednesday A, B, C
	Day of Pentecost C
	Sun btwn Aug 28 and Sep 3 B
	Sun btwn Sep 18 and 24 B
	O Praise the Lord, All Ye Nations
	3 Epiphany B
Telemann, Georg Philipp/arr. Joan Conlon	Come, Enjoy God's Festive Springtime
	Sun btwn Jun 5 and 11 A
Thiman, Eric H.	Hark! A Thrilling Voice Is Sounding
	1 Advent C
Thomas, André	African Noel
	Christmas Day (III) A, B, C
	Go Where I Send Thee
	4 Epiphany C
	Here's a Pretty Little Baby
	Christmas Day (III) A, B, C
	Keep Your Lamps
	1 Advent A, B, C
	Sun btwn Nov 6 and 12 A
	The Kingdom
	Christ the King A
	When the Trumpet Sounds
	Sun btwn Nov 6 and 12 A
Thomas, Paul	Jesus, Priceless Treasure
	Sun btwn Jul 24 and 30 B

Thomerson, Kathleen	I Want to Walk as a Child of the Light
	Epiphany of Our Lord A, B, C
	3 Epiphany B
Thompson, J. Michael	Taste and See the Lord Is Good
	4 Lent C
	5 Lent A
	Sun btwn Jul 24 and 30 B
Thompson, R. Paul	Come, Follow Me
	Sun btwn Sep 11 and 17 B
Thompson, Randall	Alleluia
	Transfiguration of Our Lord A
	Easter Evening A, B, C
	Sun btwn Aug 21 and 27 C
	Sun btwn Sep 4 and 10 B
	Blessed Be the Lord God
	2 Advent A
	Have Ye Not Known/Ye Shall Have a Song
	5 Epiphany B
	Howl Ye
	1 Advent C
	My Soul Doth Magnify the Lord
	4 Advent A
	The Best of Rooms
	Sun btwn Sep 4 and 10 C
	Sun btwn Oct 30 and Nov 5 C
	The Lord Is My Shepherd
	4 Easter A, B
Thomson, Virgil	My Shepherd Will Supply My Need
	4 Easter A, C
	Sun btwn Jul 17 and 23 B
	Sun btwn Oct 9 and 15 A
Tiefenbach, Peter	What Shall I Render to the Lord?
	3 Easter A
Titcomb, Everett	God Is Gone Up
	Ascension of Our Lord A, B, C
	I Will Not Leave You Comfortless
	Ascension of Our Lord A, B, C
	Jesus, Name of Wondrous Love
	4 Epiphany C
	O Love, How Deep
	4 Epiphany B
Tomkins, Thomas	My Shepherd Is the Living Lord
	4 Easter A
Toolan, Suzanne	I Am the Bread of Life
	Sun btwn Jul 31 and Aug 6 B
Traditional/arr. Robert Shaw, Alice Parker	My God Is a Rock
	Sun btwn Oct 9 and 15 B
Trapp, Lynn	Music for the Rite of Sprinkling
	Easter Vigil A, B, C
Trinkley, Bruce	I Want Jesus to Walk with Me
	1 Lent A
Turner, Kenneth C	O Trinity, Most Blessed Light
	Holy Trinity A
Tye, Christopher	Give Almes of Thy Goods
	Sun btwn Oct 16 and 22 A
	Christ the King A
	Lord, for Thy Tender Mercy's Sake
	Sun btwn Sep 25 and Oct 1 A
	O Jesus, King Most Wonderful
	Christ the King A
	Sing to the Lord
	Sun btwn Nov 13 and 19 C
	To Our Redeemer's Glorious Name

Tye, Christopher/arr. Carl Schalk		2 Lent A
	The Man We Crucified	
		3 Easter A
		4 Easter A
Tyler, Edward	St. Teresa's Bookmark	
		Sun btwn Nov 6 and 12 C
		Sun btwn Nov 13 and 19 B
Uhl, Dan	This Is My Beloved Son	
		Baptism of Our Lord B, C
		Transfiguration of Our Lord A
Vantine, Bruce	Now the Green Blade Rises	
		5 Lent B
Vaughan Williams, Ralph	A Choral Flourish	
		Sun btwn Oct 30 and Nov 5 C
	Antiphon	
		Christ the King B
	At the Name of Jesus	
		Passion/Palm Sunday B, C
		Ascension of Our Lord A, B, C
		Sun btwn Sep 25 and Oct 1 A
		Christ the King B, C
	Christ Our Passover	
		Easter Day A
	Come Down, Love Divine	
		5 Easter B
	He That Is Down Need Fear No Fall	
		Sun btwn Aug 28 and Sep 3 C
		Sun btwn Oct 9 and 15 B
	Lord, Thou Hast Been Our Refuge	
		Sun btwn Oct 9 and 15 B
		Sun btwn Nov 13 and 19 A
	O Clap Your Hands	
		Ascension of Our Lord A, B, C
	O How Amiable	
		5 Easter C
	O Taste and See	
		5 Lent A
		3 Easter A
		5 Easter C
		Sun btwn Aug 7 and 13 B
		Sun btwn Oct 2 and 8 C
		All Saints Day A
	The Blessed Son of God	
		1 Christmas A, C
		Baptism of Our Lord C
	The Call	
		5 Easter A, C
		Sun btwn Jul 17 and 23 C
		Sun btwn Oct 23 and 29 A
	The Old Hundredth Psalm Tune	
		Holy Trinity B
		Sun btwn Jun 12 and 18 A
		Day of Thanksgiving A
	The Song of the Tree of Life	
		Sun btwn Oct 2 and 8 A
	The Souls of the Righteous	
		All Saints Day B
	The Twenty-third Psalm	
		4 Easter C
	This Is the Truth	
		5 Easter A
Viadana, Lodovico	Exsultate justi in Domino	

	Sun btwn Aug 7 and 13 C
	Shout for Joy, Ye Righteous/Exsultate justi
	4 Lent C
	Sing, Ye Righteous
	Sun btwn Jun 19 and 25 B
Victoria, Tomás Luis de	Hosanna to the Son of David
	Passion/Palm Sunday A
	Jesu, dulcis memoria/Jesus, the Very Thought Is Sweet
	Sun btwn Nov 6 and 12 B
	Jesu, the Very Thought of Thee
	6 Epiphany C
	O magnum mysterium
	Christmas Eve (I) A, B, C
	Christmas Day (III) A, B, C
	The Passion According to St. John
	Good Friday A, B, C
	Vere langoures nostros
	Sun btwn Oct 16 and 22 B
Vierne, Louis	Benedictus
	2 Lent C
	Let All Mortal Flesh Keep Silence
	6 Epiphany C
Viner, Alan	In Heavenly Love Abiding
	Sun btwn Sep 25 and Oct 1 B
Vivaldi, Antonio	Domine fili unigenite
	2 Christmas A, B, C
Vivaldi, Antonio/arr. S. Drummond Wolff	Gloria in excelsis Deo
	Christmas Dawn (II) A, B, C
Vulpius, Melchior	Arisen Is Our Blessed Lord
	Easter Day A, C
	Easter Evening A, B, C
	Jesus Said to the Blind Man
	4 Lent A
	O Spirit of God, Eternal Source
	7 Epiphany A
	Day of Pentecost B, C
Walker, Gwyneth	Sounding Joy
	Sun btwn Jun 19 and 25 B
Walter, Johann	I Build on God's Strong Word
	1 Lent C
	Sun btwn May 29 and Jun 4 A
	Reformation Day A, B, C
	Now Sing We, Now Rejoice
	Christmas Dawn (II) A, B, C
	Rise Up, Rise Up!
	2 Advent B
	Sun btwn Aug 7 and 13 C
	Sun btwn Nov 13 and 19 A
Walton, William	A Litany/Drop, Drop Slow Tears
	5 Lent C
	Maundy Thursday A, B, C
Warland, Dale	Coventry Carol
	1 Christmas A
	Wexford Carol
	Christmas Day (III) A, B, C
Weaver, John	Epiphany Alleluias
	Epiphany of Our Lord A, B, C
	Psalm 46
	Reformation Day A, B, C
	The Easter Proclamation/The Exsultet
	Easter Vigil A, B, C
Weber, Paul D.	I Will Sing the Story of Your Love

		Sun btwn Jun 26 and Jul 2 B
		Christ the King A
		Reformation Day A, B, C
Weelkes, Thomas		Early Will I Seek Thee
		Sun btwn Jun 19 and 25 C
Weiland, Brent		Christ Is Coming
		1 Advent B
Werner, Gregor Joseph		Puer natus in Bethlehem
		Christmas Dawn (II) A, B, C
Wesley, Samuel Sebastian		Blessed Be the God and Father
		3 Easter A
		Lead Me, Lord
		Sun btwn Jul 17 and 23 A
		Sun btwn Sep 4 and 10 C
		O Lord My God
		1 Lent B
		Thou Wilt Keep Him in Perfect Peace
		3 Epiphany A
		Wash Me Thoroughly
		Ash Wednesday A, B, C
		5 Lent B
Wetzler, Robert		Peace Be with You
		2 Easter A
		Still, Still, Still
		Christmas Eve (I) A, B, C
White, David Ashley		Christians, We Have Met to Worship
		Sun btwn Aug 21 and 27 B
		Come, Ye Sinners
		3 Lent C
		Sun btwn Oct 23 and 29 C
		In Christ There Is No East or West
		Sun btwn May 29 and Jun 4 C
		O Bread of Life from Heaven
		Sun btwn Aug 7 and 13 B
		Sun btwn Aug 28 and Sep 3 C
		Sun btwn Oct 30 and Nov 5 B
		Star in the East
		Epiphany of Our Lord A, B, C
		The Call
		5 Easter A
		There's a Wideness in God's Mercy
		7 Epiphany B
		This Glimpse of Glory
		6 Epiphany C
		Transfiguration of Our Lord C
		When Peace, Like a River
		Sun btwn Nov 13 and 19 C
White, Nicholas		Steal Away
		Sun btwn Nov 6 and 12 A
		Take My Life and Let It Be Consecrated
		Sun btwn Nov 6 and 12 B
Widor, Charles Marie		Tu es Petrus
		8 Epiphany C
Wienhorst, Richard		Let Your Manner of Life
		Sun btwn Sep 18 and 24 A
		Lord, Whose Love in Humble Service
		6 Epiphany B
		Sun btwn Jul 31 and Aug 6 A
		Sun btwn Sep 18 and 24 B
		Sun btwn Oct 30 and Nov 5 A
Wilby, Philip		If Ye Love Me

Willaert, Adrian

Willan, Healey

    6 Epiphany A
    6 Easter A, C
    7 Easter C
    Day of Pentecost C
    Sun btwn Jul 10 and 16 C
The Raising of Lazarus
    5 Lent A
Arise, Shine, for Thy Light Is Come
    Epiphany of Our Lord A, B, C
Behold the Lamb of God
    Good Friday A, B, C
Behold the Tabernacle of God
    Sun btwn Oct 30 and Nov 5 B
Christ Being Raised from the Dead
    Sun btwn Jun 19 and 25 A
Christ Hath Humbled Himself
    Sun btwn Sep 25 and Oct 1 A
Christ Our Passover
    Easter Vigil A, B, C
Come unto Me, All Ye That Labor
    Sun btwn Jul 3 and 9 A
Grant Us Thy Light
    Transfiguration of Our Lord B
Holy, Holy, Holy Is the Lord
    Holy Trinity C
Hosanna to the Son of David
    Passion/Palm Sunday A
I Will Not Leave You Comfortless
    7 Easter A
Let the People Praise Thee, O God
    Sun btwn Aug 14 and 20 A
Lift Up Your Heads, Ye Mighty Gates
    3 Advent C
Lo, in the Appointed Time
    Sun btwn Nov 13 and 19 B
Magnificat and Nunc dimittis
    3 Advent A
O Sacred Feast
    3 Easter C
Oh, Send Out Thy Light
    Sun btwn Oct 30 and Nov 5 A
Rejoice in the Lord Always
    Sun btwn Oct 9 and 15 A
Rejoice, O Jerusalem
    1 Advent A
Sing to the Lord of Harvest
    Day of Thanksgiving A
Te Deum laudamus/We Praise Thee, O God
    Holy Trinity B
    All Saints Day C
The Great O Antiphons of Advent
    4 Advent A
The Seed Is the Word of God
    Sun btwn Jul 10 and 16 A
The Spirit of the Lord
    Day of Pentecost A
The Three Kings
    Epiphany of Our Lord A, B, C
The Word Was Made Flesh
    Christmas Day (III) A, B, C
    2 Christmas A, B, C
What Is This Lovely Fragrance?

	Christmas Dawn (II) A, B, C
Willcock, Christopher	Give Us a Pure Heart
	6 Epiphany C
	Sun btwn Sep 18 and 24 C
Willcocks, David	Gabriel's Message
	4 Advent C
	Hark! The Herald Angels Sing
	Christmas Day (III) A, B, C
	Love Divine, All Loves Excelling
	7 Epiphany A
	Of the Father's Love Begotten
	2 Christmas A, B, C
	Once in Royal David's City
	Christmas Dawn (II) A, B, C
	Name of Jesus A, B, C
	Sussex Carol
	Christmas Eve (I) A, B, C
	1 Christmas B
	Thou, O God, Art Praised in Zion
	Sun btwn Jul 10 and 16 A
Willcocks, Jonathan	O Holy Jesus
	3 Lent B
Williams, David McKinley	In the Year That King Uzziah Died
	5 Epiphany C
Williamson, Malcolm	Thou Art Praised in Zion
	Sun btwn Jul 10 and 16 A
Wold, Wayne L.	As This Broken Bread
	Sun btwn Jul 24 and 30 B
	Rejoice! I Found the Lost
	Sun btwn Sep 11 and 17 C
Wolff, S. Drummond	At the Lamb's High Feast
	Easter Vigil A, B, C
	Easter Day B
	Built on the Rock
	Sun btwn Aug 21 and 27 A
	Christ Is the King
	Christ the King B
	Come Down, O Love Divine
	Sun btwn Aug 14 and 20 C
	Come, You Faithful, Raise the Strain
	2 Easter B
	Holy, Holy, Holy
	Holy Trinity B
	Let All the World in Every Corner Sing
	Christ the King A
	Look, Oh, Look, the Sight Is Glorious
	7 Easter A
	Now All the Vault of Heaven Resounds
	6 Easter B
	O Day of Rest and Gladness
	Sun btwn May 29 and Jun 4 B
	Oh, Wondrous Type! Oh, Vision Fair
	Transfiguration of Our Lord C
	Praise and Thanksgiving
	Day of Thanksgiving C
	We Know That Christ Is Raised
	Easter Vigil A, B, C
	Sun btwn Jun 12 and 18 B
Wood, Charles	Jesus Had a Garden
	Sun btwn Jun 26 and Jul 2 C
(Wood, Charles)	O Thou, the Central Orb

	3 Advent A
Wood, Dale	Arise, My Soul, Arise!
	6 Epiphany B
	Built on a Rock
	Sun btwn May 24 and 28 C
	Jubilate Deo/Psalm 100
	5 Easter A
	Christ the King B
	Day of Thanksgiving C
	Rise, Shine!
	Epiphany of Our Lord A, B, C
	3 Epiphany A, B
	4 Epiphany A, B
	5 Epiphany A
	Sun btwn Jun 19 and 25 C
Wyton, Alec	Go Ye Therefore
	Holy Trinity A
	When Jesus Went to Jordan's Stream
	Baptism of Our Lord A, C
Yarrington, John	O Savior of the World
	3 Lent B
Young, Carlton R.	Bread of the World, in Mercy Broken
	Sun btwn Jul 31 and Aug 6 C
Young, Gordon	Let Not Your Heart Be Troubled
	5 Easter A
	My Master from a Garden Rose
	2 Easter C
Zacharia, Cesare de/arr. Larry Long	Magnificat
	3 Advent A
Zgodava, Richard	Out of the Orient Crystal Skies
	Epiphany of Our Lord A, B, C
Zimmermann, Heinz Werner	And the Word Became Flesh
	Christmas Day (III) A, B, C
	2 Christmas A, B, C
	Have No Fear, Little Flock
	Sun btwn Jun 5 and 11 A
	Sun btwn Aug 7 and 13 C
	Praise the Lord
	6 Epiphany B
	Sun btwn Sep 18 and 24 C
	Psalm 23
	4 Lent A
	4 Easter A
	Sun btwn Jul 17 and 23 B
	Sun btwn Oct 9 and 15 A
	The Lord is My Light
	5 Epiphany B
	2 Lent C
	Those Who Trust in the Lord
	Sun btwn Sep 4 and 10 B
Zingarelli, Niccolò Antonio	Go Not Far from Me, O God
	Sun btwn Jun 19 and 25 C
Zipp, Friedrich	Soul, Adorn Yourself with Gladness
	2 Epiphany C
	Maundy Thursday A, B, C

Index of Titles

A Babe Is Born
    Bouman, Paul
        Christmas Day (III) A, B, C

A Babe Is Born
    Mathias, William H.
        Christmas Eve (I) A, B, C

A Boy Was Born
    Britten, Benjamin
        Christmas Eve (I) A, B, C
        1 Christmas C

A Child Is Born
    Nestor, Leo
        Christmas Dawn (II) A, B, C

A Child Is Born in Bethlehem
    Proulx, Richard
        Christmas Dawn (II) A, B, C

A Choral Flourish
    Vaughan Williams, Ralph
        Sun btwn Oct 30 and Nov 5 C

A Christmas Alleluia
    Saint-Saëns, Camille
        2 Christmas A, B, C

A Contrite Heart
    Beethoven, Ludwig van/ed. K. Lee Scott
        5 Lent B

A Dove Flew Down from Heaven
    Brahms, Johannes
        4 Advent B, C

A Great Harvest
    Peloquin, Alexander
        7 Easter A

A Joyful Psalm
    Marshall, Jane
        Sun btwn Sep 25 and Oct 1 C

A Lamb Goes Uncomplaining Forth
    Distler, Hugo
        2 Lent B
        Passion/Palm Sunday B
        Good Friday A, B, C

A Lenten Love Song
    Kemp, Helen
        Maundy Thursday A, B, C

A Lenten Prayer
    Near, Gerald
        1 Lent C

A Lenten Walk
    Hopson, Hal H.
        1 Lent B, C

A Litany/Drop, Drop Slow Tears
    Walton, William
        5 Lent C
        Maundy Thursday A, B, C

A Little Advent Music
    Distler, Hugo
        1 Advent A

A Mighty Fortress
    Busarow, Donald
        1 Lent A
        Sun btwn Jun 5 and 11 B

A Mighty Fortress
    Ferguson, John
        1 Lent A, B
        Reformation Day A, B, C

A Mighty Fortress
    Schalk, Carl
        Sun btwn Jun 5 and 11 B

A Mighty Fortress Is Our God
    Hopson, Hal H.
        1 Lent A

A Mighty Fortress Is Our God/Ein feste Burg ist unser Gott
    Hassler, Hans Leo
        1 Lent A, C
        Reformation Day A, B, C

A New Creation
    Clausen, René
        4 Lent C

A New Magnificat
    Jennings, Carolyn
        3 Advent A
        4 Advent B, C

A New Year's Carol
    Britten, Benjamin
        2 Advent B

A Nobler Life	Busarow, Donald
	Sun btwn Oct 2 and 8 C
A Palm Sunday Antiphon/Hosanna to the Son of David	Morgan, David C.
	Passion/Palm Sunday A
A Parish Magnificat	Schalk, Carl
	3 Advent A
A Psalm of Confession	Hopson, Hal H.
	Ash Wednesday A, B, C
A Rose Touched by the Sun's Warm Rays	Berger, Jean
	7 Easter A
A Song of Joy	Pote, Allen
	5 Epiphany B
A Song of Praise to the Holy Trinity	Schütz, Heinrich
	Holy Trinity A
A Song of Thanksgiving/Psalm 90	Ferguson, John
	Sun btwn Oct 9 and 15 B, C
	Sun btwn Nov 13 and 19 A
	Day of Thanksgiving B, C
A Song of Trust	Scott, K. Lee
	Sun btwn Jul 3 and 9 A
A Spotless Rose	Howells, Herbert
	1 Advent C
	2 Advent A
A Vineyard Grows	Scott, K. Lee
	Sun btwn Oct 2 and 8 A
A Waiting Carol	Kemp, Helen
	4 Advent A
Abide with Me	Bertalot, John
	Easter Evening A, B, C
Above All Praise and All Majesty	Mendelssohn, Felix
	Ascension of Our Lord A, B, C
	Sun btwn Oct 9 and 15 C
Achieved Is the Glorious Work	Haydn, Franz Joseph
	Ascension of Our Lord A, B, C
	Holy Trinity C
Adoramus te	Lassus, Orlande de
	Sun btwn Jul 17 and 23 C
Adoramus te	Mozart, Wolfgang Amadeus
	5 Lent C
Adoramus te Christe	Palestrina, Giovanni Pierluigi da
	Good Friday A, B, C
Adorn Yourself, My Soul	Peter, Johann F.
	Sun btwn Aug 21 and 27 B
Advent Hymn	Jean, Martin
	2 Advent A
	3 Advent B, C
Advent Message	How, Martin
	1 Advent B
	3 Advent B
Advent Prayer	Hopson, Hal H.
	1 Advent C
Advent Processional	Ferguson, John
	2 Advent C
	3 Advent A
	4 Advent B
African Noel	Thomas, André
	Christmas Day (III) A, B, C
Agnus Dei	Basler, Paul
	2 Epiphany A
Agnus Dei	Fauré, Gabriel
	Sun btwn Nov 6 and 12 B

Agnus Dei	Hassler, Hans Leo
	Sun btwn Sep 11 and 17 B
Agnus Dei	Morley, Thomas
	2 Epiphany A
Agnus Dei	Mozart, Wolfgang Amadeus
	Good Friday A, B, C
Agnus Dei	Rutter, John
	5 Lent A
Ah, Holy Jesus	Ferguson, John
	Passion/Palm Sunday A, B
	Wednesday in Holy Week A, B, C
	Good Friday A, B, C
Ah, Holy Jesus	Jennings, Carolyn
	Passion/Palm Sunday B
	Good Friday A, B, C
Ah, Holy Jesus	Mathias, William H.
	Good Friday A, B, C
Ah, Holy Jesus	Petrich, Roger
	Passion/Palm Sunday C
Ah Thou Poor World	Brahms, Johannes
	Sun btwn Jul 31 and Aug 6 C
	Sun btwn Aug 7 and 13 C
Ain'a That Good News	Dawson, William
	Sun btwn Sep 18 and 24 C
	Christ the King C
All Creatures of Our God and King	Busarow, Donald
	6 Easter B
	Ascension of Our Lord A, B, C
All Glory Be to God Alone	Heim, Bret
	1 Christmas C
All Hail, Adored Trinity	Sowerby, Leo
	Holy Trinity A, C
All My Heart This Night Rejoices: Be Glad and Sing	Ebeling, Johann Georg
	Christmas Eve (I) A, B, C
All My Spirit Longs to Savor	Handel, George Frideric
	2 Epiphany C
	7 Easter B
	Sun btwn Jul 10 and 16 B
All on a Christmas Morning	Burt, Alfred
	Christmas Dawn (II) A, B, C
All People That on Earth Do Dwell	Tallis, Thomas
	Sun btwn Jun 12 and 18 A
All That Hath Life and Breath, Praise Ye the Lord	Clausen, René
	2 Easter C
	Sun btwn Oct 16 and 22 A
All the Ends of the Earth	Schalk, Carl
	2 Lent B
All Things Are Yours, My God	Schalk, Carl
	Sun btwn Sep 25 and Oct 1 C
All Things Bright and Beautiful	Rutter, John
	6 Easter B
	Sun btwn Oct 9 and 15 B
	Day of Thanksgiving B
All We Like Sheep Have Gone Astray	Handel, George Frideric
	4 Easter A
All Who Believe and Are Baptized	Bach, Johann Sebastian
	3 Epiphany C
	Sun btwn May 29 and Jun 4 A
	Sun btwn Jun 12 and 18 B
	Sun btwn Jun 19 and 25 C
All Ye That Cried unto the Lord	Mendelssohn, Felix
	6 Epiphany B

Title	Composer / Occasion
All You Works of the Lord, Bless the Lord	Jennings, Kenneth Easter Vigil A, B, C

Alleluia	Bach, Johann Sebastian
	  6 Easter B
	  Transfiguration of Our Lord A

Alleluia	Basler, Paul 5 Easter B
Alleluia	Handel, George Frideric Easter Day A

Alleluia	Thompson, Randall
	  Transfiguration of Our Lord A
	  Easter Evening A, B, C
	  Sun btwn Aug 21 and 27 C
	  Sun btwn Sep 4 and 10 B

Alleluia for a Festival	Hurd, David 5 Easter A
Alleluia, Christ Is Risen	Hayes, Mark Easter Day C
Alleluia! Christ Is Risen	Mathias, William H. Easter Day B
Alleluia! Risen Indeed	Petrich, Robert 3 Easter A
Alleluia! Sing to Jesus	Harrison, Benjamin 7 Easter B
Alleluia! Sing to Jesus	Pelz, Walter L. 7 Easter B
Alleluia, Song of Gladness	Proulx, Richard Transfiguration of Our Lord A
Alleluia! Voices Raise!	Hillert, Richard 7 Easter A
Alles was Odem hat	Bach, Johann Sebastian Day of Thanksgiving B

Almighty and Everlasting God	Gibbons, Orlando
	  1 Lent C
	  Sun btwn Jun 19 and 25 B
	  Sun btwn Sep 25 and Oct 1 C

Almighty God, Your Word Is Cast	DeLong, Richard P. Sun btwn Jul 10 and 16 A

Amazing Grace	Bertalot, John
	  7 Epiphany B
	  3 Lent A, B
	  4 Lent B, C
	  Sun btwn Sep 11 and 17 C
	  Sun btwn Oct 23 and 29 B

Amazing Grace	Kallman, Daniel
	  Sun btwn Jun 26 and Jul 2 B
	  Sun btwn Sep 11 and 17 C

Amazing Grace	Parker, Alice/Robert Shaw 4 Lent C
Amazing Grace	Schickele, Peter Sun btwn Jun 26 and Jul 2 A
Amid the World's Bleak Wilderness	Hillert, Richard Sun btwn Oct 2 and 8 A
An Anthem of Faith	Mueller, Carl F. Sun btwn Oct 2 and 8 C
An Easter Gloria!	Leavitt, John 2 Easter B
An Easter Greeting	How, Martin 5 Easter A

And He Shall Purify	Handel, George Frideric
	  2 Advent C
	  2 Epiphany A

And I Saw a New Heaven	Bainton, Edgar L.
	5 Easter C
	Christ the King C
	All Saints Day B
And the Glory of the Lord	Handel, George Frideric
	2 Advent B, C
And the Word Became Flesh	Martinson, Joel
	2 Christmas A, B, C
And the Word Became Flesh	Zimmermann, Heinz Werner
	Christmas Day (III) A, B, C
	2 Christmas A, B, C
And Then Shall Your Light Break Forth	Mendelssohn, Felix
	Transfiguration of Our Lord C
And with His Stripes We Are Healed	Handel, George Frideric
	4 Easter A
Angelus autem Domini	Anerio, Felice
	Easter Vigil A, B, C
	Easter Day A
Antiphon	Vaughan Williams, Ralph
	Christ the King B
Arise, My Love, My Fair One	Near, Gerald
	Easter Day C
Arise, My Soul, Arise!	Wood, Dale
	6 Epiphany B
Arise, O Zion	Jennings, Kenneth
	2 Epiphany C
Arise, Shine	Rudolph, Glen
	5 Epiphany A
Arise, Shine!	Martinson, Joel
	Epiphany of Our Lord A, B, C
Arise, Shine, for Thy Light Has Come	Jennings, Kenneth
	Epiphany of Our Lord A, B, C
Arise, Shine, for Thy Light Is Come	Willan, Healey
	Epiphany of Our Lord A, B, C
Arise, Shine, for Your Light Has Come	How, Martin
	Epiphany of Our Lord A, B, C
Arise, Shine, for Your Light Has Come	Mathias, William H.
	Baptism of Our Lord A
Arisen Is Our Blessed Lord	Vulpius, Melchior
	Easter Day A, C
	Easter Evening A, B, C
As Long as I Have Breath	Farrar, Sue
	Sun btwn Jul 17 and 23 C
As the Dark Awaits the Dawn	Schalk, Carl
	1 Advent C
	3 Advent A, B
As the Deer, for Water Yearning	Goudimel, Claude
	3 Lent C
	Easter Vigil A, B, C
As This Broken Bread	Wold, Wayne L.
	Sun btwn Jul 24 and 30 B
Ascendit Deus	Gallus, Jacobus (Handl)
	Ascension of Our Lord A, B, C
Ascension, The/Lift Up Your Heads	Moore, Philip
	Ascension of Our Lord A, B, C
At Bethlehem	Bass, Claude L.
	1 Christmas B
At the Lamb's High Feast	Leavitt, John
	Easter Vigil A, B, C
At the Lamb's High Feast	Wolff, S. Drummond
	Easter Vigil A, B, C
	Easter Day B

Title	Composer / Details
At the Lamb's High Feast We Sing	Busarow, Donald Easter Day A

At the Lamb's High Feast We Sing	Cherwien, David
	    Easter Vigil A, B, C
	    Easter Day A, B

At the Name of Jesus	Clausen, René
	    Easter Day B
	    Christ the King B

At the Name of Jesus	Vaughan Williams, Ralph
	    Passion/Palm Sunday B, C
	    Ascension of Our Lord A, B, C
	    Sun btwn Sep 25 and Oct 1 A
	    Christ the King B, C

Audivi	Taverner, John/ed. Anthony G. Petti Sun btwn Nov 6 and 12 A
Audivi, media nocte	Tallis, Thomas/ed. R.R. Terry Sun btwn Nov 6 and 12 A
Author of Life Divine	Archer, Malcolm Sun btwn Jun 19 and 25 B
Ave Maria	Biebl, Franz 4 Advent B

Ave verum corpus	Elgar, Edward
	    3 Lent B
	    Maundy Thursday A, B, C
	    Sun btwn Oct 16 and 22 B

Ave verum corpus	Mozart, Wolfgang Amadeus
	    Maundy Thursday A, B, C
	    Sun btwn Jul 31 and Aug 6 A

Ave verum corpus	Saint-Saëns, Camille Maundy Thursday A, B, C
Awake, Arise!	Martinson, Joel 3 Easter B

Awake, My Heart, with Gladness	Crüger, Johann
	    Easter Day A
	    2 Easter B
	    3 Easter A, B

Awake, O Sleeper, Rise from Death	Near, Gerald 6 Easter A
Awake, Thou Wintry Earth	Bach, Johann Sebastian Easter Day B
Balm in Gilead	Burleigh, Harry T. 6 Epiphany B

Balm in Gilead	Shepperd, Mark
	    6 Epiphany B
	    7 Epiphany B

Baptism Carol, The	Busarow, Donald Baptism of Our Lord B, C
Baptism of Christ, The	Hallock, Peter Baptism of Our Lord A
Baptism of Our Lord, The	Callahan, Charles Baptism of Our Lord A, B
Be Known to Us, Lord Jesus	Schalk, Carl Sun btwn Aug 14 and 20 B
Be Peace on Earth	Crotch, William 3 Advent C
Be Thou a Smooth Way	Johnson, Ralph M. Sun btwn Nov 6 and 12 A
Be Thou Faithful to the Truth	Mendelssohn, Felix Sun btwn Jun 5 and 11 B

Title	Composer	Occasion
Be Thou My Vision	Ferguson, John	4 Epiphany A
		Sun btwn Jul 31 and Aug 6 C
		Sun btwn Sep 18 and 24 B, C
		Sun btwn Oct 9 and 15 B
Be Thou My Vision	Parker, Alice	Sun btwn Jul 31 and Aug 6 C
Beati quorum via	Stanford, Charles Villiers	Sun btwn Oct 30 and Nov 5 B
Beautiful Savior	Cherwien, David	Transfiguration of Our Lord B, C
		Christ the King C
Beautiful Savior	Christiansen, F. Melius	Epiphany of Our Lord A, B, C
		Transfiguration of Our Lord A, B
Because You Have Seen Me, Thomas	Hassler, Hans Leo	2 Easter A
Before the Marvel of This Night	Schalk, Carl	Christmas Eve (I) A, B, C
Begin the Song of Glory Now	Fedak, Alfred V.	Easter Day B
Begone, Satan	Bender, Jan	1 Lent A
Behold, a Virgin Shall Conceive	Handel, George Frideric	4 Advent A
Behold My Servant	Bengtson, Bruce	2 Christmas A, B, C
Behold the Lamb of God	Bouman, Paul	2 Epiphany A
		Good Friday A, B, C
Behold the Lamb of God	Willan, Healey	Good Friday A, B, C
Behold, the Lord Hath Proclaimed	Berger, Jean	Christmas Dawn (II) A, B, C
Behold the Tabernacle of God	Willan, Healey	Sun btwn Oct 30 and Nov 5 B
Beloved, God's Chosen	Hobby, Robert A.	Sun btwn Jun 26 and Jul 2 C
		Sun btwn Jul 3 and 9 B
Benedictus	Fauré, Gabriel	Sun btwn Aug 14 and 20 B
Benedictus	Stanford, Charles Villiers	2 Advent C
Benedictus	Vierne, Louis	2 Lent C
Bist du bei mir	Bach, Johann Sebastian	Sun btwn Sep 18 and 24 A
Bless the Lord, My Soul	Marshall, Jane	Sun btwn Sep 11 and 17 A
Bless the Lord, O My Soul	Gibbs, Armstrong C.	3 Advent A
		5 Lent C
Bless the Lord, O My Soul	Henderson, Ruth Watson	Sun btwn Sep 11 and 17 A
Bless the Lord, O My Soul	Ippolitof-Ivanov, Mikhail	Sun btwn Aug 21 and 27 C
Blessed Are the Dead Who Die in the Lord	Schalk, Carl	All Saints Day A, B
Blessed Are the Pure in Heart	Davies, H. Walford	4 Epiphany A

Title	Composer	Occasion
Blessed Are the Pure in Spirit	Lowenberg, Kenneth	4 Lent A
Blessed Are They	Fleming, Larry L.	Sun btwn Nov 13 and 19 B All Saints Day C
Blessed Are You	Diemer, Emma Lou	All Saints Day C
Blessed Be the God and Father	Wesley, Samuel Sebastian	3 Easter A
Blessed Be the Lord God	Thompson, Randall	2 Advent A
Blessed Is He Who Cometh	Gounod, Charles	Passion/Palm Sunday A
Blessed Is the Man	Rachmaninoff, Sergei	6 Epiphany C All Saints Day A, C
Blessed Lamb, on Calvary's Mountain	Scott, K. Lee	Good Friday A, B, C
Blest Are They	Bouman, Paul	Sun btwn Jul 10 and 16 B
Blest Are They	Haas, David	6 Epiphany C All Saints Day C
Blest Be the King	Mathews, Peter	2 Advent C
Bread of Life	Farrell, Bernadette	Sun btwn Jul 31 and Aug 6 B
Bread of the World, in Mercy Broken	Young, Carlton R.	Sun btwn Jul 31 and Aug 6 C
Bread to Share	Haugen, Marty	Sun btwn Jul 24 and 30 B
Break Forth, O Beauteous Heavenly Light	Bach, Johann Sebastian	Christmas Dawn (II) A, B, C 1 Christmas A
Breath of God	Helgen, John	Vigil of Pentecost A, B, C
Breathe on Me, Breath of God	Rorem, Ned	Vigil of Pentecost A, B, C
Bridegroom of My Soul	Bach, Johann Sebastian/ed. Fritz Oberdoerffer	Sun btwn May 24 and 28 B
Bring Low Our Ancient Adam	Bach, Johann Sebastian	4 Epiphany B Ash Wednesday A, B, C Sun btwn Oct 30 and Nov 5 A
Brother James's Air	Jacob, Gordon	Sun btwn Oct 9 and 15 A
Built on a Rock	Paulus, Stephen	3 Lent C
Built on a Rock	Wood, Dale	Sun btwn May 24 and 28 C
Built on the Rock	Burkhardt, Michael	Sun btwn Aug 21 and 27 A
Built on the Rock	Christiansen, F. Melius	Sun btwn Aug 21 and 27 A
Built on the Rock	Wolff, S. Drummond	Sun btwn Aug 21 and 27 A
But Thanks Be to God	Handel, George Frideric	Sun btwn Jun 26 and Jul 2 A
But Who May Abide	Handel, George Frideric	2 Advent C Sun btwn Aug 21 and 27 C

Title	Composer	Occasion
By Gracious Powers	Ferguson, John	Sun btwn Jun 19 and 25 C Sun btwn Oct 16 and 22 C
Call to Remembrance	Farrant, Richard	1 Lent B Sun btwn Jul 10 and 16 C Sun btwn Sep 25 and Oct 1 A
Canon of Praise	Pachelbel, Johann	Sun btwn Aug 21 and 27 C
Cantate Domino	Hassler, Hans Leo	Sun btwn Sep 25 and Oct 1 B Sun btwn Oct 16 and 22 A
Cantate Domino/Psalm 98	Hurd, David	Christmas Day (III) A, B, C
Canticle II: Abraham and Isaac	Britten, Benjamin	Vigil of Easter A, B, C
Cantique de Jean Racine	Fauré, Gabriel	3 Epiphany C
Carol of the Advent	Dietterich, Philip R.	2 Advent C
Carol of the Hill	Paulus, Stephen	Good Friday A, B, C
Cast Thy Burden upon the Lord	Mendelssohn, Felix	Sun btwn Jun 19 and 25 A
Chants of the Passion	Kern, Jan	Passion/Palm Sunday A Good Friday A, B, C
Cherubic Hymn	Glinka, Mikhail	Holy Trinity A
Children of the Heavenly Father	Ferguson, John	Sun btwn May 24 and 28 B
Children of the Heavenly Father	Scholz, Robert	8 Epiphany A 6 Easter A Sun btwn May 24 and 28 A Sun btwn Jun 26 and Jul 2 B Sun btwn Sep 18 and 24 B
Children of the Heavenly Father	Sjolund, Paul	6 Easter A Sun btwn Sep 18 and 24 B
Choral Fanfare for Christmas	Nelson, Ronald A.	Christmas Dawn (II) A, B, C
Chorales for Advent	Schalk, Carl	1 Advent A
Christ Be Our Seed	Schalk, Carl	Sun btwn Jul 10 and 16 B
Christ Became Obedient for Us unto Death	Anerio, Felice/ed. Walter Ehret	Sun btwn Sep 25 and Oct 1 A
Christ Being Raised from the Dead	Willan, Healey	Sun btwn Jun 19 and 25 A
Christ for Us Became Obedient unto Death	Near, Gerald	Passion/Palm Sunday A Maundy Thursday A, B, C
Christ Goes Before	Schalk, Carl	5 Easter A Sun btwn Oct 9 and 15 B
Christ Has Arisen/Christ ist erstanden	Lassus, Orlande de	3 Easter B
Christ Hath Humbled Himself	Willan, Healey	Sun btwn Sep 25 and Oct 1 A

Title	Composer	Occasion
Christ Is Arisen	Bach, Johann Sebastian	3 Easter A
Christ Is Coming	Weiland, Brent	1 Advent B
Christ Is Living!/Cristo vive	Farlee, Robert Buckley	Easter Day C 3 Easter B
Christ Is Made the Sure Foundation	Schalk, Carl	7 Easter B Sun btwn Aug 21 and 27 A
Christ Is Risen! Alleluia!	Lau, Robert	3 Easter B
Christ Is the King	Wolff, S. Drummond	Christ the King B
Christ Jesus Lay in Death's Strong Bands	Bach, Johann Sebastian/arr. Michael Burkhardt	Easter Day A
Christ Jesus Lord, Thy Name Adored	Praetorius, Michael/ed. Francis J. Guentner	Sun btwn Sep 25 and Oct 1 A
Christ Lay in Death's Dark Tomb	Schein, Johann H.	Easter Vigil A, B, C
Christ, Our Passover	Dirksen, Richard	Easter Evening A, B, C
Christ Our Passover	Vaughan Williams, Ralph	Easter Day A
Christ Our Passover	Willan, Healey	Easter Vigil A, B, C
Christ Our Passover/Pascha nostrum	Hancock, Gerre	Easter Day B
Christ Sends the Spirit	Proulx, Richard	Vigil of Pentecost A, B, C Day of Pentecost A, B
Christ the Glory	Lallouette, Jean François/arr. Richard Proulx	Transfiguration of Our Lord B
Christ the Lord Is Risen Again	Burkhardt, Michael	Easter Day A
Christ the Lord Is Risen Again	Rutter, John	Easter Day A 5 Easter B
Christ the Lord Is Risen Today!	Ferguson, John	Easter Day A
Christ unser Herr zum Jordan kam	Bach, Johann Sebastian	Baptism of Our Lord B
Christ upon the Mountain Peak	Bertalot, John	Transfiguration of Our Lord A
Christ Upon the Mountain Peak	Bouman, Paul	Transfiguration of Our Lord A, B, C
Christ, When for Us You Were Baptized	Helman, Michael	Baptism of Our Lord C
Christ, Whose Glory	Archer, Malcolm	2 Epiphany B
Christe, adoramus te	Monteverdi, Claudio	5 Lent B
Christians, We Have Met to Worship	White, David Ashley	Sun btwn Aug 21 and 27 B
Christmas Cantata	Pinkham, Daniel	Christmas Eve (I) A, B, C
Christmas Day	Farlee, Robert Buckley	Christmas Day (III) A, B, C
Christmas Day	Holst, Gustav	Christmas Day (III) A, B, C

Christmas Night	Rutter, John
	Christmas Eve (I) A, B, C
Christus factus est	Bruckner, Anton
	3 Lent B
	Passion/Palm Sunday A, B
	Sun btwn Sep 25 and Oct 1 A
Christus Paradox	Fedak, Alfred V.
	Christ the King C
Climb to the Top of the Highest Mountain	Jennings, Carolyn
	2 Advent B
	3 Advent C
	Sun btwn Oct 2 and 8 C
Coenantibus autem illis/As They Were Eating	Lienas, Juan de
	Maundy Thursday A, B, C
Cognoverunt discipuli/The Disciples with Wondering Eyes	Byrd, William
	3 Easter A
Come and Find the Quiet Center	Organ, Anne Krentz
	Sun btwn Jul 24 and 30 C
Come, and Let Us Return unto the Lord	Harris, David S.
	Sun btwn Jun 5 and 11 A
Come Away to the Skies	Erickson, Richard
	Easter Vigil A, B, C
	Easter Day A
	6 Easter C
	Ascension of Our Lord A, B, C
	Sun btwn Jul 31 and Aug 6 C
Come Down, Love Divine	Vaughan Williams, Ralph
	5 Easter B
Come Down, O Love Divine	Busarow, Donald
	Sun btwn Aug 28 and Sep 3 C
Come Down, O Love Divine	Harris, William H.
	6 Easter C
	Sun btwn Oct 30 and Nov 5 A
Come Down, O Love Divine	Mathias, William H./arr. Donald D. Livingston
	Vigil of Pentecost A, B, C
	Day of Pentecost C
Come Down, O Love Divine	Wolff, S. Drummond
	Sun btwn Aug 14 and 20 C
Come, Enjoy God's Festive Springtime	Telemann, Georg Philipp/arr. Joan Conlon
	2 Easter A
	Sun btwn Jun 5 and 11 A
Come, Follow Me	Leavitt, John
	Sun btwn Aug 28 and Sep 3 A
Come, Follow Me	Thompson, R. Paul
	Sun btwn Sep 11 and 17 B
Come, Holy Ghost	Attwood, Thomas
	Vigil of Pentecost A, B, C
	Day of Pentecost A
	Sun btwn Aug 14 and 20 C
Come, Holy Ghost, Creator Blest	Carter, Andrew
	Day of Pentecost B
Come, Holy Ghost, God and Lord	Bach, Johann Sebastian
	Vigil of Pentecost A, B, C
Come, Holy Ghost, God and Lord	Distler, Hugo
	Day of Pentecost A, C
Come, Holy Ghost, God and Lord	Schein, Johann H.
	Day of Pentecost A
Come, Holy Ghost, Our Souls Inspire	Burkhardt, Michael
	Day of Pentecost B
Come, Holy Spirit	Gibbons, Orlando
	Day of Pentecost A

Title	Composer / Occasion
Come, Holy, Quickening Spirit	Bach, Johann Sebastian/ed. K. Lee Scott — Day of Pentecost A, B
Come, Labor On	Ferguson, John — 7 Easter B
Come My Light	Organ, Anne Krentz — 3 Advent C
Come, O Blessed of My Father	Franck, Melchior/ed. Carl Schalk — Sun btwn Sep 18 and 24 B
Come, O Creator Spirit, Come	Josquin Desprez — Day of Pentecost A
Come, O Thou Traveler Unknown	Scott, K. Lee — Sun btwn Jun 12 and 18 A — Sun btwn Oct 16 and 22 C
Come, Risen Lord	Bertalot, John — 3 Easter A, B, C
Come, Thou Fount of Every Blessing	Kosche, Kenneth T. — Sun btwn Sep 11 and 17 C
Come, Thou Long-Expected Jesus	Hillert, Richard — 4 Advent A
Come, Thou Long-Expected Jesus	Rameau, Jean Philippe — 1 Advent A — Christ the King B
Come to the Feast	Haugen, Marty — Sun btwn Jul 10 and 16 A
Come to the Waters	Ratcliff, Cary — Sun btwn Oct 30 and Nov 5 C
Come unto Him	Handel, George Frideric — Sun btwn Jul 3 and 9 A
Come unto Me, All Ye Heavy Laden	Cherubini, Luigi — Sun btwn Jul 3 and 9 A
Come unto Me, All Ye That Labor	Willan, Healey — Sun btwn Jul 3 and 9 A
Come with Rejoicing	Leaf, Robert — Sun btwn Jul 3 and 9 A
Come, Ye Sinners	White, David Ashley — 3 Lent C — Sun btwn Oct 23 and 29 C
Come, You Faithful, Raise the Strain	Wolff, S. Drummond — 2 Easter B
Comfort, Comfort	Ferguson, John — 2 Advent A, B, C
Comfort, Comfort Ye My People	Bach, Johann Sebastian — 2 Advent A
Comfort, Comfort Ye My People	Bunjes, Paul — 2 Advent A
Comfort, Comfort Ye My People	Goudimel, Claude/ed. Anne Heider — 2 Advent C
Conditor alme siderum	Rossi, Richard Robert — 1 Advent C
Coventry Antiphon	Howells, Herbert — Sun btwn Aug 14 and 20 A
Coventry Carol	Pelz, Walter L. — 1 Christmas A
Coventry Carol	Shaw, Martin — 1 Christmas A
Coventry Carol	Warland, Dale — 1 Christmas A
Create in Me	Gerike, Henry V. — Ash Wednesday A, B, C
Create in Me a Clean Heart	Christiansen, Paul J. — Ash Wednesday A, B, C — Sun btwn Sep 11 and 17 C

Title	Composer / Info
Create in Me a Clean Heart	Nelson, Ronald A. Ash Wednesday A, B, C 4 Lent C
Create in Me a Clean Heart, O God	Bouman, Paul Sun btwn Sep 11 and 17 C
Create in Me, O God	Brahms, Johannes Ash Wednesday A, B, C 5 Lent B Sun btwn Sep 11 and 17 C
Create in Me, O God	Marshall, Jane Sun btwn Sep 25 and Oct 1 A
Creating God	Hurd, David Holy Trinity A
Creator Spirit, by Whose Aid	Jennings, Carolyn Day of Pentecost A, C
Creator Spirit, Heavenly Dove	Distler, Hugo Day of Pentecost A, B
Creator Spirit, Heavenly Dove	Schalk, Carl Vigil of Pentecost A, B, C Day of Pentecost C
Credidi	Popora, Niccolo/arr. E. Hyde 3 Easter A
Crown Him with Many Crowns	Pelz, Walter L. Christ the King A
Crucifixus	Bach, Johann Sebastian Passion/Palm Sunday A Good Friday A, B, C
Day by Day	Busarow, Donald 8 Epiphany B
Day by Day	Hayes, Mark 6 Epiphany A Sun btwn Jul 17 and 23 C Sun btwn Sep 4 and 10 C Sun btwn Oct 2 and 8 B Sun btwn Nov 6 and 12 B
Day by Day	How, Martin 6 Epiphany A Sun btwn Jun 19 and 25 B Sun btwn Jul 10 and 16 C Sun btwn Aug 21 and 27 B
Day of Arising	Schalk, Carl 3 Easter A
De Profundis	Pinkham, Daniel 5 Lent A
De profundis clamavi/From the Depths I Have Called unto Thee	Mozart, Wolfgang Amadeus 3 Lent B
Dear Christians, One and All Rejoice	Distler, Hugo 5 Easter B
Dear Christians, One and All, Rejoice	Hassler, Hans Leo/Hugo Distler 6 Easter A
Dear Lord and Father	Parry, Charles Hubert H. Sun btwn Aug 28 and Sep 3 A Sun btwn Sep 25 and Oct 1 B
Deck Thyself, My Soul, with Gladness	Handel, George Frideric Sun btwn Jul 31 and Aug 6 A Sun btwn Nov 6 and 12 A
Dedication Prayer/Bist du bei mir	Bach, Johann Sebastian/ed. Patrick Liebergen 3 Epiphany B
Deep Peace	Carter, Andrew 8 Epiphany A

Title	Composer / Occasion
Der Herr ist König/The Lord God Reigneth (Psalm 99)	Pachelbel, Johann Transfiguration of Our Lord A
Domine Deus	Bach, Johann Sebastian Sun btwn Oct 16 and 22 B
Domine fili unigenite	Vivaldi, Antonio 2 Christmas A, B, C
Dona nobis pacem	Bach, Johann Sebastian Day of Pentecost A

Draw Us in the Spirit's Tether	Friedell, Harold
	  Holy Trinity A
	  Sun btwn Jun 19 and 25 C
	  Sun btwn Jun 26 and Jul 2 C
	  Sun btwn Jul 3 and 9 B
	  Sun btwn Sep 4 and 10 A
	  Sun btwn Oct 2 and 8 B

Drop Down, Ye Heavens	Statham, Heathcoat Sun btwn Aug 7 and 13 A
Dust and Ashes	Haas, David Ash Wednesday A, B, C

E'en So, Lord Jesus, Quickly Come	Manz, Paul
	  1 Advent A, C
	  3 Advent B
	  2 Easter C
	  6 Easter C
	  7 Easter C
	  Sun btwn Nov 13 and 19 A, C
	  Christ the King B

Early Will I Seek Thee	Weelkes, Thomas Sun btwn Jun 19 and 25 C
Easter	Leavitt, John Easter Day B
Easter Anthem	Billings, William Easter Day A, B
Easter Carol	Proulx, Richard 2 Easter B, C

Easter Morning	Christiansen, Paul J.
	  Easter Day A
	  2 Easter A, B, C

Easter Proclamation, The/The Exsultet	Weaver, John Easter Vigil A, B, C
Easter Sequence	Biery, James Easter Vigil A, B, C
Eat This Bread	Berthier, Jacques Sun btwn Jul 31 and Aug 6 A
Ecce virgo concipies	Isaac, Heinrich/arr. Anthony G. Petti 4 Advent A
Ego sum panis vivus	Byrd, William Sun btwn Jul 31 and Aug 6 B
Ein feste Burg	Bach, Johann Sebastian Reformation Day A, B, C
El Desembre Congelat/On December's Frozen Ground	Susa, Conrad 3 Advent B
Enatus est Emmanuel	Praetorius, Michael 1 Christmas A
Enredietur virga	Gallus, Jacobus (Handl) 2 Advent A
Entrance into Jersualem and Hymn	Proulx, Richard Passion/Palm Sunday A, C
Entrata Festiva	Peeters, Flor Easter Day C

Title	Composer	Occasion
Epiphany Alleluias	Weaver, John	Epiphany of Our Lord A, B, C
Epiphany Carol	Neswick, Bruce	Epiphany of Our Lord A, B, C Baptism of Our Lord B
Eternal Ruler of the Ceaseless Round	Busarow, Donald	Sun btwn Aug 21 and 27 B Sun btwn Oct 16 and 22 A
Ev'ry Time I Feel de Spirit	Johnson, Hall	Holy Trinity B
Ev'ry Time I Feel the Spirit	Dawson, William	Day of Pentecost A, C
Ev'ry Valley	Handel, George Frideric	8 Epiphany A Sun btwn Oct 23 and 29 C Sun btwn Oct 30 and Nov 5 A
Evening and Morning	Schalk, Carl	Sun btwn Jun 19 and 25 B Sun btwn Oct 16 and 22 A
Every Time I Feel the Spirit	Burleigh, Harry T.	Day of Pentecost C
Everything You Do	Buxtehude, Dietrich	6 Epiphany A 5 Easter B Sun btwn Oct 9 and 15 B, C
Exceeding Glad	Handel, George Frideric	4 Epiphany A
Exsultate Deo	Scarlatti, Alessandro	Sun btwn Oct 9 and 15 C
Exsultet	Repulski, John	Easter Vigil A, B, C
Exsultet/Easter Proclamation	Batastini, Robert	Easter Vigil A, B, C
Exultate jubilate	Palestrina, Giovanni Pierluigi da	Day of Thanksgiving B
Exultate justi in Domino	Viadana, Lodovico	Sun btwn Aug 7 and 13 C
Faire Is the Heaven	Harris, William H.	6 Easter C All Saints Day A, C
Fairest Lord Jesus	Forsberg, Charles	Epiphany of Our Lord A, B, C Transfiguration of Our Lord A, B, C
Fairest Lord Jesus	Hampton, Calvin	Sun btwn Jul 10 and 16 B
Fanfare for Christmas Day	Shaw, Martin	Christmas Dawn (II) A, B, C
Fanfare for Festivals	Goemanne, Noël	Easter Day A
Farewell to Alleluia	Busarow, Donald	Transfiguration of Our Lord B
Farewell to Alleluia	Farlee, Robert Buckley	Transfiguration of Our Lord A, C
Father Abraham, Have Mercy on Me	Schütz, Heinrich/ed. Richard T. Gore	Sun btwn Sep 25 and Oct 1 C
Festival Canticle	Hillert, Richard	Sun btwn Nov 13 and 19 A
Festival Magnificat	Proulx, Richard	4 Advent B
Festival Sanctus	Leavitt, John	Holy Trinity A

Title	Composer / Occasion
Festival Te Deum	Britten, Benjamin Christ the King C

Fight the Good Fight	Gardner, John
	    6 Epiphany B
	    Sun btwn Aug 14 and 20 C
	    Sun btwn Sep 25 and Oct 1 A, C
	    Sun btwn Oct 23 and 29 C

Filled with the Spirit	Burkhardt, Michael
	    Vigil of Pentecost A, B, C
	    Sun btwn Aug 14 and 20 B

Flocks in Pastures Green Abiding	Bach, Johann Sebastian 4 Easter C
For All the Saints	Mueller, Jonathan R. All Saints Day A

For as the Rain and Snow Come Down	Hopson, Hal H.
	    Easter Vigil A, B, C
	    Sun btwn Jul 10 and 16 A

For as the Rain Cometh Down	Lekberg, Sven
	    Sun btwn May 24 and 28 C
	    Sun btwn Jul 10 and 16 A

For Glory Dawns upon You	Hirten, John Karl Epiphany of Our Lord A, B, C
For God Commanded Angels to Watch Over You	Mendelssohn, Felix Sun btwn Oct 16 and 22 B

For God So Loved the World/Also hat Gott die Welt geliebet	Distler, Hugo
	    2 Lent A, C
	    4 Lent B
	    Holy Trinity B

For He Shall Give His Angels Charge Over Thee	Mendelssohn, Felix 1 Lent C
For the Beauty of the Earth	Carter, Andrew Sun btwn May 29 and Jun 4 C
For the Beauty of the Earth	Ellingboe, Bradley Sun btwn Aug 21 and 27 B

For the Beauty of the Earth	Rutter, John
	    Sun btwn Jul 10 and 16 A
	    Sun btwn Aug 14 and 20 A
	    Sun btwn Aug 21 and 27 B
	    Sun btwn Oct 2 and 8 B
	    Presentation of Our Lord A, B, C

For the Fruits of All Creation	Prower, Anthony Day of Thanksgiving A
For the Gift of Water	Pinkham, Daniel Baptism of Our Lord A

For the Lord Will Lead	Mendelssohn, Felix
	    Sun btwn Jun 19 and 25 A
	    Sun btwn Jul 3 and 9 C
	    Sun btwn Aug 21 and 27 C

For the Lord Will Lead	Mendelssohn, Felix/ed. Susan Palo Cherwien
	    6 Epiphany B
	    Sun btwn Jun 19 and 25 B

For There Is Now No Condemnation	Bach, Johann Sebastian Sun btwn Jul 10 and 16 A

For Unto Us a Child Is Born	Handel, George Frideric
	    Christmas Eve (I) A, B, C
	    2 Epiphany B

Forgive Our Sins as We Forgive	Hobby, Robert A. 7 Epiphany C
Forgive Our Sins as We Forgive	Laster, James Sun btwn Jun 12 and 18 A

From Heaven Above
    Schein, Johann H.
        Christmas Eve (I) A, B, C

From Heaven Above to Earth I Come
    Bach, Johann Sebastian
        Christmas Eve (I) A, B, C
        Christmas Dawn (II) A, B, C
        Name of Jesus A, B, C

From Heaven Above to Earth I Come
    Burkhardt, Michael
        Christmas Eve (I) A, B, C

From the Apple in the Garden
    Hopp, Roy H.
        Sun btwn Nov 6 and 12 C

Gabriel's Message
    Willcocks, David
        4 Advent C

Gather Your Children, Dear Savior, in Peace
    Schalk, Carl
        Sun btwn Jul 3 and 9 A

Gaudete
    Batastini, Robert J.
        Christmas Dawn (II) A, B, C

Get You Up
    Nystedt, Knut
        5 Epiphany B

Give Almes of Thy Goods
    Tye, Christopher
        Sun btwn Oct 16 and 22 A
        Christ the King A

Give Ear unto Me
    Marcello, Benedetto
        2 Lent C
        Sun btwn Jul 31 and Aug 6 A

Give Me Jesus
    Fleming, Larry L.
        3 Lent B
        Sun btwn Jun 26 and Jul 2 C
        Sun btwn Aug 21 and 27 B

Give Me Jesus
    Hampton, Keith
        1 Lent B

Give Rest, O Christ
    Schulz-Widmar, Russell
        All Saints Day C

Give Thanks to God
    Beethoven, Ludwig van/arr. Richard Proulx
        5 Epiphany A
        4 Lent B
        Sun btwn Jun 19 and 25 B
        Sun btwn Nov 6 and 12 B

Give Thanks to the Lord
    Satie, Erik/Luigi Zaninelli
        Sun btwn Oct 30 and Nov 5 C

Give Us a Pure Heart
    Willcock, Christopher
        6 Epiphany C
        Sun btwn Sep 18 and 24 C

Giver of Every Perfect Gift
    Scott, K. Lee
        Sun btwn Sep 4 and 10 B

Gloria in excelsis Deo
    Bach, Johann Sebastian
        Christmas Eve (I) A, B, C
        Christmas Day (III) A, B, C

Gloria in excelsis Deo
    Vivaldi, Antonio/arr. S. Drummond Wolff
        Christmas Dawn (II) A, B, C

Glorious and Powerful God
    Stanford, Charles Villiers
        Christ the King C

Glorious Things of You Are Spoken
    Hobby, Robert A.
        Sun btwn Jul 31 and Aug 6 B

Glory and Worship
    Handel, George Frideric
        7 Easter A
        Sun btwn Oct 2 and 8 A
        Christ the King A

Glory to God in the Highest
    Pergolesi, Giovanni
        Christmas Dawn (II) A, B, C

Go and Tell John
    Fleming, Larry L.
        3 Advent A

Go Down, Moses	Cherwien, David
	Easter Vigil A, B, C
Go, My Children, with My Blessing	Burkhardt, Michael
	7 Epiphany B
Go Not Far from Me, O God	Zingarelli, Niccolò Antonio
	Sun btwn Jun 19 and 25 C
Go! Tell It On the Mountain	Barnett, Steve
	Christmas Dawn (II) A, B, C
Go Therefore and Make Disciples of All Nations	Schalk, Carl
	Holy Trinity A
Go Up to the Mountain of God	Helman, Michael
	Transfiguration of Our Lord A, B, C
Go Where I Send Thee	Thomas, André
	4 Epiphany C
Go Ye Therefore	Wyton, Alec
	Holy Trinity A
God Be in My Head	Carter, Andrew
	Sun btwn Aug 28 and Sep 3 B
God Be in My Head	Davies, H. Walford
	7 Easter B
God Be in My Head	Rutter, John
	Sun btwn Jul 31 and Aug 6 C
God Be Merciful	Bouman, Paul
	Sun btwn Aug 14 and 20 A
God Be Merciful unto Us	Aston, Peter
	Sun btwn Aug 14 and 20 A
God Be Merciful unto Us	Bouman, Paul
	Sun btwn Aug 14 and 20 A
God Has Gone Up with a Shout	Hopson, Hal H.
	Ascension of Our Lord A, B, C
God Is Gone Up	Rorem, Ned
	7 Easter A
God Is Gone Up	Titcomb, Everett
	Ascension of Our Lord A, B, C
God Is Gone Up with a Merry Noise	Croft, William
	Ascension of Our Lord A, B, C
God Is Gone Up with a Merry Noise	Hutchings, Arthur
	Ascension of Our Lord A, B, C
God Is Here	Ferguson, John
	Sun btwn Sep 4 and 10 B
God Is Light	Bouman, Paul
	2 Christmas A, B, C
	2 Easter B
God Is Love	Proulx, Richard
	Maundy Thursday A, B, C
God Is My Shepherd	Dvořák, Antonín
	Sun btwn Jul 17 and 23 B
God Is Our Refuge	Mozart, Wolfgang Amadeus
	Sun btwn Aug 7 and 13 C
God Is Our Refuge	Pote, Allen
	Reformation Day A, B, C
God Is Our Refuge and Strength	Cherwien, David
	Easter Vigil A, B, C
God Is Our Refuge and Strength	Hanson, Howard
	Sun btwn May 29 and Jun 4 A
God Now Dwells among Us	Hassler, Hans Leo
	Christmas Day (III) A, B, C
God of Grace and God of Laughter	Hopp, Roy H.
	4 Epiphany C
	7 Epiphany B

Title	Composer / Occasion
God of Life	Haydn, Franz Joseph/arr. Robert Scholz Sun btwn Aug 21 and 27 B
God Remembers	Schulz-Widmar, Russell 4 Epiphany B Sun btwn Oct 23 and 29 A
God Shall Do My Advising	Buxtehude, Dietrich 5 Epiphany A
God Shall the Broken Heart Repair	Scott, K. Lee 5 Easter B Sun btwn Jun 5 and 11 A Sun btwn Jul 3 and 9 C
God So Loved the World	Bruckner, Anton/ed. Maynard Klein 2 Lent A
God So Loved the World	Goss, John 2 Lent A
God So Loved the World	Martinson, Joel 2 Lent A, B
God So Loved the World	Stainer, John 2 Lent A, C 4 Lent B Holy Trinity B
God So Loved the World/Also hat Gott die Welt geliebet	Schütz, Heinrich 2 Lent A, C 4 Lent B
God, the Lord Is Sun and Shield /Gott, der Herr, ist Sonn' und Schild	Bach, Johann Sebastian Sun btwn Oct 23 and 29 B
God, the Lord, Now Reigneth	Josquin Desprez/ed. Leonard Van Camp Ascension of Our Lord A, B, C Christ the King A
God Whose Giving Knows No Ending	Hillert, Richard Sun btwn Oct 16 and 22 A
God's Promise	Adler, Samuel 2 Lent A
God's Son Has Made Me Free	Grieg, Edvard/arr. Oscar Overby Sun btwn Jun 19 and 25 C Sun btwn Jun 26 and Jul 2 A Reformation Day A, B, C
God's Word Is Our Great Heritage	Jennings, Carolyn Sun btwn Oct 16 and 22 A
Good Christian Friends, Rejoice	Ferguson, John Christmas Dawn (II) A, B, C 1 Christmas A
Good Christians All, Rejoice and Sing	Benson, Robert A. Easter Day B
Grace Above All	Petker, Allan Sun btwn May 29 and Jun 4 B
Gracious Spirit Dwell with Me	Scott, K. Lee Vigil of Pentecost A, B, C Day of Pentecost A Sun btwn Jun 5 and 11 A Sun btwn Jun 12 and 18 C Sun btwn Jun 26 and Jul 2 A Sun btwn Sep 4 and 10 B Sun btwn Sep 18 and 24 C
Grant Peace We Pray/Verleih uns Frieden	Mendelssohn, Felix 7 Epiphany C
Grant Us Thy Light	Willan, Healey Transfiguration of Our Lord B
Great O Antiphons of Advent, The	Willan, Healey/ed. Carl Schalk 4 Advent A

Title	Composer	Occasion
Greater Love Hath No Man	Ireland, John	4 Easter A
		6 Easter B
Grieve Not the Holy Spirit	Noble, T. Tertius	2 Easter C
Haec dies	Byrd, William	Easter Day C
Hail, O Favored One	Schalk, Carl	3 Advent A
Hail to the Lord's Anointed	Bender, Mark	2 Epiphany A
		3 Epiphany C
Halleluja	Telemann, Georg Philipp/ed. Susan Palo Cherwien	Easter Day B
		3 Easter A
Hallelujah	Beethoven, Ludwig van	Transfiguration of Our Lord B
Happy Are Those Who Delight	Hillert, Richard	Sun btwn Oct 23 and 29 A
Hark! A Thrilling Voice Is Sounding	Thiman, Eric H.	1 Advent C
Hark! I Hear the Harps Eternal	Parker, Alice/Robert Shaw	All Saints Day B
Hark! The Herald Angels Sing	Willcocks, David	Christmas Day (III) A, B, C
Have Mercy on Me, O God	Schalk, Carl	Ash Wednesday A, B, C
		5 Lent B
Have Mercy, O Lord: Music for the Imposition of Ashes	Moore, Bob	Ash Wednesday A, B, C
Have No Fear, Little Flock	Pelz, Walter L.	Sun btwn Jun 5 and 11 A
Have No Fear, Little Flock	Zimmermann, Heinz Werner	Sun btwn Jun 5 and 11 A
		Sun btwn Aug 7 and 13 C
Have Ye Not Known/Ye Shall Have a Song	Thompson, Randall	5 Epiphany B
He Comes to Us as One Unknown	Ferguson, John	3 Advent A
		4 Advent A
		2 Epiphany B
		3 Epiphany A
		4 Epiphany C
		Sun btwn May 29 and Jun 4 B
He Is Born the Divine Christ Child	Averitt, William	1 Christmas C
He Never Failed Me Yet	Ray, Robert	4 Easter A
		Sun btwn Aug 7 and 13 A
He Rose	Nelson, Ronald A.	Easter Day B
He Shall Feed His Flock	Handel, George Frideric	4 Easter A
		Christ the King A
He Shall Give His Angels Charge	Hillert, Richard	1 Lent C
He That Is Down Need Fear No Fall	Dowland, John	3 Lent C
		Sun btwn Aug 21 and 27 C
		Sun btwn Oct 23 and 29 C
He That Is Down Need Fear No Fall	Moore, Philip	3 Lent C
		Sun btwn Aug 21 and 27 C

Title	Composer	Occasion
		Sun btwn Oct 23 and 29 C
He That Is Down Need Fear No Fall	Vaughan Williams, Ralph	
		Sun btwn Aug 28 and Sep 3 C
		Sun btwn Oct 9 and 15 B
He That Shall Endure	Mendelssohn, Felix	
		Sun btwn Nov 13 and 19 B
He Was Despised	Handel, George Frideric	
		Passion/Palm Sunday A
		Wednesday in Holy Week A, B, C
He, Watching Over Israel	Mendelssohn, Felix	
		Sun btwn Oct 16 and 22 C
He Who Would Be Called	Bach, Johann Sebastian	
		Sun btwn Aug 28 and Sep 3 C
He's Got the Whole World	Hampton, Keith	
		7 Epiphany B
Healer of Our Every Ill	Haugen, Marty	
		Sun btwn Oct 23 and 29 B
		Sun btwn Sep 4 and 10 B
Healing River	Cherwien, David	
		Sun btwn Jun 26 and Jul 2 B
Hear, O Thou Shepherd of Israel	Mathias, William H.	
		4 Advent A, C
		Sun btwn Oct 2 and 8 A
Hearken to My Voice, O Lord, When I Call	Neswick, Bruce	
		2 Lent B
Heavenly Light	Kopylow, Alexander/arr. Peter Wilhousky	
		3 Epiphany A, B
Heilig ist der Herr/Holy Is the Lord	Hammerschmidt, Andreas	
		5 Epiphany C
Heilig/Holy	Mendelssohn, Felix	
		5 Epiphany C
Help Us, Lord	Copland, Aaron	
		Wednesday in Holy Week A, B, C
		Sun btwn Jun 19 and 25 C
		Sun btwn Oct 23 and 29 B
Here I Am, Lord	Schutte, Daniel L./arr. Ovid Young	
		2 Epiphany B
		3 Epiphany A
		5 Epiphany C
Here Is the Little Door	Howells, Herbert	
		1 Christmas A
Here, O My Lord, I See Thee	Schalk, Carl	
		Sun btwn Aug 28 and Sep 3 C
Here's a Pretty Little Baby	Thomas, André	
		Christmas Day (III) A, B, C
Herr, ich hoffe darauf/Lord, My Hope Is in Thee	Schütz, Heinrich	
		Sun btwn Jun 26 and Jul 2 B
Hide Not Thou Thy Face	Farrant, Richard	
		Sun btwn Jun 26 and Jul 2 A
His Voice	Fleming, Larry L.	
		2 Advent B
		Sun btwn Aug 28 and Sep 3 B
His Yoke Is Easy	Handel, George Frideric	
		3 Epiphany A
		Sun btwn Jul 3 and 9 A
Hodie Christus natus est	Carter, Andrew	
		Christmas Day (III) A, B, C
Hodie Christus natus est	Mathias, William H.	
		Christmas Dawn (II) A, B, C
Hodie Christus natus est	Sweelinck, Jan Pieterszoon	
		Christmas Eve (I) A, B, C

Title	Composer	Occasion
Holy God	Farlee, Robert Buckley	Christmas Day (III) A, B, C Sun btwn Sep 11 and 17 C
Holy God, We Praise Thy Name	Arnatt, Ronald	Holy Trinity A
Holy God, We Praise Thy Name	Ferguson, John	Holy Trinity A
Holy God, We Praise Thy Name	Goemanne, Noël	Holy Trinity A
Holy God, We Praise Your Name	Busarow, Donald	Holy Trinity A
Holy God, We Praise Your Name	Ferguson, John	All Saints Day A
Holy Spirit, Ever Dwelling	Baldwin, Anthony	Vigil of Pentecost A, B, C
Holy, Holy, Holy	Scott, K. Lee	Holy Trinity B
Holy, Holy, Holy	Tchaikovsky, Pyotr Il'yich	Holy Trinity B
Holy, Holy, Holy	Wolff, S. Drummond	Holy Trinity B
Holy, Holy, Holy Is the Lord	Willan, Healey	Holy Trinity C
Holy Trinity, The	Ellingboe, Bradley	Holy Trinity A, C
Hope for Resolution	Caldwell, Paul/arr. Sean Ivory	Christmas Day (III) A, B, C
Hope of the World	Lovelace, Austin	4 Epiphany B 5 Epiphany B
Hosanna to the Son of David	Gesius, Bartholomäus	Passion/Palm Sunday C
Hosanna to the Son of David	Gibbons, Orlando	Passion/Palm Sunday B, C
Hosanna to the Son of David	Pinkham, Daniel	Passion/Palm Sunday C
Hosanna to the Son of David	Victoria, Tomás Luis de	Passion/Palm Sunday A
Hosanna to the Son of David	Willan, Healey	Passion/Palm Sunday A
How Beautiful Are the Feet	Handel, George Frideric	Sun btwn Aug 7 and 13 A
How Beautiful upon the Mountains	Stainer, John	Christmas Day (III) A, B, C
How Blest Are They	Proulx, Richard	Sun btwn Oct 23 and 29 A
How Can I Keep from Singing?	Ellingboe, Bradley	5 Epiphany B Sun btwn Jun 19 and 25 B
How Can I Keep from Singing?	Nelson, Eric	5 Epiphany B Sun btwn Jun 19 and 25 B Sun btwn Oct 30 and Nov 5 C
How Excellent Thy Name	Handel, George Frideric	Holy Trinity C
How Firm a Foundation	Busarow, Donald	Sun btwn Jun 19 and 25 B
How Great Is Your Name	Hillert, Richard	Sun btwn Oct 2 and 8 B
How Lovely Are the Messengers	Mendelssohn, Felix	4 Epiphany B

How Lovely Is Thy Dwellingplace	Brahms, Johannes
	Sun btwn Oct 23 and 29 C
	Presentation of Our Lord A, B, C
How Lovely Is Your Dwelling Place	Marshall, Jane
	Sun btwn Oct 23 and 29 C
	Christ the King B
	Presentation of Our Lord A, B, C
How Lovely Shines the Morning Star	Schalk, Carl
	Epiphany of Our Lord A, B, C
How Sweet the Name of Jesus Sounds	Frahm, Frederick
	Name of Jesus A, B, C
Howl Ye	Thompson, Randall
	1 Advent C
Humble Service	Fleming, Larry L.
	7 Epiphany A, B, C
	5 Lent C
	Sun btwn May 29 and Jun 4 C
	Sun btwn Sep 4 and 10 B
	Sun btwn Sep 18 and 24 B
	Sun btwn Oct 16 and 22 B
	Sun btwn Oct 30 and Nov 5 A
Hymn	Ives, Charles
	Sun btwn Jun 5 and 11 C
Hymn to the Trinity	Burkhardt, Michael
	Holy Trinity A
Hymns of Thanks	Goemanne, Noël
	Day of Thanksgiving A
I Am the Bread of Life	Toolan, Suzanne
	Sun btwn Jul 31 and Aug 6 B
I Am the Good Shepherd	Bender, Jan
	4 Easter A
I Am the Living Bread	Haas, David
	Sun btwn Aug 7 and 13 B
	Sun btwn Aug 14 and 20 B
I Am the Living Bread	Harwood, Basil
	Sun btwn Aug 28 and Sep 3 B
I Am the Living Bread	McCabe, Michael
	Sun btwn Aug 7 and 13 B
I Am the Resurrection	Dressler, Gallus
	5 Lent A
	Sun btwn Nov 6 and 12 C
I Am the Resurrection	Schütz, Heinrich
	5 Lent A
I Believe This Is Jesus	Moore, Undine Smith/arr. Kenneth Jennings
	2 Epiphany A, B
I Build on God's Strong Word	Walter, Johann
	1 Lent C
	Sun btwn May 29 and Jun 4 A
	Reformation Day A, B, C
I Caused Thy Grief	Manz, Paul
	Good Friday A, B, C
I Give You a New Commandment	Aston, Peter
	Maundy Thursday A, B, C
	5 Easter C
I Go My Way to Jesus Christ/So fahr ich hin zu Jesu Christ	Schütz, Heinrich
	Sun btwn Nov 13 and 19 B
I Have Set the Lord Always Before Me	Schalk, Carl
	2 Easter A
I Heard the Voice of Jesus Say	Busarow, Donald
	3 Lent A
I Know De Lord's Laid His Hands On Me	Burleigh, Harry T.

Title	Composer	Occasion
I Know That My Reedemer Lives	Beck, Theodore	Sun btwn Jun 5 and 11 C
I Know That My Redeemer Lives	Behnke, John	Sun btwn Nov 6 and 12 C
I Know That My Redeemer Lives	Bunjes, Paul	Sun btwn Nov 6 and 12 C
I Know that My Redeemer Liveth	Handel, George Frideric	Sun btwn Nov 6 and 12 C 6 Epiphany C Easter Day C Sun btwn Jun 5 and 11 B Sun btwn Nov 6 and 12 C
I Know the Lord	Parker, Alice	Sun btwn Jun 5 and 11 A
I Lift My Soul	Hobby, Robert A.	Sun btwn Jun 26 and Jul 2 B
I Lifted My Eyes to the Hills	Bouman, Paul	2 Lent A Sun btwn Jul 3 and 9 B
I Praise Thee	Mendelssohn, Felix	Sun btwn Oct 9 and 15 A
I Rejoiced When I Heard Them Say	Proulx, Richard	1 Advent A
I Sat Down under His Shadow	Bairstow, Edward C.	4 Epiphany C Sun btwn Aug 14 and 20 B
I Saw a New Heaven and a New Earth	Schalk, Carl	5 Easter C Sun btwn Oct 23 and 29 B
I to the Hills Lift Up Mine Eyes	Berger, Jean	2 Lent A Sun btwn Oct 16 and 22 C
I Wanna Be Ready	Powell, Rosephanye	Sun btwn Aug 7 and 13 C
I Want Jesus to Walk with Me	Haan, Raymond H.	4 Epiphany B 1 Lent A, C
I Want Jesus to Walk with Me	Lynn, George	Sun btwn Jun 26 and Jul 2 A
I Want Jesus to Walk with Me	Trinkley, Bruce	1 Lent A
I Want to Praise the Lord All of My Life	Telemann, Georg Philipp/ed. Susan Palo Cherwien	Sun btwn Aug 7 and 13 B
I Want to Walk as a Child of the Light	Erickson, Richard	Epiphany of Our Lord A, B, C 3 Epiphany B Presentation of Our Lord A, B, C
I Want to Walk as a Child of the Light	Lamberton, Dodd	Sun btwn Jun 26 and Jul 2 A
I Want to Walk as a Child of the Light	Manz, Paul	3 Epiphany A
I Want to Walk as a Child of the Light	Thomerson, Kathleen	Epiphany of Our Lord A, B, C 3 Epiphany B
I Was Glad	Boyce, William	1 Advent A
I Was Glad When They Said unto Me	Parry, Charles Hubert H.	1 Advent A
I Will Bless the Lord	Hobby, Robert A.	All Saints Day A
I Will Exalt You	Hallock, Peter	

	Sun btwn Sep 18 and 24 A
I Will Extol You	Diemer, Emma Lou
	Sun btwn Sep 18 and 24 A
I Will Greatly Rejoice	Nystedt, Knut
	3 Advent B
I Will Lift Up Mine Eyes	Rutter, John
	2 Lent A
I Will Magnify Thee, O Lord	Corfe, Joseph
	Sun btwn Jun 26 and Jul 2 B
I Will Not Leave You Comfortless	Byrd, William
	6 Easter A
I Will Not Leave You Comfortless	Nelson, Ronald A.
	7 Easter B
I Will Not Leave You Comfortless	Titcomb, Everett
	Ascension of Our Lord A, B, C
I Will Not Leave You Comfortless	Willan, Healey
	7 Easter A
I Will Praise Forever	Handel, George Frideric/arr. Stephen Andrews
	Sun btwn Oct 2 and 8 B
I Will Sing New Songs of Gladness	Dvořák, Antonín
	Sun btwn Jun 12 and 18 A
I Will Sing of Thy Great Mercies	Mendelssohn, Felix
	Sun btwn Jun 5 and 11 A, C
	Sun btwn Jul 10 and 16 A
	Sun btwn Aug 14 and 20 A
I Will Sing of Thy Great Mercies	Scott, K. Lee
	Sun btwn Jun 26 and Jul 2 A
I Will Sing the Story of Your Love	Weber, Paul D.
	Sun btwn Jun 26 and Jul 2 B
	Christ the King A
	Reformation Day A, B, C
I Will Trust in the Lord	Moore, Undine Smith
	Sun btwn Oct 2 and 8 A
I Will Wash My Hands in Innocency	Bairstow, Edward C.
	Sun btwn Jul 17 and 23 A
I'm Going on a Journey	Bonnemere, Edward V.
	Sun btwn Jun 12 and 18 B
I'm Gonna Sing 'til the Spirit Moves in My Heart	Hogan, Moses
	Baptism of Our Lord C
	Day of Pentecost A
If God Is for Us, Who Is against Us	Handel, George Frideric
	Sun btwn Jul 24 and 30 A
If Thou Shalt Confess with Thy Mouth	Stanford, Charles Villiers
	Sun btwn Aug 7 and 13 A
If Ye Be Risen Again with Christ	Jennings, Kenneth
	Sun btwn Jul 31 and Aug 6 C
If Ye Love Me	Tallis, Thomas
	5 Easter C
	6 Easter A, B
	Vigil of Pentecost A, B, C
	Day of Pentecost C
If Ye Love Me	Wilby, Philip
	6 Epiphany A
	6 Easter A, C
	7 Easter C
	Day of Pentecost C
	Sun btwn Jul 10 and 16 C
If You Love One Another	Nelson, Ronald A.
	Maundy Thursday A, B, C
	6 Easter C
If You Will Trust the Lord to Guide You	Kosche, Kenneth T.
	Sun btwn Sep 25 and Oct 1 B

Title	Composer / Occasion
Image of the Unseen God	Hillert, Richard 2 Easter A Sun btwn Jul 17 and 23 A
Immortal, Invisible	Proulx, Richard Sun btwn Nov 6 and 12 A
Immortal, Invisible, God Only Wise	Hobby, Robert A. Sun btwn Jul 17 and 23 C
In All These You Welcomed Me	Roberts, William Bradley 2 Easter B Ascension of Our Lord A, B, C Sun btwn Jun 26 and Jul 2 B Sun btwn Aug 28 and Sep 3 C Sun btwn Sep 18 and 24 B
In Bethlehem a Wonder	Schroeder, Hermann Christmas Eve (I) A, B, C
In Christ There Is No East or West	White, David Ashley Sun btwn May 29 and Jun 4 C
In excelsis gloria	Mathias, William H. Christmas Eve (I) A, B, C
In God, My Faithful God	Buxetude, Dietrich Sun btwn Aug 28 and Sep 3 A
In God's Presence	Helgen, John Sun btwn Jul 31 and Aug 6 B
In Heavenly Love Abiding	Viner, Alan Sun btwn Sep 25 and Oct 1 B
In paradisum	Fauré, Gabriel Sun btwn Sep 25 and Oct 1 C Christ the King C
In the Beginning	Copland, Aaron Holy Trinity A
In the Beginning	Ferguson, John Christmas Day (III) A, B, C
In the Beginning of Creation	Pinkham, Daniel Holy Trinity A
In the Beginning Was the Word	Ryan-Wenger, Michael Christmas Day (III) A, B, C 2 Christmas A, B, C
In the Bleak Midwinter	Holst, Gustav Christmas Dawn (II) A, B, C
In the Night, Christ Came Walking	Cain, Noble Sun btwn Aug 7 and 13 A
In the Resurrection Glorious	Bach, Johann Christoph Friedrich Sun btwn Jul 17 and 23 A Sun btwn Nov 6 and 12 C All Saints Day A, C
In the Splendor of the Dawn	Morton, Graeme Christmas Dawn (II) A, B, C
In the Year That King Uzziah Died	Williams, David McKinley 5 Epiphany C
In Thee Is Gladness	Kallman, Daniel 8 Epiphany C Sun btwn May 24 and 28 A Name of Jesus A, B, C
In Thee, O Lord	Haydn, Franz Joseph 5 Easter A Sun btwn May 29 and Jun 4 A
In Thee, O Lord, Do I Put My Trust	Schütz, Heinrich 5 Easter A
In Thee, O Lord, Have I Put My Trust	Stevens, Halsey Sun btwn May 29 and Jun 4 A
In You Is Gladness	Gastoldi, Giovanni

		Transfiguration of Our Lord A
In Your Mercy, Lord, You Called Me	Callahan, Charles	
		Sun btwn Jun 26 and Jul 2 C
Infant Holy, Infant Lowly	Scott, K. Lee	
		Christmas Eve (I) A, B, C
Into Jerusalem	Taranto, Steven	
		Passion/Palm Sunday C
It Came upon the Midnight Clear	Proulx, Richard	
		Christmas Eve (I) A, B, C
Jerusalem, Jerusalem	Mendelssohn, Felix	
		2 Lent C
Jerusalem, Jerusalem	Schulz-Widmar, Russell	
		Sun btwn Nov 6 and 12 C
		All Saints Day B
Jerusalem, Thou That Killest the Prophets	Mendelssohn, Felix	
		Sun btwn Jun 12 and 18 A
Jesu dulcis/The Taste of Goodness	Kreutz, Robert	
		All Saints Day A
Jesu, dulcis memoria/Jesus, the Very Thought Is Sweet	Victoria, Tomás Luis de	
		Sun btwn Nov 6 and 12 B
Jesu, Grant Me This, I Pray	Kitson, C. H.	
		1 Lent C
		Sun btwn Jul 17 and 23 B
Jesu, Joy—My Joy Forever	Bach, Johann Sebastian	
		6 Epiphany B
		Sun btwn Aug 21 and 27 B
Jesu, meine Freude/Jesus, My Sweet Pleasure	Bach, Johann Sebastian	
		8 Epiphany A, B
		Ash Wednesday A, B, C
		5 Lent B
		Sun btwn Jul 24 and 30 A, B
		Sun btwn Jul 31 and Aug 6 C
		Sun btwn Aug 7 and 13 C
		Sun btwn Sep 18 and 24 C
Jesu, Our Hope, Our Heart's Desire	Scott, K. Lee	
		5 Lent C
Jesu! Rex admirabilis/Jesus, Thou Wondrous King	Palestrina, Giovanni Pierluigi da	
		Sun btwn Jun 26 and Jul 2 B
Jesu, the Very Thought of Thee	Powell, Robert J.	
		4 Epiphany A
Jesu, the Very Thought of Thee	Victoria, Tomás Luis de	
		6 Epiphany C
Jesu, Thou Art Watching Ever	Handel, George Frideric/ed. K. Lee Scott	
		Sun btwn Jul 31 and Aug 6 B
Jesus and the Traders	Kodály, Zoltán	
		3 Lent B
Jesus Came from Nazareth	Neswick, Bruce	
		Baptism of Our Lord A
Jesus Christ Is Risen Today	Hovhannes, Alan	
		Easter Day B
Jesus Christ the Apple Tree	Poston, Elizabeth	
		5 Easter B
Jesus Christ, My Sure Defense—Alleluia	Mendelssohn, Felix	
		Easter Day A
		5 Easter A
Jesus, Good Shepherd	Ellingboe, Bradley	
		4 Lent A
		4 Easter A, B
		Sun btwn Jul 17 and 23 B
		Sun btwn Oct 9 and 15 A
Jesus Had A Garden	Wood, Charles	

Title	Composer / Occasion
Jesus Has Come and Brings Pleasure	Busarow, Donald 5 Epiphany B
Jesus Is My Joy, My All	Bach, Johann Sebastian Sun btwn Jun 5 and 11 A
Jesus Is Our Joy, Our Treasure	Buszin, Walter 5 Easter A
Jesus, Jesus, Rest Your Head	Ellingboe, Bradley Christmas Eve (I) A, B, C Christmas Dawn (II) A, B, C
Jesus Loves Me	Ferguson, John Sun btwn Sep 25 and Oct 1 A
Jesus, My All, to Heaven Is Gone	Scott, K. Lee Ascension of Our Lord A, B, C
Jesus, My Lord and God	Ferguson, John 5 Easter A 7 Easter B Sun btwn Jul 10 and 16 B
Jesus, My Sweet Pleasure/Jesu, meine Freude	Bach, Johann Sebastian 8 Epiphany A, B Ash Wednesday A, B, C 5 Lent B Sun btwn Jul 24 and 30 A, B Sun btwn Jul 31 and Aug 6 C Sun btwn Aug 7 and 13 C Sun btwn Sep 18 and 24 C
Jesus, Name of Wondrous Love	Titcomb, Everett 4 Epiphany C
Jesus, Priceless Treasure	Beck, Theodore Sun btwn Jul 24 and 30 B
Jesus, Priceless Treasure	Thomas, Paul Sun btwn Jul 24 and 30 B
Jesus Said to the Blind Man	Vulpius, Melchior 4 Lent A
Jesus, Sun of Life, My Splendor	Handel, George Frideric Sun btwn Jun 26 and Jul 2 C
Jesus, Take Us to the Mountain	Schalk, Carl Transfiguration of Our Lord A, B, C
Jesus, the Very Thought of Thee	Ashdown, Franklin D. 4 Epiphany A 6 Epiphany C 5 Lent C Sun btwn Aug 28 and Sep 3 A Sun btwn Sep 25 and Oct 1 B Sun btwn Oct 2 and 8 A Sun btwn Nov 6 and 12 B Name of Jesus A, B, C
Jesus, the Very Thought of Thee	Bairstow, Edward C. Transfiguration of Our Lord A Sun btwn Sep 25 and Oct 1 A
Jesus, Thou Joy of Loving Hearts	Scott, K. Lee 2 Lent A
Jesus Went to Jordan's Stream	Plag, Johannes/arr. Richard Proulx Baptism of Our Lord B, C
John Saw Duh Numbuh	Parker, Alice/Robert Shaw 3 Easter C
Joys Seven	Cleobury, Stephen Baptism of Our Lord A
Jubilate Deo	Britten, Benjamin 7 Epiphany B Sun btwn Jun 12 and 18 A

Title	Composer	Occasion
Jubilate Deo	Mezzogorri, Giovanni Nicolò	Sun btwn Aug 21 and 27 B Day of Thanksgiving A
Jubilate Deo	Praetorius, Michael	Sun btwn Jun 12 and 18 A
Jubilate Deo/Psalm 100	Wood, Dale	Sun btwn Jul 24 and 30 B 5 Easter A Christ the King B Day of Thanksgiving C
Just a Closer Walk	Kallman, Daniel	4 Epiphany B
Just As I Am	Chilcott, Bob	Sun btwn May 24 and 28 B
Keep Me Faithfully in Thy Paths	Handel, George Frideric	Sun btwn Jun 5 and 11 A Sun btwn Sep 4 and 10 A
Keep Silence	Helgen, John	1 Advent B 5 Epiphany C
Keep Your Lamps	Thomas, André	1 Advent A, B, C Sun btwn Nov 6 and 12 A
Keep Your Lamps Trimmed and Burning	Scott, K. Lee	Sun btwn Aug 7 and 13 C
King of All Ages, Throned on High	Isom, Paul	Christ the King B
King of Glory, King of Peace	Scott, K. Lee	Sun btwn Aug 21 and 27 A
Kingdom, The	Thomas, André	Christ the King A
Kingdom of God, The	Jennings, Carolyn	Sun btwn Sep 11 and 17 B
Laetentur coeli	Byrd, William	3 Advent C
Lamb, The	Tavener, John	4 Easter A Sun btwn Sep 18 and 24 B
Lamb of God	Christiansen, F. Melius	2 Epiphany A 5 Lent B Maundy Thursday A, B, C Good Friday A, B, C
Lamb of God	Morley, Thomas	Sun btwn Nov 6 and 12 C
Last Supper, The	Pote, Allen	Sun btwn Aug 7 and 13 A
Laudate Dominum	Mozart, Wolfgang Amadeus	2 Epiphany C Day of Thanksgiving B
Laudate pueri	Mozart, Wolfgang Amadeus	Sun btwn Sep 18 and 24 C
Laudate pueri Dominum	Handel, George Frideric	Sun btwn Sep 18 and 24 C
Lay Up for Yourselves	Rorem, Ned	Ash Wednesday A, B, C
Lead Me, Lord	Wesley, Samuel Sebastian	Sun btwn Jul 17 and 23 A Sun btwn Sep 4 and 10 C
Lenten Litany	How, Martin	5 Lent B

Let All His Saints Rejoice — Pinkham, Daniel
    All Saints Day C

Let All Mortal Flesh — Ferguson, John
    Transfiguration of Our Lord B

Let All Mortal Flesh — Holst, Gustav
    5 Epiphany C
    Sun btwn Aug 14 and 20 B

Let All Mortal Flesh Keep Silence — Bairstow, Edward C.
    4 Advent A
    5 Epiphany C
    Transfiguration of Our Lord B
    Sun btwn May 29 and Jun 4 B

Let All Mortal Flesh Keep Silence — Vierne, Louis/ed. Charles Callahan
    6 Epiphany C

Let All the Angels of God Worship Him — Handel, George Frideric
    Christmas Day (III) A, B, C

Let All the World in Every Corner Sing — Mathias, William H.
    Christ the King A

Let All the World in Every Corner Sing — Wolff, S. Drummond
    Christ the King A

Let All Together Praise Our God — Praetorius, Michael
    Christmas Day (III) A, B, C

Let Grief Not Overwhelm You — Brahms, Johannes
    Sun btwn Sep 4 and 10 B

Let Justice and Judgment — Handel, George Frideric
    Sun btwn Oct 16 and 22 C

Let Not Your Heart Be Troubled — Young, Gordon
    5 Easter A

Let Our Gladness Have No End — Schalk, Carl
    Christmas Day (III) A, B, C
    2 Christmas A, B, C

Let the People Praise Thee, O God — Hammerschmidt, Andreas
    Sun btwn Aug 14 and 20 A

Let the People Praise Thee, O God — Mathias, William H.
    6 Easter C
    Sun btwn Aug 14 and 20 A

Let the People Praise Thee, O God — Willan, Healey
    Sun btwn Aug 14 and 20 A

Let the Peoples Praise You, O God — Neswick, Bruce
    Sun btwn Aug 14 and 20 A

Let the Word Go Forth — Hayes, Mark
    Sun btwn Jul 24 and 30 A

Let the Word of Christ Dwell in You — Pinkham, Daniel
    1 Christmas C

Let Thy Blood in Mercy Poured — Rickard, Jeffrey H.
    Good Friday A, B, C

Let Thy Hand Be Strengthened — Handel, George Frideric
    Sun btwn Sep 25 and Oct 1 A

Let Us Ever Walk with Jesus — Manz, Paul
    Sun btwn Jun 26 and Jul 2 A, B
    Sun btwn Aug 7 and 13 A

Let Us Talents and Tongues Employ — Ellingboe, Bradley
    3 Epiphany A

Let Your Manner of Life — Wienhorst, Richard
    Sun btwn Sep 18 and 24 A

Life Tree — Cherwien, David/Susan Palo Cherwien
    Easter Vigil A, B, C

Lift High the Cross — Burkhardt, Michael
    Sun btwn Sep 11 and 17 B

Lift High the Cross — Busarow, Donald
    Sun btwn Sep 11 and 17 B

Lift High the Cross	Schalk, Carl
	Sun btwn Sep 11 and 17 B
Lift Thine Eyes	Mendelssohn, Felix
	2 Lent A
	Sun btwn Oct 16 and 22 C
Lift Up Your Heads	Gieseke, Richard
	1 Advent B
Lift Up Your Heads, O Ye Gates	Mathias, William H.
	Passion/Palm Sunday A, C
	Ascension of Our Lord A, B, C
Lift Up Your Heads, Ye Mighty Gates	Niedmann, Peter
	2 Advent C
	Passion/Palm Sunday C
Lift Up Your Heads, Ye Mighty Gates	Willan, Healey
	3 Advent C
Lift Up Your Voice	Schütz, Heinrich
	Sun btwn Jun 26 and Jul 2 B
	Sun btwn Aug 14 and 20 A
Light and Salt	Routley, Erik
	5 Epiphany A
Light Everlasting	Christiansen, Olaf C.
	2 Epiphany A
	3 Epiphany A
Light of the World, The	Carter, Andrew
	5 Epiphany A
	5 Easter A
Light One Candle to Watch for Messiah	Erickson, Richard
	3 Advent C
Lightener of the Stars, The	Farlee, Robert Buckley
	Transfiguration of Our Lord A
	Ascension of Our Lord A, B, C
Like as a Father	Cherubini, Luigi/arr. Austin Lovelace
	8 Epiphany B
Like As the Hart	Howells, Herbert
	3 Lent C
	Easter Vigil A, B, C
Litany to the Holy Spirit	Hurford, Peter
	7 Epiphany B
	Day of Pentecost A
Little David Play On Your Harp	Johnson, J. Rosamond
	Sun btwn Jun 5 and 11 A
Lo! He Comes with Clouds Descending	Schalk, Carl
	Christ the King A
Lo! How a Rose E'er Blooming	Distler, Hugo
	1 Advent C
	2 Advent A
	3 Advent A
	4 Advent B
	Christmas Day (III) A, B, C
Lo, How a Rose E'er Blooming	Praetorius, Michael
	2 Advent A
Lo, in the Appointed Time	Willan, Healey
	Sun btwn Nov 13 and 19 B
Lo, My Shepherd's Hand Divine	Haydn, Franz Joseph
	4 Lent A
	Sun btwn Jul 17 and 23 B
Lo, the Full Final Sacrifice	Finzi, Gerald
	Christ the King C
Locus iste	Bruckner, Anton
	Sun btwn Aug 14 and 20 A
Look at the Birds of the Air	Dengler, Lee

Title	Composer	Occasion
		Sun btwn Oct 2 and 8 C
Look, Oh, Look, the Sight Is Glorious	Wolff, S. Drummond	7 Easter A
Lord, for Thy Tender Mercy's Sake	Farrant, Richard or John Hilton	3 Epiphany B
		7 Epiphany A, C
		Ash Wednesday A, B, C
		2 Lent B
		3 Lent A
Lord, for Thy Tender Mercy's Sake	Tye, Christopher	Sun btwn Sep 25 and Oct 1 A
Lord, God of Abraham	Mendelssohn, Felix	Sun btwn May 29 and Jun 4 C
Lord God, the Holy Ghost	Schalk, Carl	Day of Pentecost A
Lord, I Trust Thee	Handel, George Frideric	Sun btwn Aug 28 and Sep 3 A
Lord, I Want to Be a Christian	Hogan, Moses	5 Lent B
Lord, in All Love	Ferguson, John	2 Lent B
		5 Lent C
		Sun btwn Jul 17 and 23 C
		Sun btwn Sep 25 and Oct 1 C
Lord, It Belongs Not to My Care	Schalk, Carl	3 Lent B
		5 Lent A
		Sun btwn Nov 6 and 12 B
Lord Jesus Christ, God's Only Son	Bach, Johann Sebastian	1 Lent B
		Easter Vigil A, B, C
Lord Jesus Christ, Thou Prince of Peace	Bach, Johann Sebastian	Sun btwn Oct 30 and Nov 5 A
Lord, Keep Us Steadfast	Bach, Johann Sebastian	1 Lent A
Lord Keep Us Steadfast in Your Word	Busarow, Donald	1 Lent B
		Sun btwn Sep 25 and Oct 1 A
Lord, Let at Last Thine Angels Come	Hassler, Hans Leo	5 Lent A
Lord, Lord, Open to Us	Bender, Jan	Sun btwn Nov 6 and 12 A
Lord, Make Me to Know Thy Ways	Byrd, William/arr. Austin Lovelace	2 Epiphany B
		Sun btwn Sep 18 and 24 B
Lord, My God, Assist Me Now	Martini, Giovanni Battista/ed. John Castellini	Sun btwn Nov 6 and 12 A
Lord of All Hopefulness	Kallman, Daniel	Sun btwn Jul 3 and 9 A
Lord of Feasting and of Hunger	Schalk, Carl	Sun btwn Jun 19 and 25 A
		Sun btwn Sep 25 and Oct 1 C
Lord of Lords Adored by Angels	Heim, Bret	Maundy Thursday A, B, C
Lord of Lords, Adored by Angels	Bouman, Paul	Maundy Thursday A, B, C
Lord of the Dance	Fleming, Larry L.	Epiphany of Our Lord A, B, C
		Ascension of Our Lord A, B, C
		Sun btwn Nov 6 and 12 B

Title	Composer / Occasion
Lord, Thee I Love with All My Heart	Bach, Johann Sebastian 2 Lent B, C Sun btwn Jul 17 and 23 C Sun btwn Sep 25 and Oct 1 C Sun btwn Oct 23 and 29 A Sun btwn Oct 30 and Nov 5 B Sun btwn Nov 13 and 19 C
Lord, Thee I Love with All My Heart	Busarow, Donald Sun btwn Oct 30 and Nov 5 B
Lord, Thou Hast Been Our Refuge	Bairstow, Edward C. Sun btwn Nov 13 and 19 A
Lord, Thou Hast Been Our Refuge	Vaughan Williams, Ralph Sun btwn Oct 9 and 15 B Sun btwn Nov 13 and 19 A
Lord, to Whom Our Prayers Ascend	Schubert, Franz Sun btwn Jul 24 and 30 C
Lord, Whose Love in Humble Service	Kallman, Daniel Sun btwn Sep 25 and Oct 1 B
Lord, Whose Love in Humble Service	Wienhorst, Richard 6 Epiphany B Sun btwn Jul 31 and Aug 6 A Sun btwn Sep 18 and 24 B Sun btwn Oct 30 and Nov 5 A
Lord's Prayer, The	Ellingboe, Bradley Sun btwn Jul 24 and 30 C
Lord's Prayer, The	Peeters, Flor Sun btwn Jul 24 and 30 C
Love Bade Me Welcome	Hurd, David 8 Epiphany B Sun btwn Nov 13 and 19 B
Love Divine, All Loves Excelling	Busarow, Donald Ascension of Our Lord A, B, C
Love Divine, All Loves Excelling	Rorem, Ned Sun btwn Jul 10 and 16 C
Love Divine, All Loves Excelling	Willcocks, David 7 Epiphany A
Love One Another	Carter, Andrew 3 Easter A
Love One Another	Ellen, Jane 7 Epiphany C
Love One Another	Organ, Anne Krentz Maundy Thursday A, B, C Sun btwn Sep 11 and 17 A
Loving Shepherd of Thy Sheep	DeLong, Richard P. 4 Easter A
Lullaby on Christmas Eve	Christiansen, F. Melius Christmas Eve (I) A, B, C
Magdalena	Brahms, Johannes Easter Day A
Magna et mirabilia	Neswick, Bruce Holy Trinity A
Magnificat	Berthier, Jacques 3 Advent A
Magnificat	Ellingboe, Bradley 4 Advent B
Magnificat	Nester, Leo 4 Advent A
Magnificat	Rachmaninoff, Sergei 4 Advent C
Magnificat	Zacharia, Cesare de/arr. Larry Long 3 Advent A

Title	Composer / Occasion
Magnificat and Nunc dimittis	Willan, Healey 3 Advent A
Magnificat anima mea	Bach, Johann Sebastian 4 Advent C

Make a Joyful Noise unto the Lord	Head, Michael
	  Sun btwn Jun 12 and 18 A
	  Day of Thanksgiving A

Make Haste	Hovhaness, Alan Sun btwn Nov 6 and 12 A

Make Me Pure, O Sacred Spirit	Telemann, Georg Philip
	  Ash Wednesday A, B, C
	  Day of Pentecost C
	  Sun btwn Aug 28 and Sep 3 B
	  Sun btwn Sep 18 and 24 B

Mandatum	Farlee, Robert Buckley
	  Maundy Thursday A, B, C
	  5 Easter C

Many Gifts, One Spirit	Pote, Allen Sun btwn Aug 21 and 27 A

Maria Walks amid the Thorn	Distler, Hugo
	  3 Advent A
	  4 Advent A, B

Mary at the Tomb	Ellingboe, Bradley
	  Easter Day A
	  2 Easter A, B, C

Mary Had a Baby	Dawson, William 4 Advent A
Mary Went Up to Hill Country	Schalk, Carl 4 Advent C
Mary's Magnificat	Carter, Andrew 4 Advent C
May I Love You, Lord	Hopp, Roy H. 2 Lent C
Meinen Jesum lass ich nicht/I Stand Fast with Jesus Christ	Reger, Max 2 Lent B
Midnight Clear	Schulz-Widmar, Russell Christmas Day (III) A, B, C
Mighty Are Your Works, O God	Mozart, Wolfgang Amadeus Holy Trinity C
Miriam's Song	Barker, Michael Easter Vigil A, B, C

Miserere mei, Deus	Allegri, Gregorio
	  Ash Wednesday A, B, C
	  5 Lent B

Miserere mei/Mercy Grant unto Me	Byrd, William Ash Wednesday A, B, C

Mizmor shir l'yom ha-Shabat	Adler, Samuel
	  Sun btwn May 24 and 28 C
	  Sun btwn Jun 12 and 18 B

Motet for Passion Sunday	Ferko, Frank Passion/Palm Sunday A
Music for the Rite of Sprinkling	Trapp, Lynn Easter Vigil A, B, C

My Eyes for Beauty Pine	Howells, Herbert
	  7 Epiphany C
	  Sun btwn Aug 21 and 27 B

My God, How Wonderful Thou Art	Christiansen, F. Melius Sun btwn Oct 23 and 29 A
My God, How Wonderful Thou Art	Clausen, René 5 Epiphany A

My God Is a Rock	Traditional/arr. Robert Shaw, Alice Parker
	Sun btwn Oct 9 and 15 B
My God, My God	Schütz, Heinrich
	Maundy Thursday A, B, C
My Heart Is Inditing	Handel, George Frideric
	Christ the King A
My Inmost Heart Now Raises	Scheidt, Samuel
	Sun btwn Jun 19 and 25 A
My Jesus Is My Lasting Joy	Buxtehude, Dietrich
	Sun btwn Jul 10 and 16 B
My Lord What a Mornin'	Burleigh, Harry T.
	1 Advent B, C
My Master from a Garden Rose	Young, Gordon
	2 Easter C
My Shepherd Is the Living Lord	Tomkins, Thomas
	4 Easter A
My Shepherd Will Supply My Need	Thomson, Virgil
	4 Easter A, C
	Sun btwn Jul 17 and 23 B
	Sun btwn Oct 9 and 15 A
My Song Is Love Unknown	Cherwien, David
	4 Lent B
My Song Is Love Unknown	Jennings, Carolyn
	Passion/Palm Sunday A
My Song Shall Be Alway of the Lovingkindness	Sampson, Godfrey
	Sun btwn Jun 26 and Jul 2 A
My Soul Doth Magnify the Lord	Thompson, Randall
	4 Advent A
My Soul Exalts Your Name, O Lord	Schütz, Heinrich/arr. Robert Buckley Farlee
	4 Advent B, C
	Sun btwn Oct 30 and Nov 5 A
My Soul Gives Glory to the Lord	Schalk, Carl
	4 Advent B, C
My Soul Proclaims the Greatness of the Lord	Hassler, Hans Leo
	3 Advent A
Nations, Listen to God's Calling	Bach, Johann Sebastian
	Sun btwn Jul 3 and 9 B
Nativity Carol	Franck, César/ed. K. Lee Scott
	Christmas Dawn (II) A, B, C
Near the Cross of Jesus/Stabat Mater	Pinkham, Daniel
	Good Friday A, B, C
New Songs of Celebration Render	Ferguson, John
	Sun btwn Nov 13 and 19 C
No Man Liveth to Himself	Schütz, Heinrich
	Sun btwn Sep 11 and 17 A
Nobody Knows the Trouble I See	Scott, K. Lee
	Sun btwn Oct 9 and 15 B
Nobody Knows the Trouble I've Seen	Burleigh, Harry T.
	Sun btwn Aug 21 and 27 C
Noel Ayisyen	Desamours, Emile
	1 Christmas B
Not for Tongues of Heaven's Angels	Hopp, Roy H.
	4 Epiphany C
Not unto Him	Mendelssohn, Felix
	Sun btwn Sep 11 and 17 A
Notre Pére	Duruflé, Maurice
	Sun btwn Jul 24 and 30 C
Now All the Vault of Heaven Resounds/ Ye Watchers and Ye Holy Ones	Hobby, Robert A.
	Easter Vigil A, B, C
	6 Easter B

Title	Composer / Occasion
Now All the Vault of Heaven Resounds	Wolff, S. Drummond 6 Easter B
Now Is Christ Risen	Nystedt, Knut Easter Day C
Now Join We to Praise the Creator	Biery, James Day of Thanksgiving A, C
Now Sing We, Now Rejoice	Walter, Johann Christmas Dawn (II) A, B, C
Now Thank We All Our God	Bach, Johann Sebastian Sun btwn Oct 9 and 15 C Day of Thanksgiving A, B, C
Now Thank We All Our God/Nun danket alle Gott	Pachelbel, Johann Day of Thanksgiving A, B, C
Now the Green Blade Rises	Johnson, Carolyn 3 Easter C
Now the Green Blade Rises	Vantine, Bruce 5 Lent B
Nun lob, mein Seel	Bach, Johann Sebastian Sun btwn Aug 21 and 27 C
Nunc dimittis	Clausen, René 1 Christmas B Presentation of Our Lord A, B, C
Nunc dimittis	Scholz, Robert 1 Christmas B
'O' Antiphons, The	Hallock, Peter 4 Advent A
O Be Joyful in the Lord	Rutter, John Sun btwn Nov 6 and 12 B
O Be Joyful in the Lord	Sowerby, Leo Sun btwn Jun 12 and 18 A
O Bless the Lord	Gabrieli, Giovanni Sun btwn Aug 21 and 27 C
O Blessed Spring	Farlee, Robert Buckley 3 Lent A Easter Vigil A, B, C 5 Easter B 7 Easter C Day of Pentecost A Sun btwn Sep 25 and Oct 1 A Sun btwn Oct 9 and 15 C
O Bread of Heaven	Franck, César/ed. Susan Palo Cherwien Sun btwn Jul 24 and 30 B
O Bread of Life from Heaven	Bach, Johann Sebastian 3 Lent C Sun btwn Jul 31 and Aug 6 B
O Bread of Life from Heaven	White, David Ashley Sun btwn Aug 7 and 13 B Sun btwn Aug 28 and Sep 3 C Sun btwn Oct 30 and Nov 5 B
O Bread of Life from Heaven/O esca viatorum	Isaac, Heinrich Sun btwn Jul 31 and Aug 6 B Sun btwn Aug 7 and 13 B Sun btwn Oct 2 and 8 A
O Bread of Life/Panis angelicus	Franck, César/ed. Susan Palo Cherwien Sun btwn Jul 31 and Aug 6 A
O Child of Promise Come	Larkin, Michael 2 Advent B
O Christ, Our Light, O Radiance True/ Jesus, Thy Church with Longing Eyes	Hobby, Robert A. Sun btwn Jul 3 and 9 B

O Clap Your Hands	Dengler, Lee
	Ascension of Our Lord A, B, C
O Clap Your Hands	Gibbons, Orlando
	Ascension of Our Lord A, B, C
O Clap Your Hands	Mathias, William H.
	Ascension of Our Lord A, B, C
O Clap Your Hands	Rutter, John
	Ascension of Our Lord A, B, C
O Clap Your Hands	Vaughan Williams, Ralph
	Ascension of Our Lord A, B, C
O Come, Every One that Thirsteth	Mendelssohn, Felix
	3 Lent A, C
	Sun btwn Jul 31 and Aug 6 A
O Come, Let Us Sing Unto the Lord	How, Martin
	3 Lent A
O Come, Let Us Sing unto the Lord	Piccolo, Anthony
	Sun btwn May 29 and Jun 4 B
	Christ the King A
O Come Let Us Worship	Rachmaninoff, Sergei
	3 Lent A
	Christ the King A
O Come, O Come, Emmanuel	Ferguson, John
	4 Advent A
O Day Full of Grace	Christiansen, F. Melius
	3 Epiphany B
	Vigil of Pentecost A, B, C
	Day of Pentecost A, B
O Day Full of Grace	Schalk, Carl
	Vigil of Pentecost A, B, C
	Day of Pentecost A, B
O Day of Peace	Hopson, Hal H.
	3 Advent B
O Day of Peace	Parry, Charles Hubert H.
	Sun btwn Nov 6 and 12 A
O Day of Rest and Gladness	Wolff, S. Drummond
	Sun btwn May 29 and Jun 4 B
O Dearest Lord, Thy Sacred Head	Johnson, David N.
	Passion/Palm Sunday B
	Good Friday A, B, C
O Death, Where Is Thy Sting?	Handel, George Frideric
	Sun btwn Jun 26 and Jul 2 A
O for a Closer Walk with God	Stanford, Charles Villiers
	Sun btwn Sep 4 and 10 C
	Sun btwn Oct 23 and 29 A
O Give Thanks unto the Lord	Croft, William
	Sun btwn Sep 18 and 24 A
O God Beyond All Praising	Proulx, Richard
	Day of Thanksgiving C
O God, My Heart Is Ready	Lindley, Simon
	Sun btwn Aug 28 and Sep 3 A
O God, O Lord of Heaven and Earth	Bender, Jan
	3 Epiphany C
	7 Epiphany C
	Sun btwn Jun 12 and 18 A
	Sun btwn Jul 3 and 9 B
	Sun btwn Oct 16 and 22 A
O God of Light	Hobby, Robert A.
	4 Epiphany C
O God of Light	Rotermund, Melvin
	3 Epiphany C

Title	Composer / Occasion
O God of Light	Sowerby, Leo
	Sun btwn Jun 19 and 25 C
O God of Mercy	Bouman, Paul
	Sun btwn Jul 10 and 16 C
	Sun btwn Sep 11 and 17 B
O God of Mercy	Hancock, Gerre/arr. Paul Bouman
	Sun btwn Jul 3 and 9 C
	Sun btwn Aug 28 and Sep 3 C
O God, Our Help in Ages Past	Ferguson, John
	Sun btwn Jun 5 and 11 B
	Sun btwn Nov 13 and 19 A
O God the King of Glory	Purcell, Henry
	7 Easter A
O God, Thou Art My God	Purcell, Henry
	3 Lent C
O God, You Are My Refuge	Bach, Johann Sebastian
	4 Epiphany C
O Gracious Lord, Our God	Schütz, Heinrich
	4 Advent A
O Healing River	Hellerman, Fred, and Fran Minkoff/ arr. David Cherwien
	Sun btwn Jun 26 and Jul 2 B
	Sun btwn Aug 14 and 20 A
O Holy and Glorious Trinity	Palestrina, Giovanni Pierluigi da
	Holy Trinity B
O Holy Jesus	Willcocks, Jonathan
	3 Lent B
O Holy Spirit	Moore, Don Andrew
	Sun btwn Aug 28 and Sep 3 B
O Holy Spirit, Lord of Grace	How, Martin
	Day of Pentecost A
O How Amiable	Vaughan Williams, Ralph
	5 Easter C
O Jesu, fili David	Josquin Desprez
	Sun btwn Aug 14 and 20 A
O Jesus Christ, My Life, My Light/ O Jesu Christ, meins Lebens Licht	Bach, Johann Sebastian
	2 Christmas A, B, C
	Sun btwn Nov 13 and 19 B
O Jesus, Crucified for Man/Begrabt dem Leib in seinen Gruft	Schubert, Franz
	Sun btwn Sep 11 and 17 B
O Jesus, King Most Wonderful	Hogan, David
	Sun btwn Oct 23 and 29 A
O Jesus, King Most Wonderful	Tye, Christopher
	Christ the King A
O Little One, Sweet	Bach, Johann Sebastian
	Christmas Day (III) A, B, C
O Lord, Give Thy Holy Spirit	Tallis, Thomas
	Vigil of Pentecost A, B, C
	Holy Trinity B
O Lord, I Love the Habitation of Your House	Bender, Mark
	Sun btwn Aug 28 and Sep 3 A
O Lord, I Trust Your Shepherd Care	Schütz, Heinrich
	4 Lent A
	4 Easter B, C
	Sun btwn Oct 9 and 15 A
O Lord I Will Praise Thee	Jacob, Gordon
	3 Advent C
O Lord, Increase My Faith	Gibbons, Orlando
	Sun btwn Oct 2 and 8 C
O Lord, Increase Our Faith	Loosemore, Henry
	Sun btwn Sep 4 and 10 C

O Lord Most High, Eternal King	Benson, Robert A.
	Ascension of Our Lord A, B, C
O Lord My God	Wesley, Samuel Sebastian
	1 Lent B
O Lord, Our Governor	Marcello, Benedetto
	Holy Trinity C
O Lord Our Lord, How Excellent Thy Name	Hanson, Howard
	Holy Trinity A, C
O Lord, Thou Art My God and King	Sateren, Leland
	Sun btwn Sep 18 and 24 A
O Lord, Thou Hast Been Our Dwelling Place	Schalk, Carl
	Sun btwn Nov 13 and 19 A
O Lord, We Praise Thee	Praetorius, Michael
	Maundy Thursday A, B, C
O Lord, You Are My God and King	Busarow, Donald
	Ascension of Our Lord A, B, C
	Christ the King A, B
O Love, How Deep	Titcomb, Everett
	4 Epiphany B
O Love, How Deep, How Broad, How High	Schalk, Carl
	7 Easter A
O magnum mysterium	Near, Gerald
	Christmas Eve (I) A, B, C
O magnum mysterium	Poulenc, Francis
	Christmas Eve (I) A, B, C
O magnum mysterium	Victoria, Tomás Luis de
	Christmas Eve (I) A, B, C
	Christmas Day (III) A, B, C
O Mighty Word from God Come Down	Josquin Desprez
	3 Easter C
O Morning Star, How Fair and Bright	Bach, Johann Sebastian
	Epiphany of Our Lord A, B, C
O Morning Star, How Fair and Bright	Busarow, Donald
	Epiphany of Our Lord A, B, C
	7 Easter C
O Morning Star, How Fair and Bright	Hobby, Robert A.
	Epiphany of Our Lord A, B, C
O Morning Star, How Fair and Bright	Pelz, Walter L.
	7 Easter C
O Morning Star, How Fair and Bright!	Praetorius, Michael
	Epiphany of Our Lord A, B, C
	Transfiguration of Our Lord A
O Mortal World	Bach, Johann Sebastian
	Sun btwn Jul 17 and 23 A
	Sun btwn Jul 31 and Aug 6 C
O My People, Turn to Me	Farlee, Robert Buckley
	Sun btwn Jul 10 and 16 A
O My Soul, Bless God the Father	Ehret, Walter
	Sun btwn Sep 11 and 17 A
O nata lux	Lauridsen, Morten
	Epiphany of Our Lord A, B, C
O nata lux	Tallis, Thomas
	Epiphany of Our Lord A, B, C
	Transfiguration of Our Lord C
O Paschal Lamp of Radiant Light	Owens, Sam Batt
	Easter Evening A, B, C
O Praise the Lord, All Ye Nations	Telemann, Georg Philipp
	3 Epiphany B
O Praise the Lord Who Made All Beauty	Hopson, Hal H.
	Easter Vigil A, B, C
O Pray for the Peace of Jerusalem	Howells, Herbert

Title	Composer	Occasion
O Rest in the Lord	Mendelssohn, Felix	1 Advent A Sun btwn Aug 7 and 13 C
O Sacred and Blessed Feast/O sacrum convivium	Fay, Peter	Sun btwn Jul 31 and Aug 6 B
O Sacred Feast	Willan, Healey	3 Easter C
O Sacred Head, Now Wounded	Leaf, Robert	Passion/Palm Sunday B Good Friday A, B, C
O sacrum convivium	Biery, James	Easter Vigil A, B, C
O sacrum convivium	Messiaen, Olivier	Maundy Thursday A, B, C
O sacrum convivium	Moore, Philip	Maundy Thursday A, B, C
O sacrum convivium	Tallis, Thomas	Maundy Thursday A, B, C
O salutaris	Dupré, Marcel	Sun btwn Nov 13 and 19 C
O salutaris hostia	Nicholson, Sydney	Sun btwn Nov 13 and 19 C
O Savior of the World	Yarrington, John	3 Lent B
O Savior Rend the Heavens Wide/ O Heiland, reiss die Himmel auf	Brahms, Johannes	1 Advent B
O Savior, Rend the Heavens Wide	Distler, Hugo	1 Advent A
O Sifuni Mungu	Maddux, David	Day of Pentecost B
O Sing to the Lord a New Song	Bengtson, Bruce	6 Easter B Sun btwn Nov 13 and 19 C
O Sing unto the Lord	Hassler, Hans Leo	Christmas Eve (I) A, B, C
O Sing unto the Lord	Purcell, Henry	Christmas Eve (I) A, B, C Sun btwn Oct 16 and 22 A
O Sons and Daughters	Davies, H. Walford	2 Easter A
O Sons and Daughters of the King	Hillert, Richard	2 Easter B
O Spirit of God, Eternal Source	Vulpius, Melchior	7 Epiphany A Day of Pentecost B, C
O Splendor of God's Glory Bright	Bisbee, B. Wayne	2 Christmas A, B, C 7 Epiphany A Transfiguration of Our Lord C
O Taste and See	Neswick, Bruce	Easter Vigil A, B, C Sun btwn Aug 7 and 13 B Sun btwn Oct 2 and 8 A, C Sun btwn Oct 16 and 22 A All Saints Day A
O Taste and See	Vaughan Williams, Ralph	5 Lent A 3 Easter A 5 Easter C Sun btwn Aug 7 and 13 B Sun btwn Oct 2 and 8 C

O the Lamb	All Saints Day A
	Bell, John L.
O Thou Sweetest Source of Gladness	Passion/Palm Sunday B
	Bach, Johann Sebastian
O Thou That Tellest	Sun btwn Sep 25 and Oct 1 A
	Handel, George Frideric
O Thou, the Central Orb	4 Advent A
	Wood, Charles
O Trinity Most Blessed Light	3 Advent A
	Turner, Kenneth C.
O vos omnes	Holy Trinity A
	Casals, Pablo
	Passion/Palm Sunday C
	Good Friday A, B, C
O vos omnes	Dering, Richard
	Passion/Palm Sunday C
O World So Vain	Brahms, Johannes
	Ash Wednesday A, B, C
O World, I Must Be Parting	Isaac, Heinrich
	Sun btwn Nov 13 and 19 A
O Zion, Herald of Good News	Handel, George Frideric
	Sun btwn Jun 12 and 18 C
Of the Father's Love Begotten	Behnke, John
	2 Christmas A, B, C
Of the Father's Love Begotten	Gieschen, Thomas
	Christmas Day (III) A, B, C
Of the Father's Love Begotten	Willcocks, David
	2 Christmas A, B, C
Offertory for All Saints Day	Hobby, Robert A.
	All Saints Day C
Offertory for the Transfiguration of Our Lord	Hobby, Robert A.
	Transfiguration of Our Lord A, C
Oh, Hold Thou Me Up	Marcello, Benedetto
	Sun btwn Jun 5 and 11 A
	Sun btwn Jul 3 and 9 B
Oh, Pray for the Peace of Jerusalem	Howells, Herbert
	Sun btwn Jul 3 and 9 A
Oh, Send Out Thy Light	Willan, Healey
	Sun btwn Oct 30 and Nov 5 A
Oh, That Bleeding Lamb	Moore, Undine Smith
	Good Friday A, B, C
Oh, Wondrous Type! Oh, Vision Fair	Scholz, Robert
	Transfiguration of Our Lord C
Oh, Wondrous Type! Oh, Vision Fair	Wolff, S. Drummond
	Transfiguration of Our Lord C
Oh, Wondrous Type, Oh, Vision Fair	Schalk, Carl
	Transfiguration of Our Lord B
Old Hundredth Psalm Tune, The	Vaughan Williams, Ralph
	Holy Trinity B
	Sun btwn Jun 12 and 18 A
	Day of Thanksgiving A
On Earth Has Dawned This Day of Days	Benson, Robert A.
	Easter Day A
On Easter Morn	Parker, Alice/Robert Shaw
	Easter Day A
On God Alone My Faith I Build	Mendelssohn, Felix
	4 Epiphany B
	Sun btwn May 29 and Jun 4 A
	Sun btwn Aug 21 and 27 A
	Sun btwn Sep 11 and 17 B
	Sun btwn Oct 2 and 8 A

On God and Not on Human Trust	Pachelbel, Johann
	Sun btwn Sep 18 and 24 A
On Jordan's Banks	Cherwien, David
	2 Advent A
On Jordan's Banks the Baptist's Cry	Busarow, Donald
	2 Advent A
On My Heart Imprint Thine Image	Manz, Paul
	4 Lent A
On the Third Day	Pote, Allen
	Easter Day A
On This Bright Easter Morn	Philips, Craig
	Easter Evening A, B, C
On This Day Earth Shall Ring	Hillert, Richard
	Christmas Dawn (II) A, B, C
Once He Came in Blessing	Sedio, Mark
	Sun btwn Jun 19 and 25 A
	Sun btwn Sep 11 and 17 B
	Sun btwn Nov 13 and 19 A
Once in Royal David's City	Proulx, Richard
	Christmas Dawn (II) A, B, C
Once in Royal David's City	Willcocks, David
	Christmas Dawn (II) A, B, C
	Name of Jesus A, B, C
Open My Eyes	Scott, K. Lee
	Sun btwn Jul 24 and 30 A
	Sun btwn Oct 2 and 8 B
Open Thou Mine Eyes	Rutter, John
	4 Lent A
	Sun btwn Jun 26 and Jul 2 C
	Sun btwn Sep 18 and 24 B
	Sun btwn Sep 25 and Oct 1 B
Our Father	Schütz, Heinrich
	Sun btwn Jul 24 and 30 C
Our Father, by Whose Name	Busarow, Donald
	Sun btwn Oct 2 and 8 B
Our Father, by Whose Name	Cherwien, David
	Sun btwn Oct 2 and 8 B
Our Father, Thou in Heaven Above	Franck, Melchior
	Sun btwn Jul 24 and 30 C
Our Lady's Vision	Reger, Max
	Sun btwn Oct 23 and 29 B
Our Paschal Lamb, That Sets Us Free	Proulx, Richard
	Easter Vigil A, B, C
	Easter Day C
	3 Easter C
	6 Easter C
Our Soul Waits for the Lord	Schalk, Carl
	Sun btwn Aug 7 and 13 C
	Sun btwn Oct 2 and 8 C
Out of the Depths	Schalk, Carl
	Ash Wednesday A, B, C
	5 Lent A
Out of the Depths Have I Cried to Thee	Oldham, Kevin
	Ash Wednesday A, B, C
Out of the Depths I Cry to Thee	Scott, K. Lee
	Ash Wednesday A, B, C
	5 Lent A
	Sun btwn Jun 5 and 11 B
Out of the Orient Crystal Skies	Zgodava, Richard
	Epiphany of Our Lord A, B, C
Over the Hills Maria Went	Eccard, Johannes

		4 Advent C
Passion According to St. John, The	Byrd, William	
		Good Friday A, B, C
Passion According to St. John, The	Victoria, Tomás Luis de	
		Good Friday A, B, C
	see also St. John Passion	
Passion of Our Lord According to St. Luke	Bertalot, John	
		Passion/Palm Sunday C
	see also St. Luke Passion	
Passion of Our Lord According to St. Matthew	Bertalot, John	
		Passion/Palm Sunday A
	see also St. Matthew Passion	
Peace Be with You	Wetzler, Robert	
		2 Easter A
Peace Came to Earth	Manz, Paul	
		Christmas Day (III) A, B, C
Peace Came to Earth	Scott, K. Lee	
		4 Advent A
Peace I Leave with You	Clausen, René	
		6 Easter C
Peace I Leave with You	Nystedt, Knut	
		2 Easter A
		6 Easter C
		Day of Pentecost A
Peace I Leave with You	Pelz, Walter L.	
		2 Easter A, B, C
		5 Easter A
		6 Easter A
		7 Easter B
Pentecost Hymn	Grieg, Edvard	
		Day of Pentecost B
Poor Man Laz'rus	Hairston, Jester	
		Sun btwn Sep 25 and Oct 1 C
Praise and Thanksgiving	Wolff, S. Drummond	
		Day of Thanksgiving C
Praise God in Heaven	Schütz, Heinrich	
		Sun btwn Jul 3 and 9 B
Praise God, Ye Lands	Schütz, Heinrich	
		Sun btwn Jul 3 and 9 C
Praise, My Soul, the God of Heaven	Jennings, Carolyn	
		Sun btwn Oct 9 and 15 C
Praise, O Praise	How, Martin	
		Day of Thanksgiving B
Praise the Living God Who Sings	Helgen, John	
		Day of Pentecost B
		Sun btwn May 24 and 28 A
		Sun btwn Oct 9 and 15 C
Praise the Lord	Praetorius, Michael	
		Holy Trinity A
Praise the Lord	Zimmermann, Heinz Werner	
		6 Epiphany B
		Sun btwn Sep 18 and 24 C
Praise the Lord! O Heavens Adore Him	Burkhardt, Michael	
		5 Easter C
Praise the Lord, O My Soul	Peter, Johann F.	
		Sun btwn Sep 11 and 17 A
Praise the Lord, O My Soul	Rutter, John	
		Sun btwn Sep 25 and Oct 1 C
Praise the Lord, O My Soul/Psalm 146	Rorem, Ned	
		Sun btwn Sep 4 and 10 B
		Sun btwn Sep 25 and Oct 1 C

Praise to the Lord	Christiansen, F. Melius
	Sun btwn Jun 19 and 25 B
Praise to the Lord	Distler, Hugo
	Sun btwn Oct 9 and 15 C
Praise to You, Lord Jesus	Schütz, Heinrich
	3 Lent B
	5 Lent C
	Good Friday A, B, C
Praise Ye the Lord	Diemer, Emma Lou
	Sun btwn Sep 4 and 10 B
Praise Ye the Lord	Rutter, John
	Sun btwn Jul 3 and 9 C
Prayer	Beethoven, Ludwig van/ed. K. Lee Scott
	Sun btwn Jun 26 and Jul 2 A, B
	Sun btwn Jul 24 and 30 B
Prayer of Thanksgiving	Kremser, Eduard
	Day of Thanksgiving A
Prayer of St. Francis, The	Ellingboe, Bradley
	Sun btwn Jul 10 and 16 B
Prayer of St. Francis, The	Mathews, Peter
	Sun btwn Jul 10 and 16 B
Prayer to Jesus	Oldroyd, George
	Sun btwn Sep 11 and 17 A
Prepare Thyself, Zion	Bach, Johann Sebastian/arr. Michael Burkhardt
	3 Advent C
Proclaim with Me	Busarow, Donald
	Sun btwn Aug 14 and 20 B
Psallite	Praetorius, Michael
	Christmas Eve (I) A, B, C
	Christmas Dawn (II) A, B, C
Psalm 1	Goudimel, Claude
	Sun btwn Oct 23 and 29 A
Psalm 1	Schütz, Heinrich/arr. George Lynn
	Sun btwn Sep 4 and 10 C
Psalm 15	Martinson, Joel
	4 Epiphany A
Psalm 22	Cherwien, David
	Maundy Thursday A, B, C
Psalm 23/The Lord Is My Shepherd	Cherwien, David
	4 Easter B, C
Psalm 23	How, Martin
	4 Lent A
	4 Easter A
	Sun btwn Oct 9 and 15 A
23rd Psalm, The	McFerrin, Bobby
	4 Easter A
Psalm 23	Pelz, Walter L.
	Sun btwn Oct 9 and 15 A
Psalm 23	Zimmermann, Heinz Werner
	4 Lent A
	4 Easter A
	Sun btwn Jul 17 and 23 B
	Sun btwn Oct 9 and 15 A
Psalm XXIV/Psaume XXIV	Boulanger, Lili
	Christ the King B
Psalm 29	Schütz, Heinrich
	Baptism of Our Lord C
Psalm 46	Weaver, John
	Reformation Day A, B, C
Psalm 46/The Lord of Hosts	Ferguson, John
	Christ the King C

Psalm 50/Offer unto God	Christiansen, F. Melius
	Sun btwn Aug 21 and 27 C
	Sun btwn Nov 6 and 12 B
Psalm 84/Cantique de Jean Racine	Fauré, Gabriel/ed. Hal H. Hopson
	Sun btwn Oct 23 and 29 C
Psalm 90/A Song of Thanksgiving	Ferguson, John
	Sun btwn Oct 9 and 15 B, C
	Sun btwn Nov 13 and 19 A
	Day of Thanksgiving B, C
Psalm 96: Sing to the Lord a New Song	Hurd, David
	Sun btwn Oct 16 and 22 A
Psalm 97	Schütz, Heinrich
	7 Easter C
Psalm 98	Marshall, Jane
	Easter Vigil A, B, C
Psalm 98	Martinson, Joel
	Sun btwn Nov 13 and 19 C
Psalm 98/Cantate Domino	Hurd, David
	Christmas Day (III) A, B, C
Psalm 98/Sing a New Song to the Lord	Bell, John L.
	Christmas Day (III) A, B, C
Psalm 100	Sweelinck, Jan Pieterszoon
	Sun btwn Jun 12 and 18 A
Psalm 100/Jubilate Deo	Wood, Dale
	5 Easter A
	Christ the King B
	Day of Thanksgiving C
Psalm 130/Out of the Depths	Ferguson, John
	Ash Wednesday A, B, C
	5 Lent A
Psalm 133	Proulx, Richard
	7 Epiphany C
Psalm 146/Praise the Lord, O My Soul	Rorem, Ned
	Sun btwn Sep 4 and 10 B
	Sun btwn Sep 25 and Oct 1 C
Psalm 147	Folkening, John
	2 Christmas A, B, C
Psalm 148	Holst, Gustav
	5 Easter C
Psalm 148	Rorem, Ned
	1 Christmas A
Psalm 148/Praise Ye the Lord	Stevens, Halsey
	1 Christmas A
Psalm 150	Hobby, Robert A.
	2 Easter C
Psalm 150/Salmo 150	Aguiar, Ernani
	2 Easter C
	Day of Thanksgiving B
Psalm for Holy Week	Peloquin, Alexander
	Maundy Thursday A, B, C
Puer natus in Bethlehem	Werner, Gregor Joseph
	Christmas Dawn (II) A, B, C
Pues si vivimos/While We Are Living	Parker, Alice
	Sun btwn Sep 11 and 17 A
Purge Me, O Lord	Tallis, Thomas
	Ash Wednesday A, B, C
Put Ye On the Lord Jesus	Roff, Joseph
	Sun btwn Sep 4 and 10 A
Quaerite primum regnum Dei/Seek Ye First	Mozart, Wolfgang Amadeus
	Sun btwn May 24 and 28 A
Quia vidisti me, Thomas/Because You Have Seen Me, Thomas	Marenzio, Luca

Title	Composer	Occasion
		2 Easter A, B, C
Raise a Song, Let Praise Abound	Eccard, Johannes	1 Christmas A
Redeeming Grace	Scott, K. Lee	1 Lent B
		Sun btwn Jun 19 and 25 C
		Sun btwn Jul 17 and 23 C
		Sun btwn Jul 24 and 30 A
		Sun btwn Aug 14 and 20 C
Rejoice Greatly, O Daughter of Zion	Handel, George Frideric	Sun btwn Jul 3 and 9 A, C
Rejoice in God	Schütz, Heinrich/arr. Nancy Grundahl	Sun btwn Oct 9 and 15 A
Rejoice in the Lord	Mathias, William H.	Sun btwn Sep 25 and Oct 1 B
Rejoice in the Lord Always	Anonymous sixteenth century/arr. John Redford	3 Advent C
		Sun btwn Oct 9 and 15 A
Rejoice in the Lord Always	Purcell, Henry	3 Advent C
		Sun btwn Sep 4 and 10 B
		Sun btwn Oct 9 and 15 A
Rejoice in the Lord Always	Willan, Healey	Sun btwn Oct 9 and 15 A
Rejoice Ye Shining Worlds on High	Billings, William	Ascension of Our Lord A, B, C
Rejoice! I Found the Lost	Wold, Wayne L.	Sun btwn Sep 11 and 17 C
Rejoice, O Jerusalem	Willan, Healey	1 Advent A
Rejoice, Rejoice Believers	Bouman, Paul	Sun btwn Nov 6 and 12 A
Rejoice, Rejoice, This Happy Morn	Ferguson, John	Christmas Day (III) A, B, C
Rejoice, Ye Shining Worlds on High	Billings, William	2 Advent A
Repleti sunt omnes/And They All Were Filled	Gallus, Jacobus (Handl)	Day of Pentecost B, C
Richard de Castre's Prayer to Jesus	Decastre, Richard	Sun btwn Sep 11 and 17 C
Ride On! Ride On in Majesty!	Benson, Robert A.	Passion/Palm Sunday A, C
Ride On, King Jesus	Fleming, Larry L.	Passion/Palm Sunday A, B
Ring Glad Bells	Morton, Graeme	Christmas Dawn (II) A, B, C
		Christmas Day (III) A, B, C
Rise Up, Rise Up!	Walter, Johann	2 Advent B
		Sun btwn Aug 7 and 13 C
		Sun btwn Nov 13 and 19 A
Rise, Shine!	Wood, Dale	Epiphany of Our Lord A, B, C
		3 Epiphany A, B
		4 Epiphany A, B
		5 Epiphany A
		Sun btwn Jun 19 and 25 C
Rolling In Foaming Billows	Haydn, Franz Joseph	Sun btwn Jun 19 and 25 B
St. John Passion	Ferguson, John	Good Friday A, B, C

St. Matthew Passion	*see also* The Passion According to St. John
	Schütz, Heinrich
	Passion/Palm Sunday A
	see also The Passion According to St. Matthew
St. Teresa's Bookmark	Tyler, Edward
	Sun btwn Nov 6 and 12 C
	Sun btwn Nov 13 and 19 B
Salvation Is Created	Tchesnokov, Pavel
	5 Lent B
Salvation unto Us Has Come	Bach, Johann Sebastian
	8 Epiphany B
	Sun btwn May 29 and Jun 4 A
	Sun btwn Jun 5 and 11 C
	Sun btwn Jun 19 and 25 C
	Sun btwn Sep 18 and 24 A
	Reformation Day A, B, C
Salvation unto Us Has Come	Chemin-Petit, Hans
	Sun btwn May 29 and Jun 4 A
Salvation unto Us Has Come	Distler, Hugo
	8 Epiphany B
	Sun btwn May 29 and Jun 4 C
	Sun btwn Sep 18 and 24 A
	Sun btwn Oct 30 and Nov 5 C
	Reformation Day A, B, C
Sanctus	Bernstein, Leonard
	Holy Trinity B
Sanctus	Duruflé, Maurice
	5 Epiphany C
Saul	Hovland, Egil
	3 Easter C
Savior of the Nations, Come	Bach, Johann Sebastian
	1 Advent B, C
Savior, Like a Shepherd Lead Us	Roberts, William Bradley
	4 Easter A, B, C
Search Me, O God	Dvořák, Antonín
	Sun btwn Jul 17 and 23 A, C
See Amid the Winter's Snow	Bertalot, John
	Christmas Day (III) A, B, C
See God to Heaven Ascending	Riegal, Friedrich Samuel
	Ascension of Our Lord A, B, C
See the Land, Her Easter Keeping	Jordan, Alice
	Easter Evening A, B, C
See What Love	Mendelssohn, Felix
	4 Epiphany C
	Maundy Thursday A, B, C
	3 Easter B
Seek the Lord	Clausen, René
	Sun btwn Jul 10 and 16 A
Seek Ye First the Kingdom of God	Glarum, L. Stanley
	Sun btwn May 24 and 28 A
Seek Ye the Lord	DeLong, Richard P.
	Easter Vigil A, B, C
Set Me As a Seal	Clausen, René
	2 Epiphany C
Shall We Gather at the River	Schultz, Donna Gartman
	All Saints Day A
Sheep May Safely Graze	Bach, Johann Sebastian
	4 Easter A
Shepherd Me, O God	Haugen, Marty
	4 Easter B
Shepherd's Carol	Chilcott, Bob

Shout for Joy, Ye Righteous/Exsultate justi	Viadana, Lodovico
	4 Lent C
Show Me Thy Ways	Pelz, Walter L.
	1 Advent C
	1 Lent B
	Sun btwn Jul 10 and 16 C
	Sun btwn Sep 4 and 10 C
	Sun btwn Sep 25 and Oct 1 A
Show Me Your Ways, O Lord	Haydn, Franz Joseph
	Sun btwn Jul 10 and 16 C
Show Me Your Ways, O Lord	Schalk, Carl
	1 Lent B
	Sun btwn Jul 10 and 16 C
Show Us Your Kindness	Hurd, David
	Sun btwn Aug 7 and 13 A
Simeon's Song	Ellingboe, Bradley
	1 Christmas B
	Presentation of Our Lord A, B, C
Simile est regnum	Morales, Cristóbal de
	Sun btwn Sep 18 and 24 A
Since by Man Came Death	Handel, George Frideric
	1 Lent A
	Easter Vigil A, B, C
	Easter Day C
	Sun btwn Jun 19 and 25 A
	Sun btwn Oct 2 and 8 A
	Sun btwn Oct 9 and 15 C
	Sun btwn Nov 6 and 12 C
Sing a New Song to the Lord/Psalm 98	Bell, John L.
	Christmas Day (III) A, B, C
Sing a Song of Joy	Scott, K. Lee
	Sun btwn Jul 31 and Aug 6 C
Sing Aloud to God	Hopson, Hal H.
	Sun btwn Oct 23 and 29 B
Sing Aloud to God Our Strength	Scott, K. Lee
	Sun btwn Oct 16 and 22 A
	Reformation Day A, B, C
Sing and Ponder	Fleming, Larry L.
	Maundy Thursday A, B, C
	Good Friday A, B, C
Sing Hosanna to the Son of David	Gesius, Bartholomäus
	Passion/Palm Sunday B
Sing of Mary, Pure and Lowly	Laster, James
	1 Christmas C
	Presentation of Our Lord A, B, C
Sing, My Soul, His Wondrous Love	Rorem, Ned
	3 Lent A
	6 Easter B
	Sun btwn Jul 10 and 16 C
	Christ the King B
Sing, O Heavens	Diemer, Emma Lou
	2 Epiphany A
Sing Praise to Christ	Bach, Johann Sebastian
	3 Easter A
	Sun btwn Sep 4 and 10 A
Sing Praise to God This Holy Day	Byrd, William
	Easter Day B
Sing Praise to the Lord	Hopson, Hal H.
	Sun btwn Oct 9 and 15 C
Sing Praises	Glarum, L. Stanley

Title	Composer	Occasion
Sing, Rejoice/Psallite unigenito	Scheidt, Samuel	8 Epiphany A Christmas Day (III) A, B, C
Sing to God	Marshall, Jane	2 Christmas A, B, C
Sing to the Lord	Schein, Johann H.	Sun btwn Oct 16 and 22 A
Sing to the Lord	Schütz, Heinrich	Sun btwn Jul 24 and 30 A Sun btwn Nov 13 and 19 C
Sing to the Lord	Tye, Christopher	Sun btwn Nov 13 and 19 C
Sing to the Lord a New Song	Pachelbel, Johann/ed. Donald Rotermund	6 Easter B
Sing to the Lord of Harvest	Blake, Leonard	Day of Thanksgiving A
Sing to the Lord of Harvest	Willan, Healey	Day of Thanksgiving A
Sing to the Lord, New Songs Be Raising	Sweelinck, Jan Pieterszoon	3 Easter C Sun btwn May 29 and Jun 4 C Sun btwn Oct 16 and 22 A Christ the King C Day of Thanksgiving A, C
Sing unto God	Fetler, Paul	7 Easter A
Sing unto the Lord	Dengler, Lee	Sun btwn Jun 12 and 18 C Sun btwn Jun 19 and 25 B
Sing We Merrily	Proulx, Richard	Sun btwn May 29 and Jun 4 B
Sing We Merrily Unto God Our Strength	Campbell, Sidney	Sun btwn Oct 23 and 29 B
Sing with All the Saints in Glory	Gerike, Henry V.	Sun btwn Nov 6 and 12 C
Sing Ye Praises to Our King	Copland, Aaron	Sun btwn Jul 3 and 9 C Christ the King A
Sing, Ye Righteous	Viadana, Ludovico	Sun btwn Jun 19 and 25 B
Sing Ye to the Lord	Bairstow, Edward C.	Easter Vigil A, B, C
Sleeper Wake	Mendelssohn, Felix	Sun btwn Nov 6 and 12 A
So Art Thou to Me	Scott, K. Lee	6 Easter A Sun btwn Jun 12 and 18 B Sun btwn Jul 24 and 30 A Sun btwn Aug 7 and 13 B Sun btwn Aug 28 and Sep 3 A, B
Solemn Reproaches of the Cross	Farlee, Robert Buckley	Passion/Palm Sunday B Good Friday A, B, C
Solus ad victimam/Alone to Sacrifice	Leighton, Kenneth	Maundy Thursday A, B, C Good Friday A, B, C
Son of God, Eternal Savior	Bouman, Paul	Sun btwn Oct 9 and 15 B
Son of God, Eternal Savior	Pearce, Thomas	Sun btwn Aug 28 and Sep 3 A
Song of Simeon	Marshall, Jane	

Title	Composer	Occasion
Song of the Three Children	Proulx, Richard	1 Christmas B Easter Vigil A, B, C
Songs of Gladness I Will Sing Thee	Dvořák, Antonín	Sun btwn Jun 5 and 11 A
Soon and Very Soon	Crouch, Andraé/Jack Schrader	Sun btwn Nov 13 and 19 B
Soul, Adorn Yourself with Gladness	Zipp, Friedrich	2 Epiphany C Maundy Thursday A, B, C
Soul Adorn Yourself with Gladness/Vengo a ti, Jesús amado	Ellingboe, Bradley	2 Advent B, C 2 Epiphany C Sun btwn Aug 7 and 13 B Sun btwn Nov 6 and 12 A Sun btwn Nov 13 and 19 C
Souls of the Righteous	Johnson, David N.	All Saints Day A
Sounding Joy	Walker, Gwyneth	Sun btwn Jun 19 and 25 B
Spirit of God, Descend	Helgen, John	Vigil of Pentecost A, B, C Sun btwn Jul 10 and 16 C Sun btwn Sep 4 and 10 C
Spirit of God, Descend upon My Heart	Ellingboe, Bradley	Baptism of Our Lord A
Springs in the Desert	Jennings, Arthur	3 Advent A
Star in the East	White, David Ashley	Epiphany of Our Lord A, B, C
Stars in the Sky Proclaim	Lassus, Rudolph de/arr. Richard Proulx	Epiphany of Our Lord A, B, C
Stay with Us	Hovland, Egil	Easter Evening A, B, C 3 Easter A
Stay with Us	Pelz, Walter L.	Easter Evening A, B, C 3 Easter A, B
Stay with Us, Lord/Bleib bei uns, Herr	Praetorius, Michael	Easter Evening A, B, C 3 Easter A
Steal Away	White, Nicholas	Sun btwn Nov 6 and 12 A
Stetit Iesus/There Came Jesus	Gallus, Jacobus (Handl)	2 Easter B
Still, Still, Still	Wetzler, Robert	Christmas Eve (I) A, B, C
Strengthen for Service	Proulx, Richard	6 Epiphany A Sun btwn Jun 5 and 11 B Sun btwn Jun 19 and 25 A Sun btwn Aug 21 and 27 B Sun btwn Sep 25 and Oct 1 B
Surely He Has Borne Our Griefs	Copley, R. Evan	Good Friday A, B, C
Surely He Hath Borne Our Griefs	Handel, George Frideric	3 Lent A Good Friday A, B, C Sun btwn Oct 16 and 22 B
Surely He Hath Borne Our Griefs	Hillert, Richard	Good Friday A, B, C

Title	Composer	Occasion
Surge illuminare	Byrd, William	2 Epiphany C
Surgens Jesus/He Is Risen	Philips, Peter	3 Easter B
Surrexit Christus	Berthier, Jacques	Easter Vigil A, B, C
Sussex Carol	Willcocks, David	Christmas Eve (I) A, B, C 1 Christmas B
Take Heart, Contented Be, and Restful	Bach, Johann Sebastian	Sun btwn Jun 5 and 11 C
Take Me to the Water	Parker, Alice	1 Lent B
Take My Life and Let It Be Consecrated	White, Nicholas	Sun btwn Nov 6 and 12 B
Take My Life, That I May Be	Hobby, Robert A.	Sun btwn Sep 11 and 17 B Sun btwn Oct 9 and 15 B
Take My Life, That I May Be/Toma, oh Dios, mi voluntad	Sedio, Mark	2 Epiphany B, C Sun btwn Oct 9 and 15 B Sun btwn Nov 6 and 12 B
Take Up Your Cross, the Savior Said	Bouman, Paul	Sun btwn Aug 28 and Sep 3 A Sun btwn Sep 4 and 10 C
Tantum ergo	Duruflé, Maurice	Sun btwn Nov 13 and 19 B
Tantum ergo	Sitton, Michael	1 Lent C
Taste and See	Gehring, Philip	Sun btwn Oct 2 and 8 B
Taste and See	Haugen, Marty	Sun btwn Aug 14 and 20 B
Taste and See	Moore, James	Sun btwn Aug 7 and 13 B
Taste and See the Lord Is Good	Thompson, J. Michael	4 Lent C 5 Lent A Sun btwn Jul 24 and 30 B
Te Deum in C	Britten, Benjamin	Holy Trinity C
Te Deum laudamus/We Praise Thee, O God	Willan, Healey	Holy Trinity B All Saints Day C
Teach Each Other in Wisdom	Ellingboe, Bradley	1 Christmas C
Teach Me, My God and King	Scott, K. Lee	Sun btwn Jul 24 and 30 A Sun btwn Sep 4 and 10 A
Teach Me Now, O Lord	Marcello, Benedetto/arr. Dale Grotenhuis	Sun btwn Jul 17 and 23 A, B Sun btwn Sep 4 and 10 A Sun btwn Oct 30 and Nov 5 B
Teach Me, O Lord	Attwood, Thomas	7 Epiphany A Sun btwn Jul 10 and 16 C Sun btwn Sep 4 and 10 A Sun btwn Oct 16 and 22 C
Teach Me, O Lord	Byrd, William	7 Epiphany A
Teach Me, O Lord	Hurd, David	

Title	Composer	Occasion
		Sun btwn Sep 4 and 10 A
Teach Me, O Lord	Nystedt, Knut	
		Sun btwn Jul 17 and 23 A
		Sun btwn Sep 4 and 10 A
		Sun btwn Oct 16 and 22 B
Teach Me Your Way, O Lord	Bisbee, B. Wayne	
		Sun btwn Jun 5 and 11 A
		Sun btwn Jun 19 and 25 A, B
		Sun btwn Jul 3 and 9 B
		Sun btwn Jul 17 and 23 A, B
		Sun btwn Aug 28 and Sep 3 B
		Sun btwn Sep 4 and 10 A
		Sun btwn Oct 30 and Nov 5 B
Teach Me Your Way, O Lord	Sedio, Mark	
		Sun btwn Jul 3 and 9 B
Thank the Lord	Clausen, René	
		Sun btwn Oct 30 and Nov 5 C
That Priceless Grace	Helgen, John	
		2 Lent C
		Sun btwn May 24 and 28 B
		Sun btwn Sep 25 and Oct 1 C
The 'O' Antiphons	Hallock, Peter	
		4 Advent A
The 23rd Psalm	McFerrin, Bobby	
		4 Easter A
The Angel Gabriel	Goetze, Mary	
		4 Advent C
The Angel Gabriel	Schroeder, Hermann	
		4 Advent B
The Angel Gabriel from Heaven Came	Prower, Anthony	
		4 Advent C
The Apple Tree	Poston, Elizabeth	
		4 Epiphany B
The Ascension/Lift Up Your Heads	Moore, Philip	
		Ascension of Our Lord A, B, C
The Baptism Carol	Busarow, Donald	
		Baptism of Our Lord B, C
The Baptism of Christ	Hallock, Peter	
		Baptism of Our Lord A
The Baptism of Our Lord	Callahan, Charles	
		Baptism of Our Lord A, B
The Best of Rooms	Grundahl, Nancy	
		Sun btwn Oct 30 and Nov 5 C
The Best of Rooms	Near, Gerald	
		Sun btwn Oct 30 and Nov 5 C
The Best of Rooms	Thompson, Randall	
		Sun btwn Sep 4 and 10 C
		Sun btwn Oct 30 and Nov 5 C
The Blessed Son of God	Neswick, Bruce	
		2 Christmas A, B, C
The Blessed Son of God	Vaughan Williams, Ralph	
		1 Christmas A, C
		Baptism of Our Lord C
The Call	Paynter, John	
		5 Easter A
The Call	Scott, K. Lee	
		5 Easter A
		Sun btwn Jul 17 and 23 A
		Sun btwn Aug 14 and 20 B
		Sun btwn Oct 30 and Nov 5 B

Title	Composer	Occasions
The Call	Vaughan Williams, Ralph	5 Easter A, C Sun btwn Jul 17 and 23 C Sun btwn Oct 23 and 29 A
The Call	White, David Ashley	5 Easter A
The Chief Cornerstone	Ellingboe, Bradley	8 Epiphany C Tuesday in Holy Week A, B, C Easter Day A 3 Easter C 5 Easter A Sun btwn May 24 and 28 C
The Christ-Child Lay on Mary's Lap	Carnahan, Craig	1 Christmas C
The Church of Christ in Every Age	Busarow, Donald	Sun btwn Oct 16 and 22 B
The Church's One Foundation	Ferguson, John	Sun btwn Jun 19 and 25 A Reformation Day A, B, C
The Church's One Foundation	Powell, Robert J.	Reformation Day A, B, C
The Church's One Foundation	Schalk, Carl	Reformation Day A, B, C
The Crown of Roses	Tchaikovsky, Pyotr Il'yich	Passion/Palm Sunday A
The Cup of Blessing	Gehring, Philip	Sun btwn Oct 16 and 22 B
The Day Draws on the Golden Light	Bairstow, Edward C.	Easter Day A
The Days of Summer	Busarow, Donald	Sun btwn Jul 17 and 23 B
The Earth Adorned/Sommersalm	Åhlén, Waldemar	6 Easter C Sun btwn Jun 19 and 25 A Sun btwn Aug 14 and 20 C
The Easter Proclamation/The Exsultet	Weaver, John	Easter Vigil A, B, C
The Eyes of All	Larkin, Michael	Sun btwn Jul 31 and Aug 6 A
The Eyes of All	Proulx, Richard	Sun btwn Jul 24 and 30 B, C Sun btwn Jul 31 and Aug 6 A Day of Thanksgiving C
The Eyes of All Wait upon Thee	Berger, Jean	Day of Pentecost A, C Sun btwn Jun 19 and 25 C Sun btwn Jul 24 and 30 B Sun btwn Jul 31 and Aug 6 A Sun btwn Oct 2 and 8 C Day of Thanksgiving C
The Food of Life	Ellingboe, Bradley	Sun btwn Jul 31 and Aug 6 C
The Gift of Love	Hopson, Hal H.	Sun btwn Oct 2 and 8 B
The Glory of the Father	Hovland, Egil	Christmas Day (III) A, B, C 2 Christmas A, B, C 3 Epiphany B
The Glory of These Forty Days	Below, Robert	1 Lent A

Title	Composer	Occasion
The God of Love My Shepherd Is	Schalk, Carl	4 Easter B Sun btwn Oct 9 and 15 A
The Great Creator of the Worlds	Powell, Robert J.	5 Epiphany B 7 Epiphany B
The Great Day of the Lord	Stout, Alan	Sun btwn Nov 13 and 19 A
The Great O Antiphons of Advent	Willan, Healey/ed. Carl Schalk	4 Advent A
The Greatest of These Is Love	Clausen, René	4 Epiphany C
The Head That Once Was Crowned	Behnke, John	Christ the King A
The Head That Once Was Crowned with Thorns	Ferguson, John	7 Easter A Sun btwn Jun 12 and 18 B Christ the King A
The Heavens Are Telling	Haydn, Franz Joseph	Sun btwn Sep 25 and Oct 1 B
The Heavens Sing Praises	Beethoven, Ludwig van/ed. K. Lee Scott	Sun btwn Jun 5 and 11 A Sun btwn Aug 21 and 27 C
The Holy City	Adams, Stephen	Passion/Palm Sunday B
The Holy Trinity	Ellingboe, Bradley	Holy Trinity A, C
The King of Love My Shepherd Is	Bairstow, Edward C.	4 Easter A
The King of Love My Shepherd Is	Krapf, Gerhard	4 Easter A, C
The King of Love My Shepherd Is	Pelz, Walter L.	4 Easter A, C Sun btwn Jul 17 and 23 B
The King Shall Rejoice	Handel, George Frideric	Christ the King A, C
The Kingdom	Thomas, André	Christ the King A
The Kingdom of God	Jennings, Carolyn	Sun btwn Sep 11 and 17 B
The Lamb	Tavener, John	4 Easter A Sun btwn Sep 18 and 24 B
The Last Supper	Pote, Allen	Sun btwn Aug 7 and 13 A
The Light of the World	Carter, Andrew	5 Epiphany A 5 Easter A
The Lightener of the Stars	Farlee, Robert Buckley	Transfiguration of Our Lord A Ascension of Our Lord A, B, C
The Lone, Wild Bird	Johnson, David N.	7 Easter A
The Lord Is a Mighty God	Mendelssohn, Felix/arr. Olaf C. Christiansen	Christ the King A
The Lord Is Ever Watchful	Mendelssohn, Felix/ed. K. Lee Scott	Sun btwn Aug 7 and 13 A
The Lord Is My Light	Zimmermann, Hans Werner	3 Epiphany A 5 Epiphany B 2 Lent C

The Lord Is My Light and My Salvation	Hillert, Richard
	Sun btwn Aug 21 and 27 A
The Lord Is My Shepherd	Bouman, Paul
	4 Easter C
	Sun btwn Oct 9 and 15 A
The Lord Is My Shepherd	Goodall, Howard
	4 Easter C
The Lord Is My Shepherd	Liddle, Samuel
	Sun btwn Jul 17 and 23 B
The Lord Is My Shepherd	Pote, Allen
	4 Easter A, B
	Sun btwn Jul 17 and 23 B
	Sun btwn Oct 9 and 15 A
The Lord Is My Shepherd	Rutter, John
	4 Lent A
	4 Easter C
	Sun btwn Oct 9 and 15 A
The Lord Is My Shepherd	Schubert, Franz
	4 Easter B
The Lord Is My Shepherd	Smith, Gregg
	4 Lent A
The Lord Is My Shepherd	Thompson, Randall
	4 Easter A, B
The Lord Is Risen Indeed	Billings, William
	2 Easter B
The Lord Shall Reign	Hurd, David
	Ascension of Our Lord A, B, C
The Lord Will Guide Our Ways	Powell, Robert J.
	6 Epiphany A
	Sun btwn Oct 9 and 15 B
The Lord Will Soon Appear	Bach, Johann Sebastian/arr. Hal H. Hopson
	2 Advent B
The Lord's My Shepherd	Archer, Malcolm
	4 Easter A
The Lord's My Shepherd	Ellingboe, Bradley
	4 Easter A
	Sun btwn Oct 9 and 15 A
The Lord's Prayer	Ellingboe, Bradley
	Sun btwn Jul 24 and 30 C
The Lord's Prayer	Peeters, Flor
	Sun btwn Jul 24 and 30 C
The Man We Crucified	Tye, Christopher/ed. Carl Schalk
	3 Easter A
	4 Easter A
The New Covenant	Mueller, Carl F.
	Sun btwn Oct 16 and 22 C
The Old Hundredth Psalm Tune	Vaughan Williams, Ralph
	Holy Trinity B
	Sun btwn Jun 12 and 18 A
	Day of Thanksgiving A
The Only Son from Heaven	Bach, Johann Sebastian
	Epiphany of Our Lord A, B, C
	Baptism of Our Lord A, C
	2 Epiphany A
The Passion According to St. John	Byrd, William
	Good Friday A, B, C
The Passion According to St. John	Victoria, Tomás Luis de
	Good Friday A, B, C
	see also St. John Passion
The Peace of God	Rutter, John
	Sun btwn Oct 9 and 15 A
The People That Walked in Darkness	Handel, George Frideric

Title	Composer	Occasion
The Pharisee and the Publican	Schütz, Heinrich	3 Epiphany A Sun btwn Oct 23 and 29 C
The Prayer of St. Francis	Ellingboe, Bradley	Sun btwn Jul 10 and 16 B
The Prayer of St. Francis	Mathews, Peter	Sun btwn Jul 10 and 16 B
The Raising of Lazarus	Willaert, Adrian	5 Lent A
The Risen Christ	Noble, T. Tertius	6 Epiphany C
The Savior of the World Is Born	Bach, Johann Sebastian	Christmas Dawn (II) A, B, C
The Seed Is the Word of God	Willan, Healey	Sun btwn Jul 10 and 16 A
The Song of the Tree of Life	Vaughan Williams, Ralph	Sun btwn Oct 2 and 8 A
The Souls of the Righteous	Marchant, Stanley	All Saints Day C
The Souls of the Righteous	Pavlechko, Thomas	All Saints Day B, C
The Souls of the Righteous	Vaughan Williams, Ralph	All Saints Day B
The Spirit of the Lord	Willan, Healey	Day of Pentecost A
The Spirit of the Lord Is upon Me	Elgar, Edward	3 Epiphany C
The Strife Is O'er	Ley, Henry G.	Easter Vigil A, B, C
The Strife Is O'er, the Battle Done	Gerike, Henry V.	Easter Vigil A, B, C 3 Easter B
The Strife Is O'er, the Battle Done	Praetorius, Michael	Easter Day A
The Thirsty Fields Drink In the Rain	Sedio, Mark	Sun btwn Jul 10 and 16 A, B
The Three Kings	Willan, Healey	Epiphany of Our Lord A, B, C
The Twenty-third Psalm	Vaughan Williams, Ralph	4 Easter C
The Virgin's Slumber Song	Reger, Max	Christmas Eve (I) A, B, C
The Virgin's Slumber Song	Reger, Max/ed. K. Lee Scott	Christmas Eve (I) A, B, C
The Vision of John	Nelson, Ronald A.	All Saints Day C
The Voice of the Lord Sounds upon the Waters	Schütz, Heinrich	Baptism of Our Lord A
The Waters of Life	Biery, James	Baptism of Our Lord A, C 7 Easter A Vigil of Pentecost A, B, C Sun btwn Aug 7 and 13 A
The Way to Jerusalem	Friedell, Harold	Sun btwn Jun 26 and Jul 2 C
The Wells of Salvation	Parker, Alice	5 Easter A
The Wisdom, Riches, and Knowledge of God	Powell, Robert J.	Sun btwn Jul 3 and 9 B
The Wise Confine Their Choice in Friends	Bach, Johann Sebastian/ed. Fritz Oberdoerffer	Sun btwn Jun 12 and 18 C

Title	Composer	Occasion
The Word Became Flesh	Roberts, Paul	2 Christmas A, B, C
The Word Was God	Powell, Rosephayne	2 Christmas A, B, C
The Word Was Made Flesh	Willan, Healey	Christmas Day (III) A, B, C
		2 Christmas A, B, C
Thee Will I Love	Jennings, Kenneth	7 Easter B
		Sun btwn Jun 12 and 18 C
		Sun btwn Jul 10 and 16 C
Then Mary Said to the Angel	Hassler, Hans Leo	4 Advent C
Then Shall the Righteous Shine Forth	Mendelssohn, Felix/arr. Wilbur Held	Sun btwn Jul 17 and 23 A
There Is a Balm in Gilead	Dawson, William	6 Epiphany B
		7 Epiphany B
		Sun btwn Jul 3 and 9 C
		Sun btwn Jul 17 and 23 C
There Is a Green Hill Far Away	Ellingboe, Bradley	4 Lent B
		Good Friday A, B, C
There Is No Rose of Such Vertu	Sedio, Mark	Christmas Day (III) A, B, C
There Shall a Star Come Out of Jacob	Mendelssohn, Felix	2 Christmas A, B, C
		Epiphany of Our Lord A, B, C
There'll Be Something In Heaven	Svedlund, Karl-Erik/arr. Bruce Bengtson	Sun btwn Nov 6 and 12 B, C
		All Saints Day A
There's a Wideness in God's Mercy	Ellingboe, Bradley	3 Epiphany B
		8 Epiphany B
		2 Lent A
		Sun btwn May 24 and 28 B
		Sun btwn Jun 5 and 11 A
		Sun btwn Sep 18 and 24 A
There's a Wideness in God's Mercy	White, David Ashley	7 Epiphany B
These Are They Which Follow the Lamb	Goss, John	2 Epiphany A
They Shall Shine as the Stars	Haan, Raymond H.	Sun btwn Nov 13 and 19 B
They That Shall Endure to the End	Mendelssohn, Felix	Sun btwn Jun 12 and 18 A
They That Wait upon the Lord	Near, Gerald	Sun btwn Oct 2 and 8 C
Thine Is the Glory	Handel, George Frideric	2 Easter C
Thine the Amen, Thine the Praise	Schalk, Carl	4 Easter C
		6 Easter C
		7 Easter A, C
		Sun btwn Nov 6 and 12 A
		Christ the King C
Third Mass of Christmas	Binkerd, Gordon	Christmas Dawn (II) A, B, C
This Glimpse of Glory	White, David Ashley	6 Epiphany C
		Transfiguration of Our Lord C

Index of Titles / 279

Title	Composer / Occasion
This Is de Healin' Water	Johnson, Hall Sun btwn Jun 19 and 25 A
This Is My Beloved Son	Nystedt, Knut Baptism of Our Lord C Transfiguration of Our Lord A
This Is My Beloved Son	Uhl, Dan Baptism of Our Lord B, C Transfiguration of Our Lord A
This Is My Son	Ore, Charles W. Baptism of Our Lord B
This Is the Bread	Pinkham, Daniel Sun btwn Aug 7 and 13 B
This Is the Day	Gallus, Jacobus (Handl) Easter Day A, C
This Is the Hour of Banquet and of Song	DeLong, Richard P. Sun btwn Aug 14 and 20 B
This Is the Night	Farlee, Robert Buckley Christmas Eve (I) A, B, C
This Is the Record of John	Gibbons, Orlando 3 Advent B
This Is the Truth	Vaughan Williams, Ralph 5 Easter A
This Joyful Eastertide	Harris, William H. Easter Day B
This Little Babe	Britten, Benjamin 1 Christmas B
This Touch of Love	Fedak, Alfred V. Sun btwn Aug 28 and Sep 3 C
This Touch of Love	Schalk, Carl 2 Epiphany C
Those Who Trust in the Lord	Zimmermann, Heinz Werner Sun btwn Sep 4 and 10 B
Thou Art Ascended Up on High	Pinkham, Daniel 7 Easter A
Thou Art My Strength	Sowerby, Leo Sun btwn May 29 and Jun 4 A
Thou Art Peter	Hewitt-Jones, Tony Sun btwn Aug 21 and 27 A
Thou Art Praised in Zion	Williamson, Malcolm Sun btwn Jul 10 and 16 A
Thou Art the Vine	Carter, Andrew 5 Easter B Sun btwn Sep 18 and 24 A
Thou Knowest, Lord, the Secrets of Our Hearts	Purcell, Henry 3 Advent A 4 Lent C Sun btwn Jul 10 and 16 C Sun btwn Jul 17 and 23 A Sun btwn Nov 6 and 12 A
Thou O God Art Praised in Zion	Boyle, Malcolm 6 Easter C
Thou, O God, Art Praised in Zion	Willcocks, David Sun btwn Jul 10 and 16 A
Thou Shalt Know Him When He Comes	Sirett, Mark G. 1 Advent B, C Easter Evening A, B, C Sun btwn Nov 13 and 19 B Christ the King B
Thou Wilt Keep Him in Perfect Peace	Wesley, Samuel Sebastian 3 Epiphany A
Though We Are Many, in Christ We Are One	Proulx, Richard 4 Easter A

Three Days Had Passed	Martinson, Joel
	Easter Day A
Three Kings, The	Willan, Healey
	Epiphany of Our Lord A, B, C
Thy Holy Wings	Ellingboe, Bradley
	2 Lent C
	Monday in Holy Week A, B, C
Thy Holy Wings	Erickson, Karle
	1 Lent B
	Monday in Holy Week A, B, C
Thy Holy Wings	Ferguson, John
	Sun btwn May 24 and 28 A
Thy Mercy, O Lord, Reacheth unto the Heavens	Edwards, Paul
	2 Epiphany C
Thy Perfect Love	Rutter, John
	Sun btwn Jun 12 and 18 C
	Sun btwn Sep 18 and 24 C
Thy Perfect Love	Scott, K. Lee
	7 Easter C
	Sun btwn May 29 and Jun 4 B
	Sun btwn Jun 26 and Jul 2 A
Thy Strong Word	Busarow, Donald
	3 Epiphany A
Thy Strong Word	Schalk, Carl
	3 Epiphany A
Thy Word Is a Lantern	Bertalot, John
	Sun btwn May 29 and Jun 4 A
	Sun btwn Jul 10 and 16 A
	Reformation Day A, B, C
Thy Word Is a Lantern	Purcell, Henry
	Sun btwn Oct 9 and 15 B
'Tis Finished	Shaw, Robert/Alice Parker
	Good Friday A, B, C
'Tis Well with Me, for by Thy Might	Bach, Johann Sebastian/ed. Fritz Oberdoerffer
	Sun btwn May 29 and Jun 4 B
To Our Redeemer's Glorious Name	Tye, Christopher
	2 Lent A
To Thee O Lord	Rachmaninoff, Sergei
	Sun btwn Sep 25 and Oct 1 A
To Thee We Sing	Rachmaninoff, Sergei
	Sun btwn Aug 28 and Sep 3 B
To Thee We Turn Our Eyes	Schütz, Heinrich
	Sun btwn Jul 3 and 9 A
To Us Is Born Emmanuel/Enatus est Emanuel	Praetorius, Michael
	Christmas Dawn (II) A, B, C
	Christmas Day (III) A, B, C
Today Hath Salvation Come	Rachmaninoff, Sergei
	Easter Vigil A, B, C
	Easter Day C
	Sun btwn Oct 9 and 15 A
Today in Triumph Christ Arose	Gesius, Bartholomäus
	Easter Day C
Tomorrow Shall Be My Dancing Day	Gardner, John
	Christmas Eve (I) A, B, C
	2 Christmas A, B, C
Torches	Joubert, John
	1 Christmas C
Transcendent, Holy God	Bach, Johann Sebastian
	Transfiguration of Our Lord C
Transfiguration	Martinson, Joel
	Transfiguration of Our Lord A, B

Title	Composer / Occasion
Triduum Hymn: Wondrous Love	Haugen, Marty Maundy Thursday A, B, C
Trinitarian Blessings	Scott, K. Lee Holy Trinity A, B, C
Trinity Sunday	Smith, Carl Holy Trinity B
Tu es Petrus	Duruflé, Maurice Sun btwn Aug 21 and 27 A
Tu es Petrus	Morales, Cristóbal de Sun btwn Aug 21 and 27 A
Tu es Petrus	Palestrina, Giovanni Pierluigi da Sun btwn Aug 21 and 27 A
Tu es Petrus	Widor, Charles Marie/ed. David Cherwien 8 Epiphany C
Turn Back O Man	Holst, Gustav Sun btwn Sep 4 and 10 A
Turn Thee Again, O Lord	Attwood, Thomas Sun btwn Nov 13 and 19 A
Turn Thy Face from My Sins	Attwood, Thomas Ash Wednesday A, B, C
Twenty-third Psalm, The	Vaughan Williams, Ralph 4 Easter C
Ubi caritas	Basler, Paul Maundy Thursday A, B, C
Ubi caritas	Duruflé, Maurice 4 Epiphany C Maundy Thursday A, B, C 5 Easter C 6 Easter B Sun btwn Jun 26 and Jul 2 C Sun btwn Sep 11 and 17 A
Ubi caritas	Raminsh, Imant Maundy Thursday A, B, C
Ubi caritas et amor	Proulx, Richard Maundy Thursday A, B, C
Universal Praise	Billings, William All Saints Day C
Unto Us Is Born God's Son	Ferguson, John Christmas Dawn (II) A, B, C 2 Christmas A, B, C
Up Through Endless Ranks of Angels	Cherwien, David Ascension of Our Lord A, B, C
Up Through Endless Ranks of Angels	Gerike, Henry V. Ascension of Our Lord A, B, C
Up Through Endless Ranks of Angels	Pelz, Walter L. Ascension of Our Lord A, B, C
Upon the Cross Extended	Isaac, Heinrich Good Friday A, B, C
Verbum caro factum est	Proulx, Richard, ed 2 Christmas A, B, C
Vere langoures nostros	Victoria, Tomás Luis de Sun btwn Oct 16 and 22 B
Verily, Verily I Say unto You	Tallis, Thomas Sun btwn Aug 14 and 20 B
Wade in the Water	Boatner, Edward Sun btwn Aug 7 and 13 A
Wake, Awake	Christiansen, F Melius 1 Advent C Sun btwn Nov 6 and 12 A
Wake, Awake, for Night Is Flying	Bach, Johann Sebastian 1 Advent B, C

Title	Composer	Occasion
		Sun btwn Nov 6 and 12 A
Wake, O Shepherds	Rameau, Jean Philippe/ed. Ronald A. Nelson	
		Christmas Eve (I) A, B, C
Walk Humbly with Thy God	Darst, W. Glen	
		Sun btwn Nov 6 and 12 A
Wash Me Thoroughly	Wesley, Samuel Sebastian	
		Ash Wednesday A, B, C
		5 Lent B
Wash Me Through and Through	Hallock, Peter	
		Ash Wednesday A, B, C
Wash Yourself in the Jordan	Pinkham, Daniel	
		6 Epiphany B
Watchman, Tell Us of the Night	Hovhaness, Alan	
		1 Advent A
We Adore You O Christ	Proulx, Richard	
		Passion/Palm Sunday C
We Are a Garden Walled Around	Farlee, Robert Buckley/ed. Susan Palo Cherwien	
		Easter Evening A, B, C
		Sun btwn Jul 31 and Aug 6 B
We Are Not Our Own	Schulz-Widmar, Russell	
		7 Epiphany C
We Bless the Father and the Son and the Holy Ghost	Reger, Max	
		Holy Trinity A
We Know That Christ Is Raised	Hopson, Hal H.	
		Sun btwn Jun 12 and 18 B
We Know That Christ Is Raised	Stanford, Charles Villiers	
		Easter Vigil A, B, C
We Know That Christ Is Raised	Wolff, S. Drummond	
		Easter Vigil A, B, C
		Sun btwn Jun 12 and 18 B
We Offer Our Thanks and Praise	Schütz, Heinrich	
		Sun btwn Sep 25 and Oct 1 B
		Sun btwn Nov 6 and 12 C
		Day of Thanksgiving C
We Praise You, O God	Jennings, Carolyn	
		Day of Thanksgiving A, B, C
We Sing to Him	Purcell, Henry	
		Holy Trinity C
We Thank Thee, Lord	Bortniansky, Dmitri/ed. Peter Tkach	
		Sun btwn Aug 21 and 27 A
We Wait for Thy Loving Kindness, O God	McKie, William	
		4 Epiphany C
We Walk by Faith	Helman, Michael	
		2 Easter B
We Will March thro' the Valley	Parker, Alice	
		1 Lent B
Weary of All Trumpeting	Proulx, Richard	
		5 Lent C
		Sun btwn Jun 19 and 25 A
		Sun btwn Oct 9 and 15 B
		Sun btwn Oct 16 and 22 B
		Sun btwn Oct 23 and 29 B
Were You There	Burleigh, Harry T.	
		Good Friday A, B, C
Were You There	Chilcott, Bob	
		Good Friday A, B, C
Were You There	Proulx, Richard	
		Passion/Palm Sunday A
		Good Friday A, B, C
Wexford Carol	Sedio, Mark	
		2 Christmas A, B, C

Wexford Carol

What Child Is This?

What Does the Lord Require?

What God Ordains Is Good Indeed

What Is This Lovely Fragrance?

What Shall I Render to the Lord?

What Shall We Offer

What Sweeter Music

What Sweeter Music

What Then

What Wondrous Love

When Christmas Morn Is Dawning

When Fully Came the Day of Pentecost

When I Survey the Wondrous Cross

When I Survey the Wondrous Cross

When I Survey the Wondrous Cross

When I Survey the Wondrous Cross

When Jesus Went to Jordan's Stream

When Long Before Time

When Peace, Like a River

When the Morning Stars Together

When the Trumpet Sounds

When Twilight Comes

Where Charity and Love Prevail

Who Himself Exalteth

Who Is the One We Love the Most

Who Shall Abide

Who Shall Separate Us

Warland, Dale
    Christmas Day (III) A, B, C
Sutcliffe, James
    1 Christmas C
    Presentation of Our Lord A, B, C
Routley, Erik/arr. John Hakes
    4 Epiphany A
Bach, Johann Sebastian
    Sun btwn Jul 17 and 23 B
Willan, Healey
    Christmas Dawn (II) A, B, C
Tiefenbach, Peter
    3 Easter A
Proulx, Richard
    Day of Thanksgiving C
Rutter, John
    2 Advent B
Sirett, Mark G.
    Christmas Dawn (II) A, B, C
Ferguson, John
    8 Epiphany C
    Sun btwn May 24 and 28 C
Scholz, Robert
    4 Lent B
Scott, K. Lee
    Christmas Dawn (II) A, B, C
Palestrina, Giovanni Pierluigi da
    Day of Pentecost A
Ferguson, John
    2 Lent B
Lenel, Ludwig
    Sun btwn Oct 2 and 8 A
Martin, Gilbert
    5 Lent C
    Tuesday in Holy Week A, B, C
Saylor, Bruce
    5 Lent C
Wyton, Alec
    Baptism of Our Lord A, C
Erickson, Richard
    Easter Vigil A, B, C
    Holy Trinity C
White, David Ashley
    Sun btwn Nov 13 and 19 C
Arnatt, Ronald
    Holy Trinity A
Thomas, André
    Sun btwn Nov 6 and 12 A
Farlee, Robert Buckley
    2 Lent C
    Maundy Thursday A, B, C
Schalk, Carl
    Maundy Thursday A, B, C
    Sun btwn Sep 11 and 17 A
Bach, Johann Sebastian
    Sun btwn Aug 28 and Sep 3 C
Schalk, Carl
    7 Epiphany B
Pelz, Walter L.
    4 Epiphany A
Schütz, Heinrich/ed. Larry Fleming

Title	Composer	Occasion
		Sun btwn Jul 24 and 30 A
Who Shall Separate us from the Love of Christ	Pinkham, Daniel	
		Sun btwn Jul 24 and 30 A
Who Was the Man	Davis, Katherine	
		Sun btwn Aug 7 and 13 A
Whoever Would Be Great among You	Nelson, Ronald A.	
		5 Epiphany C
		Sun btwn Sep 18 and 24 A, B
		Sun btwn Oct 16 and 22 B
		Sun btwn Oct 30 and Nov 5 A
Why Do the Nations So Furiously Rage?	Handel, George Frideric	
		Sun btwn Aug 14 and 20 C
		Sun btwn Nov 13 and 19 C
Will You Come and Follow Me	Bell, John L.	
		Sun btwn Jul 3 and 9 B
Wilt Thou Forgive?/A Hymne to God the Father	Hilton, John/ed K. Lee Scott	
		1 Lent A
		Sun btwn May 24 and 28 B
With a Voice of Singing	Jennings, Kenneth	
		5 Easter A
		6 Easter B
		7 Easter A
		Sun btwn Jul 3 and 9 C
With a Voice of Singing	Shaw, Martin	
		5 Easter A
With High Delight Let Us Unite	Pelz, Walter L.	
		3 Easter A
With the Lord, There Is Mercy	Rowan, William P.	
		1 Lent C
		5 Lent A
Witness	Halloran, Jack	
		3 Lent C
		Sun btwn Aug 28 and Sep 3 B
Witness	Johnson, Hall	
		Sun btwn Jun 19 and 25 B
Woman in the Night	Rowan, William P.	
		Sun btwn Aug 14 and 20 A
Wondrous Love	Benson, Robert A.	
		Maundy Thursday A, B, C
Wondrous Love	Christiansen, Paul J.	
		3 Lent A
		4 Lent B
Word of God Come Down on Earth	Ferguson, John	
		Sun btwn May 29 and Jun 4 A
		Sun btwn Jul 10 and 16 A
Worthy Is the Lamb	Handel, George Frideric	
		3 Easter C
Worthy to Be Praised	Smith, Byron J.	
		Easter Vigil A, B, C
		Sun btwn Sep 18 and 24 A
Ye Are Not of the Flesh	Bach, Johann Sebastian	
		5 Lent A
		Sun btwn Jul 10 and 16 A
Ye Choirs of New Jerusalem	Rose, Michael	
		Ascension of Our Lord A, B, C
Ye Choirs of New Jerusalem	Stanford, Charles Villiers	
		Easter Day A
Ye Watchers and Ye Holy Ones	Powell, Robert J.	
		Ascension of Our Lord A, B, C
Yea Though I Wander	Schumann, Georg/ed. Paul Christiansen	
		4 Easter C

You Are God: We Praise You	Proulx, Richard
	Holy Trinity C
You Are Peter!	Ellingboe, Bradley
	Sun btwn Aug 21 and 27 A
You Are the Light of the World	Hillert, Richard
	4 Epiphany A
You Visit the Earth	Greene, Maurice/ed. K. Lee Scott
	Sun btwn Jul 10 and 16 A
	Day of Thanksgiving A
Your Love, O Lord, For Ever I Will Sing	Hallock, Peter
	Sun btwn Jun 26 and Jul 2 A
Your Love, O Lord, Reaches to the Heavens	Stearns, Peter Pindar
	2 Epiphany C
Your Savior Comes	Nystedt, Knut
	Christmas Dawn (II) A, B, C
Zion Hears the Watchmen Singing	Bach, Johann Sebastian
	1 Advent A
	3 Advent C
	Sun btwn Aug 7 and 13 C
Zion's Walls	Copland, Aaron
	Sun btwn Jul 3 and 9 C